Complex Analysis

Anuradha Gupta

Associate Professor,
Department of Mathematics,
Delhi College of Arts and Commerce
(University of Delhi).

Ane Books Pvt. Ltd.

New Delhi ♦ Chennai

Complex Analysis

Anuradha Gupta

First Edition : 2011

Reprint : **2017, 2018, 2020, 2023**

Published by

Ane Books Pvt. Ltd.

4821, Parwana Bhawan, 1st Floor, 24 Ansari Road, Darya Ganj,
New Delhi - 110 002, Tel.: +91(011) 23276843-44, Fax: +91(011) 23276863
e-mail: kapoor@anebooks.com, Website: www.anebooks.com

Branch Office:

- Avantika Niwas, 1st Floor, 19 Doraiswamy Road, T. Nagar,
  Chennai - 600 017, Tel.: +91(044) 28141554, 28141209
  e-mail: anebookschennai@gmail.com, rathinam@anebooks.com

ISBN : 978-93-8116-224-8

Printed at : Repro Knowledgecast Limited, Thane

Complex Analysis

Dedicated to

My Husband

Late Sh. Sanjay Gupta

Preface

Complex Analysis known as theory of functions of complex variable is one of the most useful branch of Mathematics that investigates functions of complex numbers. It is useful in many branches of Mathematics and science including number theory, applied mathematics, physics, hydrodynamics and electrical engineering.

This book has been written for B. Sc (H) Mathematics, Part III students of University of Delhi. This is an elementary text in Complex Variables for undergraduate and postgraduate students of University of Delhi. The basic techniques and theorems are presented in such a way that students having prior knowledge of real analysis can easily understand the text.

Features of this text:

This book presented the theory of analytic functions in a more accessible way in the early stages of his/her complex analysis study. Each chapter begins with the introductory comments on the specifics covered in that chapter. Almost every section ends with a remark in which the comparison between real and complex analysis is given where we talk about those areas where real and complex calculus differ. Several of the larger sections have been divided in sub-sections. I have also provided lots of examples and have tried very hard to supply all pertinent details of their solutions. The corresponding exercise sets are divided in order to make the study easier.

Acknowledgements:

I would like to express my thanks to professor S.C. Arora, Former Head, Department of Mathematics, Dr. Pawan Bala and Dr. Dinesh Khattar, Kirori Mal College, University of Delhi for their word of encouragement and their suggestions. Thanks are also due to my parents and children for their constant support. I want to extend my appreciation to the editors, Mr. Nishant Saini and Ms. Pinki Singh for their help in proof reading. Lastly, I would like to thank Ane Books Pvt. Ltd. for encouraging me to write the book and for their assistance during its production.

Request: This mathematics text entails thousands of Mathematical symbols and words, but text book writing seems to be inescapable from typo-graphical mistakes or plain mistakes. I apologize in advance for any errors that you may find and request you to bring them to my attention.

Anuradha Gupta

Contents

1

Complex Numbers and The Complex Plane

The formula for solving a quadratic equation has been known for hundreds of years. A quadratic equation $ax^2 + bx + c = 0$ has two solutions

$$x = \frac{-b+\sqrt{b^2-4ac}}{2a} \text{ and } x = \frac{-b-\sqrt{b^2-4ac}}{2a}.$$

But if the term $b^2 - 4ac < 0$, then the roots are not real. To overcome this problem, the imaginary unit was introduced as the square root of minus one.

i.e., $$i = \sqrt{-1} \quad \text{or} \quad i^2 = -1.$$

Using this notion, the solutions for quadratic equation $x^2 + 1 = 0$ are i and $-i$. However, until complex numbers were widely accepted, such solutions were simply ignored or considered meaningless. The Italian Mathematician Raffaele Bombelli (1572) introduced imaginary and complex numbers in connection with the solving of cubic equations of the form

$$ax^3 + bx^2 + cx + d = 0.$$

In methods developed by Tartaglia and Cardano, the calculations that needed to be done to find the solution of a cubic equation often involved manipulating square roots of negative numbers, even if the actual solutions were all real numbers. This led to the serious study of complex numbers.

Bombelli started the process by defining i and explaining rules for mathematical operations with complex numbers. In 1799, John Wallis gave the idea of representing complex numbers with points in a coordinate plane. But in the eighteenth century, the number concept took a gigantic evolutionary step forward when the German Mathematician Carl Friedrich Gauss put the so-called imaginary numbers or complex numbers on a logical and consisting footing by treating them as an extension of the real number system.

The goal in the first section is to examine basic definitions and arithmetic of complex numbers.

The complex number system denoted by **C**, is the set of all pairs of real numbers (*i.e.* $\mathbb{R} \times \mathbb{R}$) with the operations of addition and multiplication defined by

$$(a, b) + (c, d) = (a + c, b + d)$$

$$(a, b)\,(c, d) = (ac - bd, bc + ad)$$

for all $(a, b), (c, d) \in \mathbf{C}$.

It is easy to check using the properties of real numbers that '+' and '×' are both commutative and associative and that '×' is distributive over '+'. The additive identity is (0, 0) and additive inverse of (a, b) is $(-a, -b)$. The multiplicative identity is (1, 0). For multiplicative inverse of any non-zero (a, b) we proceed in the following way:

Let (α, β) be the multiplicative inverse of (a, b), therefore

$$(\alpha, \beta)\,(a, b) = (1, 0)$$

$$\Rightarrow \quad (\alpha a - \beta b, \alpha b + a\beta) = (1, 0)$$

which is equivalent to the linear system of equations

$$\alpha a - \beta b = 1$$

$$\alpha b + \beta a = 0$$

and the solution is

$$\alpha = \frac{a}{a^2 + b^2}, \quad \beta = \frac{-b}{a^2 + b^2}$$

Thus, the set of complex numbers forms a field.

We note that the subset $\{(a, 0)/a \in \mathbb{R}\}$ of **C** is isomorphic to $\mathbb{R}$ such that the complex number $(a, 0)$ corresponds to the real number a. Thus, it is more convenient to write a instead of $(a, 0)$ and since

$$(a, 0) \times (c, d) = (ac, ad).$$

We can write $a \times (c, d) = (ac, ad)$

$$a(c, d) = (ac, ad)$$

Thus, a complex number (a, b) can be written as

$$(a, b) = (a, 0) + (0, b) = a(1, 0) + b(0, 1).$$

Put $(1, 0) = 1$ and $(0, 1) = i$, then

$$(a, b) = a + ib$$

represents the same complex number. Thus, a complex number can be written in the form $a + ib$, where a and b are real numbers and $i = \sqrt{-1}$.

The real number a in $z = a + ib$ is called the **real part of z;** the real number b is called the **imaginary part of z.** The real and imaginary parts of a complex number z are abbreviated ***Re*(*z*)** and ***Im*(*z*)**, respectively.

Two complex numbers are equal if their corresponding real and imaginary parts are equal. We write the formal definition in the following way:

1.1 DEFINITION

Two complex numbers $z_1 = a_1 + ib_1$ and $z_2 = a_2 + ib_2$ are equal if $a_1 = a_2$ and $b_1 = b_2$ or symbolically,

$$Re(z_1) = Re(z_2) \quad \text{and} \quad Im(z_1) = Im(z_2).$$

1.1.1 Arithmetic Operations on Complex Numbers

We know addition and multiplication of complex numbers (regarded as an element of $\mathbb{R} \times \mathbb{R}$) are commutative, associative and distributive over addition. Thus, the complex numbers of the form $a + ib$ can be manipulated according to the laws of algebra as follows:

If $z_1 = a_1 + ib_1$ and $z_2 = a_2 + ib_2$ are two complex numbers, then

Addition: $$z_1 + z_2 = (a_1 + ib_1) + (a_2 + ib_2) = (a_1 + a_2) + i(b_1 + b_2)$$

Subtraction: $$z_1 - z_2 = (a_1 + ib_1) - (a_2 + ib_2) = (a_1 - a_2) + i(b_1 - b_2)$$

Multiplication: $$z_1 z_2 = (a_1 + ib_1)(a_2 + ib_2) = (a_1 a_2 - b_1 b_2) + i(b_1 a_2 + a_1 b_2)$$

Division: $$\frac{z_1}{z_2} = \frac{a_1 + ib_1}{a_2 + ib_2}, \quad a_2 \neq 0 \text{ or } b_2 \neq 0$$

$$= \frac{(a_1 + ib_1)(a_2 - ib_2)}{(a_2 + ib_2)(a_2 - ib_2)}$$

$$= \frac{a_1 a_2 + b_1 b_2}{a_2^2 + b_2^2} + \frac{i(b_1 a_2 - a_1 b_2)}{a_2^2 + b_2^2}.$$

Solution of quadratic equations with complex coefficients: We know that the square roots of -1 are i and $-i$. Moreover, there are two square roots of any non-zero complex number $a + ib$.

i.e. $(x + iy)^2 = a + ib$

$\Rightarrow$ $x^2 - y^2 = a$ ...(1)

and $2xy = b$ ...(2)

Substituting the value of y from (2) in (1), we get

$$x^2 - \frac{b^2}{4x^2} = a$$

i.e. $4x^4 - 4ax^2 - b^2 = 0$ ...(3)

and $y = \dfrac{b}{2x}.$

Solving (3) for x, we get

$$x = \pm\sqrt{\frac{a \pm \sqrt{a^2 + b^2}}{2}},$$

$$y = \frac{b}{2x} = \pm\sqrt{\frac{-a + \sqrt{a^2 + b^2}}{2}} \text{ (sign } b)$$

where sign $b = \begin{cases} 1 \text{ if } b \geq 0 \\ -1 \text{ if } b < 0 \end{cases}.$

Example 1.1

Find $(2i)^{1/2}$.

Solution

The solutions are $x = \pm\sqrt{\dfrac{\sqrt{4}}{2}} = \pm 1$

and $y = \pm\sqrt{\dfrac{\sqrt{4}}{2}}$ (Sign of *Im* part)

$= +1$

Thus, $x + iy = +1 \pm i$ are the solutions of $(2i)^{1/2}$.

Example 1.2

Find $(-3-4i)^{1/2}$.

Solution

The solution are

$$x = \pm\sqrt{\frac{-3+\sqrt{9+16}}{2}}$$

$$= \pm\sqrt{\frac{-3+5}{2}}$$

$$= \pm 1$$

$$y = \pm\sqrt{\frac{3+\sqrt{25}}{2}} \quad \text{(Sign of } Im \text{ part)}$$

$$= \pm\, 2\,(-1)$$

$$= \mp 2$$

The solutions are $1-2i$ and $-1+2i$.

It follows that any quadratic equation with complex coefficients admits a solution in complex field.

Let $\quad az^2 + bz + c = 0, \quad a, b, c \in \mathbf{C}$ and $a \neq 0$, then

$$z^2 + \frac{b}{a}z + \frac{c}{a} = 0$$

$$\Rightarrow \quad \left(z + \frac{b}{2a}\right)^2 = \frac{b^2 - 4ac}{4a^2}$$

Thus,
$$z = \frac{-b \pm \sqrt{b^2 - 4ac}}{2a}.$$

1.1.2 The Complex Conjugate

If $z = a + ib$ is a complex number, then the complex number obtained by changing the sign of imaginary part of z is called the **complex conjugate** of z *i.e.*, the complex conjugate $\bar{z}$ of z is $a - ib$.

Using the addition, subtraction and multiplication of complex numbers, the following properties of conjugate of complex numbers can be proved easily.

Properties of Conjugate: Let $z_1, z_2 \in \mathbf{C}$, then

(i) $\overline{z_1 + z_2} = \bar{z}_1 + \bar{z}_2$

(ii) $\overline{z_1 - z_2} = \bar{z}_1 - \bar{z}_2$

(iii) $\overline{z_1 z_2} = \bar{z}_1 \, \bar{z}_2$

(iv) $\overline{\left(\dfrac{z_1}{z_2}\right)} = \dfrac{\bar{z}_1}{\bar{z}_2}$ (provided $z_2 \neq 0$)

(v) $\bar{\bar{z}} = z \quad \forall \quad z \in \mathbf{C}$

(vi) $z + \bar{z} = 2Re\, z, \quad z - \bar{z} = 2iIm z.$

Comparison with Real Numbers

Many of the properties of the real number system $\mathbb{R}$ hold in the complex number system **C** but there are remarkable differences between the two system of numbers.

The concept of 'order' in the real number system does not carry over to the complex number system. In other words, if $z_1 = a_1 + ib_1$ $(b_1 \neq 0)$ and $z_2 = a_2 + ib_2$ $(b_2 \neq 0)$ are two complex numbers then the statements $z_1 < z_2$ or $z_2 \geq z_1$ have no meaning in **C**.

EXERCISE

1. Write the following numbers in the form $a + ib$

(i) $i(2 + 7i)$

(ii) $2(4 - i) - 3(3 + 2i)$

(iii) $(4 - 3i)(4 + i)$

(iv) $\left(\dfrac{3}{2} - \dfrac{1}{4}i\right)\left(\dfrac{2}{3} + \dfrac{5}{3}i\right)$

(v) $\dfrac{4 - 2i}{3 + 8i}$

(vi) $\dfrac{-i}{1 + i}$

(vii) $\dfrac{(1 - i)(1 + 2i)}{(4 + i)(4 + 3i)}$

(viii) $\dfrac{(4 - 5i) + 2i^4}{(3 + i)^2}$

(ix) $i(1 + i)(2 + i)(2 - 6i)$

(x) $(2 + 6i)\left(\dfrac{2 + i}{1 - 2i}\right)^2$

(*xi*) $3i^5 - i^4 + 7i^3 - 10i^2 - 9$ (*xii*) $\frac{3}{i} + \frac{2}{i^3} - \frac{20}{i^{18}}$.

2. In each of the following cases, indicate whether the statement is True or False.

(*i*) $Re\,(5 + 3i) = 5$ (*ii*) $Im(3 + 2i) = 2i$

(*iii*) If $z_1 z_2$ is a real number, then z_1 and z_2 must be real.

(*iv*) If $z_1 + z_2$ is a real number, then z_1 and z_2 must be real

3. Let $z = x + iy$. Express the following in terms of the symbols $Re(z)$ and $Im(z)$.

(*i*) $Re(-iz)$ (*ii*) $Im(iz)$

(*iii*) $Im((2 + i)z)$ (*iv*) $Im(z^2)$

(*v*) $Re(i - z)^2$.

4. Solving the following equations for $z = a + ib$.

(*i*) $z^2 = i$ (*ii*) $\overline{z}^2 = 4z$

(*iii*) $4z = i(1 + 9i)$ (*iv*) $z - 2\overline{z} + 7 - 6i = 0$

(*v*) $z + 2\overline{z} = \frac{2-i}{1+3i}$ (*vi*) $\frac{z}{1+\overline{z}} = 3 + 4i$

(*vii*) $z = \frac{5+6i}{1+i}$.

5. Find all possible values of z satisfying

(*i*) $z^2 = -9$ (*ii*) $z^2 = -k^2,\ k \in \mathbb{R}$

(*iii*) $z^2 + i = 0$ (*iv*) $z^4 = -4$.

ANSWERS

1. (*i*) $-7 + 2i$ (*ii*) $-1 - 8i$

(*iii*) $19 - 8i$ (*iv*) $\frac{17}{12} + \frac{14}{6}i$

(*v*) $\frac{-4 - 38i}{73}$ (*iv*) $\frac{-1}{2} - \frac{i}{2}$

(*vii*) $\frac{11}{85} - \frac{7i}{85}$ (*viii*) $\frac{9}{50} - \frac{19}{25}i$

(ix) $20i$ (x) $\frac{-14}{25} - \frac{42}{25}i$

(xi) $-4i$ (xii) $-i + 20$

2. (i) T (ii) F

(iii) F (e.g. if $z_1 = 3 + i$, $z_2 = 3 - i$, $z_1 z_2 = 10$)

(iv) F ($z_1 = 4 + i$, $z_2 = 5 - i$, $z_1 + z_2 = 9$)

3. (i) y (ii) x

(iii) $x + 2y$ (iv) $2xy$

(v) $-1 + x^2 - y^2 + 2y$

4. (i) $z = \pm\left(\frac{1}{\sqrt{2}} + \frac{1}{\sqrt{2}}i\right)$ (ii) $-2 + 2\sqrt{3}i$

(iii) $\frac{-9}{4} + \frac{i}{4}$ (iv) $7 + 2i$

(v) $\frac{-1}{30} + \frac{7}{10}i$ (vi) $\frac{-7}{6} - \frac{1}{6}i$

(viii) $\frac{11}{2} + \frac{i}{2}$

5. (i) $+ 3i$ (ii) $+ ki$

(iii) $\pm\frac{1}{\sqrt{2}} \mp \frac{1}{\sqrt{2}}i$ (iv) $1, i, \frac{-\sqrt{3}}{2} + \frac{i}{2}, \frac{1}{2} - \frac{\sqrt{3}}{2}i$

1.2 COMPLEX PLANE

In 1779, Casper Wessel first gave representation of complex number, but in 1806, J.R. Argand published in a privately printed edition, a method of representing imaginary numbers geometrically. But later the geometrically interpretation of complex numbers was developed by Carl Friedrich Gauss in the following way:

A complex number $z = a + ib$ is uniquely determined by an ordered pair of real numbers (a, b). Therefore, 'a' corresponds to the horizontal real axis and 'b' corresponds to the vertical imaginary axis of a Cartesian coordinate system. Thus, the horizontal axis is called the **real axis** and vertical axis is called the **imaginary axis**.

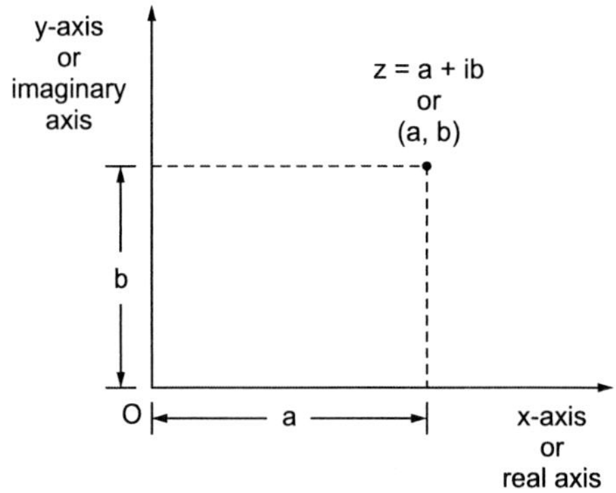

(1) Vector Form: The numbers in an ordered pair of real numbers can be interpreted as the component of a vector in a two-dimensional plane. Thus, a complex number $z = x + iy$ can be viewed as a two-dimensional position vector with initial point, the origin and terminal point (x, y). This vector representation of a complex number leads us to define length of the vector z as the distance $\sqrt{x^2 + y^2}$ from the origin to the point (x, y). This length is called the **modulus** of complex number z.

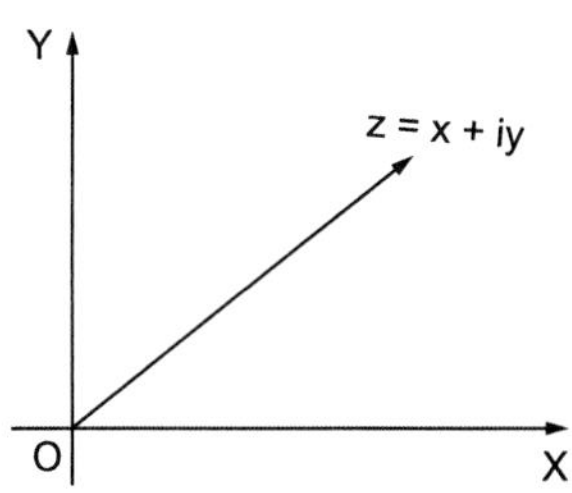

z as a position vector in two-dimensional plane.

Definition 1.2

(2) Modulus: The modulus of complex number $z = x + iy$ is the real number

$$|z| = \sqrt{x^2 + y^2}.$$

Modulus of z is also called absolute value of z.

Properties of Modulus:

(*i*) If $z = x + iy$ is a complex number, then

$$z\bar{z} = (x + iy)(x - iy)$$
$$= x^2 - y^2$$
$$= |z|^2$$

$\Rightarrow$ $$|z| = \sqrt{z\bar{z}}$$

(*ii*) If z_1 and z_2 are two complex numbers, then

$$|z_1 z_2| = |z_1||z_2|$$

and $$\left|\frac{z_1}{z_2}\right| = \frac{|z_1|}{|z_2|} (z_2 \neq 0)$$

If $|z_1| = |z_2| = z$, then

$$|z^2| = |z|^2.$$

(*iii*) Triangular inequality: $|z_1 + z_2| \leq |z_1| + |z_2|$ ...(1)

We know $$|z_1| \leq |z_1 + z_2| + |-z_2|$$

(Using triangular inequality)

$$= |z_1 + z_2| + |z_2|$$

$\Rightarrow$ $$|z_1| - |z_2| \leq |z_1 + z_2| \quad ...(2)$$

Interchanging z_1 and z_2, we get

$$|z_2| - |z_1| \leq |z_1 + z_2|$$

$\Rightarrow$ $$-(|z_1| - |z_2|) \leq |z_1 + z_2| \quad ...(3)$$

From (2) and (3), we get

$$||z_1| - |z_2|| \leq |z_1 + z_2|$$

If we replace z_2 by $-z_2$ in (1), we get

$$|z_1 - z_2| \leq |z_1| + |z_2|$$

Remark 1

(*a*) Let z_1 and z_2 be two sides of the triangle as shown in the figure. Then $z_1 + z_2$ is the largest side of the triangle. From geometry, we know the length of the side of the triangle corresponding to the vector $z_1 + z_2$ cannot be larger than the sum of the lengths of the remaining two sides.

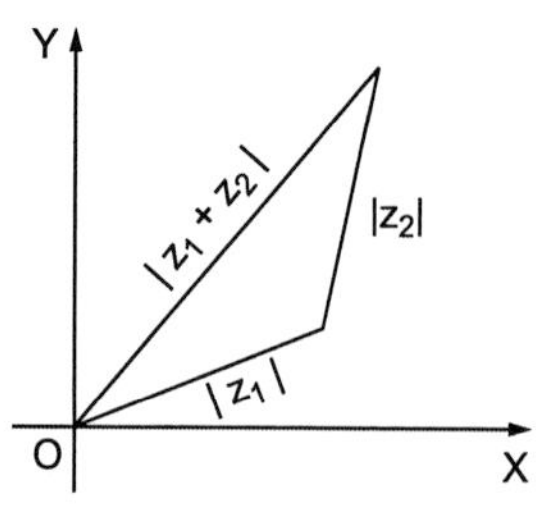

(*b*) The triangular inequality (*i*) can be extended to any finite sum of complex numbers:

$$|z_1 + z_2 + ... + z_n| \leq |z_1| + |z_2| + ... + |z_n|.$$

1.2.1 Polar Form of Complex Numbers

The polar coordinate system was invented by Isaac Newton which consists of a point O called the pole and the horizontal line with pole as initial point called polar axis. If $P(x, y)$ is any point with rectangular coordinates (x, y) and r is the distance from the pole to P and θ is the angle of inclination measured from the polar axis to the line OP. Then x, y, r and θ are related by the equation

$$x = r\cos\theta, \quad y = r\sin\theta.$$

Thus, the complex number $z = x + iy$

$$= r\cos\theta + ir\sin\theta$$

$$= r(\cos\theta + i\sin\theta) \qquad ...(1)$$

Equation (1) is called polar form of the complex number z where

$$r = \sqrt{x^2 + y^2}, \quad \cos\theta = \frac{x}{r}, \sin\theta = \frac{y}{r}.$$

The positive number r is called the modulus and θ is an argument of z and is

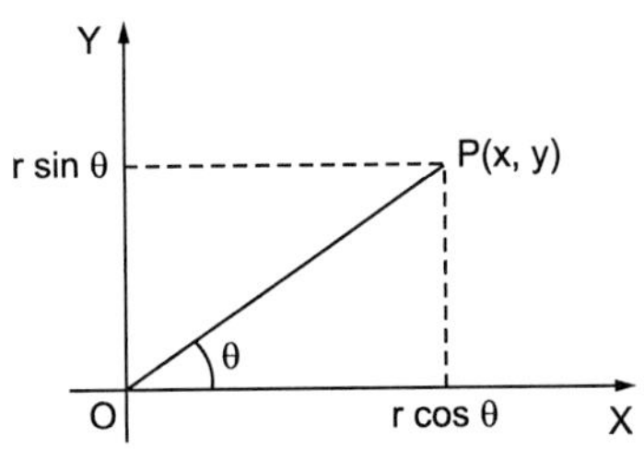

denoted by $\theta = \arg(z)$. Since $\sin\theta$ and $\cos\theta$ are 2π-periodic, therefore argument of z is not unique. In other words, if θ_0 is an argument of z, then the angles $\theta_0 + 2\pi$, $\theta_0 + 4\pi$ are necessarily arguments of z.

Example 1.3

Express $1 + i$ in the polar form.

Solution

$|z| = \sqrt{1+1} = \sqrt{2} = r$. Then $\cos\theta = \frac{1}{\sqrt{2}}, \sin\theta = \frac{1}{\sqrt{2}},$

$$\tan\theta = 1 \Rightarrow \theta = \tan^{-1}1 = \pi/4. \text{ Thus,}$$

$$1+i = \sqrt{2}\left(\cos\frac{\pi}{4} + i\sin\frac{\pi}{4}\right).$$

Remark 2

An argument of $1 + i$ can be any element from $\left\{\frac{\pi}{4}, \frac{9\pi}{4}, \frac{-7\pi}{4}, \frac{17\pi}{4}, \frac{-15\pi}{4}, \ldots\right\}$. Nevertheless any one element from this set is sufficient to identify the set and whatever the number $z(\neq 0)$ there is only one of its arguments in the internal $(-\pi, \pi)$.

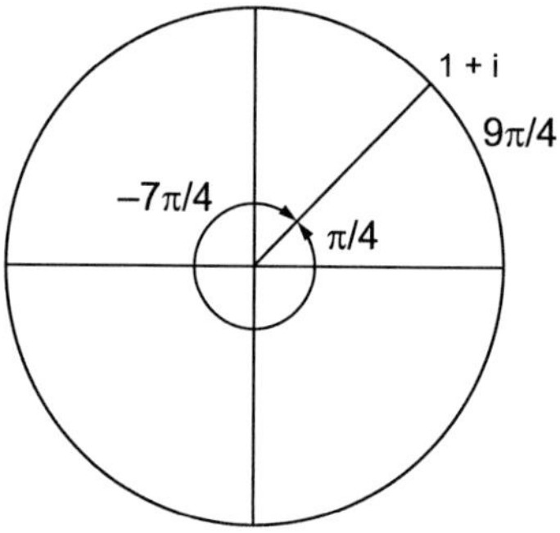

(1) Principal Argument: If θ is an argument of z and $-\pi < \theta \leq \pi$, then θ is called the principal value of the argument of z. The principal argument of z is unique and is represented by the symbol Arg (z).

i.e., $$-\pi < \text{Arg}(z) \leq \pi.$$

(2) Multiplication and Division: The polar form of a complex number is convenient when we multiply and divide two complex numbers.

Suppose $z_1 = r_1(\cos\theta_1 + i\sin\theta_1)$ and $z_2 = r_2(\cos\theta_2 + i\sin\theta_2)$ where θ_1 and θ_2 are any arguments of z_1 and z_2 respectively.

Then,
$$\begin{aligned} z_1 z_2 &= r_1 r_2[\cos\theta_1\cos\theta_2 - \sin\theta_1\sin\theta_2 \\ &\qquad + i(\sin\theta_1\cos\theta_2 + \cos\theta_1\sin\theta_2)] \\ &= r_1 r_2[\cos(\theta_1+\theta_2) + i\sin(\theta_1+\theta_2)] \qquad \ldots(1) \end{aligned}$$

and for $z_2 \neq 0$

$$\begin{aligned} \frac{z_1}{z_2} &= \frac{r_1}{r_2}(\cos\theta_1\cos\theta_2 + \sin\theta_1\sin\theta_2 \\ &\qquad + i(\sin\theta_1\cos\theta_2 - \cos\theta_1\sin\theta_2)] \\ &= \frac{r_1}{r_2}[\cos(\theta_1-\theta_2) + i\sin(\theta_1-\theta_2)] \qquad \ldots(2) \end{aligned}$$

The expressions in (1) and (2) show that the length of the vectors z_1z_2 and $\frac{z_1}{z_2}$ are the product of the lengths of z_1 and z_2 and the quotient of the lengths of z_1 and z_2, respectively and arguments are given by

$$\arg(z_1\ z_2) = \arg z_1 + \arg z_2 \text{ and } \arg\left(\frac{z_1}{z_2}\right) = \arg z_1 - \arg z_2.$$

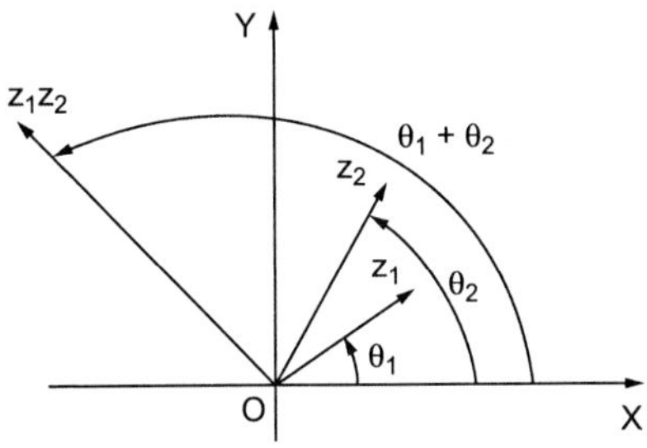

1.2.2 Integral Powers of z

The most impressive payoff from writing complex number in polar form is the solution of an equation of the form

$$z^n = a$$

where a is a non-zero complex number. If $z = r(\cos\theta + i\sin\theta)$ then putting $z_1 = z_2 = z$ in (1), we get

$$\begin{aligned} z^2 &= r^2[\cos(\theta+\theta) + i\sin(\theta+\theta)] \\ &= r^2(\cos 2\theta + i\sin 2\theta) \end{aligned}$$

Thus, $|z^2| = |z|^2$. In general $|z^n| = |z|^n$ and if θ is the argument of z, then $n\theta$ is the argument of z^n.

Example 1.4

Find a value of z^4 such that $z = -\sqrt{3} - i$.

Solution

The polar form of

$$\begin{aligned} z &= -\sqrt{3} - i \\ &= 2\left(\cos\frac{7\pi}{6} + i\sin\frac{7\pi}{6}\right) \end{aligned}$$

Then, $$z^4 = 2^4\left(\cos\left(4.\frac{7\pi}{6}\right) + i\sin\left(4.\frac{7\pi}{6}\right)\right)$$

$$= 16\left[\cos\frac{14\pi}{3} + i\sin\frac{14\pi}{3}\right]$$

$$= 8[-1 + i\sqrt{3}].$$

Definition 1.3

The solutions of $z^n = a$ are called nth roots of a, where n is a positive integer.

We will now show that there are exactly n solutions of the equation $z^n = a$.

Suppose $z = r(\cos\theta + i\sin\theta)$ and $a = \rho(\cos\phi + i\sin\phi)$ are polar forms of z and a. Then $z^n = a$ becomes

$r^n(\cos n\theta + i\sin n\theta) = \rho(\cos\phi + i\sin\phi)$. ...(1)

From (1), we calculate that

$$r^n = \rho \qquad ...(2)$$

and $\quad \cos n\theta + i\sin n\theta = \cos\phi + i\sin\phi$ ...(3)

From (2), we define $r = \rho^{1/3}$ to be the unique positive nth root of the positive real number ρ. From (3), we get

$$\cos n\theta = \cos\phi, \quad \sin n\theta = \sin\phi.$$

Thus, the arguments θ and ϕ are related by $n\theta = \phi + 2k\pi$, where k is an integer. Thus, $\theta = \dfrac{\phi + 2k\pi}{n}$ where $k = 0, 1, \ldots n - 1$. Thus, we obtain n distinct nth roots of z.

The n nth roots of a non-zero complex number $a = \rho(\cos\phi + i\sin\phi)$ are given by

$$z_k = \rho^{1/3}\left[\cos\left(\frac{\theta + 2k\pi}{n}\right) + i\sin\left(\frac{\theta + 2k\pi}{n}\right)\right] \qquad ...(4)$$

where $k = 0, 1, 2 \ldots, n - 1$.

Example 1.5

Find the three cube roots of i.

Solution

We solve the equation $z^3 = i$

$$= \cos\frac{\pi}{2} + i\sin\frac{\pi}{2}.$$

From (4) with $n = 3$, we get

$$z_k = \sqrt[3]{1}\left(\cos\left(\frac{\frac{\pi}{2}+2k\pi}{3}\right)+i\sin\left(\frac{\frac{\pi}{2}+2k\pi}{3}\right)\right),\ k=0,1,2$$

Hence, the three roots are

$$k=0,\ z_0 = \cos\frac{\pi}{6}+i\sin\frac{\pi}{6}=\frac{\sqrt{3}}{2}+\frac{i}{2}$$

$$k=1,\ z_1 = \cos\frac{5\pi}{6}+i\sin\frac{5\pi}{6}=\frac{-\sqrt{3}}{2}+\frac{i}{2}$$

$$k=2,\ z_2 = \cos\frac{3\pi}{2}+i\sin\frac{3\pi}{2}=-i$$

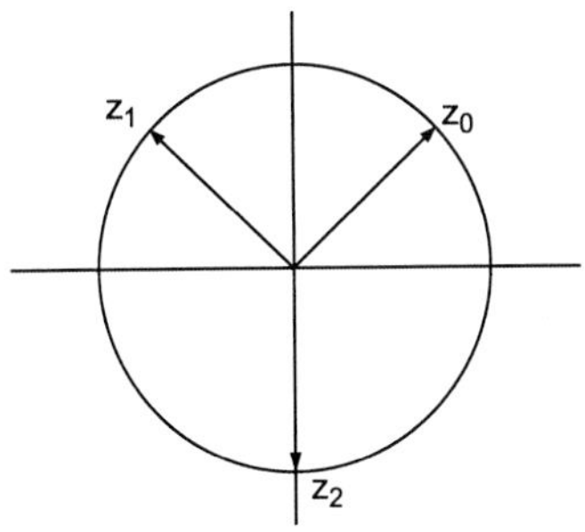

Example 1.6

Find the fourth root of $16i$.

Solution

We need to solve $z^4 = 16i$

$$= 16\left(\cos\frac{\pi}{2}+i\sin\frac{\pi}{2}\right)$$

Thus, for $n = 4$, we get

$$z_k = \sqrt[4]{16}\left(\cos\left(\frac{\frac{\pi}{2}+2k\pi}{4}\right)+i\left(\frac{\frac{\pi}{2}+2k\pi}{4}\right)\right),\ k=0,1,2,3.$$

Hence, the four roots are

$$k=0,\ z_0 = 2\left(\cos\frac{\pi}{8}+i\sin\frac{\pi}{8}\right)$$

$$k=1,\ z_1 = 2\left(\cos\frac{5\pi}{8}+i\sin\frac{5\pi}{8}\right)$$

$$k = 2,\ z_2 = 2\left(\cos\frac{9\pi}{8} + i\sin\frac{9\pi}{8}\right)$$

$$k = 3,\ z_3 = 2\left(\cos\frac{13\pi}{8} + i\sin\frac{13\pi}{8}\right).$$

Comparison with Real Numbers

As a consequence of (4), the complex number system is closed under the operation of extracting roots. This means that for any z in **C**, $z^{1/n}$ is also in **C**. But the real number system does not possess a similar closure property since, if $x \in \mathbb{R}$, then $x^{1/n}$ may not be in $\mathbb{R}$.

EXERCISE

1. Find $|z|$ and Arg z for the following complex numbers:

(*i*) $z = -i$

(*ii*) $z = -\sqrt{3} - i$

(*iii*) $z = \cos\alpha - i\sin\alpha,\ \alpha \in (-\pi, \pi)$

(*iv*) $z = -10$

(*v*) $z = -2 - 2\sqrt{3}i$

(*vi*) $z = \dfrac{12}{\sqrt{3}+i}$

(*vii*) $z = \dfrac{3}{-1+i}$

(*viii*) $z = 5 - 5i$

2. Show that Arg $\left(\dfrac{z-1}{z+1}\right) = \begin{cases} \pi/2 & \text{if } Im\, z > 0 \\ -\pi/2 & \text{if } Im\, z < 0 \end{cases}$

where z is a point on the unit circle $|z| = 1$.

3. Write the complex number whose polar form is given in the following:

(*i*) $Z = 5\left(\cos\dfrac{7\pi}{6} + i\sin\dfrac{7\pi}{6}\right)$

(*ii*) $Z = 8\sqrt{2}\left(\cos\dfrac{11\pi}{4} + i\sin\dfrac{11\pi}{4}\right)$

(*iii*) $Z = 6\left(\cos\dfrac{\pi}{8} + i\sin\dfrac{\pi}{8}\right)$

(*iv*) $Z = \sqrt{2}\left(\cos\dfrac{\pi}{4} + i\sin\dfrac{\pi}{4}\right)$

4. Express the following in the polar form and then in the form $a + ib$.

(*i*) $$\frac{\left[8\left(\cos\frac{3\pi}{8} + i\sin\frac{3\pi}{8}\right)\right]^3}{\left[2\left(\cos\frac{\pi}{16} + i\sin\frac{\pi}{16}\right)\right]^{10}}$$

(*ii*) $$\left(\cos\frac{\pi}{9} + i\sin\frac{\pi}{9}\right)^{12}\left[2\left(\cos\frac{\pi}{6} + i\sin\frac{\pi}{6}\right)\right]^5$$

5. Find a positive integer n for which the equality holds

(*i*) $\left(\frac{\sqrt{3}}{2} + \frac{1}{2}i\right)^n = -1$ (*ii*) $\left(\frac{-\sqrt{2}}{2} + \frac{\sqrt{2}}{2}i\right)^n = 1.$

6. Compute all roots of the following:

(*i*) $(-i)^{1/3}$ (*ii*) $(-1 - \sqrt{3}\,i)^{1/4}$

(*iii*) $(-1+i)^{1/3}$ (*iv*) $\left(\frac{16i}{1+i}\right)^{1/8}$

(*v*) $(-32)^{1/5}$ (*vi*) $\left(\frac{1+i}{\sqrt{3}+i}\right)^{1/6}$.

7. Solve the equation $z^4 + 4z^2 + 8 = 0$.

8. Use the fact that $8i = (2 + 2i)^2$ to find all solutions of the equation

$$z^2 - 8z + 16 = 8i$$

9. For $z \neq 1$, verify the identity

$$1 + z + z^2 + \ldots + z^n = \frac{1 - z^{n+1}}{1 - z}.$$

10. For the complex number $z_1 = -1$ and $z_2 = 5i$, verify that

(*i*) $\text{Arg}(z_1 z_2) \neq \text{Arg}(z_1) + \text{Arg}(z_2)$

(*ii*) $\text{Arg}(-z_2/z_1) \neq \text{Arg}(-z_2) - \text{Arg}(z_1)$.

11. For the complex numbers given in problem (10), verify that

(*i*) $\arg(z_1 z_2) = \arg(z_1) + \arg(z_2)$

(*ii*) $\arg(-z_2/z_1) = \arg(-z_2) - \arg(z_1)$.

ANSWERS

1. (i) $1, \frac{3\pi}{2}$ (ii) $2, \frac{7\pi}{6}$

(iii) $1, -\alpha$ (iv) $10, \pi$

(v) $4, \frac{4\pi}{3}$ (vi) $6, \frac{11\pi}{6}$

(viii) $\frac{3}{\sqrt{2}}, \frac{5\pi}{4}$ (viii) $5\sqrt{2}, \frac{7\pi}{4}$

3. (i) $\frac{-5\sqrt{3}}{2} \frac{-5}{2}i$ (ii) $-8 + 8i$

(iii) $5.5433 + 2961i$ (iv) $1 + i$

4. (i) $\frac{i}{2}$ (ii) $16\sqrt{3} + 16i$

5. (i) $n = 6$ (ii) $n = 0$

6. (i) $\frac{\sqrt{3}}{2} - \frac{i}{2}, \frac{-\sqrt{3}}{2} - \frac{i}{2}, i$

(ii) $2^{1/4}\left\{\cos\frac{(6k+4)\pi}{12} + i\sin\frac{(6k+4)\pi}{12}\right\}, k = 0, 1, 2, 3$

(iii) $\frac{1}{2^{1/3}}(1+i), -1.0842 + 0.2905i, 0.2905 - 1.0842i$

(iv) $1.3477 + 0.1327\,i, 0.8591 + 1.0469\,i, -0.1327 + 1.3477\,i,$
$-1.0469 + 0.8591\,i, -1.3477 - 0.1327\,i, -0.8591 - 1.0469\,i$

(v) $2\left[\cos\frac{(2k-1)\pi}{5} + i\sin\frac{(2k-1)\pi}{5}\right] k = 0, 1, 2, 3, 4$

(vi) $\frac{1}{2^{1/2}}\left\{\cos\left(\frac{(4k-1)\pi}{72}\right) + i\sin\left(\frac{24k-1}{72}\right)\pi\right\} k = 0, 1, 2, 3, 4, 5$

(vii) $\pm 8^{1/2}\left(\cos\frac{3\pi}{8} + i\sin\frac{3\pi}{8}\right)$

(viii) $z = 6 + 2i$

1.3 SETS OF POINT IN THE COMPLEX PLANE

The aim of this section is to state some essential definitions and terminology about sets in complex plane.

1. The modulus of $z = x + iy$ is the distance of the point (x, y) from the origin (Fig 1.1).

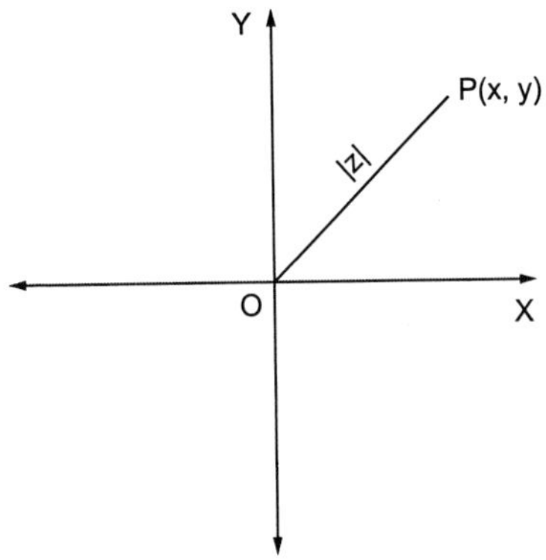

Fig. 1.1

2. The set $\{z : Re\, z > 0\}$ is represented geometrically by the right half-plane (Fig 1.2).

Fig. 1.2

3. The **real axis** (x-axis) is given by any of the following equations:

   (*i*) $Imz = 0$ (*ii*) $z = \bar{z}$

   (*iii*) $|z - i| = |z + i|$ or in general $|z - a| = |z + a|$ if $Im\, a \neq 0$.

4. The imaginary (y-axis) axis can be described in one of the following ways:

   (*i*) $Re\, z = 0$

   (*ii*) $|z - 1| = |z + 1|$ or in general $|z - b| = |z + b|$ if $Re\, b \neq 0$.

5. The **upper half-plane** can be described as

   (*i*) $\{z : |\arg z - \pi/2| < \pi/2\} = \{z : Im\, z > 0\}$

   (*ii*) $\{z : |z - i| < |z + i|\}$ (Fig 1.3)

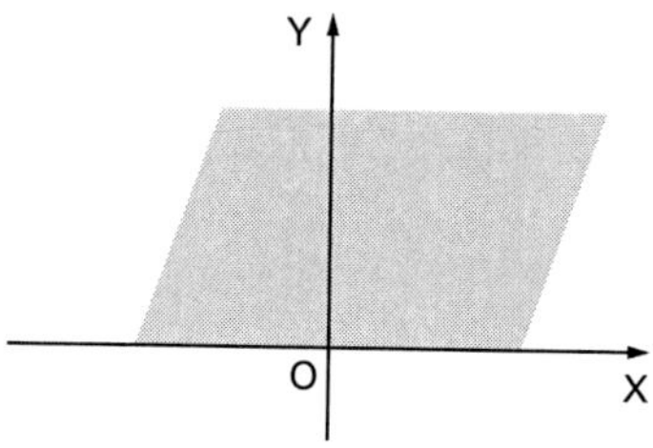

Fig. 1.3

6. $|z - w|$ represents the distance between the complex numbers z and w in the plane.

7. **Circles:**

   (*i*) Let $z_0 = x_0 + iy_0$. Since, $|z - z_0| = \sqrt{(x - x_0)^2 + (y - y_0)^2}$ is the distance between z and z_0, thus, the set $\{z \in \mathbf{C} : |z - z_0| = r, r > 0\}$ represents a circle of radius r and centered at the point z_0 (Fig 1.4).

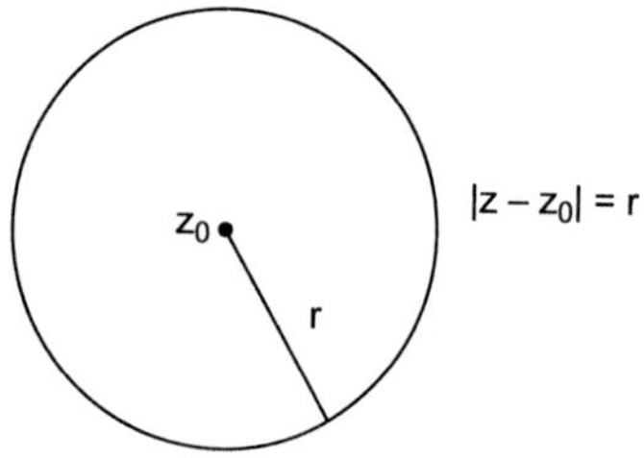

Fig. 1.4

   (*ii*) $z(\theta) = z_0 + re^{i\theta}$, $0 < \theta < 2\pi$ also represents the same circle.

Example 1.7

(*i*) $|z| = 1$ is the equation of a unit circle centered at the origin (Fig 1.5).

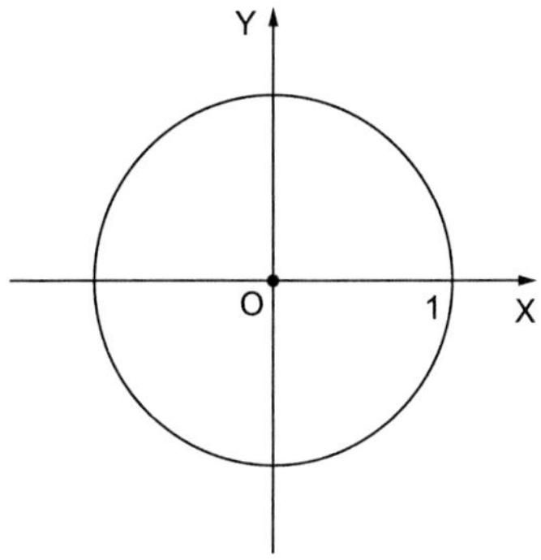

Fig. 1.5

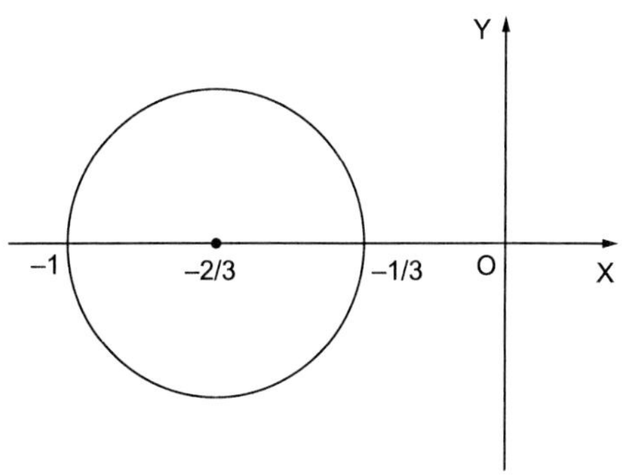

Fig. 1.6

(*ii*) The set $\left\{z \in \mathbf{C} : \left|z + \frac{2}{3}\right| = \frac{1}{3}\right\}$ is the equation of a circle with radius $\frac{1}{3}$ and centered at $-\frac{2}{3}$ (Fig 1.6).

8. **Interior of a circle:** The set $\{z \in \mathbf{C} : |z - z_0| < r\}$ represents the interior of a circle with radius r centered at z_0 (Fig 1.7).
   Exterior of a circle: The set $\{z \in \mathbf{C} : |z - z_0| > r\}$ represents the exterior of a circle with radius r centered at z_0 (Fig 1.8).

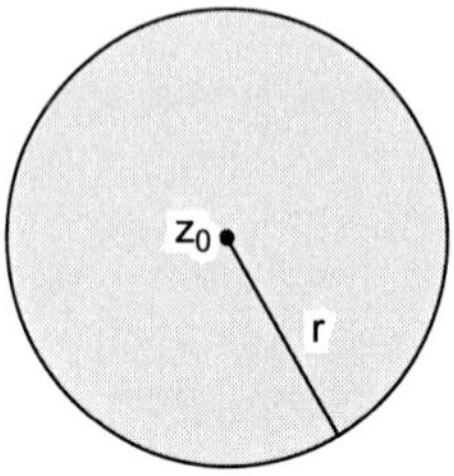

Fig. 1.7

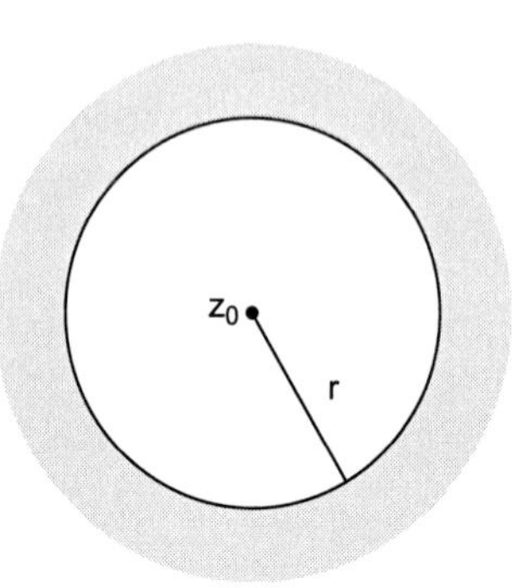

Fig. 1.8

9. **Annulus:** The set S_1 of points satisfying the inequality $r_1 < |z - z_0|$ lies exterior to the circle of radius r_1 centered at z_0, whereas the set S_2 of points satisfying $|z - z_0| < r_2$ lies interior to the circle of radius r_2 centered at z_0. Thus, if $0 < r_1 < r_2$, then the set of point satisfying the simultaneous inequality

$$r_1 < |z - z_0| < r_2,$$

is the intersection of the sets S_1 and S_2 (Fig. 1.9).

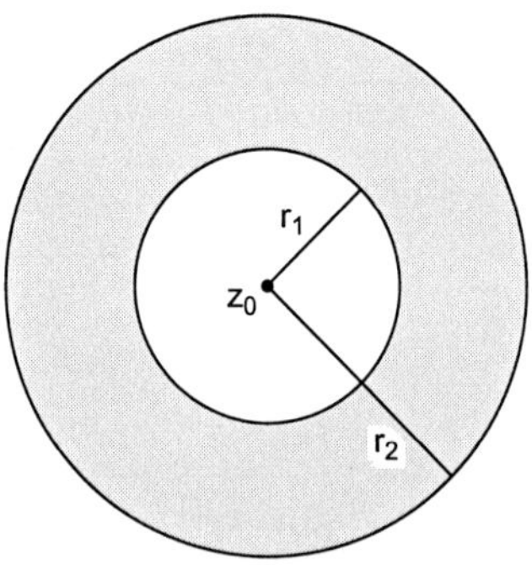

Fig. 1.9

10. **Discs and neighbourhood:** $D(z_0; \in)$ denotes the open disc of radius $\in > 0$ centered at z_0 *i.e.*, $D(z_0; \in) = \{z : |z - z_0| < \in\}$, $D(z_0; r)$ is called a neighbourhood (or $\in$-neighbhourhood) of z_0.

11. **Open set:** A set $S \subseteq C$ is said to be open if for any $z \in S$ there exists $\delta > 0$ such that $D(z, \delta) \subset S$.

12. Complement of a set: For any set $S \subseteq C$, $\tilde{S} = \mathbf{C} \sim S$ denotes the complement of S. *i.e.*, $\tilde{S} = \{z \in \mathbf{C}: z \notin S\}$.

13. Closed set: A set is closed if its complement is open. Equivalently, S is closed if $\tilde{S}$ is open.

14. Boundary of a set: The boundary of a set $S \subseteq \mathbf{C}$, denoted by ∂S, is the set of points whose δ-neighbourhood have a non-empty intersection with both S and $\tilde{S}$, for every $\delta > 0$.

$\bar{S}$, the closure of S is given by $\bar{S} = S \cup \partial S$.

15. Bounded set: S is bounded if it is contained in $D(0; M)$ for some $M > 0$. Sets that are closed and bounded are called **compact.**

Examples 1.8

(*i*) Every open disc is an open set.

(*ii*) The quadrant $Q = \{z \in \mathbf{C} : Rez > 0, Imz > 0\}$ is open, since for $z \in Q$, $D(z, r) \subset Q$ for $0 < r < \min\{Rez, Imz\}$.

(*iii*) Any closed disc $\bar{D}(a; r)$ is a closed set for if $z \notin D(a; r)$ then $D(z, \delta) \subseteq \mathbf{C} \sim D(a; r)$ whenever $0 < \delta \leq |z - a| - r$.

(*iv*) $\{z : Re\, z \geq 0\}$, $\{z : Imz \geq 0\}$ are closed.

(*v*) The set $S = \{z : 1 \leq |z| < 2\}$ is neither open nor closed.

16. Connected set: A set S is said to be connected if there do not exist two disjoint open sets A and B whose union contains S *i.e.*,

$$S \subset A \cup B, A \cap B = \phi, A \neq \phi, B \neq \phi.$$

If S is not connected then it is called disconnected.

17. $[z_1, z_2]$ denotes the straight line segment with end points z_1 and z_2.

18. A **polygonal line** is the join of finite number of line segments of the form $[z_0, z_1] \cup [z_1, z_2] \cup \ldots \cup [z_{n-1}, z_n]$.

19. Polygonally connected set: A set $S \subseteq \mathbf{C}$ is said to be polygonally connected if every pair $z, w \in S$ can be joined by polygonal line contained in S.

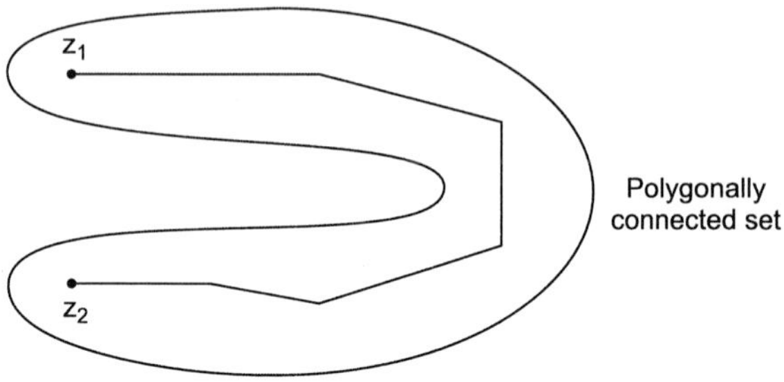

20. Convex set: A set $S \subseteq \mathbf{C}$ is said to be convex if for any two points $z_1, z_2 \in S$, $[z_1, z_2] \subseteq S$.

Remark

(*i*) Every polygonally-connected set is connected. But converse is not true.

For example, the set $S = \{z = x + iy/y = x^2\}$ is connected but not polygonally connected because the set does not contain straight line segments.

(*ii*) There are connected sets whose points cannot be connected to one another by any curve in the set.

For example, the set $S = \{z = x + iy : x = 0 \text{ or } x > 0, y = \sin \frac{1}{x}\}$ is connected, but $x = 0$ is the point in S that cannot be connected by any curve in S.

(*iii*) Every convex set is polygonally connected but converse is not true (Fig 1.10).

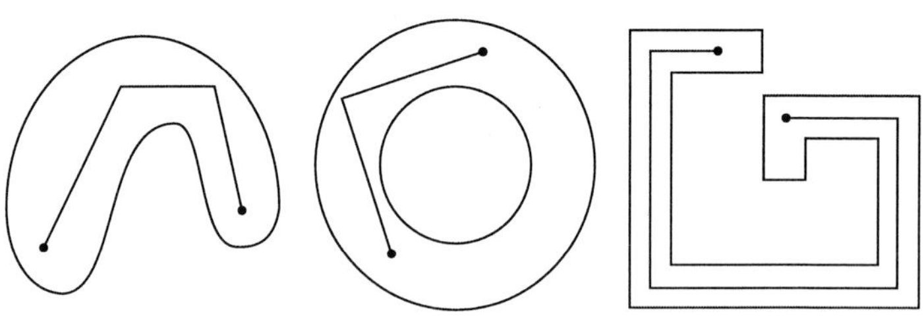

Fig. 1.10

(*iv*) In every open set, connectedness and polygonally connectedness are equivalent.

21. An open connected set is a region.

Let z_0 be a given point in an open set G and G_1 be the set of points z in G polygonally connected to z_0 in G, and G_2 be the set of points z in G not-polygonally connected to $z_0 \in G$. The sets G_1 and G_2 are opens it is shown in the following lemma:

Lemma 1.1

The sets G_1 and G_2 are open sets.

Proof

Let $z \in G_1$. Then, since G is open, there is $\delta > 0$ such that $w \in G$ whenever $|w - z| < \delta$. If $|w - z| < \delta$ then $[z, w] \subseteq G$ and since there is polygonal line $[z_0, z_1, ..., z_{n-1}, z] \subseteq G$, the line $[z_0, z_1 ... z_{n-1}, z, w] \subseteq G$, then $w \in G_1$. Z is an arbitrary point of G_1, then G_1 is open.

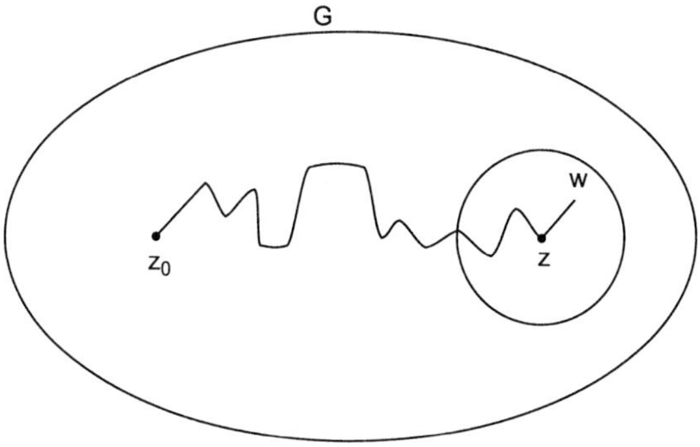

Let $z \in G_2 \subseteq G$. Since G is open, there is $\delta > 0$ such that $w \in G$ whenever $|w - z| < \delta$. If z_0 is not polygonally connected to w in G, then z_0 is not polygonally connected to z in G ($[w, z] \subseteq G$) hence $w \notin G_1$ and so $w \in G_2$. Thus G_2 is also open.

Theorem 1.2

A region G is polygonally connected.

Proof

Fix $z_0 \in G$. Let G_1 and G_2 be as defined above. Then $G = G_1 \cup G_2$, $G_1 \cap G_2 = \phi$ and G_1 and G_2 are open (by Lemma 1.1). As G is connected and $G_1 \neq \phi$, $G_2 = \phi$. Then $G = G_1$ and so every point of G is polygonally connected to z_0. Since $z_0 \in G$ is arbitrary, G is polygonally connected.

EXERCISE

1. Prove that every convex open set is connected.
2. Prove that every open polygonally connected set is connected.
3. Describe the sets whose points satisfy the following relations. Which of the sets are regions?

   (*i*) $\{z : |z - i| \neq |z|\}$ (*ii*) $\{z : 0 < |z| < 3\}$

   (*iii*) $\{z : |z - i| \leq 1\}$ (*iv*) $\left\{z : \left|\frac{z-1}{z+1}\right| = 1\right\}$

   (*v*) $\{z : |z| < 1 \text{ and } Imz > 0\}$ (*vi*) $\{z : Rez > 0 \text{ or } Im\ z \neq 0\}$

   (*vii*) $\left\{z : \frac{1}{z} = \overline{z}\right\}$ (*viii*) $|z : 2 < |z| < 3\}$

   (*ix*) $\{z : |z|^2 = Im\ z\}$ (*x*) $\{z : |Imz| > (Rez)^2\}$.
4. Which of the following sets are compact?

   (*i*) $\{z : Rez = Imz\}$ (*ii*) $\{z : z^9 + 3z^2 + 1 = 0\}$

   (*iii*) $[0, 1]$ (*iv*) $\{z : |z| < 1\}$.
5. What is the distance from z to A when

   (*i*) $z = 1, A = \{z : |z| < 1\}$ (*ii*) $z = 2, A = \{z : |z| \leq 1\}$

   (*iii*) $z = 0, A = \{z : Rez + Imz = 1\}$
6. Describe the following sets as open, closed, neither, or both. Also give a sketch of each

   (*i*) $\{z : Imz > (Rez)^2\}$ (*ii*) $\{z : 1 \leq |z - 2| < 3\}$

   (*iii*) $\{z : (|z| + 2)^2 \geq 4\}$ (*iv*) $\{z : 2Rez + 3Imz \leq 2\}$

   (*v*) $\{z : |z - 1| > |z + 1|\}$

ANSWERS

1. Join two point z, z' in convex open sets such that $[z, z_1], [z_1, z_2]$ ....$[z_{n-1}, z_1] \subseteq G$.

3. (*i*) 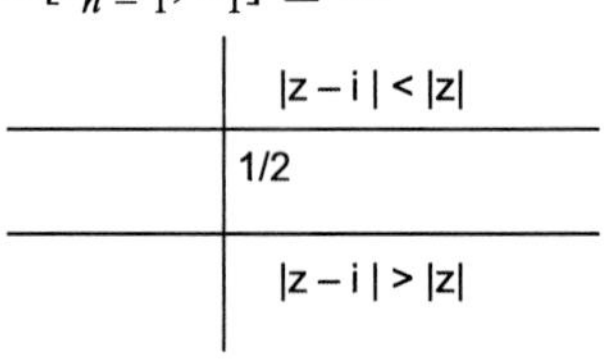

not a region.

(*ii*) 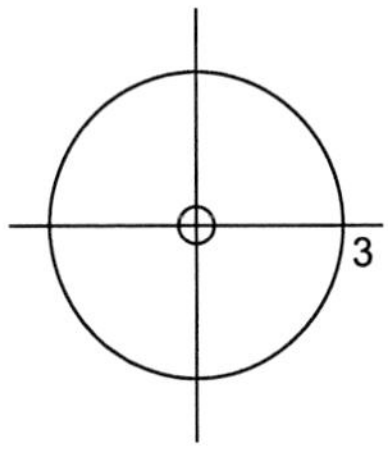

Region

(*iii*) 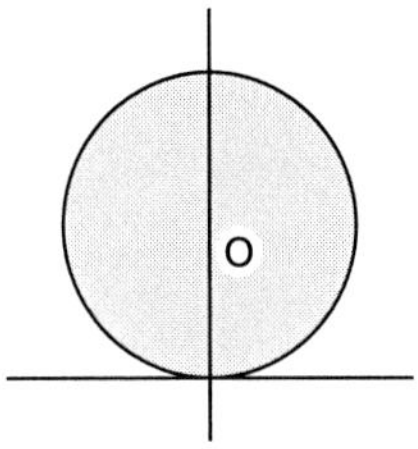

Connected but not open

(*iv*) $\{z : |z - 1| = |z + 1| = Imz$ open and connected

(*v*) 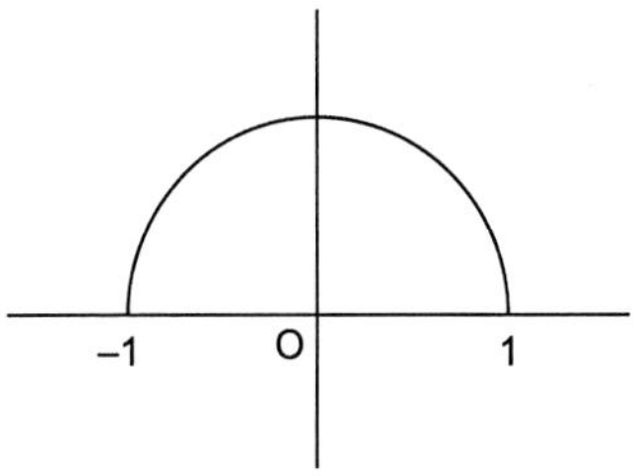

not a region

(*vi*) 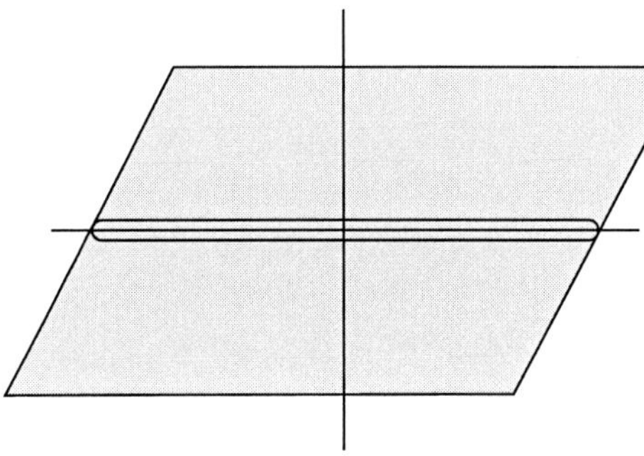
Region

(*vii*) $\{z : |z|^2 = 1\}$ not a region.

(*viii*) 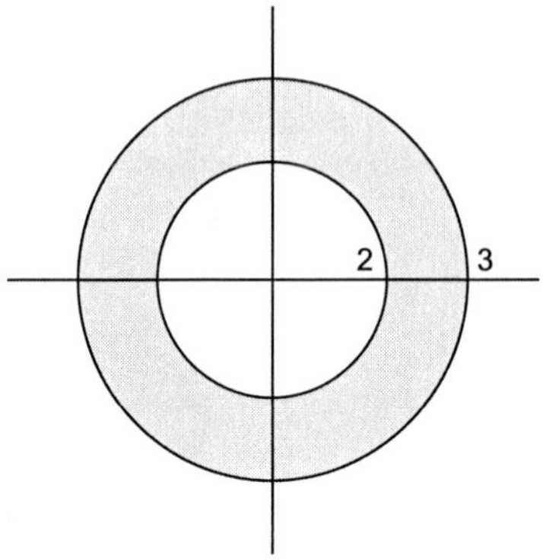

Region

(*ix*) 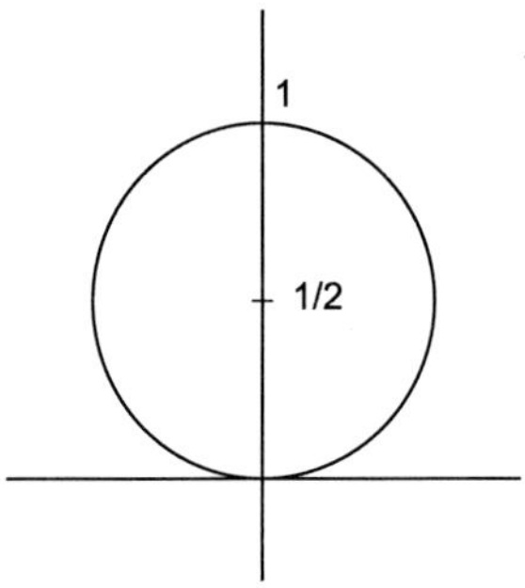

not a region

(*x*) 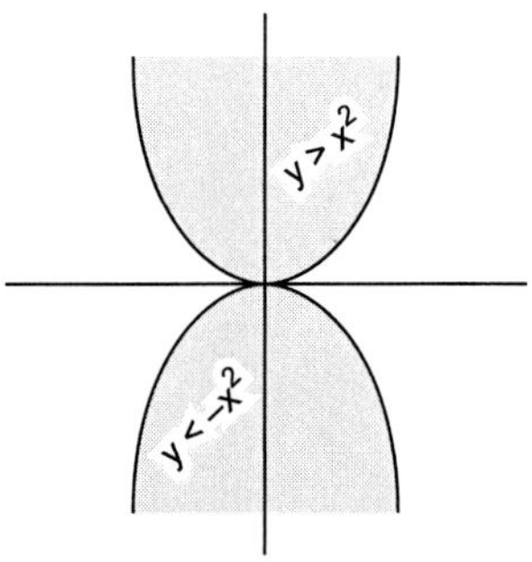

open but not a region

4. (*i*) not compact (because unbounded)

(*ii*) Compact (it has at most nine pts)

(*iii*) compact

(*iv*) Not compact (because not closed)

5. (*i*) $d_A(1) = 0$ ($1 \notin A$, A is open)

(*ii*) $d_A(2) = 1$

(*iii*) $d_A(0) = \dfrac{1}{\sqrt{2}}$

6. (*i*) open

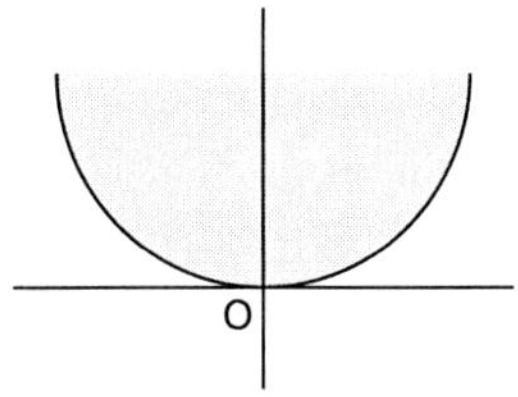

(*ii*) Neither open not closed

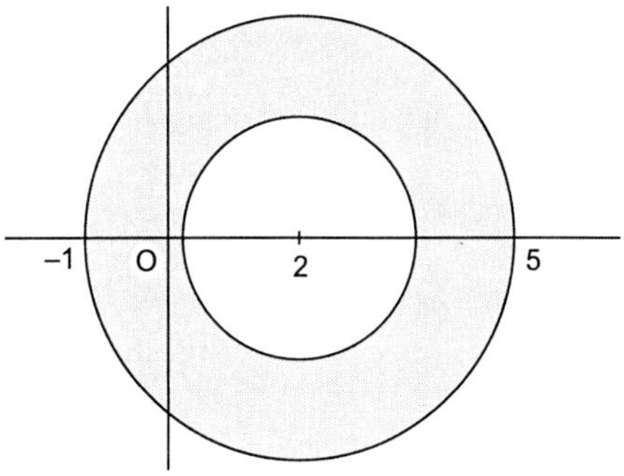

(*iii*) $(|z| + 2)^2 > 4 \Leftrightarrow |z| > 0$ *i.e.*, whole complex plane $\notin$. Both open and closed.

(*iv*) Closed

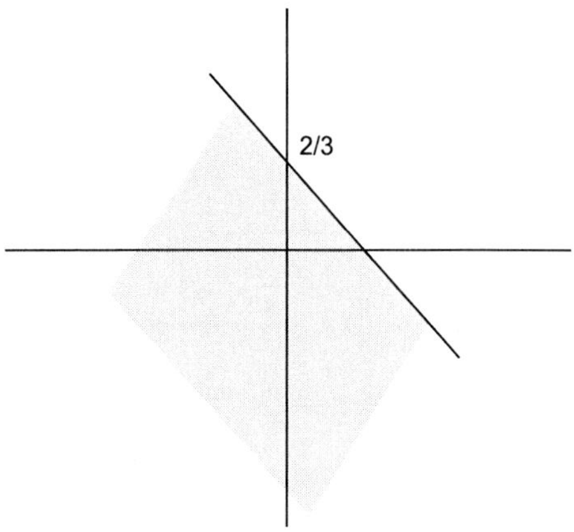

(v) Open

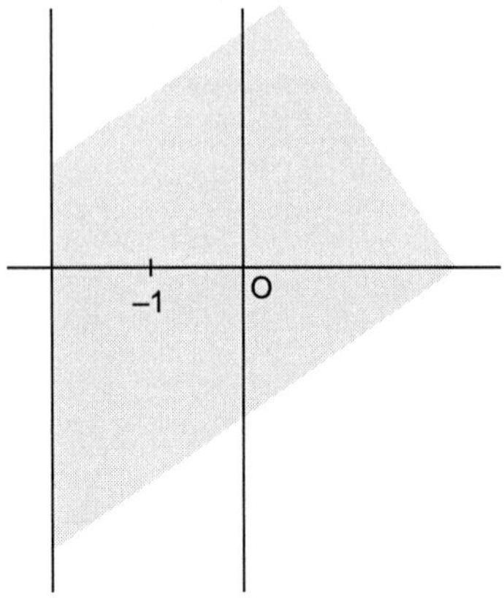

1.4 STEREOGRAPHIC PROJECTION

Let $\Sigma = \{(x_1, x_2, x_3) : x_1^2 + x_2^2 + x_3^2 = 1\}$ be a unit sphere. The plane $x_3 = 0$ coincides with the complex plane **C** and suppose that x_1, x_2 axes are x and y axes, respectively. To $(x_1, x_2, x_3) \in \Sigma$ we associate a complex number $z = x + iy$, where the ray from (0, 0, 1) through (x_1, x_2, x_3) intersects **C**. This establishes a one-to-one correspondence between **C** and the points on Σ.

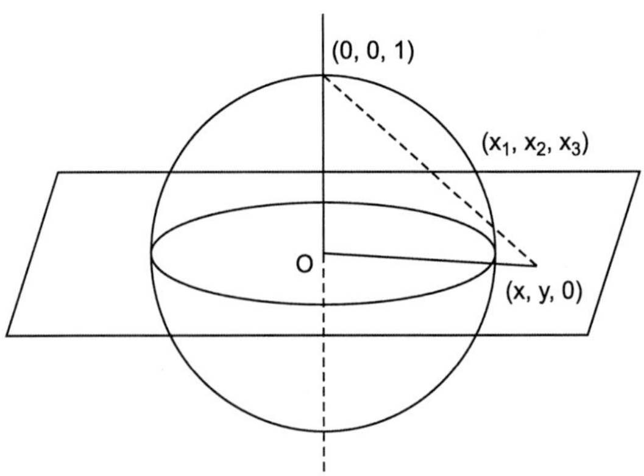

Since (0, 0, 1), (x_1, x_2, x_3), $(x, y, 0)$ are collinear, therefore $\{(1-t)x, (1-t)y, t; 0 \le t \le 1\}$ lies on Σ. Therefore,

$$(1-t)^2 x^2 + (1-t)^2 y^2 + t^2 = 1$$

$$\Rightarrow \quad (1-t)^2 (x^2 + y^2) = 1 - t^2$$

$$\Rightarrow \quad (1-t)^2 |z|^2 = (1-t)(1+t)$$

$$\Rightarrow \quad t(1 + |z|^2) = -1 + |z|^2$$

$$\Rightarrow \quad t = \frac{|z|^2 - 1}{|z|^2 + 1}$$

$$\Rightarrow \quad 1 - t = \frac{2}{1 + |z|^2}$$

Thus, $$x_1 = \frac{2x}{1+|z|^2}, x_2 = \frac{2x}{1+|z|^2}, x_3 = \frac{|z|^2 - 1}{|z|^2 + 1} \qquad ...(1)$$

Also, $$x_1 + ix_2 = \frac{2(x+iy)}{1+|z|^2} \text{ and } 1 - x_3 = \frac{2}{1+|z|^2} \qquad ...(2)$$

Let $\{\sigma_k\} = \{(x_k, y_k, z_k)\}$ is a sequence of points of Σ which converges to (0, 0, 1). Let $\{Z_k\}$ be the corresponding sequence in **C**. By (2), we get

$$x^2 + y^2 = \frac{x_1^2 + x_2^2}{(1-x_3)^2} = \frac{1-x_3^2}{(1-x_3)^2} = \frac{1+x_3}{1-x_3}.$$

Thus, if $\sigma_k = (x_k, y_k, z_k) \to (0, 0, 1)$ then $|Z_k| \to \infty$. Conversely, if $|Z_k| \to \infty$, then $\sigma_k \to (0, 0, 1)$ (from (1)).

Roughly speaking, this suggests that the point (0, 0, 1) on Σ corresponds to ∞ in the complex plane. More precisely, by adjoining to **C** a "point at infinity" and defining its neighbourhood as the sets in **C** corresponding to the spherical neighbourhood of (0, 0, 1). The unit sphere Σ is called Riemann sphere and the system consisting of **C** adjoined with the 'ideal point' ∞ is called the extended complex-number system.

This way of corresponding or mapping the complex numbers onto a sphere is called a **stereographic projection.**

Remark

By a circle on Σ we mean the intersection of Σ with a plane of the form

$$Ax_1 + Bx_2 + Cx_3 = D.$$

If S is the circle on Σ and T be the corresponding set in **C**, then by (1), we get

$$A\left(\frac{2x}{1+x^2+y^2}\right)+\frac{2By}{1+x^2+y^2}+\frac{C(x^2+y^2-1)}{x^2+y^2+1}=D$$

$\Rightarrow \quad 2Ax + 2By + C(x^2 + y^2) - C = D(x^2 + y^2 + 1)$

$\Rightarrow \; 2Ax + 2By + (C - D)(x^2 + y^2) = C + D$ for $(x, y) \in T$ ...(3)

If $C \neq D$ then (3) represents a circle and if $C = D$ it represents a straight line.

Comparison with Real Numbers

In calculus, we deal with limits at infinity, where the behaviour of functions are examined as x is either increased or decreased without bound. We move in two directions on a number line, it is convenient to represent the notions of "increasing without bound" and "decreasing without bound, *i.e.*, $x \to \infty$ or $x \to -\infty$, respectively. But without the designation $\pm\infty$, we can get along with just an ideal point called the 'point at infinity, which is denoted by ∞. We identify any real number a with a point (x_0, y_0) on a unit circle $x^2 + y^2 = 1$ by drawing a straight line from the point $(a, 0)$ on the x-axis or horizontal number line to the point $(0, 1)$ on the circle. The point (x_0, y_0) is the point of intersection of the line with the circle. If we move the point $(a, 0)$ further from the origin, (x_0, y_0) goes nearer to $(0, 1)$. The only point on the circle that does not correspond to a real number a is $(0, 1)$. We identify $(0, 1)$ with ∞ just to complete the correspondence with all the points on the circle. The set consisting of the real number R adjoining with ∞ is called the extended real-number system.

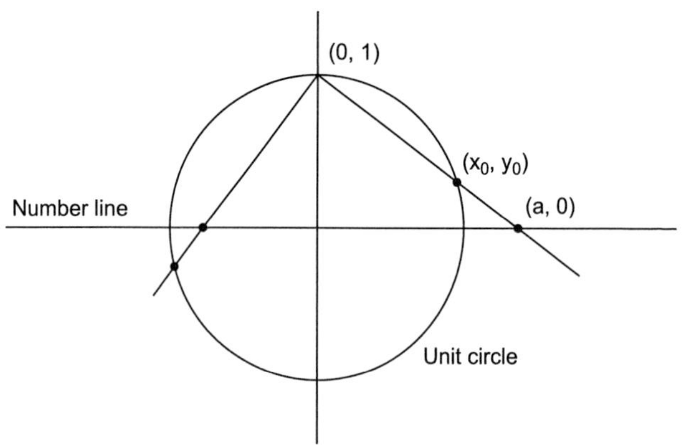

EXERCISE

1. Find a point (x_0, y_0, z_0) on the unit sphere that corresponds to the complex number $2 + 5i$.
2. Describe the set of points on the unit sphere that corresponds to each of the following sets in the complex plane:
   (*i*) The numbers on the unit circle $|z| = 1$.
   (*ii*) The numbers within the open disc $|z| < 1$.
   (*iii*) The numbers that are exterior to unit circle.
3. Which subsets of S corresponds to the real and imaginary axes in **C**.
4. Let z and z' be points on S corresponding to z and z' respectively. Let w be the point on S corresponding to $z + z'$. Find the coordinates of w in terms of the coordinates of z and z'.
5. Let $S = \{(x_1, x_2, x_3) \in \Sigma; x_3 \geq x\}$ where $0 < x < 1$ and let T be the corresponding set in **C**. Show that T is the exterior of a circle centered at 0.
6. Suppose $T \subset \mathbf{C}$ show that the corresponding set S **C** Σ is
   (*i*) a circle if T is a circle.
   (*ii*) a circle minus (0, 0, 1) if T is a line.

ANSWERS

1. $(x_0, y_0, z_0) = \left(\dfrac{2}{15}, \dfrac{1}{3}, \dfrac{14}{15}\right)$
2. (*i*) $(x, y, 0)$
   (*ii*) the set of points in the interior of the circle.
   (*iii*) Outside the unit sphere.
3. Real axis means $y = 0$, then $\left(\dfrac{2x}{x^2+1}, 0, \dfrac{x^2-1}{x^2-1}\right)$ lies on the unit sphere.

4. Imaginary axis means $x = 0$, $\left(0, \frac{2y}{1+y^2}, \frac{y^2-1}{1+y^2}\right)$ lies on the unit sphere.

5. Since $s > s_0$, $0 < s_0 < 1$, then $x^2 + y^2 > \frac{s_0}{1-s_0}$.

❑❑❑

2

Functions of Complex Variable

In this chapter, our aim is to define a function from a set of complex numbers to another set of complex numbers. The concept of limit of a complex-valued function and continuity of a complex function are also introduced in this chapter.

2.1 COMPLEX-VALUED FUNCTION

In elementary calculus, we have studied that if the range of a function f is contained in $\mathbb{R}$, then it is called real-valued function. In this section, we discuss the basic notions connected with the idea of complex-valued function. Since we are dealing with complex numbers, therefore we shall use the term 'function' to mean a function sending complex numbers to complex numbers.

Recall from calculus that a function is a certain kind of correspondence between two sets. Thus,

A function f from a non-empty set A to a non-empty set B is a rule of correspondence that assigns to each element of A one and only one element of B. The set A is called the domain of f and the set of images in B is called range of f of Domain $f = A = \mathbb{R}$ and range $f_C B = \mathbb{R}$, then f is called a real-valued function. Correspondingly, we define a complex function in the following way:

Definition 2.1: Complex Function

A complex function is a function whose domain and range are subsets of the set **C** of complex numbers. A complex function is called a complex-valued function of a complex variable. In other words, *a* function

$f: \mathbf{C} \to \mathbf{C}$ is said to be complex-valued if for each $z \in \mathbf{C}$ in the domain there is one $\omega \in \mathbf{C}$ in the codomain and we write $f(z) = \omega$.

Example 2.1

$$f(z) = z + 2$$
$$f(z) = \frac{1}{z}$$
$$f(z) = |z|^2 \text{ (we regand } \mathbb{R} \subset \mathbf{C})$$
$$f(z) = i \sin z$$

are complex-valued functions.

Operation on the Complex-Valued Functions

If $f: \mathbf{C} \to \mathbf{C}$ and $g: \mathbf{C} \to \mathbf{C}$ are two complex-valued functions, then

(*i*) $(f + g)(z) = f(z) + g(z)$ (*ii*) $(f - g)(z) = f(z) + g(z)$

(*iii*) $\left(\frac{f}{g}\right)(z) = \frac{f(z)}{g(z)}, g(z) \neq 0$ (*iv*) $(f g)(z) = f(z) g(z)$

(*v*) $(\text{fog})(z) = f(g(z))$.

are complex-valued functions.

It is easy to work-out the domains of the combinations, given those of f and g. For example, if f has domain A and g has domain B, then $f + g$ and fg have domain $A \cap B$. For the composite map fog. Range $g \subseteq$ domain f.

2.1.1 Real and imaginary parts of a function

If $w = f(z)$ is a complex function, then the image of complex number $z = x + iy$ under f is a complex number $w = u + iv$. Then,

$$f(x + iy) = u + iv$$

where u and v are real-valued functions of real variables x and y. Thus, any complex function $w = f(z)$ in terms of two real functions can be written as

$$f(z) = u(x, y) + iv(x, y)$$

It means that any complex-valued function can be decomposed into two real-valued functions. We write $u(x, y) = Re\, f(z)$ and $v(x, y) = Imf(z)$. Thus,

$$f(z) = Ref(z) + iImf(z)$$

Example 2.2

(*a*) If $z = x + iy$ then $z^3 = x(x^2 - 3y^2) + iy(3x^2 - y^2)$

Thus, $f(z) = z^3$ can be written as $f(z) = u(z) + iv(z)$ where $u(z) = x(x^2 - 3y^2)$ and $v(z) = y(3x^2 - y^2)$.

(*b*) If
$$\begin{aligned} g(z) &= z + 2Rez \\ &= x + iy + 2\ Re\ (x + iy) \\ &= x + iy + 2x \\ &= 3x + iy. \end{aligned}$$

Thus, $g(z) = u(z) + iv(z)$ where $u(x, y) = 3x$ and $v(x, y) = y$.

(*c*) If
$$\begin{aligned} h(z) &= z + \frac{1}{z} \\ &= (x + iy) + \frac{1}{x+iy} \times \frac{x-iy}{x-iy} \\ &= (x + iy) + \frac{x-iy}{x^2+y^2} \end{aligned}$$

Thus, $h(z) = u(x, y) + ix(x, y)$ where $u(x, y) = x + \dfrac{x}{x^2+y^2}$

and $v(x, y) = y - \dfrac{y}{x^2+y^2}$.

Geometry of Complex-Valued Functions

In real analysis the graph of a function provides very useful visualisation of its properties. However, the graph of a function $f: \mathbf{C} \to \mathbf{C}$ is a subset of $\mathbf{C} \times \mathbf{C}$ $(= \mathbb{R} \times \mathbb{R} \times \mathbb{R} \times \mathbb{R})$ and so a four-dimensional object. Thus, it is not possible to represent it on a two-dimensional page.

But we can study the behaviour of complex function f by the following approach. Draw two complex planes side by side. The left hand plane is called z-plane and the right hand plane w-plane because we normally write a function in complex variables as $w = f(z)$. If we take a point z_0 in the z-plane, we can locate the value $w_0 = f(z_0)$, in the w-plane. We could do this for a whole set S of points in the z-plane and look at the corresponding set of values in w-plane and we name this set S'.

Definition 2.2: The image of *S* under *f*:

If $w = f(z)$ is a complex function and if S is a set of points in z-plane then we call the set of images of the points in S under f, the image of S under f and denote it by S'.

The following illustrations would give us insight into how points in the z-plane are mapped onto points in the w-plane by f.

Example 2.3

Image of a half-plane under $w = iz$. Find the image of half-plane $Re(z) \geq 2$ under the complex mapping $w = iz$ and represent the mapping graphically.

Solution

Let $S = \{z : Rez \geq 2\}$ be the half-plane (as shown in (Fig 2.1(a)). For any point z on the line, we have

$z = 2 + iy, -\infty < y < \infty$. Thus, $w = f(z)$

$$w = f(2 + iy)$$

$$w = i(2 + iy)$$

$$w = 2i - y$$

which is a line $v = 2$ in the w-plane. We conclude that the vertical line $x = 2$ in the z-plane is mapped onto the horizontal line $v = 2$ in the w-plane by the mapping $w = iz$. (Fig 2.1.(b)).

Now, consider the entire half-plane S. We describe S in the following way in terms of the two horizontal inequalities

$$x \geq 2, \quad -\infty < y < \infty \qquad ...(1)$$

In order to describe the image of S, we express the mapping $w = iz$ in terms of its real and imaginary parts u and v.

If $z = x + iy$, then $w = i(x + iy)$

$$\Rightarrow \qquad u + iv = ix - y$$

$$\Rightarrow \qquad u = -y, \quad v = x \qquad ...(2)$$

From (1) and (2), we get $v \geq 2, -\infty < u < \infty$.

Thus, the set S', the image of S under $w = iz$, consists of all points $w = u + iv$ in the ω-plane that satisfy the simultaneous inequalities $v \geq 2$, $-\infty < u < \infty$. In other words, the set S' consists of all points in the half-plane lying on or above $v = 2$.

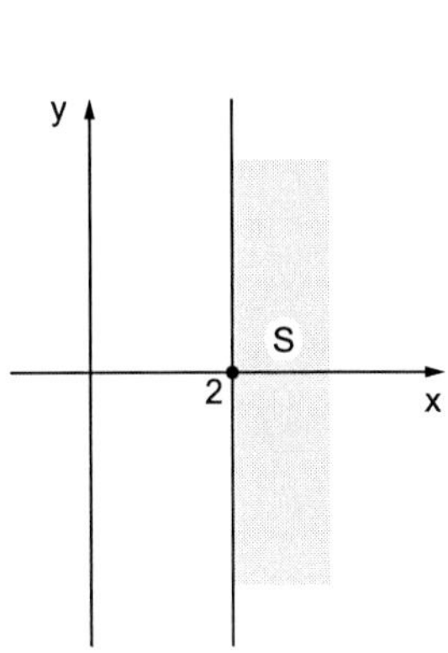

Fig. 2.1 (a)

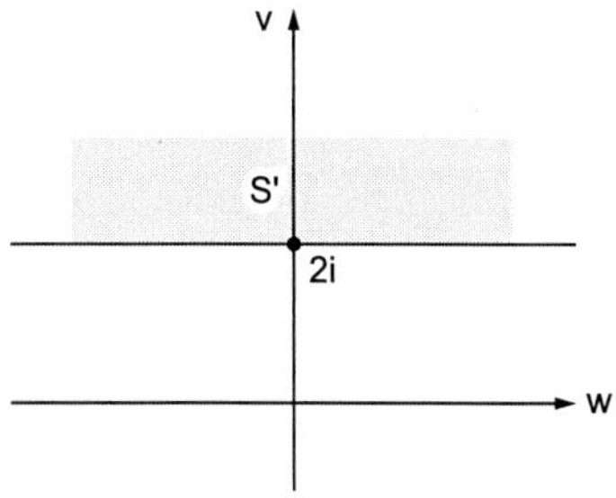

Fig. 2.1 (b)

In Example 2.3, the image S' and the set S are both half-plane. But this is not the case in all complex functions. This is illustrated in the following example:

Example 2.4

Sketch the image of $S = \{(x, y): 1 < x < 2, y \in \mathbb{R}\}$ under the function $w = f(z) = z^2$.

Solution

Since $w = z^2 = (x + iy)^2 = x^2 - y^2 + 2ixy$.

$\Rightarrow u(x, y) + iv(x, y) = x^2 - y^2 + 2ixy.$

Comparing real and imaginary point, we get point (u, v) in the w-plane such that $u = x^2 - y^2$, $v = 2xy$.

If $(u, v) \in f(s)$, then we have the following two cases:

(*i*) $x = 0$ then $u = -y^2$, $v = 0$ for same $y \in \mathbb{R}$.

(*ii*) $x \neq 0$, $1 < x < 2$ then

$$u = x^2 - \left(\frac{v}{2x}\right)^2$$

Thus, $f(s)$ is the set consisting of the parabolas

$P_x = \left\{(u, v); u = x^2 - \dfrac{v^2}{4x^2}\right\}$ for $1 < x < 2$. Now, if $1 < x < 2$ then

P_x lies between the parabolas P_1 and P_2 (Fig 2.2 (b)).

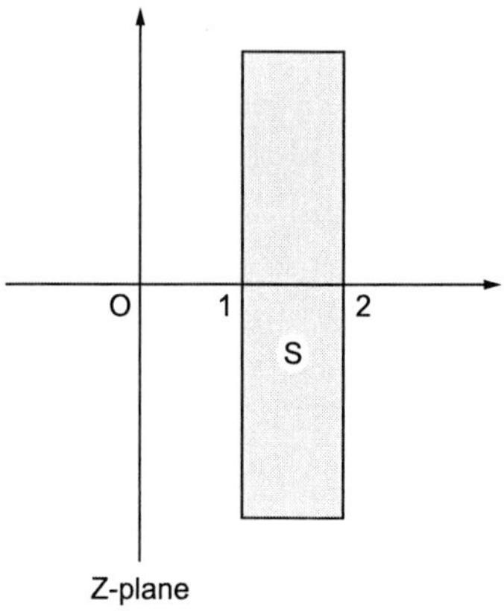

Fig. 2.2 (a)

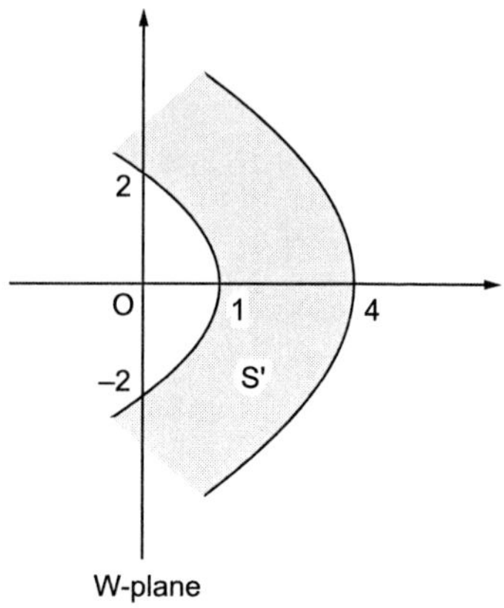

Fig. 2.2 (b)

Comparison with Real Numbers

1. In this section, we made the important observation that every complex function can be defined in terms of two real-valued functions $u(x, y)$ and $v(x, y)$ as $f(x, y) = u(x, y) + iv(x, y)$. This shows that the study of complex-valued functions are closely related to the study of real multi-variable functions of two real variables.
2. If f is a real-valued function then the graph of f is a curve in the Cartesian plane. Graphs are used extensively to investigate properties of real functions in elementary courses. The graph of a complex-valued function lies in four-dimensional space. Thus, we cannot draw the graph of complex function in one graph. The geometric representation of a complex function $w = f(z)$ consists of two figures (as shown in Examples 2.3 and 2.4): the first a subset S in the complex plane, and the second, the image S' of the set S under a complex mapping.

EXERCISE

1. Find the real and imaginary parts u and v of the following complex functions f as functions of x and y:

(*i*) $f(z) = 6z - 5 + 9i$ (*ii*) $f(z) = e^{z^2}$

(*iii*) $f(z) = z^2 + \overline{z}^2$ (*iv*) $f(z) = \dfrac{\overline{z}}{z+1}$

(*v*) $f(z) = e^{2z + i}$ (*vi*) $f(z) = -5z + 2\overline{z} - i.$

2. Find the natural domain of the given complex functions

(*i*) $f(z) = 2Re\, z - iz^2$ (*ii*) $f(z) = \dfrac{3z+2i}{z^3+4z^2+z}$

(*iii*) $f(z) = \dfrac{iz}{|z-1|}$ (*iv*) $f(z) = \dfrac{iz}{|z|-1}$

(*v*) $f(z) = \dfrac{1}{|z|-3}.$

3. Find the range of each of the following complex functions:

(*i*) $f(z) = Im\, z$ defined on the closed disc $|z| \le 2$.

(*ii*) $f(z) = (1 + i)\,|z|$ defined on the square $0 \le Re\, z \le 1$, $0 \le Im\, z \le 1$.

(*iii*) $f(z) = \overline{z}$ defined on the upper half-plane $Im\, z > 0$.

4. If $f(z) = \dfrac{z}{z+4}$ and $z = i$, evaluate

(*i*) $\overline{f}\,(\overline{z}-1)$ (*ii*) $|\,f\,|(z+1)$ (*iii*) $\dfrac{1}{\overline{f}}\,(\overline{z}).$

5. Find the image of the given line under the complex mapping $w = z^2$.

(*i*) $y = 1$ (*ii*) $x = -3$ (*iii*) $x = 0$

(*iv*) $y = 0$ (*v*) $y = -x.$

6. Find the images of the strip $A = \{z : 0 \le Re\, z \le 1\}$ and the circle $C = \{z : |\,z\,| = 1\}$ under the functions

(*i*) $f(z) = (2 + i)\, z + 3$ (*ii*) $g(z) = z^2.$

7. Find the image S' of the set S under the given complex mapping $w = f(z)$.

(*i*) $f(z) = i\overline{z}$; S is the horizontal line $y = 3$

(*ii*) $f(z) = \overline{z}$, S is the line $y = x$

(*iii*) $f(z) = iz + 4$, S is the half-plane $Im(z) \le 1$

(*iv*) $f(z) = iz + \overline{z}$; S is the vertical line $x = 3$.

ANSWERS

1. (*i*) $u(z) = 6x - 5, v(z) = 6y + 9$

(*ii*) $u(z) = e^{|z|^2} \cos 2xy$, $v(z) = e^{|z|^2} \sin 2xy$

(*iii*) $u(z) = 2(x^2 + y^2), v(z) = 0$

(*iv*) $u(z) = \dfrac{x(x+1) - y^2}{(x+1)^2 + y^2}$ $v(z) = \dfrac{-xy - y(x+1)}{(x+1)^2 + y^2}$

(*v*) $u(z) = e^{2x} \cos(2y + 1), v(z) = e^{2x} \sin(2y + 1)$

(*vi*) $u(z) = -3x, v(z) = -7y - 1$

2. (*i*) **C** (*ii*) **C** (*iii*) **C** $\sim \{1\}$

(*iv*) Whole complex plane **C** except the boundary of the unit circle

(*v*) All complex numbers except boundary of the circle centred at 0 and radius 3.

3. (*i*) $-2 < Im\ z < 2$ (*ii*) $(1 + i)$

(*iii*) Lower half plane $Im\ z < 0$

4. (*i*) $\dfrac{-1+2i}{5}$ (*ii*) $\dfrac{1}{\sqrt{13}}$

(*iii*) $1 - 4i$

5. (*i*) the parabola $u = \dfrac{1}{4}v^2 - 1$ (*ii*) the parabola $u = 9 - \dfrac{v^2}{36}$

(*iii*) the ray $-\infty < u < 0, v = 0$ (*iv*) $0 < u < \infty, v = 0$

(*v*) $u = 0, -\infty < v < 0$

6. (*i*) $f(c)$ is the circle with centre 3 and radius $\sqrt{5}$.

(*ii*) $f(c)$ is the unit circle.

7. (*i*) The vertical line $u = 3$ (*ii*) The line $u = -v$

(*iii*) The half plane $Re(w) > 3$ (*iv*) The line $u = v$

2.2 LIMITS AND CONTINUITY

The concept of limit plays an important role in elementary calculus. Recall that $\lim_{x \to a} f(x) = L$ means that value of the function $f(x)$ can be made arbitrarily close to the real number L if the values of x are chosen sufficiently close to, but not equal to, the real number a. The concept of continuity, the derivatives, the definite integral were all defined in terms of the concept of a limit. The limit of complex-valued functions also plays very important role in complex analysis. The complex limit is analogous to the concept of limit in real analysis in the sense that $\lim_{z \to z_0} f(z) = L$ will mean that the values of $f(z)$ of the complex function f can be made arbitrarily close to the complex number L if values of $f(z)$ are chosen sufficiently close to, but not equal to the complex number L if values of z are chosen sufficiently close to, but not equal to, the complex number z_0.

In this section, we will define the limit of a complex functions, examine some of its properties, and introduce the concept of continuity for functions of complex variables.

2.2.1 Complex Limit

A concept of limit is, in essence, the same as a real limit except that it is based on a notion of "close" in the complex plane. In complex plane, the distance between two complex numbers z_1 and z_2 is the modulus of the difference $z_2 - z_1$, thus the phrase "$f(z)$ can be made arbitrarily close to the complex number L," can be stated precisely as: for every $\in > 0$, z can be chosen so that $|f(z) - L| < \in$. Since, the modulus of a complex number is a real number, both $\in$ and δ still represent positive real numbers in the following definition of complex limit.

Definition 2.3

Let f be a complex function, z_0 and L be complex numbers. We say that f has limit L near z_0 if for every $\in > 0$ there is some $\delta > 0$ such that for all z, if

$$0 < |z - z_0| < \delta \text{ then } |f(z) - L| < \in.$$

Complex and real limits have several common properties but there is an important difference between the two. For real function $\lim_{x \to a} f(x) = L$ exists if and only if $\lim_{x \to a^+} f(x) = \lim_{x \to a^-} f(x) = L$. That is, there are two directions from which x can approach a on the real line, from the right or from the left. The real limit exists if and only if the values of limit from both the sides are equal.

For complex limit, z is allowed to approach z_0, from any directions in the complex plane. In order that $\lim_{z \to z_0} f(z)$ exists and equals L, we require that $f(z)$ approach the same complex number L along every possible curve through z_0. Thus, if f approaches two complex numbers L_1 and L_2 such that $L_1 \neq L_2$ along two different curves or paths through z_0, then $\lim_{z \to z_0} f(z)$ does not exist. It is shown in the following example:

Example 2.5

Show that $\lim_{z \to 0} \frac{z}{\bar{z}}$ does not exist.

Solution

Firstly, we assume that z approaches zero along the real axis. For this we consider complex number z in the form $z = x + 0i$ where x approaches 0. For these points, we have

$$\lim_{z \to 0} \frac{z}{\bar{z}} = \lim_{x \to 0} \frac{x + 0i}{x - 0i} = 1 \qquad \text{...(1)}$$

But, if z approaches to zero along the imaginary axis, then $z = 0 + iy$ where the real number y is approaching 0. For this, we have

$$\lim_{z \to 0} \frac{z}{\bar{z}} = \lim_{y \to 0} \frac{0 + iy}{0 - iy} = \lim_{y \to 0} (-1) = -1. \qquad \text{...(2)}$$

Since the values in (1) and (2) are not the same, we conclude that $\lim_{z \to 0} \frac{z}{\bar{z}}$ does not exist.

In general, by computing values of $\lim_{z \to z_0} f(z)$ as z approaches z_0 from different directions, it can be shown that limit of a function does not exist (Example 2.5), but this technique cannot be used to prove the existence of a limit. In order to prove that a limit does not exist we must use definition 2.3 directly. This requires that for every positive real number $\in$ there is an appropriate choice of δ that meets the requirement of definition 2.3.

Example 2.6

Show that $\lim_{z \to a} z^2 = a^2$.

Solution

Let $f(z) = z^2$. Consider

$$\begin{aligned} |f(z) - f(a)| &= |z^2 - a^2| = |z + a|\,|z - a| \\ &= |z - a + 2a| \,.\, |z - a| \\ &\le (1 + 2|a|)\,|z - a| \text{ if } |z - a| < 1 \end{aligned}$$

Thus, let $\delta = \min\left(1, \dfrac{\in}{1+2|a|}\right)$ if $|z - a| < \delta$ then $|f(z) - f(a)| < \in$

Example 2.7

Prove that $\lim_{z \to 1+i} (2+i)z = 1+3i$.

Solution

Let $f(z) = (2 + i)z$

Let $\in > 0$ be given, consider

$$\begin{aligned} |f(z) - l| &= |(2 + i)z - (1 + 3i)| \\ &= |2 + i| \left| z - \frac{(1+3i)}{2+i} \right| < \in \qquad \text{...(1)} \end{aligned}$$

Also $\dfrac{1+3i}{2+i} = 1 + i$ and $|2 + i| = \sqrt{5}$, then (1) is equivalent to:

$$\sqrt{5}\,|z - (1+i)| < \in$$

or $$|z - (1+i)| < \frac{\in}{\sqrt{5}}.$$

Take $\delta = \dfrac{\in}{\sqrt{5}}$. Thus, given $\in > 0$, let $\delta = \dfrac{\in}{\sqrt{5}}$. If $0 < |z - (1 + i)|$ $< \dfrac{\in}{\sqrt{5}}$ then $|(2 + i)z - (1 + 3i)| < \in$. Thus, $\lim_{z \to (1+i)} (2+i)z = 1+3i$.

Theorem 2.1: Real and Imaginary parts of a Limit

Suppose that $f(z) = u(x, y) + iv(x, y)$, $z_0 = x_0 + iy_0$ and $L = u_0 + ix_0$.

Then, $\lim_{z \to z_0} f(z) = L$ if and only if

$$\lim_{(x,y)(x_0,y_0)} u(x,y) = u_0 \text{ and } \lim_{(x,y)\to(x_0,y_0)} v(x,y) = v_0.$$

i.e., $\lim_{z \to z_0} Re(f(z)) = Re(L)$ and $\lim_{z \to z_0} Im(f(z)) = Im(L)$.

We obtain many properties of complex numbers from properties of real numbers. The following general theorem describes how the limit operation relates to the various operations on the complex plane.

Theorem 2.2: Properties of limit of complex functions.

Suppose *f* and *g* are two complex functions. If $\lim_{z \to z_0} f(z) = L$ and $\lim_{z \to z_0} g(z) = M$, then

(*i*) $\lim_{z \to z_0} cf(z) = CL$, c is a complex number

(*ii*) $\lim_{z \to z_0} (f(z) \pm g(z)) = L \pm M$

(*iii*) $\lim_{z \to z_0} f(z).g(z) = LM$

(*iv*) $\lim_{z \to z_0} \dfrac{f(z)}{g(z)} = \dfrac{L}{M}$, provided $M \neq 0$

(*v*) $\lim_{z \to z_0} \overline{f}(z) = \overline{L}$

(*vi*) $\lim_{z \to z_0} |f|(z) = |L|$.

Proof:

(*i*) Let $f(z) = u(x, y) + iv(x, y)$, $z_0 = x_0 + iy_0$, $L = u_0 + iv_0$ and $c = a + ib$. Since $\lim_{z \to z_0} f(z) = L$, then by Theorem 2.1, we get

$$\lim_{(x,y)\to(x_0,y_0)} u(x,y) = u_0$$

and $$\lim_{(x,y)\to(x_0,y_0)} v(x, y) = v_0$$

Since, $u(x, y)$ and $v(x, y)$ are real valued function. Then

$$\lim_{(x,y)\to(x_0,y_0)} au(x, y) = au_0$$

and $$\lim_{(x,y)\to(x_0,y_0)} bv(x, y) = bv_0$$

$$\Rightarrow \quad \lim_{(x,y)\to(x_0,y_0)} (au(x, y) - bv(x, y) = au_0 - bv_0.$$

and $$\lim_{(x,y)\to(x_0,y_0)} (bu(x, y) + av(x, y) = bu_0 + av_0$$

Thus, $Re(cf(z)) = au(x, y) - bv(x, y)$ and $Im(cf(z)) = bu(x, y) + av(x, y)$. Therefore,

$$\lim_{z\to z_0} cf(z) = (au_0 - bv_0) + i(bu_0 + av_0) = CL.$$

(*ii*) and (*iii*) can be proved easily using the techniques of real analysis.

(*iv*) We shall first prove that $\lim_{z\to z_0}\left(\frac{1}{g(z)}\right)=\frac{1}{M}$ if $M \neq 0$.

Now, $$\left|\frac{1}{g(z)}-\frac{1}{M}\right| = \left|\frac{1}{g(z)}-\frac{1}{M}\right| = \frac{|g(z)-M|}{|M||g(z)|} \quad ...(1)$$

Let $\in = \frac{1}{2}|M| > 0$ there is $\delta_0 > 0$ such that whenever $0 < | z - a | < \delta_0$, we have

$$|g(z) - M| < \frac{1}{2}|M|. \text{ Then}$$

$$\begin{aligned} |g(z)| &> -|g(z) - M| + |M| \\ &> |M| - \frac{1}{2}|M| \\ &= \frac{|M|}{2} > 0 \end{aligned}$$

From (1), we get

$$\left|\frac{1}{g}(z)-\frac{1}{M}\right| \leq \frac{2}{|M|^2}|g(z)-M|$$

Thus, given $\in > 0$ there exists $\delta_1 > 0$ such that

$$|g(z)-M| < \frac{1}{2}|M|^2 \in \text{ whenever } 0 < |z-a| < \delta_1$$

Let $\delta = \min(\delta_0, \delta_1)$, then

$$\left|\frac{1}{g}(z)-\frac{1}{M}\right| < \frac{2}{|M|^2}\times\frac{|M|^2}{2}\in = \in .$$

Using (*iii*) and $\lim\limits_{z\to z_0}\frac{1}{g}(z)=\frac{1}{M}$, we get

$$\lim_{z\to z_0}\frac{f}{g}(z) = \lim_{z\to z_0}\left(f(z)\frac{1}{g(z)}\right) = \frac{L}{M}.$$

(*v*) Since $|\overline{f(z)-L}|=|f(z)-L|$. Since $\lim\limits_{z\to z_0} f(z)=L$. Then, $\lim\limits_{z\to z_0}\overline{f}(z)=\overline{L}$.

(*vi*) Since $||f|(z) - |L|| = ||f(z) - |L|| \le |f(z) - L|$. Thus, $\lim\limits_{z\to z_0}|f|(z)=|L|$.

The following examples illustrate how Theorem 2.2 can be applied in computing limits of complex functions.

Example 2.8

Compute

(*i*) $\lim\limits_{z\to i}(z^5 - z^2 + z)$

(*ii*) $\lim\limits_{z\to(2+i)}\dfrac{z^2-(2+i)^2}{z-(2+i)}$

(*iii*) $\lim\limits_{z\to i}\dfrac{(3+i)z^4 - z^2 + 2z}{z+1}$

Solution

$$\begin{aligned}(i)\ \lim_{z\to i}(z^5 - z^2 + z) &= \lim_{z\to i} z^5 - \lim_{z\to i} z^2 + \lim_{z\to i} z\\ &= i^5 - i^2 + i\\ &= i + 1 + i\\ &= 2i + 1\end{aligned}$$

(ii) $$\lim_{z \to (2+i)} \frac{z^2-(2+i)^2}{z-(2+i)} = \lim_{z \to (2+i)} \frac{(z-(2+i)(z+(2+i)}{z-(2+i)}$$

$$= \lim_{z \to (2+i)} (z+(2+i)) = 4+2i.$$

(iii) $$\lim_{z \to i} \frac{(3+i)z^4 - z^2 + 2z}{z+1} = \frac{(3+i)\lim_{z\to i} z^4 - \lim_{z\to i} z^2 + 2\lim_{z\to i} z}{\lim_{z\to i}(z+1)}$$

$$= \frac{(3+i)(i)^4 - i^2 + 2i}{i+1}$$

$$= \frac{3+i+1+2i}{i+1}$$

$$= \frac{3i+4}{i+1} = \frac{4+3i}{1+i} \times \frac{1-i}{1-i} = \frac{7}{2} - \frac{1}{2}i.$$

2.2.2 Continuity of Complex Functions

A real valued function $y = f(x)$ is said to be continuous at a if $\lim_{x\to a} f(x)$ is equal to the value of the function at a. The definition of continuity for a complex function is the same as that of real numbers. This gives the following definition for a continuous complex function at a point.

Definition 2.4

A complex function f is continuous at a point z_0 if $\lim_{z\to z_0} f(z) = f(z_0)$.

If a complex function f is not continuous at a point z_0 then f is said to be discontinuous at z_0. For example, the function $f(z) = \dfrac{1}{1+z^2}$ is discontinuous at $z = i$ and $z = -i$.

Example 2.9

Show that the complex function $f(z) = z^2 - iz + 2$ is continuous at $z_0 = 1 - i$.

Solution

$$\lim_{z\to z_0} f(z) = \lim_{z\to 1-i} (z^2 - iz + 2)$$

$$= (1-i)^2 - i(1-i) + 2$$

$$= 1 - 3i$$

Furthermore, at $z_0 = 1 - i$,

$$f(z_0) = f(1 - i) = (1 - i)^2 - i(1 - i) + 2 = 1 - 3i.$$

Thus, $\lim_{z \to (1-i)} f(z) = f(1-i)$, we conclude that $f(z) = z^2 - iz + 2$ is continuous at the point $z_0 = 1 - i$.

In Definition 2.4, we have defined continuity at a point z_0. But in the subsequent chapter we will deal with the continuity of a function on a set of points in the complex plane. A complex function f is continuous on a set S if f is continuous at z_0 for each z_0 in S.

Clearly each constant function $z \to c$ and identify function $z \to z$ are continuous. Since the concept of continuity depends on the concept of limit, therefore, we have an analogous result for the continuous functions.

Theorem 2.3

Let f and g be continuous at z_0, then

(*i*) $f + g$ is continuous at z_0,

(*ii*) $f \cdot g$ is continuous at z_0,

(*iii*) f/g is continuous at z_0, provided $g(z_0) \neq 0$.

It follows easily by induction on n if $f_1, f_2 \ldots f_n$ are continuous at z_0, then $f_1 + f_2 + \ldots + f_n$ and $f_1 \cdot f_2 \ldots\ldots\ldots\ldots f_n$ are also continuous at z_0. Hence, every polynomial function is continuous. Also, every rational function is continuous.

2.2.3 Bounded Functions

Continuous complex functions have many important properties that are analogous to properties of continuous real functions. One of the important global property of continuous function in real analysis is the Boundedness.

Theorem 2.4

If f is a function continuous on a closed interval I, then f is bounded on I.

Recall that f is bounded on I if there is $M > 0$ such that $|f(x)| \leq M$ for all x in I. This definition can be generalised in case of complex analysis in the following form:

Definition 2.5

A complex function f is bounded on a set S (contained in the domain of f) if there is $K > 0$ such that $|f(z)| \leq K$ for all $z \in S$.

A result for real multi-variable functions states that if $F(x, y)$ is continuous on a closed and bounded region R of the Cartesian plane then there is a real number $M > 0$ such that $|F(x, y)| \leq M$ for all $(x, y) \in R$ then F is bounded on R. Let $f(z) = u(x, y) + iv(x, y)$ is defined on a closed and bounded region R if there exists a real constant $M > 0$ such that $|f(z)| < M$ for all z in R then f is bounded on $\mathbf{C}$.

If f is continuous, then $Ref = u(x, y)$ and $Imf = v(x, y)$ are also continuous real functions on R. Then

$$|f(z)| = \sqrt{|u(x, y)|^2 + |v(x, y)|^2}$$

is also continuous on R.

Since $|f|$ is real valued and it is closed and bounded in the region R, we conclude $|f|$ is bounded on R. That is, there is a real constant $M > 0$ such that $|f(z)| \leq M$ for all $(x, y) = z$ in R. Thus, this establishes the following important property of continuous complex functions.

Theorem 2.5

If a complex function f is continuous on a closed and bounded region R, then f is bounded on R. It means there is a real constant $M > 0$ such that $|f(z)| \leq M$ for all z in R.

Comparison with Real Numbers

In real analysis a function is continuous if there are no breaks or holes in the graph of f. There is also an analogous property in complex analysis. We begin by recalling that a parametric curve defined by parametric equation $x = x(t), y = y(t)$ is continuous if real functions x and y are continuous. Similarly, we say that a complex parametric curve defined by $z(t) = x(t) + iy(t)$ is continuous if both $x(t)$ and $y(t)$ are continuous real functions. With the help of such curves we are able to visualise continuous complex function.

If a complex function f is continuous on a set S, then the image of every continuous parametric curve in S must be a continuous curve.

For this, consider a continuous complex function $f(z) = u(x, y) + iv(x, y)$ and a continuous parametric curve defined by $z(t) = x(t) + iy(t)$. Since $u(x, y)$ and $v(x, y)$ are continuous real functions. It follows from multi-variable calculus that the composition $u(x(t)), y(t))$ and $v(x(t), y(t))$ are continuous functions. Therefore, the image of the parametric curve given by $f(z(t)) = u(x(t), y(t)) + iv(x(t), y(t))$ is continuous.

EXERCISE

1. Find the following limits:

(i) $\lim_{z\to 2} \bar{z}^2$ (ii) $\lim_{z\to 1} \frac{z^3+1}{z+1}$ (iii) $\lim_{z\to 1} \frac{z^3+i}{z-i}$

(iv) $\lim_{z\to 1-i} (|z|^2 - i\bar{z})$ (v) $\lim_{z\to 3i} \frac{Im(z^2)}{z+Rez}$

(vi) $\lim_{z\to 0} \frac{z^2+\bar{z}^2}{Re(z)+Im(z)}$ (vii) $\lim_{z\to 2-i} (z^2 - z)$

(viii) $\lim_{z\to i} (z^5 - z^2 + z)$ (ix) $\lim_{z\to -i} \frac{z^4-1}{z+i}$

(x) $\lim_{z\to -3+i\sqrt{2}} \frac{z+3-i\sqrt{2}}{z^2+6z+11}$.

2. Show that the function $\frac{\bar{z}}{z}$ has no limit near zero.

3. Consider the $\lim_{z\to 0} \frac{Re(z)}{Im(z)}$.

(i) What value does the limit approach as z approaches 0 along the line $y = x$?

(ii) What value does the limit approach as z approaches zero along the imaginary axis?

(iii) What can you say about $\lim_{z\to 0} \frac{Re(z)}{Im(z)}$?

4. Consider the limit $\lim_{z \to i} (|z| + i \operatorname{Arg}(iz))$.

(*i*) What value does the limit approach as z approaches i along the unit circle $|z| = 1$ in the first quadrant?

(*ii*) What value does the limit approach as z approaches i along the unit circle $|z| = 1$ in the second quadrant?

(*iii*) What can you say about $\lim_{z \to i} (|z| + i \operatorname{Arg}(iz))$?

5. Given that f and g are continuous at a, which of the following must be true? Give your reasons.

(*i*) $z \to [f(z)]^2 + 2g(z) + 3$ is continuous at a,

(*ii*) $f/|g|$ is continuous at a,

(*iii*) gof is continuous at a,

(*iv*) $Re(f) + Im(g)$ is continuous at a.

6. Prove that the function $f(z) = 3|z|$ is continuous at each point of **C**.

7. Show that the function f is continuous at the given point.

(*i*) $f(z) = z^2 - iz + 3 - 2i;\ z_0 = 2 - i$

(*ii*) $f(z) = \dfrac{z^3}{z^3 + 3z^2 + z};\ z_0 = i$

(*iii*) $f(z) = \begin{cases} \dfrac{z^3 - 1}{z - 1}, & |z| \neq 1 \\ 3, & |z| = 1 \end{cases};\ z_0 = 1$

(*iv*) $f(z) = \bar{z} - 3Re(z) + i;\ z_0 = 3 - 2i$

(*v*) $f(z) = z^3 - \dfrac{1}{z};\ z_0 = 3i$

(*vi*) $f(z) = \dfrac{Re(z)}{z + iz} - 2z^2;\ z_0 = e^{i\pi/4}$.

8. Show that the function f is discontinuous at the given point.

(*i*) $f(z) = \dfrac{1}{|z| - 1};\ z_0 = i$

(*ii*) $f(z) = \operatorname{Arg}(z);\ z_0 = -1$

(*iii*) $f(z) = \operatorname{Arg}(iz);\ z_0 = i$

(*iv*) $f(z)=\begin{cases}\dfrac{z}{|z|}, & z\neq 0\\ 1, & z=0\end{cases}$ at $z_0=0$

(*v*) $f(z)=\begin{cases}\dfrac{z^3-1}{z-1}, & |z|\neq 1\\ 3, & |z|=1\end{cases}$; $z_0=i$

9. Let $\lim\limits_{z\to a} f(z) = l$. Define g by

$$g(z)=\begin{cases}f(z), & \text{if } z\neq a\\ l, & \text{if } z=a\end{cases}$$

show that g is continuous at a.

ANSWERS

1. (*i*) 4 (*ii*) 1

(*iii*) $\dfrac{z^3+i}{z-i}=z^2+iz+i^2, -3$ (*iv*) $3-i$

(*v*) 0 (*vi*) 0

(*vii*) $1-3i$ (*viii*) $2i+1$

(*ix*) $4i$ (*x*) $\dfrac{-3-\sqrt{2}i}{44}$

2. $f(z) = e^{-2i\theta} \to 1$ as $\theta \to 0$ along x-axis.

$\to -1$ as $\theta \to 0$ along y-axis.

3. (*i*) 1 (*ii*) 0

(*iii*) does not exist.

4. (*i*) $1+i\pi$ (*ii*) $1+i\pi$

(*iii*) $1+i\pi$

5. (*i*) T (*ii*) T provided $|g| \neq 0$

(*iii*) F (*iv*) T

7. (*i*) $5-8i$ (*ii*) $\dfrac{1}{3}i$

(*iii*) 3 (*iv*) $-6 + 3i$

(*v*) $\dfrac{-80}{3}$ (*vi*) $-\dfrac{5}{2}i$

8. (*i*) $\dfrac{1}{|z|-1}$ is not defined at $z_0 = i$.

(*ii*) $\lim\limits_{z \to -1} f(z)$ does not exist.

(*iii*) $\lim\limits_{z \to i} f(z)$ does not exist

(*iv*) $\lim\limits_{z \to 0} \dfrac{z}{|z|}$ does not exist.

(*v*) $\lim\limits_{z \to i} f(z) \neq f(i)$

9. $\lim\limits_{z \to a} g(z) = \lim\limits_{z \to a} f(z) = l = g(a)$

2.3 POWER SERIES

The theory of complex sequences and series is analogous to the one encountered in real analysis. In this section, we explore the convergence and divergence of complex sequences and complex infinite series. But in the last part of the section our main interest is power series, in which variables can take complex values. So we shall go through the essential definitions for complex series but we shall not be comprehensive in our study of complex series. Our aim is to get sufficient information that is needed to tackle power series.

Sequences: An infinite sequence of complex numbers is a function from the natural numbers $\mathbb{N}$ to the complex numbers **C**. In other words, to each integer $n = 1, 2, 3$ ... we assign a single complex number z_0. For example, the sequence $\{i^n\}$ is $\{i, i^2, i^3, i^4, ...\}$

If $\lim\limits_{n \to \infty} z_n = l$, then we say the sequence $\{z_n\}$ is convergent. In other words, $\{z_n\}$ converges to the number l if for each positive real number $\in$, a positive integer N can be found such that $|z_n - l| < \in$ whenever $n > N$.

Although this definition seems to be identical with the convergence of real sequences, but the interpretation is different in the sense that all terms 'eventually' lie in the open disc $\{z : |z - l| < \in\}$, instead of the internal $]\, l - \in, l + \in [$.

The convergence of complex sequences can be considered in terms of the convergence of real sequences in the following theorem.

Theorem 2.6

A sequence $\{z_n\}$ converges to a complex number $l = a + ib$ if and only if $Re(z_n)$ converges to $Rel = a$ and $Im(z_n)$ converges to $Iml = b$.

Example 2.10

Consider the sequence $\left\{\dfrac{3+ni}{n+2ni}\right\}$.

Solution

$$\text{Let } z_n = \frac{3+ni}{n+2ni} = \frac{3+ni}{n+2ni} \times \frac{n-2ni}{n-2ni}$$

$$= \frac{2n^2+3n}{5n^2} + \frac{(in^2-6n)}{5n^2}.$$

But $$Re(z_n) = \frac{2n^2+3n}{5n^2} \to \frac{2}{5} \text{ as } n \to \infty$$

$$Im(z_n) = \frac{n^2-6n}{5n^2} \to \frac{1}{5} \text{ as } n \to \infty$$

Thus, the given sequence $\{z_n\}$ converges to $a + ib = \frac{2}{5} + \frac{i}{5} = \frac{1}{5}(2+i)$.

Series: A complex series

$$\sum_{k=1}^{\infty} z_k = z_1 + z_2 + \ldots + z_n + \ldots$$

is convergent if the sequence of partial sums $\{S_n\}$ where

$$S_n = z_1 + z_2 \ldots + z_n,$$

converges: The series $\sum_{k=1}^{\infty} z_k$ converges to l if $S_n \to l$ as $n \to \infty$ and the sum of the series is l.

Many of the properties of convergent series of real numbers have direct analogous for convergent series of complex numbers. We list some of them below (without proof) as the proofs can be constructed on the basis of the corresponding proofs of real series.

Results about sequences and series of complex numbers.

(*i*) If $\{z_n\}$ converges then its limit is unique. That is, if $l = \lim_{n \to \infty} z_n$ and $l' = \lim_{n \to \infty} z_n$ then $l = l'$.

(*ii*) If Σz_n converges then its sum is unique. In other words, if $\sum_{n=1}^{\infty} z_n$ converges to the sum s and s' then $s = s'$.

(*iii*) If $\{z_n\}$ converges to l and $\{z_n'\}$ converges to m, then $\{z_n + z_n'\}$ converges to $l + m$; if c is any complex number, then $\{cz_n\}$ converges to cl.

(*iv*) If $\sum_{n=1}^{\infty} z_n$ converges to the sum s and $\sum_{n=1}^{\infty} z_n$, converges to the sum t, then $\sum_{n=1}^{\infty} (z_n + z_n')$ converges to $s + t$, if c is any complex number then $\sum_{n=1}^{\infty} cz_n$ converges to the sum cs.

(*v*) A geometric series $\sum_{k=1}^{\infty} a\, z^{K-1} = a + az + az^2 + \dots$ is convergent if $|z| < 1$ and sum of the geometric series is $\dfrac{a}{1-z}$; is divergent if $|z| \geq 1$.

(*vi*) If $\sum_{n=1}^{\infty} z_n$ converges then $\lim_{n \to \infty} z_n = 0$.

(*vii*) If $\sum_{n=1}^{\infty} z_n$ converges then given any $\in > 0$ there is a positive integer N such that $|z_{n+1} + z_{n+2} \,..+ z_{n+p}| < \in$ whenever

$n \geq N, p \geq 1$. The Cauchy's criterion for convergence plays an important role in the study of convergence of real sequences. The following theorem gives Cauchy's criterion for complex series.

Theorem 2.7

The series of complex numbers $\sum_{n=1}^{\infty} z_n$ converges if and only if for every $\in > 0$ there is a natural number N such that $|z_{n+1} + z_{n+2} \dots + z_{n+p}| < \in$, whenever $n \geq N$ and $p \geq 1$.

Proof

The necessary part is mentioned in (*vii*) we shall prove that sufficient part.

Let $S_n = \sum_{k=1}^{n} z_k$ then for every $\in > 0$ there is some integer N such that $|S_{n+p} - S_n| < \in$ whenever $n \geq N$, $p \geq 1$. Let $S_n = x_n + iy_n$.

Then, the sequence of real numbers $\{x_n\}$ and $\{y_n\}$ both are Cauchy sequences because

$$|x_{n+p} - x_n| \leq |(x_{n+p} - x_n) + i(y_{n+p} - y_n)\}$$
$$= |S_{n+p} - S_n|,$$

Similarly

$$|y_{n+p} - y_n| \leq |S_{n+p} - S_n|,$$

Then, $|x_{n+p} - x_n| < \in$ and $|y_{n+p} - y_n| < \in$ whenever $n \geq N, p \geq 1$.

Since every Cauchy sequence of real numbers converges, therefore let $x = \lim_{n \to \infty} x_n$, $y = \lim_{n \to \infty} y_n$. Then, $S_n = x_n + iy_n \to x + iy$ and the series $\sum_{n=1}^{\infty} z_n$ converges to s.

One of the consequences of the Cauchy's criterion for real series is that every absolutely convergent series is convergent. If this result is true for complex series, it ought to be helpful because $\sum_{n=1}^{\infty} |z_n|$ will be a series of real non-negative terms which is useful in proving some tests for convergence. We begin with the following definition.

Definition 2.6

The series of complex numbers $\sum_{n=1}^{\infty} z_n$ is absolutely convergent (or converges absolutely) if the series $\sum_{n=1}^{\infty} |z_n|$ converges.

Theorem 2.8

If the series of complex numbers $\sum_{n=1}^{\infty} z_n$ is absolutely convergent, then it is convergent.

Proof

By hypothesis, $\sum_{n=1}^{\infty} |z_n|$ converges, so by the Cauchy criterion for real series, given $\in > 0$, there is some natural N such that

$$||z_{n+1}| + |z_{n+2}| + ... + |z_{n+p}|| < \in \text{ whenever } n \geq N, p \geq 1.$$

But $||z_{n+1}| + |z_{n+2}| + ... + |z_{n+p}||$

$$= |z_{n+1}| + |z_{n+2}| + ... + |z_{n+p}|$$

and $|z_{n+1} + z_{n+2} + ... + z_{n+p}| \leq |z_{n+1}| + |z_{n+2}| + ... + |z_{n+p}|$

Thus, whenever $n \geq N$ and $p \geq 1$,

$$|z_{n+1} + z_{n+2} + ... + z_{n+p}| < \in.$$

Hence, $\sum_{n=1}^{\infty} z_n$ converges by the Cauchy's criterion for complex series.

As we mentioned earlier, absolute convergence is useful because if $z_n \neq 0$, $\sum_{n=1}^{\infty} |z_n|$ is a series of positive real numbers, to which we can apply tests of real analysis.

Two of the most frequently used tests for the convergence of infinite series are given in the following theorems:

Theorem 2.9: Ratio Test

Suppose $\sum_{n=1}^{\infty} z_n$ is a series of non-zero complex terms such that

$$\lim_{n \to \infty} \left| \frac{z_{n+1}}{z_n} \right| = l.$$

(*i*) If $l < 1$, then the series converges absolutely.
(*ii*) If $l > 1$ or $l = \infty$, then the series diverges.
(*iii*) If $l = 1$, the test fails.

Theorem 2.10: Root Tests

Suppose $\sum_{n=1}^{\infty} z_n$ is a series of complex terms Such that

$$\lim_{n \to \infty} (|z_n|)^{1/n} = l.$$

(*i*) If $l < 1$, then the series converges absolutely.
(*ii*) If $l > 1$ or $L = \infty$, then the series diverges.
(*iii*) If $l = 1$, the test fails.

Example 2.11

Show that the series $\sum_{n=1}^{\infty} \frac{z^n}{n!}$ is convergent for any complex number z.

Solution

If $z \neq 0$, the ratio of successive terms of the series $\sum_{n=0}^{\infty} \left| \frac{z^n}{n!} \right|$ is

$\left| \frac{z^{n+1}}{(n+1)!} \right| \left| \frac{n!}{z^n} \right| = \left| \frac{z}{n+1} \right|$ and $\lim_{n \to \infty} \left| \frac{z}{n+1} \right| = 0$. Thus, the series $\sum \frac{z^n}{n!}$ converges absolutely when $z \neq 0$ and so converges. The series is also convergent when $z = 0$.

Definition 2.7

Power Series

An infinite series of the form

$$\sum_{n=1}^{\infty} a_n(z-z_0)^n = a_0 + a_1(z-z_0) + a_2(z-z_0)^2 + \ldots + \quad \ldots(1)$$

where the coefficients a_k are complex constants, is called a power series centered at z_0 $((z-z_0)^0 = 1)$. The complex point z_0 is referred as the centre of the series. If we put $z_0 = 0$, then from (1), we have

$$\sum_{n=0}^{\infty} a_n z^n = a_0 + a_1 z + a_2 z^2 + \ldots \quad \ldots(2)$$

(2) is a power series centred at the point $z = 0$.

To simplify the exposition slightly, we shall concentrate on power series of the form $\sum_{n=0}^{\infty} a_n z^n$ as mentioned in (2). There are analogous of the results we are about to prove for power series centred at $z_0 \neq 0$. The situation for complex power series is the same as real power series except that we replace interval by disc. To show the sets on which complex power series converges are disc, we first show that if the series $\sum_{n=0}^{\infty} a_n z_0^n$ converges for some $z_0 \neq 0$, then $\Sigma a_n z^n$ converges absolutely whenever $|z| < |z_0|$.

Lemma 2.11

If $\sum_{n=0}^{\infty} a_n z_0^n$ converges and $z_0 \neq 0$, then $\sum_{n=0}^{\infty} a_n z^n$ converges absolutely for all z such that $|z| < |z_0|$.

Proof

Since $\sum_{n=0}^{\infty} a_n z_0^n$ converges, $\lim_{n\to\infty} |a_n z_0^n| = 0$. In particular $\left\{|a_n z_0^n|\right\}$ is bounded, therefore, there is some K such that $|a_n z_0^n| \leq K$ for all n. Then,

$$| a_n z^n | = | a_n z_0^n | \left| \frac{z}{z_0} \right|^n \leq K \left| \frac{z}{z_0} \right|^n$$

Since $\left| \frac{z}{z_0} \right| < 1$, the real series $\sum_{n=0}^{\infty} K \left| \frac{z}{z_0} \right|^n$ converges and so does $\sum_{n=0}^{\infty} | a_n z^n |$ by comparison test for real series. Thus, $\sum a_n z^n$ is absolutely convergent and hence convergent when $| z | < | z_0 |$.

Theorem 2.12

Let $A = \{z : \Sigma a_n z^n \text{ converges}\}$. Then, one of the following possibilities must hold:

(*i*) $A = \{0\}$;

(*ii*) there is $r > 0$ such that A consists of the disc $\{z : | z | < R\}$,

(*iii*) $A = C$.

Proof

If $A \neq \{0\}$ or $A \neq \mathbf{C}$ then we can find z_1 and z_2 such that $| z_1 | > 0$ and $\sum_{n=0}^{\infty} a_n z_1^n$ converges and $\sum_{n=0}^{\infty} a_n z_2^n$ diverges.

From Lemma 2.11 we get that $| z_1 | \leq | z_2 |$ (for if $| z_2 | < | z_1 |$, then $\sum a_n z_2^n$ converges, but this is not so).

Let $R = Sup \{| z | : z \in A\}$. $R \neq \phi$ as it contains $| z_1 |$ and is bounded above (by $| z_2 |$) for if $z \in R$ such that $| z_1 | > | z_2 |$ then $\sum_{n=0}^{\infty} a_n z_2^n$ is convergent and $z_2 \in A$, *a* contradiction. Also $R > 0$ because $| z_1 | > 0$.

Let z be such that $| z | < R$. Then by the definition of supremum of a set there exists $z_0 \in A$ such that

$$| z | < | z_0 | < R,$$

and by Lemma 2.11, $\sum_{n=0}^{\infty} a_n z^n$ converges absolutely and hence converges and so $z \in A$.

Thus, A contains an open disc $\{z; |z| < R\}$. From the definition of R, it follows that A cannot contain any z for which $|z| > R$.

We have proved in the above theorem that the set of points on which a power series converges is a disc. The radius of the disc is called **radius of convergence** of the power series. The boundary of the disc is called the **circle of convergence**. The set of points in the interior of the disc is called the **domain of convergence** for a power series.

If $0 < R = Sup\ \{|z|: \Sigma\, |a_n z^n| \text{ converges}\} < \infty$ then $\{z : |z| = R\}$ is the circle of convergence.

To study the concept of radius of convergence of power series we recall the notion of the $\overline{\lim}$ of positive real sequences. That is,

$$\overline{\lim_{n\to\infty}}\ z_n = \lim_{n\to\infty} \left(\underset{K \geq n}{Sup}\ z_K\right)$$

Since $\underset{K \geq n}{Sup}\ z_K$ is non-increasing function of n, the limit always exists or equals $+\infty$. The properties of the $\overline{\lim}$ which will be useful, are the following:

Theorem 2.13

If $\overline{\lim_{n\to\infty}}\ z_n = L$, then

(*i*) for each N and for each $\varepsilon > 0$, there exists some $K > N$ such that $z_k \geq L - \varepsilon$.

(*ii*) for each $\varepsilon > 0$, there is some N such that $z_k \leq L + \varepsilon$ for all $K > n$.

(*iii*) $\overline{\lim}\ cz_n = cL$ for any non-negative constant c.

Formula for Radius of Convergence.

Consider the power series $\sum_{n=0}^{\infty} a_n z^n$. Then,

(*i*) If $\lim_{n\to\infty} Sup\, |a_n\, z^n|^{1/n} < 1$, then the series $\Sigma\, |a_n z^n|$ is convergent.

i.e., $\lim_{n\to\infty} Sup\, |a_n|^{1/n}\, |z_n| < 1$, then the series $\sum_{n=0}^{\infty} a_n z^n$ is absolutely convergent. Thus,

$$|z| < \frac{1}{\lim\limits_{x \to \infty} Sup\, |a_n|^{1/n}}.$$

(*ii*) If $\lim\limits_{n\to\infty} Sup\,|a_n|^{1/n} > 1$, then the series $\Sigma|a_n z^n|$ is divergent

i.e., if $|z| > \dfrac{1}{\lim\limits_{n \to \infty} Sup\, |a_n|^{1/n}}$ then the series $\Sigma a_n z^n$ is divergent.

Thus, from Theorem 2.12, we get

$$R = \frac{1}{\lim\limits_{n \to \infty} Sup\, |a_n|^{1/n}}.$$

We conclude the following:

Theorem 2.14

Suppose $\lim\limits_{n \to \infty} Sup\, |a_n|^{1/n} = L$. Then,

(*i*) If $L = 0$, $\sum\limits_{n=0}^{\infty} a_n z^n$ converges for all z.

(*ii*) If $L = \infty$, $\sum a_n z^n$ converges for $z = 0$ only.

(*iii*) If $0 < L < \infty$, Set $R = \dfrac{1}{L}$. Then $\sum a_n z^n$ converges for $|z| < R$ and diverges for $|z| > R$.

If $\sum a_n z^n$ has radius of convergence R, then the series converges uniformly in any small disc: $|z| \leq R - \delta$. For this

$$\sum_{n=0}^{\infty} |a_n z^n| \leq \sum_{n=0}^{\infty} |a_n|(R - \delta)^n$$

also converges. Hence, the power series is continuous through its domain of convergence.

All the three cases in Theorem 2.14 can be combined by stating that a power series always converges inside a disc of radius

$$R = \frac{1}{\lim\limits_{n \to \infty} Sup\, |a_n|^{1/n}}$$

We conclude the following:

(*i*) If $R = 0$, then the series converges at $z = 0$ only.

(*ii*) If $R = \infty$, means that the series converges for all z.

(*iii*) If $0 < R < \infty$, then the series converges for $|z| < R$ and diverges for $|z| > R$.

Example 2.12

(1) Since $\overline{\lim_{n\to\infty}}\, n^{1/n} = 1$, $\sum_{n=1}^{\infty} n\, z^n$ converges for $|z| < 1$ and diverges for $|z| > 1$. The series also diverges for $|z| = 1$. Because $|n\, z^n| = n \to \infty$ if $n \to \infty$.

(2) $\sum_{n=1}^{\infty} \frac{z^n}{n^2}$ has radius of convergence equal to 1. But for $|z| = 1$

$$\left|\frac{z^n}{n^2}\right| = \frac{1}{n^2}.$$

Thus, $\sum \frac{z^n}{n^2}$ converges on the unit circle.

(3) $\sum_{n=0}^{\infty} [1+(-1)^n]^n z^n$ has radius of convergence $\frac{1}{2}$. Since

$\lim_{n\to\infty} Sup\, ([1+(-1)^n]^n)^{1/n} = \lim_{n\to\infty} 2 = 2.$

(4) $\sum_{n=0}^{\infty} z^{n2} = 1 + z + z^4 + z^9 + z^{16} + \ldots$ has radius of convergence 1.

In this case $\overline{\lim_{n\to\infty}}\, |a_n|^{1/n} = \lim_{n\to\infty} 1 = 1.$

(5) $\sum_{n=0}^{\infty} (-1)^n z^n$ has radius of convergence 1. It converges for all points inside a unit circle. For $|z| = 1$, it is divergent.

(6) $\sum_{n=0}^{\infty} z^{n!} = z + z^2 + z^6 + z^{24} + \ldots$ has radius of convergence

1. As $\lim_{n\to\infty} Sup\, |a_n|^{1/n} = \lim 1 = 1.$

In the examples, we observe that the behaviour of a power series is not definite on the circle of convergence, the series may converge for all or some or none of the points on the circle of convergence. The following example shows that their are some points on the circle of convergence where the series is convergent.

Example 2.13

Show that $\sum_{n=1}^{\infty} \frac{z^n}{n}$ converges at all points on the unit circle except $z = 1$.

Solution

$\sum_{n=1}^{\infty} \frac{z^n}{n}$ has radius of convergence 1 ($\because \lim_{n\to\infty} Sup\,|a_n|^{1/n} = \lim_{n\to\infty} Sup\left(\frac{1}{n}\right)^{1/n} = 1$). Thus, the series $\sum_{n=1}^{\infty}\left|\frac{z^n}{n}\right|$ is convergent for $\{z : |z| < 1\}$ and is divergent for all $z \in \{z : |z| > 1\}$. For $z = 1$ the series $\sum_{n=1}^{\infty} \frac{z^n}{n} = \sum_{n=1}^{\infty} \frac{1}{n}$ is divergent ($\because \sum \frac{1}{n} = 1 + \frac{1}{2} + \frac{1}{3} + \ldots$ is harmonic series).

For $z = -1$ the series $\sum_{n=1}^{\infty} \frac{z^n}{n} = \sum_{n=1}^{\infty} \frac{(-1)^n}{n}$ is convergent. If $z = e^{i\theta} = \cos\theta + i\sin\theta$, $0 < \theta < 2\pi$, then the series becomes

$$\sum_{n=1}^{\infty} \frac{z^n}{n} = \sum_{n=1}^{\infty} \frac{(\cos\theta + i\sin\theta)^n}{n} = \sum_{n=1}^{\infty}\left(\frac{\cos n\theta}{n} + \frac{i\sin n\theta}{n}\right)$$

Consider the series $\sum_{n=1}^{\infty} \frac{\cos n\theta}{n}$ and $\sum_{n=1}^{\infty} \frac{\sin n\theta}{n}$.

Let $\qquad C = \cos\theta + \cos 2\theta + \ldots + \cos n\theta.$

$\qquad S = \sin\theta + \sin n\theta + \ldots + \sin n\theta.$

then, $\qquad C + iS = e^{i\theta} + e^{i\theta} + \ldots + e^{in\theta}$

$$= \frac{e^{i\theta}(1 - e^{ni\theta})}{1 - e^{i\theta}} \times \frac{1 - e^{-i\theta}}{1 - e^{-i\theta}}$$

$$= e^{i\theta}\left[\frac{1+e^{(n-1)i\theta}-e^{-i\theta}-e^{ni\theta}}{2-(e^{i\theta}+e^{-i\theta})}\right]$$

$$= \frac{e^{i\theta}+e^{ni\theta}-1-e^{(n+1)i\theta}}{2-2\cos\theta}$$

$$\left(\because \frac{e^{i\theta}+e^{-i\theta}}{2} = \cos\theta,\ 0<\theta<2\pi\right)$$

$$= \frac{e^{i\theta}+e^{ni\theta}-1-e^{(n+1)i\theta}}{2\sin^2\theta/2.}$$

Thus, $$C = \frac{\cos\theta+\cos n\theta-1-\cos(n+1)\theta}{2\sin^2\theta/2}$$

and $$S = \frac{\sin\theta+\sin n\theta-\sin(n+1)\theta}{2\sin^2\theta/2}$$

Also $|C| \le \dfrac{1}{\sin^2\theta/2}$ and $\sum\frac{1}{n}\to 0$ as $n\to\infty$. Also $\sum\frac{1}{n}$ is monotonically decreasing series. Then, by Dirichlet's Test $\sum\frac{\cos n\theta}{n}$ is convergent. Similarly we can have that $\sum\frac{\sin n\theta}{n}$ is convergent.

Thus, $\sum\frac{z^n}{n}$ is convergent for all $z \in \{z : |z| = 1\}$ except at $z = 1$.

Alternate formula for radius of convergence.

Theorem 2.15

If $\sum a_n$ is a positive term series of real numbers then

$$\lim_{n\to\infty}\frac{a_{n+1}}{a_n} \le \lim inf\,(a_n)^{1/n} \le \lim_{n\to\infty} Sup\, a_n^{1/n} \le \lim_{n\to\infty} Sup\frac{a_{n+1}}{a_n}.$$

Proof

If $\lim\limits_{n\to\infty} inf\dfrac{a_{n+1}}{a_n} = 0$ then $\lim\limits_{n\to\infty} inf\dfrac{a_{n+1}}{a_n} = 0 \le \lim inf\,(a_n)^{1/n}$.

Suppose that $\lim inf \dfrac{a_{n+1}}{a_n} = l > 0$. Let $0 < \varepsilon < l$ then by the definition there exists a positive integer m such that

$$\frac{a_{n+1}}{a_n} > l - \varepsilon \ \forall\ n \geq m. \qquad ...(1)$$

Putting $n = m, m + 1, ... n$ and multiplying the corresponding sides, we get

$$\frac{a_n}{a_m} > (l - \varepsilon)^{n-m}$$

$$\Rightarrow \qquad a_n > \frac{a_m}{(l-\varepsilon)^m}(l-\varepsilon)^n$$

Thus, $\lim\limits_{n\to\infty} inf\ (a_n)^{1/n} > l - \varepsilon$. This is true for all $\varepsilon > 0$. Thus,

$$\lim_{n\to\infty} inf\ (a_n)^{1/n} > \lim_{n\to\infty} inf \frac{a_{n+1}}{a_n}$$

Now, if $\lim\limits_{n\to\infty} Sup \dfrac{a_{n+1}}{a_n} = \infty$, then $\lim\limits_{n\to\infty} Sup\ (a_n)^{1/n} < \infty = \lim\limits_{n\to\infty} Sup \dfrac{a_{n+1}}{a_n}$

Let $\in\ > 0$ be any real number. Suppose $\lim\limits_{n\to\infty} Sup \dfrac{a_{n+1}}{a_n} = l < \infty$, then

by Theorem 2.13 (*ii*) there is a positive integer p, such that

$$\frac{a_{n+1}}{a_n} \leq l + \in\ \forall\ n \geq p \qquad ...(2)$$

Putting $n = p, p + 1, ... n$ and multiplying the corresponding sides, we get

$$\frac{a_n}{a_p} < (l + \in)^{n-p}$$

$$\Rightarrow \qquad a_n < \frac{a_p}{(l+\in)^p}(l+\in)^n$$

$$\lim_{n\to\infty} Sup\ (a_n)^{1/n} < l + \in \forall \in > 0$$

Thus, $\lim\limits_{n\to\infty} Sup\ (a_n)^{1/n} < \lim\limits_{n\to\infty} Sup \dfrac{a_{n+1}}{a_n}$.

Theorem 2.16

Suppose $\{a_n\}$ is a sequence of positive real numbers and $\lim\limits_{n\to\infty} \frac{a_{n+1}}{a_n} = l$,

then $\lim\limits_{n\to\infty} a_n^{1/n} = l$.

Proof

Since $\lim\limits_{n\to\infty} \frac{a_{n+1}}{a_n} = l$ then $\lim\limits_{n\to\infty} Sup \frac{a_{n+1}}{a_n} = \lim inf \frac{a_{n+1}}{a_n} = l$, then by Theorem 2.15, we get

$$\lim_{n\to\infty} \frac{a_{n+1}}{a_n} \le \lim_{n\to\infty} inf\,(a_n)^{1/n} \le \lim_{n\to\infty} Sup\,(a_n)^{1/n} \le \lim_{n\to\infty} \frac{a_{n+1}}{a_n}.$$

Thus, $\lim\limits_{n\to\infty} \frac{a_{n+1}}{a_n} = \lim\limits_{n\to\infty} \text{Sup}\,(a_n)^{1/n} = \lim\limits_{n\to\infty} \inf\,(a_n)^{1/n} = l$

Hence, $\lim\limits_{n\to\infty} (a_n)^{1/n} = l$.

From the above result we obtain that

$$\lim_{n\to\infty} \frac{a_{n+1}}{a_n} = \lim_{n\to\infty} (a_n)^{1/n}.$$

Therefore, if $\sum\limits_{n=0}^{\infty} a_n z^n$ is a power series with radius of convergence

$$R = \frac{1}{\lim\limits_{n\to\infty} Sup\,|a_n|^{1/n}} = \frac{1}{\lim\limits_{n\to\infty} Sup \left|\frac{a_{n+1}}{a_n}\right|}$$

Thus, $$R = \frac{1}{\lim\limits_{n\to\infty} Sup \left|\frac{a_{n+1}}{a_n}\right|}$$

can be used in manipulating the radius of converges. This is demonstrated in the following examples.

Example 2.14

Find the radius of convergence of the following series:

$$(i)\ \sum_{n=0}^{\infty}\frac{(-1)^n z^n}{n!} \qquad (ii)\ \sum_{n=0}^{\infty}\frac{z^{2n+1}}{(2n+1)!} \qquad (iii)\ \sum_{n=1}^{\infty}\frac{n!\,z^n}{n^2}$$

$$(iv)\ \sum_{n=0}^{\infty}\frac{2^n z^n}{n!}.$$

Solution

(*i*) $$a_n = \frac{(-1)^n}{n!}$$

$$a_{n+1} = \frac{(-1)^{n+1}}{(n+1)!}$$

Then, $$\left|\frac{a_{n+1}}{a_n}\right| = \frac{1}{n+1} \to 0 \text{ as } n \to \infty.$$

Then, $$R = \frac{1}{\limsup\limits_{n\to\infty}\left|\frac{a_{n+1}}{a_n}\right|} = \infty.$$

(*ii*) Let $$a_n = \begin{cases} 0 & \text{if } n \text{ is even} \\ \dfrac{1}{(2n+1)!} & \text{if } n \text{ is odd.} \end{cases}$$

$$a_{n+1} = \begin{cases} 0 & \text{if } n \text{ is odd} \\ \dfrac{1}{(2n+3)!} & \text{if } n \text{ is even.} \end{cases}$$

$\Rightarrow$ $$\sup\left|\frac{a_{n+1}}{a_n}\right| = \frac{1}{2n+3} \to 0 \text{ as } n \to \infty$$

Thus, $$R = \infty.$$

(*iii*) Let $$a_n = \frac{n!}{n^n}$$

$\Rightarrow$ $$a_{n+1} = \frac{(n+1)!}{(n+1)^{n+1}}$$

Then,
$$\frac{a_{n+1}}{a_n} = \frac{(n+1)!}{(n+1)^{n+1}} \times \frac{n^n}{n!}$$
$$= \frac{n+1}{n+1} \times \left(\frac{n}{n+1}\right)^n = \frac{1}{\left(1+\frac{1}{n}\right)^n}$$

Thus, $\lim\limits_{n\to\infty} \sup \left|\frac{a_{n+1}}{a_n}\right| = \lim\limits_{n\to\infty} \frac{1}{\left(1+\frac{1}{n}\right)^n} = \frac{1}{e}$. Hence $R = e$.

(*iv*) Here, $a_n = \frac{2^n}{n!}$

then $a_{n+1} = \frac{2^{n+1}}{(n+1)!}$

$$\Rightarrow \quad \overline{\lim_{n\to\infty}} \left|\frac{a_{n+1}}{a_n}\right| = \overline{\lim_{n\to\infty}} \left|\frac{2}{n+1}\right| = 0. \text{ Then } R = \infty.$$

We know if $\sum a_n x^n$ and $\sum b_n x^n$ are two real power series then their sum is convergent whenever both of the original power series are convergent. A similar result for complex power series can be proved in the following:

Theorem 2.17

Let $\sum\limits_{n=0}^{\infty} a_n z^n$ and $\sum\limits_{n=0}^{\infty} b_n z^n$ are two power series with radius of convergence R and R', respectively. Then $\sum\limits_{n=0}^{\infty} (a_n + b_n)\, z^n$ is also convergent and radius of convergence is max $\{R, R'\}$.

Proof

Let $\{s_n\}$ and $\{t_n\}$ be the sequences of partial sums of $\sum a_n z^n$ and $\sum b_n z^n$, respectively, then $\{s_n + t_n\}$ converges for $|z| < \min\{R, R'\}$.

But $\sum\limits_{n=0}^{\infty} (a_n + b_n)\, z^n$ has radius of convergence $\dfrac{1}{\overline{\lim}\, [a_n + b_n]^{1/n}}$

and so, $\dfrac{1}{\overline{\lim}\,[a_n,b_n]^{1/n}} = \min\{R, R'\}$

or $\overline{\lim}\,[a_n,b_n]^{1/n} = \max\left\{\dfrac{1}{R}, \dfrac{1}{R'}\right\}$

$$= \max\left\{\overline{\lim}\,|a_n|^{1/n}, \overline{\lim}\,|b_n|^{1/n}\right\}.$$

Example 2.15

Find the radius of convergence of $\sum_{n=0}^{\infty}(n+2^n)z^n$.

Solution

Using the above theorem

$$\overline{\lim_{n\to\infty}}\,|n+2^n| = \max\left\{\overline{\lim_{n\to\infty}}\,|n|^{1/n}, \overline{\lim_{n\to\infty}}\,|2^n|^{1/n}\right\}$$
$$= \max\{1, 2\}$$
$$= 2$$

Thus, $R = \dfrac{1}{2}$ is the radius of convergence of $\sum_{n=0}^{\infty}(n+2^n)z^n$.

Example 2.16

Suppose $\sum_{n=0}^{\infty} a_n = A$ and $\sum_{n=0}^{\infty} b_n = B$. Suppose that each of the series is absolutely convergent. Show that if the Cauchy's product.

$C_n = \sum_{K=0}^{\infty} a_k b_{n-1}$ then $\sum_{K=0}^{\infty} C_K = AB$.

Solution

If $\Sigma|a_k|$ and $\Sigma|b_k|$ converge and

$$d_k = \sum_{j=0}^{K}|a_j||b_{K-j}| \text{ then } \sum_{K=0}^{n} d_K \le \sum_{K=0}^{n}|a_K|\sum_{K=0}^{\infty}|b_K|$$

so Σd_k converges in particular

$d_{n+1} + d_{n+2} + \ldots \to 0$ as $n \to \infty$.

Let
$$A_n = a_0 + a_1 + \ldots + a_n$$
$$B_n = b_0 + b_1 + \ldots + b_n$$
$$C_n = c_0 + c_1 + \ldots + c_n$$

Then, $A_n B_n = C_n + R_n$ where $R_n = \sum_{j,K=0}^{\infty} a_K\, b_j, n < k + j \le 2n$,

$|R_n| \le d_{n+1} + d_{n+2} + \ldots + d_{2n}$.

Taking limit as $n \to \infty$, we get $\sum_{n=0}^{\infty} C_n = AB$.

Using Example 2.16, we conclude that if $\sum_{n=0}^{\infty} a_n z^n = A$ and $\sum_{n=0}^{\infty} b_n z^n = B$ are absolutely convergent sequences then the series $\sum_{n=0}^{\infty} C_n z^n$ converges absolutely to AB where $C_n = \sum_{K=0}^{n} a_k\, b_{n-K}$ is the Cauchy's product. Furthermore, if $\sum a_n z^n$ and $\sum b_n z^n$ have radii of convergence R_1 and R_2 respectively, then the series $\sum c_n z^n$ converges for $|z| < \min\{R_1, R_2\}$.

Theorem 2.18

The radii of convergence for $\sum_{n=0}^{\infty} C_n z^n$ and $\sum_{n=1}^{\infty} n\, C_n z^{n-1}$ are same.

Proof:

Let R and R' be the radii of convergence of $\sum_{n=0}^{\infty} C_n z^n$ and $\sum_{n=1}^{\infty} n\, C_n z^{n-1}$ respectively. Let $|z| < R$, choose a real number ρ such that $a < |z| < \rho < R$. Thus, $\sum C_n \rho^n$ is convergent. Consider

$$|n\,C_n z^{n-1}| = \frac{n}{|z|}|C_n z^n| = \frac{n}{|z|}\left(\frac{z}{\rho}\right)^n |C_n \rho^n|$$

Since $\frac{|z|}{\rho} < 1$, there $\sum\left|\frac{z}{\rho}\right|^n$ is convergent. Thus, $\sum nC_n z^{n-1}$ is convergent for all $z \in \{z : |z| < R\}$. Hence $R \le R'$. Now, let $|z| < R'$ and $\sum_{n=1}^{\infty}|n\,C_n\,z^{n-1}|$ is convergent for all $z \in \{z : |z| < R'\}$. Also

$$|C_n\,z^n| = |z|\,|C_n\,z^{n-1}| \le |z|\,|n\,C_n\,z^{n-1}|$$

Then, $\sum|C_n z^n|$ is convergent for all $z \in \{z : |z| < R'\}$.

Thus, $R' \le R$. Hence $R = R'$.

EXERCISE

1. Write the first five terms of the given sequences in the following:

   (i) $\{6i^n\}$ (ii) $\{2 + (-i)^n\}$

   (iii) $\{(1 + i)^n\}$ (iv) $\{1 + (i)^{2n}\}$.

2. Determine whether the given sequences converge or diverge

   (i) $\left\{\frac{(ni+2)^2}{n^2 i}\right\}$ (ii) $\left\{\frac{n(1+i^n)}{n+1}\right\}$

   (iii) $\left\{\frac{n+i^n}{\sqrt{n}}\right\}$ (iv) $\left\{\frac{n^2 i + 2^n}{3ni + 5^n}\right\}$.

3. Determine whether the following series converge or diverge

   (i) $\sum_{n=0}^{\infty}(1-i)^n$ (ii) $\sum_{n=0}^{\infty}\frac{1}{2}i^n$

   (iii) $\sum_{n=0}^{\infty}3\left(\frac{2}{1+2i}\right)^n$ (iv) $\sum_{n=2}^{\infty}\frac{i^n}{(1+i)^{n-1}}$

   (v) $\sum_{n=1}^{\infty}z^{2^n}$.

4. Find the circle of convergence and radius of convergence of the given power series

(*i*) $\sum_{n=1}^{\infty} n z^n$ (*ii*) $\sum_{n=0}^{\infty} \frac{(z-4-3i)^n}{5^{2n}}$

(*iii*) $\sum_{n=0}^{\infty} \frac{n!}{(2n)^n} z^{3n}$ (*iv*) $\sum_{n=1}^{\infty} \frac{z^n}{n^n}$.

5. Show that the power series $\sum_{n=1}^{\infty} \frac{z^n}{n^2}$ converges at every point on its circle of convergence, but $\sum_{n=1}^{\infty} n z^n$ diverges at every point of the circle.

6. Suppose $\{z_n\}$ and $\{w_n\}$ are two sequences such that $\{z_n + w_n\}$ converges. Does it follow that at least one of the sequence $\{z_n\}$ or $\{w_n\}$ converges.

7. Show that there is no power series $f(z) = \sum_{n=0}^{\infty} C_n z^n$ such that

(*i*) $f(z) = 1$ for $z = \frac{1}{2}, \frac{1}{3}, \frac{1}{4}, \ldots$ (*ii*) $f'(0) > 0$.

8. Suppose $\Sigma c_n z^n$ has radius of convergence R. Find the radius of convergence of

(*i*) $\sum n^p c_n z^n$ (*ii*) $\sum |c_n| z^n$

(*iii*) $\sum c_n^2 z^n$

9. Find the domain of convergence of

(*i*) $\sum_{n=0}^{\infty} n(z-i)^n$ (*ii*) $\sum_{n=0}^{\infty} \frac{(-1)^n}{n!} (z+1)^n$

(*iii*) $\sum_{n=0}^{\infty} n^2 (2z-1)^n$

ANSWERS

1. (*i*) $6i, -6, -6i, 6, 6i$ (*ii*) $2-i, 1, 2+i, 3, 2-i$
   (*iii*) $1+i, 2i, 2i-2, -4, -4(1+i)$
   (*iv*) 0,2,0,2,0
2. (*i*) Convergent (*ii*) divergent
   (*iii*) divergent (*iv*) divergent
3. (*i*) Divergent (*ii*) Convergent
   (*iii*) Convergent (*iv*) Convergent
   (*v*) Convergent in the unit circle.
4. (*i*) $R = 1, |z| = 1$ (*ii*) $R = 25, |z-4-3i| = 5$
   (*iii*) $R = 2, |z| = 2$ (*iv*) $R = \infty$, **C**
5. The series is convergent for $z = 1, -1$ and is also convergent for $z = e^{i\theta}, 0 < \theta < 2\pi$. The series is divergent for $z = 1, -1$ and for $z = e^{i\theta}, 0 < \theta < 2\pi$.
7. $f(z) = 1$ for $z = \frac{1}{2}, \frac{1}{3}, \frac{1}{4}$ .... then $f'(0) = 0$.
8. (*i*) R (*ii*) R
   (*iii*) R^2
9. (*i*) $|z-i| < 1$ (*ii*) **C**
   (*iii*) $|z - \frac{1}{2}| < 1$.

2.4 UNIFORM CONVERGENCE OF SEQUENCE OF FUNCTIONS

A sequence of function $\{f_n\}$ converges to f uniformly in a domain D if for each $\varepsilon > 0$ there is a positive integer N such that $n > N$ implies $|f_n(z) - f(z)| < \varepsilon$ for all $z \in D$. By referring to the real and imaginary parts of $\{f_n\}$, it is clear that uniform limit of continuous functions is continuous (See Rudin p. 137).

Theorem 2.18

Suppose $\sum_{K=1}^{\infty} f_K$ is a series of continuous functions in a domain D. If

$|f_K(z)| \le M_K$ for all $z \in D$ and if $\sum_{K=1}^{\infty} M_K$ converges then $\sum_{K=1}^{\infty} f_K(z)$ converges to a function f which is continuous in D.

Proof

Let $\in > 0$ be given. Since $\sum_{K=1}^{\infty} M_K$ converges, therefore there exists $N > 0$ such that

$$|M_{n+1} + M_{n+2} \,..| < \in \forall\, n \ge N.$$

Consider

$$\left| f(z) - \sum_{K=1}^{n} f_K(z) \right| = \left| \sum_{K=n+1}^{\infty} f_K(z) \right| < |M_{n+1} + M_{n+2} \,..| < \in \forall\, n \ge N.$$

Thus, the convergence is uniform and f is continuous.

Example 2.17

Let $f(z) = \sum_{K=1}^{\infty} Kz^K$ is continuous in $D = \{z : |z| \le \frac{1}{2}\}$.

Solution

Since $$|Kz^K| \le \frac{K}{2^K}$$

Since $\sum \frac{K}{2^K}$ converges, then the series $\sum_{K=1}^{\infty} Kz^K$ is informly convergent and f is continuous in D.

Example 2.18

Show that the function $f(z) = \sum_{K=1}^{\infty} \frac{1}{K^2 + Z}$ is continuous in $\{z : Re\, z > 0\}$.

Solution

Since $\left|\dfrac{1}{K^2+z}\right| \leq \dfrac{1}{K^2} \; \forall \; z \in \{z : Re\, z > 0\}.$

Since $\sum\limits_{K=1}^{\infty} \dfrac{1}{K^2}$ is convergent, therefore by Compression Test $\sum\limits_{K=1}^{\infty} \dfrac{1}{K^2+z}$ is convergent in $\{z : Re\, z > 0\}$.

❑❑❑

3

Analytic Functions

In this chapter, we study complex-valued functions properly by studying differentiation of complex functions.

The definition of differentiability and the properties of differentiable functions are similar to the corresponding definition and properties of real analysis except the geometrical interpretation of differentiability of a function at a point. In case of real functions, the derivative in geometric terms is the slope of the graph of the function, but for complex function we cannot very usefully think of it as the slope of a graph, since too many dimensions are involved.

We also experience differentiability of complex-valued functions in two much stronger ways. Firstly, in terms of nice and strong properties of differentiable complex functions and secondly the condition of differentiability is more restrictive than we might imagine. Several examples of this phenomenon occur in the present unit.

We shall also deal with a topic which is traditionally part of elementary complex analysis courses—the Cauchy-Riemann equations.

3.1 DERIVATIVE OF COMPLEX-VALUED FUNCTION

The calculus of complex functions deals with the usual concept of differentiation and its basic properties, but most of the results are similar to the corresponding results in real analysis. We begin with the following definition:

Definition 3.1

A complex-valued function f defined in a neighbourhood of a point z_0, is said to be differentiable at z_0 if

$$\lim_{h \to 0} \frac{f(z_0 + h) - f(z_0)}{h}$$

exists and is denoted by $f'(z_0)$.

In definition 3.1, h is not necessarily real. Thus, to find the limit as h approaches to zero in the complex plane. We proceed in the following way:

Example 3.1

Find the derivative of z^2.

Solution

$$f(z + h) = (z + h)^2 = z^2 + 2zh + h^2$$

Therefore, $$\frac{f(z+h) - f(z)}{h} = \frac{z^2 + 2zh + h^2 - z^2}{h}$$

$$= 2z + h$$

Taking limit as h approaches zero, we get

$$\lim_{h \to 0} \frac{f(z+h) - f(z)}{h} = \lim_{h \to 0} (2z + h)$$

$$\Rightarrow \qquad f'(z) = 2z.$$

Example 3.2

Show that the function $f(z) = \bar{z}$ is nowhere differentiable.

Solution

Consider $$\frac{f(z+h) - f(z)}{h} = \frac{\overline{z+h} + \bar{z}}{h}$$

$$= \frac{\bar{h}}{h}$$

If $h \to 0$ along a line parallel to x-axis, then $\bar{h} = h$ and

$$\lim_{h \to 0} \frac{f(z+h) - f(z)}{h} = \lim_{h \to 0} \frac{\bar{h}}{h} = 1$$

Also, if $h \to 0$ along a line parallel to y-axis, and

$$\lim_{h \to 0} \frac{f(z+h) - f(z)}{h} = \lim_{h \to 0} \frac{-ih}{ih} = -1$$

Thus, using the definition of limit we conclude that $\lim_{h \to 0} \frac{f(z+h) - f(z)}{h}$ does not exist. Thus, $f(z) = \bar{z}$ is nowhere differentiable.

The next result gives the necessary condition for a differentiable function which is same as real valued function.

Theorem 3.1

Every differentiable function is continuous at a point.

Proof

Let $f(z)$ be differentiable at a point $z_0 \in \mathbf{C}$. Then by the definition.

$$f'(z_0) = \lim_{h \to 0} \frac{f(z_0 + h) - f(z_0)}{h}$$

Thus, $\lim_{h \to 0} (f(z_0 + h) - f(z_0)) = \lim_{h \to 0} \frac{f(z_0 + h) - f(z_0)}{h} \times \lim_{h \to 0} h$

$$= f'(z_0) \times 0 = 0.$$

Hence, f is continuous at z_0.

3.1.1 Rules of Differentiation

The familiar rules of differentiation in calculus of real variables carry over to the calculus of complex variables.

Theorem 3.2

If f and g are differentiable at a point $z \in \mathbf{C}$, then

(*i*) $(cf(z))' = cf'(z)$

(*ii*) $(f(z) \pm g(z))' = f'(z) \pm g'(z)$

(*iii*) $(f(z)\, g(z))' = f(z)\, g'(z) + f'(z)\, g(z)$

(*iv*) $\left[\dfrac{f(z)}{g(z)}\right]' = \dfrac{f'(z)\,g(z) - g'(z)f(z)}{(g(z))^2}$, provided $g(z) \neq 0$.

Proof

Since f and g are differentiable at z, therefore

$$\lim_{h \to 0} \frac{f(z+h) - f(z)}{h} = f'(z),$$

$$\lim_{h \to 0} \frac{g(z+h) - g(z)}{h} = g'(z).$$

(*i*) Consider $\displaystyle\lim_{h \to 0} \frac{c(f(z+h)) - cf(z)}{h} = c \lim_{h \to 0} \frac{f(z+h) - f(z)}{h}$

$\Rightarrow \qquad (cf(z))' = cf'(z)$

(*ii*) Now, $\displaystyle\lim_{h \to 0} \frac{(f+g)(z+h) - (f+g)(z)}{h}$

$$= \lim_{h \to 0} \frac{f(z+h) - f(z)}{h} + \lim_{h \to 0} \frac{g(z+h) - g(z)}{h}$$

$\Rightarrow \qquad (f+g)'(z) = f'(z) + g'(z)$

(*iii*) $\displaystyle\lim_{h \to 0} \frac{(f.g)(z+h) - (f.g)(z)}{h}$

$$= \lim_{h \to 0} \frac{f(z+h)\,g(z+h) - f(z)g(z)}{h}$$

$$= \lim_{h \to 0} g(z+h) \frac{[f(z+h) - f(z)]}{h}$$

$$+ \lim_{h \to 0} \frac{f(z)\,[g(z+h) - g(z)]}{h}$$

$\Rightarrow \qquad (f\,g)'(z) = g(z)\,f'(z) + f(z)\,g'(z).$

(*iv*) To establish the differentiability of $\dfrac{f}{g}$; we first prove the differentiability of $\dfrac{1}{g}(g \neq 0)$.

Consider $\displaystyle\lim_{h \to 0} \frac{1}{h}\left[\frac{1}{g(z+h)} - \frac{1}{g(z)}\right] = \lim_{h \to 0} -\left[\frac{g(z+h) - g(z)}{h\,g(z+h)\,g(z)}\right]$

$$= \frac{-g'(z)}{[g(z)]^2}$$

Now, $$\left(\frac{f(z)}{g(z)}\right)' = \left[f(z).\frac{1}{g(z)}\right]'$$

$$= f'(z)\times\frac{1}{g(z)} + f(z)\times\frac{-g'(z)}{[g(z)]^2}$$

$$= \frac{f'(z)\,g(z) - f(z)\,g'(z)}{[g(z)]^2}.$$

Theorem 3.3: Chain Rule

If g is differentiable at $a \in \mathbf{C}$ and f is differentiable at $g(a)$, then fog is differentiable at a and

$$(fog)'\ (a) = f'(g(a))\ g'(a).$$

Proof

Define a function $\phi(h)$ as follows:

$$\phi(h) = \begin{cases} f(g(a+h) - f(g(a)) & \text{if } g(a+h) \neq g(a) \\ f'(g(a)) & \text{if } g(a+h) = g(a) \end{cases}$$

Then $\phi(0) = f'(g(a))$. Also $\phi(h)$ is continuous at 0. Consider

$$\frac{f(g(a+h) - f(g(a))}{h} = \frac{f(g(a+h) - f(g(a))}{g(a+h) - g(a)} \times \frac{g(a+h) - g(a)}{h} \qquad ...(1)$$

We know $\lim\limits_{h\to 0} \frac{g(a+h) - g(a)}{h} = g'(a)$, therefore taking limit as $h \to 0$ on both sides, we get

$$\lim_{h\to 0} \frac{f(g(a+h) - f(g(a))}{h} = \lim_{h\to 0} \frac{f(g(a+h) - f(g(a))}{g(a+h) - g(a)} \times g'(a)$$

Now, it remains to prove that

$$\lim_{h\to 0} \phi(h) = \lim_{h\to 0} \frac{f(g(a+h)) - f(g(a))}{g(a+h) - g(a)}$$

$$= f'(g(a)) \qquad ...(2)$$

Let $g(a+h) \neq g(a)$. If $|\,h\,|$ is sufficiently small then since f is continuous at $g(a)$, therefore given $\in > 0$ there exists $\delta_1 > 0$ such that

$$\left|\frac{f(g(a)+h)-f(g(a))}{h}-f'(g(a))\right|<\in, 0<|(g(a)+h)-g(a)|<\delta_1$$

...(3)

Also, g is continuous at a, therefore given $\delta_1 > 0$, there exists $\delta > 0$ such that

$|g(a+h)-g(a)| < \delta$ if $0 < |h| < \delta$

Put $g(a+h) - g(a) = h$ in (1), then

$$\left|\frac{f(g(a+h))-f(g(a))}{h}-f'(g(a))\right|<\in, 0<|h|<\delta$$

Thus, $\lim\limits_{h\to 0}\dfrac{f(g(a+h))-f(g(a))}{g(a+h)-g(a)} = f'(g(a))$.

If $g(a+h) = g(a)$, then the result is trivial.

The rules of differentiation in real analysis apply in Complex analysis, too, provided the appropriate modifications are made. We need to be careful about the fact that none of the new functions of complex analysis, namely conjugation, modulus and the real and imaginary part functions, is differentiable.

Example 3.3

Show that $z \to Im\, z$ is nowhere differentiable.

Solution

Let $f(z) = Im\, z$ for all $z \in \mathbf{C}$. Consider

$$\frac{f(z+h)-f(z)}{h} = \frac{Im\,(z+h)-Imz}{h}$$

$$= \frac{Im\, h}{h} \text{ provided } h \neq 0.$$

If h is real, $\dfrac{Im\, h}{h} = 0$; if h is imaginary, $\dfrac{Im\, h}{h} = \dfrac{1}{i} = -i$.

Thus, $\lim\limits_{h\to 0}\dfrac{f(z+h)-f(z)}{h}$ does not exist. Thus, $z \to Im\, z$ is nowhere differentiable.

Example 3.4

Show that $f(z) = |z|$ is continuous but not differentiable at $z = 0$.

Solution

Consider $\lim_{h \to 0} (f(z) - f(0)) = \lim_{z \to 0} |z| = 0$

Thus, f is continuous at $z = 0$. Now,

$$\frac{f(z) - f(0)}{z - 0} = \frac{|z|}{z} \qquad \text{...(1)}$$

If we write $z = re^{i\theta}$ then $|z| = r$, therefore, we can write from (1)

$$\frac{f(z) - f(0)}{z - 0} = e^{-i\theta}$$

If $z \to 0$ along a line parallel to x-axis, then $\theta \to 0$ and we get

$$\lim_{z \to 0} \frac{f(z) - f(0)}{z - 0} = \lim_{\theta \to 0} (\cos\theta - i \sin\theta) = 1$$

If $z \to 0$ along a line parallel to y-axis, then $\theta \to \pi/2$ and

$$\lim_{z \to 0} \frac{f(z) - f(0)}{z - 0} = \lim_{\theta \to \pi/2} (\cos\theta - i \sin\theta) = -i$$

Thus, $\lim_{z \to 0} \frac{f(z) - f(0)}{z - 0}$ does not exists. Hence, f is not differential at $z = 0$.

The next rule is also an important rule of differentiation; differentiation of an inverse function.

Theorem 3.4

Let f be a one-one function defined on a region R and let a be an interior point of $f(R)$. Suppose f is continuous at a, and that f is differentiable at $f^{-1}(a)$, with $f'(f^{-1}(a)) \neq 0$ then f^{-1} is differentiable at a and

$$(f^{-1})'(a) = \frac{1}{f'(f^{-1}(a))}$$

Proof

Let $f(b) = a$. If $h(\neq 0)$ is any non-zero complex number such that $a + h \in f(R)$, there is a unique complex number $\phi(h)$, such that $f(b + \phi(h)) = a + h$. The function $h \to \phi(h)$ satisfies the following properties:

$$\phi(h) = f^{-1}(a + h) - f^{-1}(a)$$

$$f(b + \phi(h)) - f(b) = h$$

Consider $\dfrac{f^{-1}(a+h) - f^{-1}(a)}{h} = \dfrac{\phi(h)}{f(b+\phi(h)) - f(b)}$ ...(1)

Since f is differentiable at b, and $f'(b) \neq 0$, thus for given $\in > 0$, there is some $\delta_1 > 0$ such that

$$\left|\frac{h}{f(b+h) - f(b)} - \frac{1}{f'(b)}\right| < \in \text{ whenever } 0 < |h| < \delta_1.$$

Since f^{-1} is continuous at a, therefore $\lim\limits_{h \to 0} \phi(h) = 0$, therefore, there is $\delta > 0$ such that

$$|\phi(h)| < \delta_1, \text{ whenever } 0 < |h| < \delta$$

and since $\phi(h) \neq 0$ for $h \neq 0$, we have

$0 < |\phi(h)| < \delta_1$ whenever $0 < |h| < \delta$.

So, if $0 < |h| < \delta$, then

$$\left|\frac{\phi(h)}{f(b+\phi(h)) - f(b)} - \frac{1}{f'(b)}\right| < \in$$

$$\Rightarrow \qquad \lim_{h \to 0} \frac{\phi(h)}{f(b+\phi(h)) - f(b)} = \frac{1}{f'(b)}$$

Now from (1), we get

$$\lim_{h \to 0} \frac{f^{-1}(a+h) - f^{-1}(a)}{h} = \frac{1}{f'(b)} = \frac{1}{f'(f^{-1}(a))}.$$

Thus, f^{-1} is differentiable at a and $(f^{-1})\,(a) = \dfrac{1}{f'(f^{-1}(a))}$.

Comparison with Real Analysis

1. The geometrical interpretation of derivative of a real function $y = f(x)$ is the slope of the tangent at a point $(x, f(x))$ on the curve. If $f'(x) > 0, < 0, = 0$ then f is increasing, decreasing or possibly has an absolute value. $f'(x)$ is also the rate of change of one variable with respect to the other. But these interpretations cannot be carried over to complex analysis.
2. The function $f(z) = |z|^2$ is differentiable only at $z = 0$, but a real function $f(x) = |x|^2$ is differentiable everywhere. The real function $f(x) = x$ is differentiable everywhere but the complex-valued function $f(z) = Rez$ is nowhere differentiable.
3. In real analysis, inverse of a continuous one-one function must be continuous. In the proof, we used the fact that a continuous one-one function must either increasing or decreasing. But the increasingness or decreaseness does not make any sense in complex analysis. We shall prove the result later on by adopting another technique (using theory of analytic functions).

EXERCISE

1. Find the derivatives of the following functions:

   (*i*) $z \to \dfrac{z^2 + 2z + i}{2iz + 1}$ (*ii*) $z \to [(z + i)^2 + (z - i)^2]^2$

   (*iii*) $z \to \dfrac{az + b}{cz + d}$, where a, b, c and d are complex constants.

   (*iv*) $z \to [(z^2 + 1)^2 + 1]^2$ (*v*) $z \to z - \dfrac{1}{z}$

   (*vi*) $z \to \dfrac{1}{z^2}$ (*vii*) $z \to iz^3 - 7z^2$

   (*viii*) $z \to aiz + 2 - 3i$ (*ix*) $z \to 15z^2 - 4z + 1 - 3i$

2. The function $f(z) = |z|^2$ is continuous at the origin.

   (*i*) Show that f is differentiable at the origin.

   (*ii*) Show that f is not differentiable at any point $z \neq 0$.

3. Let $p(z) = az^2 + bz + c$, where a, b, c are complex constants. Show that $q(z) = \overline{p(\overline{z})}$ is given by $\overline{a}z^2 + \overline{b}z + \overline{c}$. Then show that the derivative of q at $\overline{\alpha}$ is $q'(\overline{\alpha}) = \overline{p'(\alpha)}$.

4. The function f is differentiable at α. Define the function g by $g(z) = \overline{f(\overline{z})}$. Show that g is differentiable at $\overline{\alpha}$ and that $g'(\overline{\alpha}) = \overline{f'(\alpha)}$.

ANSWERS

1. (i) $\dfrac{2\left(iz^2+2z+2\right)}{(2iz+1)^3}$ (ii) $8z\left[(z+i)^2+(z-i)^2\right]$

(iii) $\dfrac{ad-bc}{(cz+d)^2}$ (iv) $8z\left(z^2+1\right)\left(\left(z^2+1\right)^2+1\right)$

(v) $1+\dfrac{1}{z^2}$ (vi) $\dfrac{-2}{z^3}$

(viii) $3iz^2 - 14z$ (viii) ai

(ix) $30z - 4$

2. (i) $\lim\limits_{z\to 0}\dfrac{f(z)-f(0)}{z-0}=0$

(ii) $a \neq 0$ $\lim\limits_{z\to a}\dfrac{f(z)-f(a)}{z-a}$ does not exist

3. If $p(z) = az^2 + bz + c$, $q(z) = \overline{p(\overline{z})} = \overline{a}z^2 + \overline{b}z + \overline{c}$

$q'(\overline{\alpha}) = 2\overline{a}\,\overline{\alpha} + \overline{b} = \overline{p'(\alpha)}$

4. $\lim\limits_{z\to\alpha}\dfrac{g(z)-g(\overline{\alpha})}{z-\overline{\alpha}} = \overline{f'(\alpha)}$

3.2 THE CAUCHY-RIEMANN EQUATIONS

We have emphasised on the similarities between complex analysis and real analysis but in this section we take a different point of view. We have studied in the previous section about the differentiability of functions of z and various rules of differentiation. Now, we look at the properties of differentiability and its relation with Cauchy-Riemann equations. We shall show that Cauchy-Riemann equations are only necessary for the differentiability of a complex-valued function. We begin with a result in which a function $f(z) = u(x, y) + iv(x, y)$ is differentiable at a point z, then the real functions u and v must satisfy the equations that relate their first order partial derivatives.

Theorem 3.5

Suppose $f(z) = u(x, y) + iv(x, y)$ is differentiable at a point $z_0 = x_0 + iy_0$. Then, the first order partial derivatives of u and v exist at z and satisfy the Cauchy-Riemann equations

$$\frac{\partial u}{\partial x} = \frac{\partial v}{\partial y} \quad \text{and} \quad \frac{\partial u}{\partial y} = -\frac{\partial v}{\partial x}.$$

Proof

Consider

$$f(z_0 + \delta z) - f(z_0) = u(x_0 + \delta x, y_0 + \delta y) + iv(x_0 + \delta x, y_0 + \delta y) - u(x_0, y_0) - iv(x_0, y_0)$$

Now

$$\frac{f(z_0 + \delta z) - f(z_0)}{\delta z} = \frac{u(x_0 + \delta x, y_0 + \delta y) - u(x_0, y_0)}{\delta x + i\delta y} + \frac{i(v(x_0 + \delta x, y_0 + \delta y) - v(x_0, y_0)}{\delta x + i\delta y} \quad ...(1)$$

Since f is differentiable at $z_0 = x_0 + iy_0$, therefore

$$f'(z_0) = \lim_{\delta z \to 0} \frac{f(z_0 + \delta z) - f(z_0)}{\delta z}.$$

If we take limit on both sides of (1) as $\delta z \to 0$ along a line parallel to x-axis, then $\delta y = 0$ and $\delta z = \delta x \to 0$. Thus,

$$\lim_{\delta z \to 0} \frac{f(z_0+\delta z)-f(z_0)}{\delta z} = \lim_{\delta x \to 0} \frac{u(x_0+\delta x, y_0)-u(x_0, y_0)}{\delta x} + \lim_{\delta x \to 0} \frac{v(x_0+\delta x, y_0)-v(x_0, y_0)}{\delta x}$$

$$\Rightarrow \qquad f'(z_0) = \frac{\partial u}{\partial x} + i\frac{\partial v}{\partial x} \qquad ...(2)$$

Now, if $\delta z \to 0$ along a line parallel to y-axis, *i.e.*, $\delta z = i\delta y \to 0$ then from (1), we get

$$\lim_{\delta z \to 0} \frac{f(z_0+\delta z)-f(z_0)}{\delta z} = \lim_{\delta y \to 0} \frac{u(x_0, y_0+\delta y)-u(x_0, y_0)}{i\delta y} + \lim_{\delta y \to 0} \frac{v(x_0, y_0+\delta y)-v(x_0, y_0)}{\delta y}$$

$$\Rightarrow \qquad f'(z_0) = \frac{\partial u}{i\partial y} + \frac{\partial v}{\partial y}$$

$$= -i\frac{\partial u}{\partial y} + \frac{\partial u}{\partial y} \qquad ...(3)$$

From (2) and (3), we get

$$\frac{\partial u}{\partial x} + \frac{i\partial v}{\partial x} = -\frac{i\partial u}{\partial y} + \frac{\partial v}{\partial y}$$

Equating real and imaginary parts, we get

$$\frac{\partial u}{\partial x} = \frac{\partial v}{\partial y}, \quad \frac{\partial v}{\partial x} = -\frac{\partial u}{\partial y}.$$

The converse of the above theorem is not true. The next example shows a function which is not differentiable at a point although the partial derivatives exist and the Cauchy-Riemann equation are satisfied.

Example 3.5

Let $f(z) = f(x, y) = \begin{cases} \dfrac{xy(x+iy)}{x^2+y^2}, & z \neq 0 \\ 0, & z = 0 \end{cases}$

then, $u(x, y) = \begin{cases} \dfrac{x^2 y}{x^2 + y^2}, & z \neq 0 \\ 0 & , z = 0 \end{cases}$

and $v(x, y) = \begin{cases} \dfrac{xy^2}{x^2 + y^2}, & z \neq 0 \\ 0 & , z = 0 \end{cases}$

Consider

$$\lim_{x \to 0} \frac{u(x, 0) - u(0, 0)}{x} = 0, \lim_{x \to 0} \frac{v(x, 0) - v(0, 0)}{x} = 0$$

$$\lim_{y \to 0} \frac{u(0, y) - u(0, 0)}{y} = 0, \lim_{x \to 0} \frac{v(0, y) - v(0, 0)}{y} = 0$$

Thus, the Cauchy-Riemann equations are satisfied at $z = 0$, but

$$\lim_{z \to 0} \frac{f(z) - f(0)}{z} = \lim_{(x, y) \to (0, 0)} \frac{xy}{x^2 + y^2} \quad ...(1)$$

Put $y = mx$ in (1), then

$$\lim_{z \to 0} \frac{f(z) - f(0)}{z} = \frac{m}{1 + m^2}$$

If $z \to 0$ along a line parallel to x-axis, then $m = 0$

$$\lim_{z \to 0} \frac{f(z) - f(0)}{z} = 0$$

If $z \to 0$ along a line $y = x$, then

$$\lim_{z \to 0} \frac{f(z) - f(0)}{z} = \frac{1}{2}$$

Thus, the function f is not differentiable at $z = 0$.

Example 3.6

Show that $f(z) = |z|$ is nowhere differentiable using Cauchy-Riemann equations.

Solution

Since $f(z) = |z|$ is a real function for all $z \in \mathbf{C}$ therefore, $u(x, y) = \sqrt{x^2 + y^2}$ and $v(x, y) = 0$

Since $|z|$ is not differentiable at $z = 0$, therefore, the partial derivatives do not exist at $z = 0$. If $(x, y) \neq (0, 0)$, then

$$\frac{\partial U(x, y)}{\partial x} = \frac{x}{\sqrt{x^2 + y^2}} \quad , \quad \frac{\partial u(x, y)}{\partial y} = \frac{y}{\sqrt{x^2 + y^2}}$$

$$\frac{\partial V(x, y)}{\partial x} = 0 \quad , \quad \frac{\partial v(x, y)}{\partial y} = 0.$$

Thus, $\frac{\partial u}{\partial x} \neq \frac{\partial v}{\partial y}$ and $\frac{\partial u}{\partial y} \neq -\frac{\partial v}{\partial x}$, so f is nowhere differentiable.

From Example 3.5, we conclude that if the real and imaginary parts of a function satisfy the Cauchy-Riemann equations then the function may not be differentiable. An extra hypothesis is needed before we can conclude that the function is differentiable. The most useful theorem is the following one:

Theorem 3.6

Suppose that $f = u + iv$, where the functions $u(x, y)$ and $v(x, y)$ have partial derivatives which are continuous and satisfy the Cauchy-Riemann equations at (x_0, y_0). Then, f is differentiable at, $z_0 = x_0 + iy_0$, and its derivative is

$$f'(z_0) = \frac{\partial u}{\partial x}(x_0, y_0) + i\frac{\partial v}{\partial x}(x_0, y_0) = \frac{\partial v}{\partial y}(x_0, y_0) - i\frac{\partial u}{\partial y}(x_0, y_0).$$

Proof

Let $f(z) = u(x, y) + iv(x, y)$ such that $u(x, y)$ and $v(x, y)$ admit first order continuous partial derivatives and satisfy Cauchy-Riemann equations at (x_0, y_0). Consider

$$\frac{f(z_0 + \delta z) - f(z_0)}{\delta z} = \frac{u(x_0 + \delta x, y_0 + \delta y) + iv(x_0 + \delta x, y_0 + \delta y) - u(x_0, y_0) - iv(x_0, y_0)}{\delta x + i\delta y}$$

$$= \frac{(u(x_0 + \delta x, y_0 + \delta y) - u(x_0, y_0) + i[v(x_0 + \delta x, y_0 + \delta y) - v(x_0, y_0)]}{\delta x + i\delta y} \quad ...(1)$$

Now, $u(x_0 + \delta x, y_0 + \delta y) - u(x_0, y_0) = u(x_0 + \delta x, y_0 + \delta y) - u(x_0 + \delta x, y_0) + u(x_0 + \delta x, y_0) - u(x_0, y_0)$ ...(2)

Set $\phi(t) = u(x_0 + \delta x, t), \quad y_0 \leq t \leq y_0 + \delta y$

ϕ is continuous on $[y_0, y_0 + \delta y]$ and differentiable on $]y_0, y_0 + \delta y[$, then by Lagrange's Mean value theorem there is $\theta_1 \in]0, 1[$ such that

$\phi(y_0 + \delta y) - \phi(y_0) = u_y (x_0 + \delta x, y_0 + \theta_1 \delta y)\delta y, 0 < \theta_1 < 1$

$\Rightarrow u(x_0 + \delta x, y_0 + \delta y) - u(x_0 + \delta x, y_0) = u_y(x_0 + \delta x, y_0 + \theta_1 \delta y) \delta y$

Also $u(x_0 + \delta x, y_0) - u(x_0, y_0) = \delta_x u_x (x_0 + \theta_2 \delta x, y_0)$.

Thus from (2), we get

$$u(x_0 + \delta x, y_0 + \delta y) - u(x_0, y_0) = \delta_y u_y (x_0 + \delta x, y_0 + \theta_1 \delta y) + \delta_x u_x (x_0 + \theta_2 \delta x, y_0), 0 < \theta_1 < 1, 0 < \theta_2 < 1 \quad ...(3)$$

Let $u_y(x_0 + \delta x, y_0 + \theta_1 \delta y) - u_y(x_0, y_0) = \phi_1$ such that $\phi_1 \to 0$ as $\delta x, \delta y \to 0$.

Similarly $u_x (x_0 + \theta_2 \delta x, y_0) - u_x (x_0, y_0) = \phi_2$ such that $\phi_2 \to 0$ as $\delta x, \delta y \to 0$.

From (2), we have

$$u(x_0 + \delta x_1 y_0 + \delta y) - u(x_0, y_0) = \delta y[u_y (x_0, y_0) + \phi_1] + \delta_x [u_x(x_0, y_0) + \phi_2] \quad ...(4)$$

Such that $\phi_1 \to 0, \phi_2 \to 0$ as $\delta x, \delta y \to 0$.

Similarly $v(x_0 + \delta x, y_0 + \delta y) - v(x_0, y_0) = \delta x[v_x(x_0, y_0) + \phi_3] + \delta y[v_y(x_0 y_0) + \phi_4]$ ...(5)

Such that $\phi_3 \to 0, \phi_4 \to 0$ as $\delta x, \delta y \to 0$.

From (1), (4) and (5), we get

$$\frac{f(z_0 + \delta z) - f(z_0)}{\delta z} = \frac{\delta_y u_y + \delta_x u_x + i v_x \delta_x + i \delta_y v_y + \phi_1 \delta_y + \phi_2 \delta x + i\phi_3 \delta x + i\phi_4 \delta y}{\delta x + i\delta y}$$

$$= \frac{(u_x + iv_x)(\delta x + i\delta y) + \phi_1 \delta_y + \phi_2 \delta x + i\phi_3 \delta x + i\phi_4 \delta y}{\delta x + i\delta y}$$

Taking limit as $\delta z \to 0$, we get

$$\lim_{\delta z \to 0} \frac{f(z_0 + \delta z) - f(z_0)}{\delta z} = u_x + iv_x$$

Thus,
$$f'(z_0) = u_x(x_0, y_0) + iv_x (x_0, y_0)$$
$$= v_y(x_0, y_0) - iu_y (x_0, y_0)$$

One of most important and useful consequences of these theorems is a technique which helps us to know whether or not a function is differentiable. We demonstrate this technique in the following examples.

Example 3.7

Show that the function $f(z) = \frac{1}{z}$ $(z \neq 0)$ is differentiable.

Solution

$$\text{Since } f(z) = \frac{1}{z} = \frac{1}{x+iy} = \frac{x-iy}{x^2+y^2}$$

Then, $\quad u(x, y) = \dfrac{x}{x^2+y^2}, \; v(x, y) = \dfrac{-y}{x^2+y^2}$

The partial derivative are

$$\frac{\partial u(x, y)}{\partial x} = \frac{y^2 - x^2}{(x^2+y^2)^2}, \quad \frac{\partial u(x, y)}{\partial y} = \frac{-2xy}{(x^2+y^2)^2}$$

$$\frac{\partial v(x, y)}{\partial x} = \frac{2xy}{(x^2+y^2)^2}, \quad \frac{\partial v(x, y)}{\partial y} = \frac{y^2 - x^2}{(x^2+y^2)^2}$$

Thus, $\dfrac{\partial u}{\partial x} = \dfrac{\partial v}{\partial y}$ and $\dfrac{\partial v}{\partial x} = \dfrac{-\partial u}{\partial y}$ when $(x, y) \neq (0, 0)$.

Since the partial derivative are continuous provided $(x, y) \neq (0, 0)$ and Cauchy-Riemann equations are satisfied, the function is differentiable on $\{z : z \neq 0\}$.

Example 3.8

Show that the function $f(z) = z^2$ is differentiable everywhere.

Solution

Let $f(z) = u(x, y) + iv(x, y) = (x + iy)^2$.

Then, $\quad u(x, y) = x^2 - y^2, \; v(x, y) = 2xy$.

The partial derivatives of u and v are

$$\frac{\partial u(x, y)}{\partial x} = 2x \quad \frac{\partial u(x, y)}{\partial y} = -2y$$

$$\frac{\partial v(x, y)}{\partial x} = 2y \quad \frac{\partial v(x, y)}{\partial y} = 2x$$

Thus, the partial derivatives u_x, u_y, v_x and v_y are continuous and satisfies Cauchy-Riemann equation. Thus, $f(z) = z^2$ is differentiable for all z.

Definition 3.2

Analytic Functions: A complex function $w = f(z)$ is said to be analytic at a point $z_0 \in \mathbf{C}$ if f is differentiable at z_0 and at every point in some neighbourhood of z_0.

A function f is analytic in a domain D if it is analytic at every point of D. A function f analytic through a domain D is also called holomorphic or regular.

We can talk about the differentiability at a point but analyticity at a point has different meaning. We say a function is analytic at a point if it is differentiable in an open set containing that point. The following example shows that a function is differentiable at a point but not analytic at a point.

Example 3.9

$$\text{Consider } f(z) = |z|^2, \text{ then}$$

$$u(x, y) + iv(x, y) = x^2 + y^2$$

$$\Rightarrow \qquad u(x, y) = x^2 + y^2,\ v(x, y) = 0$$

If $(x, y) \neq (0, 0)$. Then $u_x(x, y) = 2x$, $u_y(x, y) = 2y$.

and $\quad v_x(x, y) = 0, \quad v_y(x, y) = 0.$

The Cauchy-Riemann equations are not satisfied for $z \neq 0$. For $(x, y) = (0, 0)$,

$$\lim_{z \to 0} \frac{f(z) - f(0)}{z - 0} = \lim_{z \to 0} \frac{|z|^2}{z} = \lim_{z \to 0} \frac{z\overline{z}}{z} = \lim_{z \to 0} \overline{z} = 0$$

Thus, $f(z) = |z|^2$ is differentiable at $z = 0$, it is not analytic at that point because there exists no neighbourhood of $z = 0$ throughout which f is differentiable. Hence f is nowhere analytic.

We conclude that every analytic function in differentiable but every differentiable function need not be analytic.

Definition 3.3

If a function f is analytic at every point z in the complex plane then it is called an entire function.

Thus, every polynomial function and rational function are entire functions provided the rational function does not vanish in the domain D.

The following results are the consequences of Cauchy-Riemann equation.

Theorem 3.7

If f is analytic in a region R and $f'(z) = 0$, then f is constant.

Proof

Let $z_0 \in R$. Since R is open therefore there is a disc D centred at z_0 and contained in R. Now,

$$f'(z) = \frac{\partial u(x, y)}{\partial x} + i\frac{\partial v(x, y)}{\partial x}$$

$$0 = \frac{\partial v(x, y)}{\partial x} - i\frac{\partial u(x, y)}{\partial x}$$

so $$\frac{\partial u(x, y)}{\partial x} = \frac{\partial u(x, y)}{\partial y} = \frac{\partial v(x, y)}{\partial x} = \frac{\partial v(x, y)}{\partial y} = 0.$$

Since $\frac{\partial u(x, y_0)}{\partial x} = \frac{\partial v(x, y_0)}{\partial x} = 0$, the functions $x \to u(x, y_0)$ and $x \to v(x, y_0)$ are constants, and if $z_1 = x_1 + iy_1$ is any point in D, then

$$\begin{aligned} f(x_1 + iy_0) &= u(x_1, y_0) + iv(x_1, y_0) \\ &= u(x_0, y_0) + iv(x_0, y_0) \\ &= f(x_0 + iy_0) \end{aligned}$$

Since $\frac{\partial u(x_1, y)}{\partial y} = \frac{\partial v(x_1, y)}{\partial y} = 0$, the function $y \to u(x_1, y)$ and $y \to v(x_1, y)$ are constant. Thus

$$\begin{aligned} f(x_1 + iy_1) &= u(x_1 , y_1) + iv\,(x_1, y_1) \\ &= u(x_1, y_0) + iv\,(x_1, y_0) \\ &= f(x_1 + iy_0) \\ &= f(x_0 + iy_0) \end{aligned}$$

$\Rightarrow f(z_1) = f(z_0)$. Thus, f is constant on D.

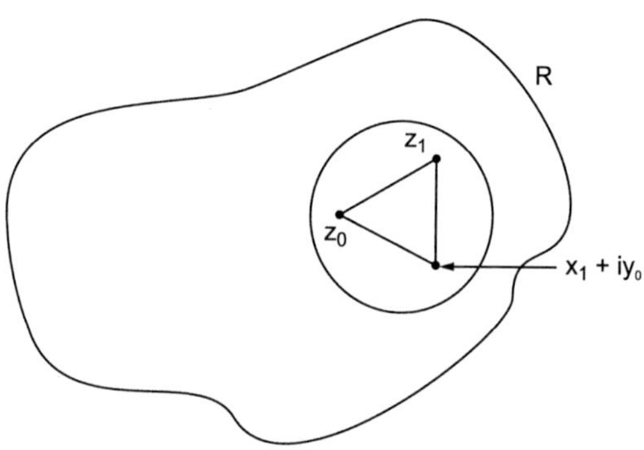

Remark

The condition of connectedness in Theorem 3.7 cannot be dropped: For example, consider

$$D = D_1 \cup D_2, \quad D_1 = \{z : |z| < 1\}, \quad D_2 = \{z : |z-2| < \frac{1}{2}\}$$

$D_1 \cap D_2 = \phi$. Thus, D is open but not connected.

Define a function $f : D \to \mathbb{R}$ by

$$f(z) = \begin{cases} 1 \text{ if } z \in D_1 \\ 2 \text{ if } z \in D_2 \end{cases}$$

Then, $f'(z) = 0$, but f is not constant on D.

The theorem 3.7 can be used in the following:

Theorem 3.8

If f is analytic on a region R and one of the following holds,

(*i*) *Re* f is constant on R,

(*ii*) *Im* f is constant on R,

(*iii*) $|f|$ is constant on R,

then, f is constant on R.

Proof

(*i*) Let $f(z) = u(x, y) + iv(x, y)$. Since $Re\, f(z) = u(x, y) =$ constant

then, $$\frac{\partial u\,(x, y)}{\partial x} = 0 = \frac{\partial v\,(x, y)}{\partial y} \text{ and } \frac{\partial u}{\partial y} = 0 = -\frac{\partial v}{\partial x}.$$

Thus, $$f'(z) = \frac{\partial u\,(x, y)}{\partial x} + \frac{i\partial v(x, y)}{\partial x}$$
$$= \frac{\partial v\,(x, y)}{\partial y} - \frac{i\partial u(x, y)}{\partial y}$$

Thus, $f'(z) = 0$ on R and hence f is constant.

(*ii*) If Im $f(z) =$ constant, then we proceed same as in part (*i*).

(*iii*) Let $f(z) = u(x, y) + iv\,(x, y)$; then

$$|f(z)|^2 = u^2 + v^2 = k^2 \text{(say)} \qquad ...(1)$$

If $k = 0$ then $|f(z)| = 0 \Leftrightarrow f(z) = 0$.

If $k \neq 0$. Differentiating (1) with respect to x and y respectively, we have

$$2uu_x + 2vv_x = 0$$

and $$2uu_y + 2vv_y = 0$$

or $$uu_x + vv_x = 0$$

$$vu_x - uv_x = 0$$

Then, $$(u^2 + v^2)u_x = 0$$

i.e., $$k^2 u_x = 0$$

i.e., $u_x = 0$ and $v_x = 0$

Thus, $f'(z) = u_x(x, y) + v_x(x, y) = 0$. Hence, f is constant.

The Cauchy-Riemann equations can also be used to know the function of the form $f(z) = u(x, y) + iv(x, y)$ if either $u(x, y)$ or $v(x, y)$ is known. This is shown in the following examples:

Example 3.10

Find the analytic function $f = u + iv$ with $u(x, y) = x^2 - y^2$.

Proof

Since f is analytic, therefore it is differentiable at $z = x + iy$ and thus, Cauchy-Riemann equations are satisfied.

Now, $u(x, y) = x^2 - y^2$, then

$$\frac{\partial u}{\partial x} = 2x = \frac{\partial v}{\partial y} \quad \Rightarrow \quad v = 2xy + c \qquad ...(1)$$

$$\frac{\partial u}{\partial y} = -2y = \frac{-\partial u}{\partial x} \quad \Rightarrow \quad v = 2xy + c \qquad ...(2)$$

Thus,
$$f(z) = u(x, y) + iv(x, y)$$
$$= x^2 - y^2 + i(2xy + c)$$
$$= x^2 - y^2 + 2ixy + ic$$

Example 3.11

Show that there are no analytic function $f = u + iv$ with $u(x, y) = x^2 + y^2$.

Solution

Let, if possible there is an analytic function $f = u + iv$ with

$$u(x, y) = x^2 + y^2$$

If f is analytic then it satisfies Cauchy-Riemann equations. Thus,

$$\frac{\partial u}{\partial x} = 2x = \frac{\partial v}{\partial y} \quad \Rightarrow \quad v = 2xy + c_1$$

and $$\frac{\partial u}{\partial y} = +2xy = \frac{-\partial v}{\partial x} \quad \Rightarrow \quad v = -2xy + c_2.$$

Thus, we cannot find analytic function $f = u + iv$ with $u(x, y) = x^2 + y^2$.

Comparison with Real Numbers

(1) Almost all the properties of differentiable complex functions is similar to differentiable real functions. But the Lagrange's Mean Value theorem (*i.e.*, if f is a real-valued function defined on $[a, b]$ such that f is continuous on $[a, b]$ and differentiable on $]\, a, b\,[$ then there exists $(\in \,]\, a, b\,[$ such that $\dfrac{f(b) - f(a)}{b - a} = f'(c))$ does not hold for complex numbers.

For example, let $f : [a, b] \rightarrow \mathbf{C}$ $(a < b)$ be defined as

$$f(x) = x^2 + ix^3$$

Then f is differentiable in $[a, b]$. Let if possible there exists $c \in \,]\, a, b\,[$ such that

$$f'(c) = \frac{f(b) - f(a)}{b - a}$$

$$\Rightarrow \qquad 2c + 3ic^2 = \frac{(b^2 + ib^3) - (a^2 + ia^3)}{b - a}$$

$$\Rightarrow \qquad c = \frac{b + a}{2} \text{ and } c^2 = \frac{b^2 + a^2 + ab}{3}$$

But $$\left(\frac{b + a}{2}\right)^2 = \frac{b^2 + a^2 + ab}{3}$$

$$\Rightarrow 3(b^2 + a^2 + 2ab) = 4(b^2 + a^2 + ab)$$

$$\Rightarrow \quad b^2 + a^2 - 2ab = 0$$

$$\Rightarrow \quad (b - a)^2 = 0$$

$\Rightarrow$ $b = a$ which is not possible.

EXERCISE

1. Suppose $f(z)$ is analytic. Show that $|f'(z)|^2 = u_x^2 + v_x^2 = u_y^2 + v_y^2$.
2. If $u(x, y)$ and $v(x, y)$ are real and imaginary parts of an analytic function f. What can you say about the analyticity of the function $g(z) = v(x, y) + iu(x, y)$.
3. Show that if f and g are analytic and $f'(z) = g'(z)$, then $f(z) = g(z) + c$, where c is constant.
4. Show that the following functions are analytic in the appropriate domain:

   (*i*) $f(z) = e^{-x} \cos y - ie^{-x} \sin y$

   (*ii*) $f(z) = 4x^2 + 5x - 4y^2 + 9 + i\,(8xy + 5y - 1)$

   (*iii*) $f(z) = \dfrac{x-1}{(x-1)^2 + y^2} - i\dfrac{y}{(x-1)^2 + y^2}$

   (*iv*) $f(z) = \dfrac{x^3 + xy^2 + x}{x^2 + y^2} + i\dfrac{x^2 y - y^3 - y}{x^2 + y^2}$.
5. Find real constant a, b, c and d so that the given function is entire

   (*i*) $f(z) = 3x - y + 5 + i(ax + by - 3)$

   (*ii*) $f(z) = x^2 + axy + by^2 + i(cx^2 + dxy + y^2)$.
6. Show that the function

$$f(z) = \begin{cases} 0, & z = 0 \\ \dfrac{z^5}{|z|^4}, & z \neq 0 \end{cases}$$

   is not differentiable at the origin, but Cauchy-Riemann equations are satisfied.
7. Show that the function $f(z) = \sqrt{|x||y|}$ $(x, y \in \mathbb{R})$, satisfies Cauchy-Riemann equations at the origin yet f is not analytic at the origin.

ANSWERS

1. f satisfies C – R equations and if $f(z) = u(z) + iv(z)$, then $|f'(z)|^2 = u_x^{\,2} + v_x^{\,2} = u_y^{\,2} + v_y^{\,2}$

2. Analytic

4. (*i*) $u(z) = e^{-x} \cos y$. $v(z) = e^{-x} \sin y$ and C – R equations are satisfied

(*ii*) $u(z) = 4x^2 + 5x - 4y^2 + 9$, $v(z) = 8xy + 5y - 1$ and show that $u_x = v_y$, $u_y = -v_x$

(*iii*) $u(z) = \dfrac{x-1}{(x-1)^2 + y^2}, v(z) = \dfrac{-y}{(x-1)^2 + y^2}$ & show CR – equations are satisfied

(*iv*) $u(z) = \dfrac{x^3 + xy^2 + x}{x^2 + y^2}, v(x) = \dfrac{x^2 y - y^3 - y}{x^2 + y^2}$ show $u_x = u_y$ & $u_y = -v_x$

5. (*i*) $a = 1, b = 3$ (*ii*) $a = 2, b = -1, c = -1, d = 2$

6. $$u(x, y) = \frac{x^5 - 10y^2x^3 + 5y^4x}{\left(x^2 + y^2\right)^2}$$

$$v(x, y) = \frac{5yx^4 - 10y^3x + y^5}{\left(x^2 + y^2\right)^2}$$

and CR– equations are satisfied. But $\lim\limits_{(x,y)\to(0,0)} \dfrac{u(x,y) - u(0,0)}{x + iy}$

and $\lim\limits_{(x,y)\to(0,0)} \dfrac{v(x,y) - v(0,0)}{x + iy}$ do not exist.

7. $\lim\limits_{(x,y)\to(0,0)} \dfrac{f(x,y) - f(0,0)}{x + iy}$ does not exist.

3.3 DIFFERENTIABILITY AND UNIQUENESS OF POWER SERIES

In this section, we shall show that a power series, like polynomials, are differentiable functions. In Theorem 2.18, we have proved that if

$\sum_{n=0}^{\infty} c_n z^n$ converges in $\{z : |z| < \mathbb{R}\}$ then $\sum_{n=1}^{\infty} nC_n z^{n-1}$ also converges

in the same disc. We begin with the following.

Theorem 3.9

Suppose $f(z) = \sum_{n=0}^{\infty} c_n z^n$ Converges in the disc $D = \{z : |z| < \mathbb{R}\}$. Then,

$f'(z)$ exists and $f'(z) = \sum_{n=0}^{\infty} nC_n z^{n-1}$ throughout D.

Proof

Case (i): If $0 < R < \infty$, Consider

$$\frac{f(z+h)-f(z)}{h} = \frac{\sum_{n=0}^{\infty} c_n (z+h)^n - \Sigma c_n z^n}{h}$$

$$= \frac{\sum_{n=0}^{\infty} c_n \{(z+h)^n - z^n\}}{h}$$

$$= \sum_{n=0}^{\infty} c_n \left\{ nz^{n-1} + \frac{n(n-1)}{2!} z^{n-2} h + \ldots + h^{n-1} \right\}$$

$$\Rightarrow \quad \frac{f(z+h)-f(z)}{h} - \sum_{n=0}^{\infty} c_n n z^{n-1}$$

$$= \sum_{n=0}^{\infty} c_n \left\{ \frac{n(n-1)}{2!} z^{n-2} h + \ldots + h^{n-1} \right\}$$

$$= \sum_{n=0}^{\infty} \frac{n(n-1)}{2} c_n h \left\{ z^{n-2} + \frac{(n-2)}{3} z^{n-3} h + \ldots \frac{2}{n(n-1)} h^{n-2} \right\}$$

$$\leq \sum_{n=0}^{\infty} \frac{n(n-1)}{2} c_n h \left\{ z^{n-2} + (n-2) z^{n-3} h + \ldots + h^{n-2} \right\}$$

$$= \sum_{n=0}^{\infty} \frac{n(n-1)}{2} c_n h \, (z+h)^{n-2} \quad \text{for } |h| \leq 1$$

Hence, for $|h| \leq 1$, choose $z + h = \rho < R$.

$$\left| \frac{f(z+h) - f(z)}{h} - \sum_{n=0}^{\infty} n c_n z^{n-1} \right| \leq |h| \sum_{n=0}^{\infty} \frac{n(n-1)}{2} |c_n| \, \rho^{n-2}$$

$$\leq A \, |h|$$

Where $A = \sum_{n=0}^{\infty} \frac{n(n-1)}{2} |c_n| \rho^{n-2}$

Since $\sum_{n=0}^{\infty} |c_n| \rho^{n-2}$ converges for all $|z| < R$. Thus, letting $h \to 0$, we get

$$f'(z) = \sum_{n=1}^{\infty} n c_n z^{n-1}.$$

Case (*ii*) Let $R = \infty$, then the series $\sum c_n z^n$ converges for all $z \in$ **C**. Then,

$$\frac{f(z+h) - f(z)}{h} - \sum n c_n z^{n-1} = \sum_{n=2}^{\infty} c_n \left\{ \frac{n(n-1)}{2!} z^{n-2} h \ldots + h^{n-1} \right\}$$

$$= \sum_{n=2}^{\infty} c_n \alpha_n \qquad \ldots(1)$$

where

$$\alpha_n = \sum_{K=2}^{\infty} {}^n c_K h^{K-1} z^{n-K} \leq |h| \sum_{K=2}^{\infty} {}^n c_K \, |z|^{n-K}$$

$$= |h| (|z| + 1)^n \text{ for } |h| \leq 1.$$

Hence, for $|h| \leq 1$, from (1), we get

$$\left|\frac{f(z+h)-f(z)}{h}-\sum{}^{n}c_n\, z^{n-1}\right|\le |h|\sum_{K=0}^{\infty}|c_n|(|z|+1)^n \le A|h|)$$

Since $\sum_{n=0}^{\infty}|c_n|\,z^n$ converges for all z. Letting $h \to 0$, we conclude that

$$f'(z) = \sum_{n=1}^{\infty} nc_n\, z^{n-1}.$$

Theorem 3.10

Let $\sum c_n z^n$ be a power series with radius of convergence $R > 0$, then $\sum c_n z^n$ is infinitely differentiable in $\{z : |z| < \mathbb{R}\}$.

Proof

Using Theorem 3.9, we have

$$f'(z) = \sum_{n=1}^{\infty} nc_n\, z^{n-1}$$

Since $\sum nc_n\, z^{n-1}$ has the same radius of convergence R, therefore using the above result

$$f''(z) = \sum_{n=2}^{\infty} n(n-1)\, c_n\, z^{n-2}$$

Then, by induction $f^{(k)}$ is differentiable for all $k > 1$ and

$$f^{k}(Z) = \sum_{n=K}^{\infty} n(n-1)\ldots(n-k+1)\, c_K\, z^{n-K} \quad \ldots(1)$$

Corollary 3.11

Let $f(z) = \sum_{n=0}^{\infty} c_n z^n$ be a power series with radius of convergence $R > 0$, then

$$C_n = \frac{f^{(n)}(0)}{n!} \text{ for all } n.$$

Proof

Putting $z = 0$ and $n = k$ in (1), we get

$$f^{(n)}(0) = (n(n-1)\,...1)C_n$$

$$\Rightarrow \qquad f^{(n)}(0) = n!\ C_n \text{ for all } n$$

$$\Rightarrow \qquad C_n = \frac{f^{(n)}(0)}{n!}.$$

From corollary 3.11, we conclude that if $f(z) = \sum_{n=0}^{\infty} c_n z^n = 0$ for all $z \in \{z : |z| < R\}$ then $f \equiv 0$ and also $f^{(n)}(0) = 0$, thus $c_n = 0$ for all n. We get a stronger result in the following form.

Theorem 3.12: Uniqueness Theorem

Let $\{z_k\}$ be a sequence converging to zero and $f(z) = \sum_{n=0}^{\infty} c_n z^n$ be a power series such that $f(z_k) = 0$ for all k then $f \equiv 0$.

Proof

Let $f(z) = c_0 + c_1 z + c_2 z^2 + ...$

Since f is continuous at the origin, therefore

$$c_0 = f(0) = \lim_{z \to 0} f(z) = \lim_{k \to \infty} f(z_k) = 0$$

Define $\qquad g : C \to \mathbf{C}$ by

$$g(z) = \frac{f(z)}{z}.$$

Since f is continuous, then g is also continuous for all z. Also,

$$g(0) = \lim_{z \to 0} g(z) = \lim_{z \to 0} \frac{f(z)}{z} = \lim_{K \to \infty} \frac{f(z_k)}{z_k} = 0$$

But $\qquad g(z) = \dfrac{f(z)}{z} = c_1 + c_2 z + c_3 z^2 + ...$

Then, $\qquad c_1 = g(0) = 0$. Similarly

$$c_n = \lim_{z \to 0} \frac{f(z)}{z^n} = \lim_{k \to 0} \frac{f(z_k)}{z_k^n} = 0.$$

Hence, $\qquad f(z) \equiv 0.$

Corollary 3.13

If a power series equals zero at all the points of a set with an accumulation point at the origin, then the power series is identically zero.

Solution

Let $\sum_{n=0}^{\infty} c_n z^n$ be a power series. Let $S = \{z_1, z_2 \ldots\}$ be such that $|z_1|$

$\leq 1, |z_2| \leq \frac{1}{2}|z_1|, |z_3| \leq \frac{1}{2^2}|z_2| \ldots$

Thus, $$|z_n| \leq \frac{1}{2^{n-1}}|z_{n-1}| \text{ for all } n$$

$$\Rightarrow \qquad \frac{|z_n|}{|z_{n-1}|} \leq \frac{1}{2^{n-1}} \to 0 \text{ as } n \to \infty. \text{(By ratio test)}$$

By ratio test $\{z_n\}$ is a sequence converging to zero. Thus, S has an accumulation point zero. By Theorem 3.12 $f \equiv 0$ on S.

Corollary 3.14

Let $f(z) = \Sigma a_n z^n$ and $g(z) = \Sigma b_n z^n$, be two power series such that $f(z) \equiv g(z)$ on a set S where S is a set with an accumulation point at the origin. Then $a_n = b_n$ for all n.

Proof

Define $$h(z) = f(z) - g(z)$$

$$= \sum_{n=0}^{\infty} (a_n - b_n) z^n$$

Since $h(z) \equiv 0$ on the set S. Then by corollary 3.13 $h \equiv 0$. Thus, $f(z) \equiv g(z)\ \forall\ z$. Hence, $a_n = b_n\ \forall\ n$.

Let $f(z) = \sum_{n=0}^{\infty} c_n (z-a)^n$ be a power series about a and has radius of convergence R. Then, we can extend all the results from Theorem 3.9 to corollary 3.14. We conclude that the power series

$\sum_{n=0}^{\infty} c_n (z-a)^n$ with radius of convergence R defines an analytic function

$$f(z) = \sum_{n=0}^{\infty} c_n (z-a)^n \text{ for all } z \in \{z : |z-a| < R\}.$$

Example 3.12

The function $z \to \sin\frac{1}{z}$ is not defined at $z = 0$, but using the above result we can define a function such that

$$f(z) = \sin\frac{1}{z} \quad \forall \quad z \in S = \left\{z : z = \frac{1}{n\pi}\right\}$$

Since $\sin\frac{1}{z} = 0$ if $z = \frac{1}{n\pi}, n = \pm 1, \pm 2, \ldots$

Using corollary 3.14, $f(z) \equiv 0$.

❑❑❑

4

Elementary Functions

In this chapter, we investigate the complex exponential, logarithmic, power, trigonometric, hyperbolic and inverse hyperbola functions. All of these functions are found to be analytic in a suitable domain and their derivatives are same as their real counterparts. The elementary complex functions are very useful source of examples for various concepts studied in the subsequent chapters

4.1 THE EXPONENTIAL FUNCTION

In this section, we study the complex exponential function and the mapping $w = e^z$. If x is a positive real number, then there is only one solution to the equation $y = e^x$, namely $x = \log_e y$ but in case of complex numbers there are infinitely many solutions to the equation $w = e^z$. Therefore, the complex logarithmic function log z is a 'multi-valued function'—this interpretation is also given in the section. Both exponential and logarithmic functions have most of the properties of those similar to real functions except the above mentioned.

The power series $\sum_{n=0}^{\infty} \frac{z^n}{n!}$ has infinite radius of convergence. We define exponential function by

$$e^z = \sum_{n=0}^{\infty} \frac{z^n}{n!}, z \in \mathbf{C}.$$

Properties of exponential functions

(*i*) $$\frac{d}{dz}(e^z) = e^z \text{ for all } z \in \mathbf{C}.$$

We know $$\frac{d}{dz}\left(\sum_{n=0}^{\infty}\frac{z^n}{n!}\right) = \sum_{n=1}^{\infty}\frac{nz^{n-1}}{n!} = \sum_{n=1}^{\infty}\frac{z^{n-1}}{(n-1)!} = \sum_{n=0}^{\infty}\frac{z^n}{n!} = e^z.$$

Thus, the exponential function is entire.

(*ii*) If $z = x + iy$, then

$$e^z = e^{x+iy} = e^x(\cos y + i\sin y)$$

(*iii*) $$e^{z+w} = e^z \,.\, e^w.$$

Let $$e^z = \sum_{n=0}^{\infty}\frac{z^n}{n!} \text{ and } e^w = \sum_{n=0}^{\infty}\frac{w^n}{n!}$$

Let c_j be the Cauchy's product of the two series, then

$$c_n = \sum_{j=1}^{n}\frac{z^j w^{n-j}}{(n-j)!}$$

$$= \frac{1}{n!}\sum_{j=1}^{n}\frac{n!}{(n-j)!}z^j\omega^{n-j}$$

$$= \frac{1}{n!}(z+w)^n$$

Thus $$e^z \,.\, e^w = \sum_{n=0}^{\infty}c_n$$

$$= \sum_{n=0}^{\infty}\frac{(z+w)^n}{n!}$$

$$= e^{z+w}.$$

OR

Let $z = x_1 + iy_1,\ w = x_2 + iy_2$

then, $e^z = e^{x_1}(\cos y_1 + i\sin y_1),\ e^w = e^{x_2}(\cos y_2 + i\sin y_2)$

$$e^z\,e^w = e^{x_1+x_2}\{(\cos y_1 + i\sin y_1)(\cos y_2 + i\sin y_2)\}$$

$$= e^{x_1+x_2}\{\cos(y_1+y_2) + i\sin(y_1+y_2)\}$$

$$= e^{z+w}$$

(*iv*) We know $e^z = \sum_{n=0}^{\infty} \frac{z^n}{n!}$

$$= 1 + z + \frac{z^2}{2!} + \frac{z^3}{3!} + \ldots$$

Put $z = 0$, then

$$e^0 = 1$$

Thus, we conclude $e^z \neq 0$ for all $z \in \mathbf{C}$.

(*v*) Using (*iii*), we get

$$e^z\, e^{-z} = e^0 = 1$$

$$\Rightarrow \qquad e^{-z} = \frac{1}{e^z} \text{ for all } z \in \mathbf{C}.$$

(*vi*) Modulus and argument of complex exponential function.

Consider the equation

$$\begin{aligned} w &= e^z \\ &= e^{x+iy} \\ &= e^x(\cos y + i \sin y) \\ &= r(\cos\theta + i \sin\theta) \qquad \text{(in polar form)} \end{aligned}$$

Comparing, we get $r = e^x$ and $\theta = y + 2k\pi$, $k = 0, \pm 1, \pm 2, \ldots\ldots.$

Since r is the modulus, therefore we can write

$$|e^z| = e^x = e^{Re\, z}$$

and $\quad \arg(e^z) = y + 2k\pi, \qquad k = 0, \pm 1, \pm 2, \ldots..$

From calculus, we know $e^x > 0$ for all $x \in \mathbb{R}$. Therefore, $|e^z| > 0$.

(*vii*) Conjugate of complex exponential function.

$$e^z = e^x(\cos y + i \sin y)$$

Then,

$$\begin{aligned} \overline{e^z} &= e^x(\cos y - i \sin y) \\ &= e^x(\cos(-y) + i \sin(-y)) \\ &= e^{x-iy} \\ &= e^{\bar{z}} \end{aligned}$$

Therefore, for all complex z, $\overline{e^z} = e^{\bar{z}}$.

(*viii*) Using (*iii*) and (*v*) we can easily show $e^{z-w} = \dfrac{e^z}{e^w}$.

(ix) $\quad (e^z)^n = e^{nz}, n = 0, \pm 1, \pm 2, \ldots$

Consider $\quad e^z \cdot e^z = e^{z+z}$

$$= e^{2z} \qquad \text{(using } (iii))$$

By mathematical induction, the result can be proved in general.

(x) $\quad e^{i\pi} = \cos \pi + i \sin \pi = -1$

and $\quad e^{2i\pi} = \cos 2\pi + i \sin 2\pi = 1.$

There is a significant difference between real and complex exponential functions. Real exponential functions are one-one but since $e^{2\pi i} = 1 = e^{\circ}$, so complex exponential functions are not one-one, in fact it is periodic. A complex function f is said to be periodic with period a if $f(z + a) = f(z)$ for all complex z. The real exponential functions are not periodic but the complex exponential function is because it depends on cosine and sine functions, which are periodic. Let a be the period of e^z. Then

$$e^{z+a} = e^z$$

$$\Rightarrow \quad e^z \cdot e^a = e^z$$

$$\Rightarrow \quad e^a = 1$$

If $a = \alpha + i\beta$, then $|e^a| = e^{\alpha} = 1 \Rightarrow \alpha = 0$

and $\cos \beta + i \sin \beta = 1$ so $\beta = 2n\pi$ for some integer n. Thus, $a = 2n\pi i$ is the periodicity of e^z. It means

$$e^{z+2\pi i} = e^z.$$

Or we say the complex exponential function e^z is periodic with a purely imaginary period $2\pi i$. We conclude that

$$e^z = e^{z+2\pi i} = e^{(z+2\pi i)+2\pi i} = \ldots = e^{z+2n\pi i}$$

Thus, the exponential function e^z is not one-one and all values of e^z are assumed in an infinite horizontal strip of width 2π in the z-plane (as shown in the Fig. 4.1).

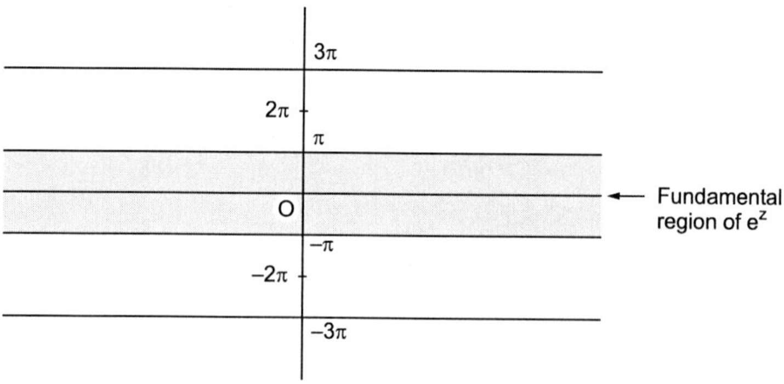

Fig. 4.1

The infinite horizontal strip defined by

$$-\infty < x < \infty, \qquad -\pi < y < \pi$$

is called the fundamental region of e^z.

Example 4.1

Find all the solutions of

(*i*) $e^z = 1$ (*ii*) $e^z = 1 + i$ (*iii*) $e^z = 3$.

Solution

(*i*) Let $z = x + iy$, then

$$e^{x + iy} = 1$$

$\Rightarrow$ $e^x(\cos y + i \sin y) = 1$

$\Rightarrow$ $e^x \cos y = 1, \quad e^x \sin y = 0$

Squaring and adding, we get

$$e^{2x} = 1 \quad \Rightarrow \quad x = 0$$

Thus, $\cos y = 1$ and $\sin y = 0 \Rightarrow y = 2n\pi$, $n = 0, \pm 1, \pm 2, \pm 3$ ...

Hence, the set $\{z : z = 2n\pi i\}$ is the set of all solutions of $e^z = 1$.

(*ii*) If $e^z = 1 + i$, then

$$e^x \cos y = 1, \quad e^x \sin y = 1$$

$\Rightarrow$ $e^{2x} = 2 \quad \Rightarrow \quad x = \frac{1}{2}\log_e 2$

Then, $\cos y = \frac{1}{\sqrt{2}}$, $\sin y = \frac{1}{\sqrt{2}} \Rightarrow y = \left(2n\pi + \frac{\pi}{4}\right)$, $n = 0, \pm 1, \pm 2$ ...

The solution set is $\left\{z : z = \frac{1}{2}\ \log_{e^2} + \left(\frac{8n+1}{4}\right)\pi i, n \in \pi\right\}$

(*iii*) If $e^z = -3$, then

$$e^x \cos y = -3, \quad e^x \sin y = 0$$

$\Rightarrow$ $e^{2x} = 9$

$\Rightarrow$ $e^x = \pm 3 \quad \Rightarrow \quad x = \log_e 3$

Now, $\cos y = -1$, $\sin y = 0 \Rightarrow y = (2n + 1)\frac{\pi}{2}$. The solution set is

$$\left\{z : z = \log_e 3 + (2n+1)\frac{\pi}{2}i, n \in I\right\}.$$

4.1.1 The Exponential Mapping

(*i*) Image of $Re\, z = \alpha$ under the map $w = e^z$ is basically the image of the line segment $z(t) = \alpha + it, -\pi < t < \pi$ under the complex mapping in parameter t is

$$w(t) = e^{z(t)} = e^{\alpha + it} = e^{\alpha}\, e^{it} = e^{\alpha}\,(\cos t + i \sin t) : t \in \mathbb{R}$$

which is a circle of radius e^{α} Fig. 4.2.

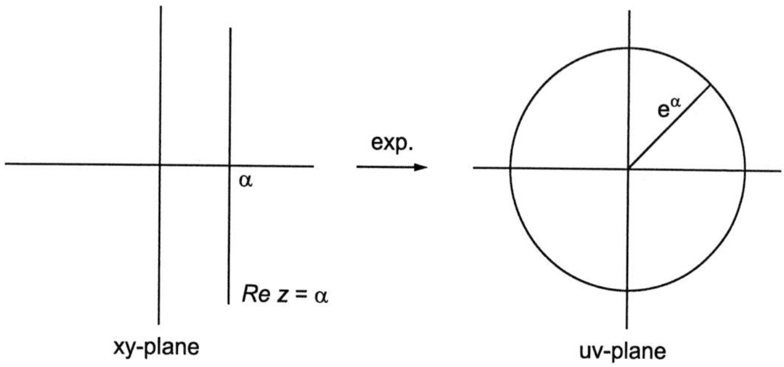

Fig. 4.2

(*ii*) Image of $Im\, z = \beta$, which is a line parallel to x-axis, under the exponential mapping to a radical half-plane or ray (not containing the origin). For if $z(t) = t + i\beta$, $t \in \mathbb{R}$, then

$$w(t) = e^{z(t)} = e^{t + i\beta} = e^{t}\{\cos \beta + i \sin \beta\}, -\infty < t < \infty.$$

Define $s = e^t$, then $0 < s < \infty$ since $-\infty < t < \infty$. Then, the image is given by $w(s) = se^{i\beta}$, the set consisting of all point $w \neq 0$ in the ray from the origin and containing the point $e^{i\beta} = \cos \beta + i \sin \beta$. Or this ray can be expressed in the form of the equation $\arg w = \beta$.

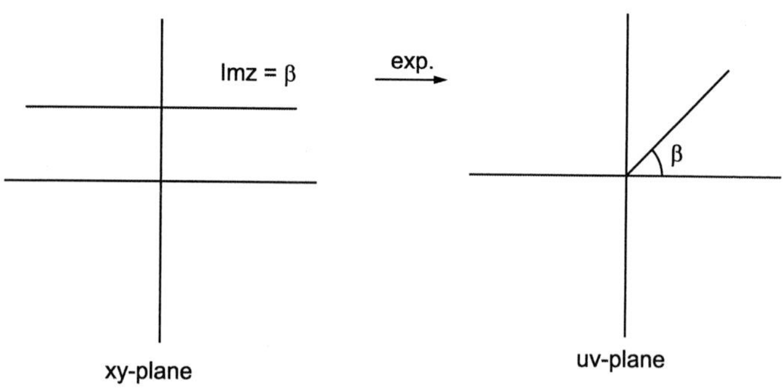

Fig. 4.3

We summarise these mapping properties in the following:

(*i*) $w = e^z$ maps the vertical line segment $x = \alpha, -\pi < y < \pi$ onto the circle $| w | = e^{\alpha}$.

(*ii*) $w = e^z$ maps the horizontal line $y = \beta, -\infty < x < \infty$ onto the ray $\arg(w) = \beta$.

(*iii*) $w = e^z$ maps the fundamental region $-\infty < x < \infty, -\pi < y < \pi$ onto the set $| w | > 0$.

In general, we conclude that the net of coordinate lines is mapped to a net of cocentric circles and radial half-planes. (Fig. 4.4).

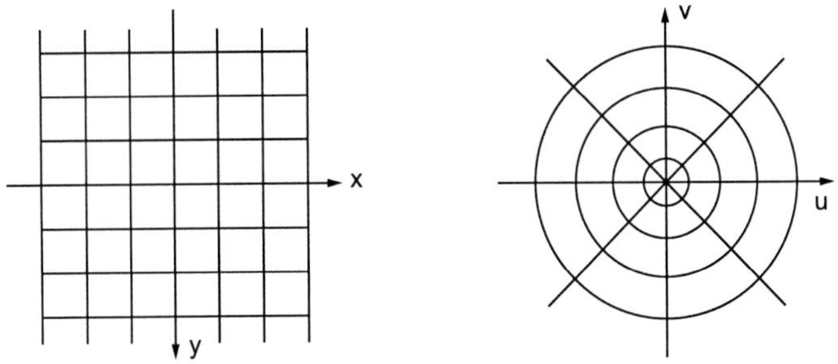

Fig. 4.4

EXERCISE

1. Find the derivative of the following functions:

(*i*) $z^2 e^{z+i}$ (*ii*) e^{2z+4}

(*iii*) $\dfrac{3e^{2z} - ie^{-z}}{z^3 - 1 + i}$ (*iv*) $e^{iz} - e^{-iz}$

(*v*) $ie^{1/z}$ (*vi*) e^{z^2+2iz}.

2. Express the given function f in the form $f(z) = u(z) + iv(z)$.

(*i*) $f(z) = e^{-iz}$ (*ii*) $f(z) = e^{2\bar{z}+i}$

(*iii*) $f(z) = e^{\frac{i}{z}}$ (*iv*) $f(z) = e^{z^2}$

(*v*) $f(z) = e^{e^z}$ (*iv*) $f(z) = e^{2z}$.

3. Find the image under the mapping $w = e^z$ of

(*i*) $Re\ z = a$

(*ii*) $Im\ z = b$ where a and b are constants.

4. Find the image under the exponential mapping

(*i*) $y = -2$ (*ii*) $x = 3$

(*iii*) $1 < x \le 2$

(*iv*) square with vertices 0, 1, $1 + i$, i

(*v*) the rectangle $0 \le x \le \log_e 2$, $-\pi/4 \le y \le \frac{\pi}{2}$.

(*vi*) $-\infty < x \le 0, \quad 0 \le y \le \pi$.

5. If z_1 and z_2 satisfy $e^{z_1} = e^{z_2} = \omega$, what is the relationship between z_1 and z_2?

6. Show that the power series

$$f(z) = 1 + z + \frac{z^2}{2!} + \ldots = \sum_{n=0}^{\infty} \frac{z^n}{n!}$$

equals e^z.

ANSWERS

1. (*i*) $z^2e^{z+i} + 2z\, e^{z+i}$ (*ii*) $2e^{2+4}$

(*iii*) $$\frac{6\left(z^3-1\right)e^{2z} - e^{-z} - 9e^{2z}z^2 + i\left(6e^{2z} - 3ie^{-z}z^2\right)}{\left(z^3-1+i\right)^2}$$

(*iv*) $i(e^{iz} + e^{-iz})$ (*v*) $\frac{-i}{z^2}e^{1/z}$

(*vi*) $(2z+2i)e^{z^2+2iz}$

2. (*i*) $(\cos y - i \sin y)\, e^x$

(*ii*) $e^{2x}(\cos(2y+1) - i\sin(2y+1))$

(*iii*) $$\frac{y}{e^{x^2+y^2}}\left\{\cos\left(\frac{x}{x^2+y^2}\right) + i\sin\left(\frac{y}{x^2+y^2}\right)\right\}$$

(*iv*) $e^{x^2-y^2}(\cos xy + i\sin xy)$

(*v*) $e^{\cos x}\left(\cos(\sin y)+i\sin(\sin y)\right)$

(*vi*) $e^{2x}\left(\cos y+i\sin y\right)$

3. (*i*) $w = e^z$ maps the vertical line $Ra\ z = a$ onto the circle $|w| = e^z$;
(*ii*) the horizintal line y = b onto the ray arg w = b.

4. (*i*) $\arg w = -2$ (*ii*) $|w| = e^3$
(*iii*) $e < |w| < e^z$ (*iv*) $0 < x < 1$
(*v*) $1 < |w| < 2,\ -\pi/4 < \arg w < \pi/2$
(*vi*) $0 < |w| < 1,\ 0 < \arg w < \pi$

5. z_1 and z_2 differ by an integer multiple of 2π

4.2 COMPLEX LOGARITHMIC FUNCTION

In real analysis, the logarithmic function is the inverse of the exponential function. In complex analysis, the exponential function is not one-one so we cannot define logarithm as an inverse of exponential directly, therefore we restrict the domain to make the exponential function one-one. Let $w = u + iv$. If $e^w = z$, then $|\,e^w\,| = |\,z\,|$, $\arg(e^w) = \arg(z)$. It follows that $e^u = |\,z\,|$ and $v = \arg z$ or $u = \log_e |\,z\,|$ and $v = \arg(z)$. Thus, if $e^w = z$, then $w = \log_e |\,z\,| + i\arg(z)$ since arg(*z*) has infinitely many values, then $e^w = z$ has infinite number of solutions. We summarize the above discussion in the form of following definition:

Definition 4.1

A multivalued function $\log z$ defined by

$$\log z = \log_e |\,z\,| + i\arg(z)$$

is called the complex logarithm. In polar form, if $z = re^{i\theta}$, then

$$\log z = \log_e r + i(\theta + 2n\pi),\ n = 0, \pm 1, \pm 2, \ldots$$

We can use the definition of log *z* in finding all solution of the exponential equations $e^w = z$ when *z* is a non-zero complex number.

Example 4.2

Find all the solutions of the following equations:

(*i*) $e^w = i$ (*ii*) $e^w = -2$ (*iii*) $e^w = 1 + \sqrt{3}i$.

Solution

Let $e^w = z$, then the solution is in the form

$$w = \log z = \log_e |z| + i \arg(z).$$

(*i*) $z = i = (\cos \pi/2 + i \sin \pi/2)$. Thus, $|z| = 1$ and $\arg(z) = \frac{\pi}{2} + 2n\pi$.

Thus, $e^w = i$ has solutions of the form

$$w = \log_e 1 + i\left(\frac{\pi}{2} + 2n\pi\right),\ n = 0, \pm 1, \pm 2, ..$$

$$= \frac{(4n+1)\pi}{2} i,\ n = 0, \pm 1, \pm 2,$$

Thus, $w = \ldots\ldots\ \frac{-7\pi}{2}i, \frac{-3\pi}{2}i, \frac{\pi}{2}i, \frac{5\pi}{2}i,$

satisfies the equation $e^w = i$.

(*ii*) $z = -2 = 2(\cos \pi + i \sin \pi)$, we have $|z| = 2$ and $\arg z = \pi + 2n\pi$

and so $w = \log(-2) = \log_e 2 + i(\pi + 2n\pi)$

Thus, $w = \log_e 2 + (2n + 1)\pi\, i,\ n = 0, \pm 1, \pm 2, \ldots$

satisfy the equation $e^w = -2$.

(*iii*) $z = 1 + \sqrt{3}i = 2\left(\cos\frac{\pi}{3} + i \sin\frac{\pi}{3}\right)$. Then, $|z| = 2$ and $\arg z = \frac{\pi}{3} + 2n\pi$.

Then, $$w = \log(1 + \sqrt{3}\, i) = \log_e 2 + i\left(\frac{\pi}{3} + 2n\pi\right)$$

$$w = \log_e 2 + \left(\frac{6n+1}{3}\right)\pi i, \quad n = 0, \pm 1, \pm 2, \pm 3 \ldots$$

are the solutions of $e^w = 1 + \sqrt{3}i$.

4.2.1 Properties of Logarithmic Function

The complex algorithmic function satisfies the following identities which are analogous to its real counterpart.

If z_1 and z_2 are non-zero complex numbers and n is an integer, then

(*i*) $\log(z_1 z_2) = \log z_1 + \log z_2$

Consider $\log z_1 + \log z_2 = \log |z_1| + \log |z_2| + i\arg(z_1) + i\arg(z_2)$ ...(1)

Since $|z_1|$ and $|z_2|$ are real number therefore, using the property of log for real numbers, we get $\log |z_1| + \log |z_2| = \log |z_1||z_2| = \log |z_1 z_2|$

and $\quad \arg(z_1 z_2) = \arg z_1 + \arg z_2$

Thus, from (1), we get

$$\begin{aligned}\log z_1 + \log z_2 &= \log |z_1 z_2| + i\arg(z_1 z_2)\\ &= \log(z_1 z_2)\end{aligned}$$

(*ii*) $\quad \log\left(\dfrac{z_1}{z_2}\right) = \log z_1 - \log z_2$

Consider $\log z_1 - \log z_2 = \log |z_1| + i\arg(z_1) - \log |z_2| + i\arg(z_2)$ ...(2)

Since, $|z_1|$ and $|z_2|$ are real, therefore, $\log |z_1| - \log |z_2| = \log \dfrac{|z_1|}{|z_2|}$.

Also, $\quad \arg\left(\dfrac{z_1}{z_2}\right) = \arg z_1 - \arg z_2$. From (2)

$$\begin{aligned}\log z_1 - \log z_2 &= \log \frac{|z_1|}{|z_2|} + i\arg\left(\frac{z_1}{z_2}\right)\\ &= \log\left(\frac{z_1}{z_2}\right).\end{aligned}$$

(*iii*) $\log z_1^{\,n} = n \log z_1$

We know $n \log z_1 = n(\log |z_1| + i\arg(z_1))$

$$\begin{aligned}&= n\log |z_1| + in\arg(z_1)\\ &= \log |z_1|^n + i\arg(z_1^{\,n})\\ &= \log z_1^{\,n}\end{aligned}$$

4.2.2 Principal Branch of a Complex Logarithm

We know there are many subsets of complex plane on which the complex exponential function is one-one, but we restrict our attention to the fundamental region of e^z *i.e.*, $\{z : -\pi < Im\, z < \pi\}$.

Definition 4.2

The exponential function with domain restricted to $\{z : -\pi < Im\, z < \pi\}$ is one-one and its inverse function is called the principal branch of the logarithm and is denoted by Log z. In other words,

$$\text{Log}\, z = \log_e |z| + i \,\text{Arg}\,(z)$$

If $\quad z = re^{i\theta}$ is the polar form, then

$$\text{Log}\, z = \log_e r + i\theta,\ -\pi < \theta \le \pi.$$

Example 4.3

Evaluate (*i*) Log i (*ii*) Log $(1 - i)$ (*iii*) Log (-2).

Solution

(*i*)
$$\text{Log}\, i = \log_e 1 + i\frac{\pi}{2}$$
$$= i\frac{\pi}{2}$$

(*ii*)
$$\text{Log}\,(1 - i) = \log_e \sqrt{2} + i\left(-\frac{\pi}{4}\right)$$
$$= \frac{1}{2}\log_e 2 - \frac{\pi i}{4}$$

(*iii*)
$$\text{Log}\,(-2) = \log_e 2 + i\pi$$

Since, $z \to \log |z|$ and $z \to \arg z$ are both continuous function therefore Log z is continuous on $\{z : z \neq 0$ or a negative real number$\}$. Since, Log z is one of the values of the complex logarithm $\log z$ therefore, we get

$$e^{\text{Log}\, z} = z \text{ for all } z \neq 0.$$

This gives Log z is the inverse of exponential function as the exponential function is one-one in $\{z : -\pi < Im\, z \le \pi\}$. To justify this consider a point $z = x + iy$ in the fundamental region $-\infty < x < \infty$, $-\pi < y \le \pi$ and $|e^z| = e^x$ and Arg $(e^z) = y + 2n\pi$, n is an integer. Thus, y is the principal argument of e^z. Thus, $\arg(e^z) = y$. Also, we know from real analysis $\log_e e^x = x$.

Thus, from definition 4.2, we obtain

$$\text{Log}\, e^z = \log_e e^x + i\,\text{Arg}\,(e^z)$$
$$= x + iy$$
$$= z.$$

Since, Log is continuous function, we may use this and theorem 3.4 to prove the analyticity of the function log.

Theorem 4.1

Log is analytic in its domain and $\text{Log}'z = \dfrac{1}{z}$.

Proof

Since Log is continuous in its domain, then using Theorem 3.4 and the fact that $\dfrac{d}{dz}(e^z) = e^z \neq 0$ for all $z \in \mathbf{C}$, we have

$$\text{Log}'(z) = \frac{1}{(e^{(\text{Log } z)})^1} = \frac{1}{e^{(\text{Log } z)}} = \frac{1}{z}.$$

We have shown in the properties of logarithmic function that for any two complex numbers z_1, z_2, $\log (z_1 z_2) = \log z_1 + \log z_2$. But this does not hold in case of principal branch of the logarithmic function. It may happen both z_1, z_2 are not in the fundamental region or if z_1 and z_2 are there but z_1z_2 may not be in the fundamental region. For example, if $z_1 = i$, $z_2 = i$, then $z_1z_2 = -1$, or if $z_1 = z_2 = i - 1$, $\text{Arg } z_1 = \text{Arg } z_2 = \dfrac{3\pi}{4}$, and $\text{Log } z_1 + \text{Log } z_2 = \log 2 + i\dfrac{3\pi}{2}$ which does not correspond to any complex number whose value is equal to $\text{Log } (z_1z_2)$.

We prove the following with a stringent condition on z_1, z_2 and z_1z_2.

Theorem 4.2

let $G = \{z : Re\, z > 0\}$ and $z_1, z_2, z_1z_2 \in G$, then

$$\text{Log } (z_1 z_2) = \text{Log } z_1 + \text{Log } z_2 + 2ni\pi \text{ where } n = -1, 0 \text{ or } 1.$$

Proof

$$\begin{aligned}\text{Log } (z_1 z_2) &= \log |z_1 z_2| + i \text{ Arg } (z_1 z_2) \\ &= \log |z_1| + \log |z_2| + i(\text{Arg } z_1 + \text{Arg } z_2 \\ &\quad + 2n\pi) \\ &= \text{Log } z_1 + \text{Log } z_2 + 2n\pi i,\ n = -1, 0, 1.\end{aligned}$$

4.2.3 Logarithmic Mapping

The logarithmic mapping $w = \text{Log}\, z$ can be better understood in terms of exponential mappings $w = e^z$ as Log z is the inverse of e^z. Since, $w = e^z$ maps the fundamental region onto the set, $w \mid > 0$ in the w-plane. Then, as an inverse mapping $w = \log z$ maps $|z| > 0$ in the z-plane onto the fundamental region in w-plane (*i.e.*, $-\infty < u < \infty$, $-\pi < v \leq \pi$). We summarize the mapping properties of Log z in the following:

(*i*) $w = \text{Log}\, z$ maps the set $\{z : |z| > 0\}$ onto the region $-\infty < u < \infty$, $-\pi < v \leq \pi$ (Fig 4.5).

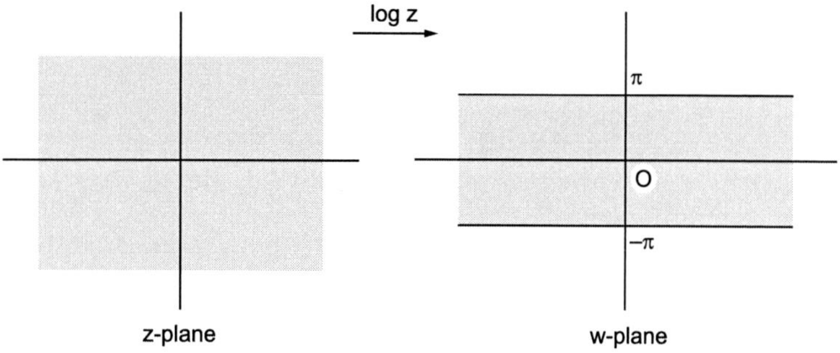

Fig. 4.5

(*ii*) $w = \log z$ maps the circle $|z| = r$ onto the vertical line segment $u = \log_e r$, $-\pi < v \leq \pi$ (Fig 4.6).

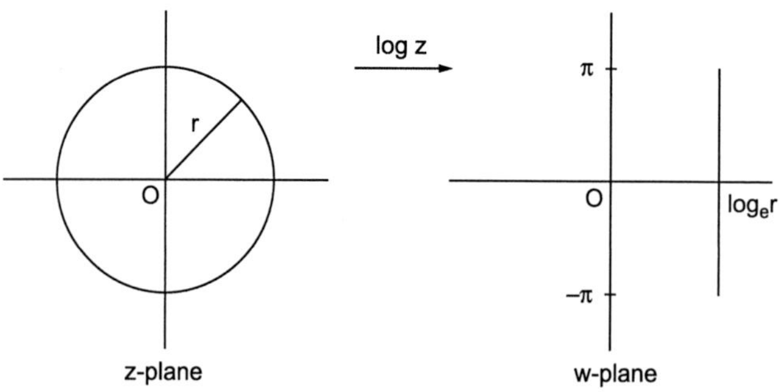

Fig. 4.6

(*iii*) $w = \log z$ maps the ray $\arg z = \theta$ onto the horizontal line $v = \theta$, $-\infty < u < \infty$ (Fig 4.7).

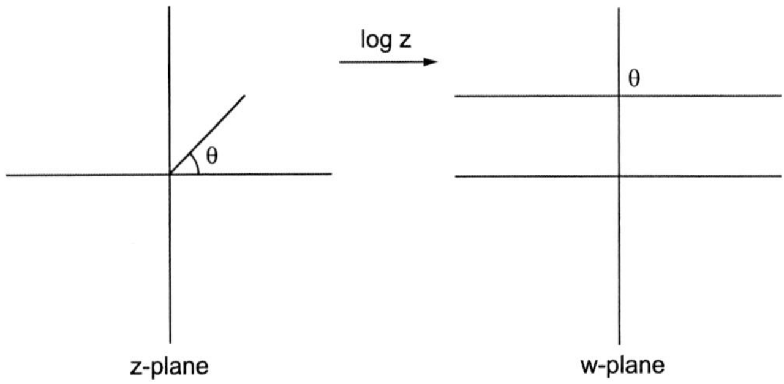

Fig. 4.7

Example 4.4

Find the image of the annulus $2 \le |z| \le 4$ under the mapping $w = \log z$.

Solution

From the above property (*ii*) of logarithmic mapping, the circle $|z| = 2$ maps onto a vertical line $u = \log_e 2$, $-\pi < v \le \pi$ and the circle $|z| = 4$ maps onto a line $u = \log_e 4$, $-\pi < v \le \pi$, respectively. Since, the real logarithmic function is increasing in its domain, then the image of the annulus $2 \le |z| \le 4$ is the rectangular region $\log_e 2 \le u \le \log_e 4$, $-\pi < v \le \pi$.

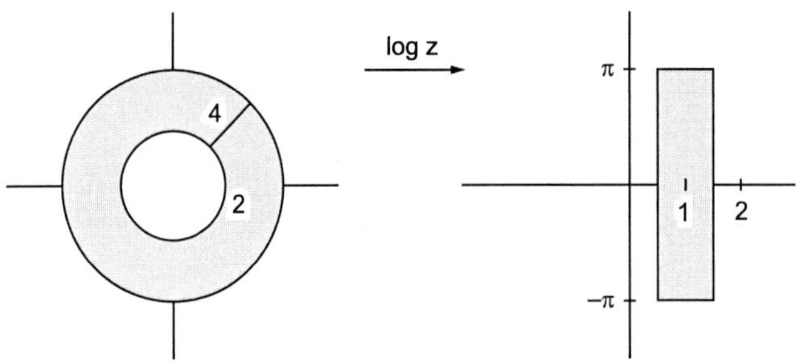

There are many branches of logarithms. Some have the same domain as the principal branch. We can define other branches by changing the internal of θ. For example, if $z = re^{i\theta}$, then

$$\log z = \log_e r + i\theta, \quad -\pi/2 < \theta < 3\pi/2$$

In general we define any branch of log as $f(z) = \log_e r + i\theta$, $\theta_0 < \theta < \theta_0 + 2\pi$

Comparison with Real Analysis

In spite of many similarities in real and complex exponential and logarithmic functions, there are many differences which are given below:

(*i*) The real exponential function is one-to-one, but the complex exponential function is not.

(*ii*) The real logarithmic function is single-valued function, whereas the complex logarithmic function is multi-valued.

(*iii*) We know if x_1 and x_2 are real numbers, then

$$\log (x_1 x_2) = \log x_1 + \log x_2.$$

But the result is not true for $\log (z_1 z_2)$ where z_1 and z_2 are complex numbers.

EXERCISE

1. Find all complex values of the given logrithms

(*i*) $\log (-5)$ (*ii*) $(1 + i)$

(*iii*) $\log (1 + \sqrt{3} i)$ (*iv*) $\log (\sqrt{2} + \sqrt{6} i)$

(v) $\log (-\sqrt{3} + i)$.

2. Find the principal value of the logarithm in the form $a + ib$

(*i*) $\text{Log} (-e^z)$ (*ii*) $\text{Log} (3 - 4i)$

(*iii*) $\text{Log} ((1 + i)^4)$ (*iv*) $\text{Log} [(1 + \sqrt{3} i)^5]$

(*v*) $\text{Log} [(1 + 2i) (1 + \sqrt{3} i)]$ (*vi*) $\text{Log} (6 - 6i)$.

3. Find

(*i*) $[\arg (-1)]$ (*ii*) $[\arg (1 + i)]$

(*iii*) $[\text{Log } e^z]$ (for $z \in \mathbf{C}$).

4. Find all complex values of z satisfying the given equation

(*i*) $e^z = 2i$ (*ii*) $e^{1/z} = -1$

(*iii*) $e^{2z} + e^z + 1 = 0$ (*iv*) $e^{z-2} = -ie^z$

(*v*) $e^z = 1 + i$ (*vi*) $e^z = -1 + i\sqrt{3}$.

5. Find the image of the following sets under the mapping $w = \text{Log } z$.

(*i*) The circle $|z| = 4$ (*ii*) The annulus $3 \le |z| \le 5$

(*iii*) The ray $\arg(z) = \frac{\pi}{3}$ (*iv*) The positive y-axis

(*v*) The region in the first quadrant bounded by the circle $|z| = 1$ and $|z| = e$.

6. Find two complex number z_1 and z_2 such that

(*i*) $\text{Log}(z_1 z_2) \neq \text{Log } z_1 + \text{Log } z_2$

(*ii*) $\text{Log}(z_1 z_2) = \text{Log } z_1 + \text{Log } z_2$

7. If $\text{Log}(z_1 z_2) = \text{Log } z_1 + \text{Log } z_2$, then what is the relationship between z_1 and z_2?

ANSWERS

1. (*i*) $\log 5 + i(2n+1)\pi$ (*ii*) $\frac{1}{2}\log 2 + i\left(2n\pi + \pi/4\right)$

(*iii*) $\log 2 + i\left(2n\pi + \pi/3\right)$ (*iv*) $\frac{3}{2}\log 2 + i\left(2n\pi - \pi/3\right)$

(*v*) $\log 2 + i(2n+3)\pi/6$

2. (*i*) $2\{1 + i\pi\}$ (*ii*) $\log 5 + i\tan^{-1}\left(\frac{4}{3}\right)$

(*iii*) $2\log 2 + i\pi$ (*iv*) $5\left\{\log 2 + i\frac{\pi}{3}\right\}$

(*v*) $\log 2\sqrt{5} + i\left\{\tan^{-1} 2 + \pi(6n+1)\right\}$

(*vi*) $\log 6\sqrt{2} - i\pi/4$

3. (*i*) $\left\{i(2n+1)\pi, n \in I\right\}$ (*ii*) $\left\{2n\pi + \pi/4, n \in I\right\}$

(*iii*) $\left\{r + i(0 + 2n\pi), n \in I\right\}$

4. (*i*) $\left\{\log_e 2 + i\pi\right\}$ (*ii*) $\frac{-i}{\pi}$

(*iii*) $\frac{2\pi}{3}i$ (*iv*) $4+\frac{i3\pi}{2}$

(*v*) $\frac{1}{2}\log_e 2+\frac{i\pi}{4}$ (*vi*) $\log_e 2 + 2i\pi/3$

5. (*i*) $u = \log_e 4$, $\pi < v < \pi$

(*ii*) The rectangle $\log_e 3 < u < \log_e 5$, $-\pi < v < \pi$

(*iii*) The horizontal line $v = \pi/3$, $-\infty < u < \infty$

(*iv*) $-\infty < \mathrm{u} < \infty$, $0 < v < \pi$

(*v*) $0 < u < 1$, $0 < v < \pi/2$

6. (*i*) Let $z_1 = i = z_2$, $z_1 z_2 = -1$ Log $z_1 = i\pi/2$, Log $z_2 = i\pi/2$ but Log$(z_1 z_2) = i\pi$. Which fails to be in $-\pi < \mathrm{Im}(\mathrm{Log} z) < \pi$

(*ii*) $z_1 = i$, $z_2 = (1 + i)$, $z_1 z_2 = -1 + i$, $\log(z_1) = i\pi/2$, $\log(z_2) = \log\sqrt{2} + i\pi/4$, $\log(z_1 z_2) = \log\sqrt{2} + 3\pi/4\ i = \log(z_1) + \log(z_2)$

4.3 POWERS

In this section, we study complex powers z^α, where α is a complex number. Complex powers of the form $(1 + i)^i$ can be expresed in terms of the complex exponential and logarithmic functions defined in section 4.1 and 4.2, respectively. If n is an integer, then

$$z^n = (e^{\log z})^n = e^{n \log z}$$

We use this to generalize the notion of power function.

Definition 4.3

If α is a complex number and $z \neq 0$, then the complex power z^α is defined to be

$$z^\alpha = e^{\alpha \log z} \qquad ...(1)$$

If $z^\alpha = e^{\alpha \log z}$ where we use principal branch of the logarithm, is called principal branch of the αth power.

Using section 4.2 we get that if n is an integer

$$z^n = e^{n \log z} = e^{n[\log_e |z| + i \arg |z|]}$$

$$= e^{n \log_e |z|} e^{ni \arg(z)} \qquad ...(2)$$

If $\theta = \text{Arg } z$, then $\arg z = \theta + 2k\pi$ where k is an integer and therefore,

$$e^{n \arg(z) i} = e^{n(\theta + 2k\pi)i} = e^{n\theta i} e^{2nk\pi i}$$

Since n and k are integers thus $2n\,k\,\pi$ is an even integer and thus

$$e^{2nk\pi i} = \cos(2nk\,\pi) + i\sin(2nk\pi) = 1$$

From (2), we get

$$z^n = e^{n \log_e |z|}$$

which is single-valued. But more generally, if α is a rational number say $\alpha = \frac{p}{q}$ where p and q are integers such that $q \neq 0$ and $z \neq 0$. Consider

$$\left(e^{\alpha \operatorname{Log}(z)}\right)^q = e^{q\,\alpha \operatorname{Log}(z)}$$

$$= e^{p \operatorname{Log}(z)}$$

$$= (e^{\operatorname{Log}(z)})^p$$

and thus $e^{\alpha \operatorname{Log}(z)}$ is a qth root of z^p. The possible values of the branches of the αth power of z are the numbers

$$e^{(\alpha[\operatorname{Log} z + 2k\pi i])} = e^{\alpha \operatorname{Log}(z)},\ k = 0, 1, 2 \dots q-1.$$

Example 4.5

Find all possible values of $(1+i)^{2/3}$ and its principal value.

Solution

$$\text{We know } (1+i) = \sqrt{2}\left(\cos\frac{\pi}{4} + i\sin\frac{\pi}{4}\right). \text{ Then,}$$

$$\operatorname{Log}(1+i) = \log_e \sqrt{2} + i\frac{\pi}{4}$$

$$\Rightarrow \qquad e^{\frac{2}{3}\operatorname{Log}(1+i)} = e^{\frac{2}{3}\left(\log_e \sqrt{2} + i\frac{\pi}{4}\right)}$$

$$= e^{\frac{1}{3}\log_e 2} e^{i\frac{\pi}{6}}$$

$$= \sqrt[3]{2}\left(\frac{\sqrt{3}}{2} + \frac{i}{2}\right).$$

Example 4.6

Find all possible values of $(-i)^i$.

Solution

$$\text{Since } -i = \cos\left(-\frac{\pi}{2}\right) + i\sin\left(-\frac{\pi}{2}\right), \text{ then}$$

$$\log(-i) = \log_e |1| + i\left(-\frac{\pi}{2} + 2n\pi\right), n = 0, \pm 1, \pm 2 \ldots$$

$$\Rightarrow \quad e^{i(\log -i)} = e^{i^2}\left(-\frac{\pi}{2} + 2n\pi\right), n = 0, \pm 1, \pm 2, \ldots..$$

$$= e^{\frac{\pi}{2}} - 2n\pi, \; n = 0, \pm 1, \pm 2, \ldots..$$

4.3.1 Properties of Power Function

The complex powers has the following properties which are analogous to real powers.

If α_1 and α_2 are two complex constants, then

(*i*) $$z_1^{\alpha_1} z_2^{\alpha_2} = z^{\alpha_1 + \alpha_2}$$

Proof

Consider
$$z^{\alpha_1} z^{\alpha_2} = e^{\alpha_1 \log z}\, e^{\alpha_2 \log z}$$
$$= e^{\alpha_1 \log z + \alpha_2 \log z}$$
$$= e^{(\alpha_1 + \alpha_2)\log z}$$
$$= z^{\alpha_1 + \alpha_2}.$$

(*ii*) $$\frac{z^{\alpha_1}}{z^{\alpha_2}} = z^{\alpha_1 - \alpha_2}$$

$$\frac{z^{\alpha_1}}{z^{\alpha_2}} = \frac{e^{\alpha_1 \log z}}{e^{\alpha_2 \log z}}$$
$$= e^{\alpha_1 \log z}\, e^{-\alpha_2 \log z}$$
$$= e^{\alpha_1 \log z - \alpha_2 \log z}$$

$$= e^{(\alpha_1 - \alpha_2)\log z}$$

$$= z^{\alpha_1 - \alpha_2}.$$

(*iii*) $(z^{\alpha})^n = z^{n\alpha}$ for $n = 0, \pm 1, \pm 2, \ldots.$

Consider $(z^{\alpha})^n = (e^{\alpha \log z})^n$

$$= z^{n\alpha}, \quad n = 0, \pm 1, \pm 2, \ldots$$

4.3.2 Analyticity of Power Function

We know the principal branch of logarithmic function Log z is not continuous on complex plane, but $e^{\alpha z}$ is continuous in the entire complex plane. However, Log z is continuous on the domain $|z| > 0, -\pi < \arg(z) < \pi$. Thus, we conclude that z^{α} is continuous on the domain $|z| > 0, -\pi < \arg(z) < \pi$. Also in polar form, the function defined by

$$f(z) = e^{\alpha(\log_e r + i\theta)}, -\pi < \theta < \pi$$

is a branch of the multi-valued function $f_1(z) = z^{\alpha} = e^{\alpha \log z}$.

This is called the principal branch of the complex power z^{α}. Using chain rule if we differentiate $g(z) = e^{\alpha \operatorname{Log} z}$, we get

$$g'(z) = e^{\alpha \operatorname{Log} z}\frac{d}{dz}(\alpha \operatorname{Log} z) = \frac{\alpha}{z}e^{\alpha \operatorname{Log} z} = \frac{\alpha}{z}g(z).$$

$$= \frac{\alpha}{z}z^{\alpha} = \alpha z^{\alpha - 1}$$

Then, $$\frac{d}{dz}(z^{\alpha}) = \alpha z^{\alpha - 1} \quad \ldots(1)$$

Example 4.7

Find the derivative of the principal value of z^{1+i} at the point $z = 1 + \sqrt{3}i$.

Solution

Since, the point $z = 1 + \sqrt{3}i$ is in the domain $|z| > 0, -\pi < \arg < \pi$. From (1), it follows that

$$\frac{d}{dz}(z^{1+i}) = (1+i)\, z^{i},$$

and $$\left.\frac{d}{dz}(z^{1+i})\right|_{z = 1+\sqrt{3}i} = (1+i)(1+\sqrt{3}i)^{i}$$

We know $(1+\sqrt{3}i) = 2\left(\cos\frac{\pi}{3} + i\sin\frac{\pi}{3}\right)$, then

$$(1+\sqrt{3i})^i = e^{i\left(\log_e 2 + \frac{i\pi}{3}\right)}$$

$$= e^{-\frac{\pi}{3} + i(\log_e 2)} \qquad ...(2)$$

Then, $$\frac{d}{dz}(z^{1+i})\bigg|_{z=1+\sqrt{3}i} = \sqrt{2}\, e^{\frac{i\pi}{4}} . e^{-\frac{\pi}{3} + i(\log_e 2)} \qquad \text{(using (2)}$$

$$= \sqrt{2}\, e^{\frac{i\pi}{4} - \frac{\pi}{3} + i(\log_e 2)}$$

$$= \sqrt{2}\, e^{-\frac{\pi}{3} + i\left(\frac{\pi}{4} - \log_e 2\right)}.$$

Comparison with Real Numbers

(*i*) If x is any real number, n_1 and n_2 are real numbers then $(x^{\alpha_1})^{\alpha_2} = x^{\alpha_1 \alpha_2}$ is true. But in case of complex numbers $(z^{\alpha_1})^{\alpha_2} \neq z^{\alpha_1\alpha_2}$ unless α_2 is an integer.

(*ii*) We know if z_1 and z_2 are two complex numbers and α is a complex constant, then $(z_1 z_2)^\alpha = z_1^\alpha z_2^\alpha$. But this is not true in case of principal values of these complex powers. For example, if $z_1 = -1$, $z_2 = i$ and $\alpha = i$, then

$$(-1 \,.\, i)^i = (-i)^i = e^{i\log(-i)} = e^{-i\frac{\pi}{2}i} = e^{\frac{\pi}{2}}$$

and $$(-1)^i\,(i)^i = e^{i\log(-1)} . e^{i\log(i)}$$

$$= e^{i\times i\pi}\, e^{i\times i\frac{\pi}{2}}$$

$$= e^{-\pi - \frac{\pi}{2}} = e^{\frac{-3\pi}{2}}$$

Then, $(-1 \,.\, i)^i \neq (-1)^i\,(i)^i$.

EXERCISE

1. Find all the values of the given complex power.

(*i*) $3^{\frac{2i}{\pi}}$ (*ii*) $(\sqrt{2})^i$ (*iii*) $(i)^{\sqrt{2}}$

(*iv*) $e^{i\pi}$ (*v*) $(ei)^{\sqrt{2}}$ (*vi*) $(-i)^i$.

2. Find the principal value of the given complex power.

(*i*) $(1+\sqrt{3}i)^{3i}$ (*ii*) $(1+i)^{2-i}$ (*iii*) $(i)^{i}$

(*iv*) $i^{i/\pi}$ (*v*) 2^{4i} (*vi*) $(-1)^{3i}$.

3. Find the derivative of the principal value of the given function at the given point.

(*i*) z^i at $z = 1 + i$ (*ii*) z^{2i} at $z = i$

(*iii*) $z^{\sqrt{2}}$ at $z = -i$ (*iv*) $z^{3/2}$ at $z = 1 + i$.

4. Evaluate z° for any complex number z.

5. If α is any complex number then what can you say about 1^{α}.

ANSWERS

1. (*i*) $e^{-4n} + \frac{2}{\pi}\log_e{}^3 i$, $n \in I$ (*ii*) $e^{-n\pi} + \frac{i}{2}\log 2$,

(*iii*) $e\sqrt{2}\left(i(2n+1)\frac{\pi}{2}\right), n \in I$ (*iv*) -1

(*v*) $e^{\sqrt{2}\left(1+(2n+1)\frac{\pi}{2}i\right)}$, $n \in I$ (*vi*) $e^{(2n+1)\frac{\pi}{2}}$, $n \in I$

2. (*i*) $2^{3i} - \pi$ (*ii*) $\left(\sqrt{2}\right)^{(2-i)} e^{\pi/4}$

(*iii*) $e^{-\pi/2}$ (*iv*) $e^{-1/2}$

(*v*) $e^{4\log 2i}$ (*vi*) $e^{-3\pi}$

3. (*i*) $e^{(i-1)}\left(\log\sqrt{2} + \pi/4\right)$ (*ii*) $2e^{-\pi - i\pi/4}$

(*iii*) $\sqrt{2}\, e^{-i\pi/\sqrt{2} + i\pi/2}$ (*iv*) $\frac{3}{2}(2)^{1/4} e^{i\pi/8}$

4. $z^{\circ} = e^{\circ}\log z = e^{\circ} = 1$

5. $e^{\alpha \log 1} = e^{\alpha \times 0} = 1$

4.4 TRIGONOMETRIC FUNCTIONS

The real cosine and sine series are defined as

$$\cos x = \sum_{n=0}^{\infty} \frac{(-1)^n x^{2n}}{(2n)!}, \quad \sin x = \sum_{n=0}^{\infty} \frac{(-1)^n x^{2n+1}}{(2n+1)!}$$

Analogously, we define complex cosine and sine series by power series as:

$$\cos z = \sum_{n=0}^{\infty} \frac{(-1)^n z^{2n}}{(2n)!}, \quad \sin z = \sum_{n=0}^{\infty} \frac{(-1)^n z^{2n+1}}{(2n+1)!} \quad ...(1)$$

Both the power series has infinite radius of convergence and thus are analytic in **C**. Using theorem 3.9, differentiating (1), we get

$$\frac{d}{dz}(\cos z) = -\sin z, \quad \frac{d}{dz}(\sin z) = \cos z.$$

Also, we know

$$e^z = 1 + z + \frac{z^2}{2!} + \frac{z^3}{3!} + ...$$

then,

$$e^{iz} = 1 + (iz) + \frac{(iz)^2}{2!} + \frac{(iz)^3}{3!} + ...$$

$$= \left(1 - \frac{z^2}{2!} + \frac{z^4}{4!} + ...\right) + i\left(z - \frac{z^3}{3!} + \frac{z^5}{5!} ...\right)$$

$$e^{iz} = \cos z + i \sin z \quad ...(2)$$

and

$$e^{-iz} = \cos z - i \sin z \quad ...(3)$$

From (2) and (3), we get

$$\cos z = \frac{e^{iz} + e^{-iz}}{2}, \quad \sin z = \frac{e^{iz} - e^{-iz}}{2i}. \quad ...(4)$$

We say the complex cosine and sine function are defined by (4). The other trigonometric functions tangent, cotangent, secant and cosecant functions using sine and cosine are defined as follows:

$$\tan z = \frac{\sin z}{\cos z}, \quad \cot z = \frac{\cos z}{\sin z}, \quad \sec z = \frac{1}{\cos z} \text{ and } \operatorname{cosec} z = \frac{1}{\sin z}$$

Example 4.8

Using (4) express the following trigonometric functions in the form $a + ib$.

(*i*) $\sin 4i$ (*ii*) $\cos(-3i)$.

Solution

(*i*)
$$\sin 4i = \frac{e^{i(4i)} - e^{-i(4i)}}{2i}$$
$$= \frac{e^{-4} - e^{4}}{2i}$$
$$= \frac{i}{2}(e^{4} - e^{-4})$$

(*ii*)
$$\cos(-3i) = \frac{e^{i(-3i)} + e^{-i(-3i)}}{2}$$
$$= \frac{e^{3} + e^{-3}}{2}.$$

We know several trigonometric identities for real trigonometric functions but most of these identity also hold for complex trigonometric functions. We now prove some of them in the following:

Proposition 4.3

If z is a complex number, then

(*i*) $\sin^2 z + \cos^2 z = 1$

Consider
$$\sin^2 z + \cos^2 z = \frac{(e^{iz} + e^{-iz})^2}{4} - \frac{(e^{iz} - e^{-iz})^2}{4}$$
$$= \frac{e^{2iz} + e^{-2iz} + 2 - (e^{2iz} + e^{-2iz} - 2)}{4}$$
$$= 1$$

(*ii*) Sin $2z = 2 \sin z \cos z$.

Consider
$$2 \sin z \cos z = \frac{2(e^{iz} - e^{-iz})}{2i} \times \frac{(e^{iz} + e^{-iz})}{2}$$
$$= \frac{e^{2iz} - e^{-2iz}}{2i}$$
$$= \sin^2 z$$

Similarly, we can also prove the following:

(*i*) $\cos 2z = \cos^2 z - \sin^2 z$

(*ii*) $\sin (z_1 \pm z_2) = \sin z_1 \cos z_2 \pm \cos z_1 \sin z_2$.

$\cos(z_1 \pm z_2) = \cos z_1 \cos z_2 \mp \sin z_1 \sin z_2$.

(*iii*) $\cos (-z) = \cos z$

(*iv*) $\sin (-z) = -\sin z$

(*v*) $\sin (z + \pi) = - \sin z$

(*vi*) $\cos (z + \pi) = -\cos z$.

4.4.1 Periodicity

We know real trigonometric functions are periodic with period 2π. Similarly we can also prove that the complex trigonometric functions are periodic with the same period 2π. Consider

$$\begin{aligned}\sin (z + 2\pi) &= \frac{e^{i(z+2\pi)} - e^{-i(z+2\pi)}}{2i} \\ &= \frac{e^{iz+2\pi i} - e^{-iz+2\pi i}}{2i} \\ &= \frac{e^{iz} - e^{-iz}}{2i} = \sin z\end{aligned}$$

using the fact that the periodicity of complex exponential function is $2\pi i$. Also, $\cos(z + 2\pi) = f(z)$. Thus, the complex sine and cosine functions are periodic with real period 2π. We can also conclude that secant and cosecant also have periodicity 2π. Using the identities $\sin (z + \pi) = -\sin z$ and $\cos (z + \pi) = -\cos z$, we can prove that tangent and cotengent are periodic with period π.

4.4.2 Modulus of Trigonometric Functions

To define the modulus of cosine and sine complex functions, we use the definition of real hyperbolic sine and cosine functions as

$$\sinh y = \frac{e^y - e^{-y}}{2}, \quad \cosh y = \frac{e^y + e^{-y}}{2}.$$

Let $z = x + iy$, then

$$|\sin z| = |\sin (x + iy)| = \left|\frac{e^{i(x+iy)} - e^{-i(x+iy)}}{2i}\right|$$

$$= \left| \frac{e^{ix-y} - e^{-ix+y}}{2i} \right|$$

$$= \left| \frac{e^{-y}(\cos x + i \sin x) - e^{y}(\cos x - i \sin x)}{2i} \right|$$

$$= \left| \sin x \left(\frac{e^{-y} + e^{y}}{2} \right) + \cos x \left(\frac{e^{-y} - e^{y}}{2i} \right) \right|$$

$$= |\sin x \cos hy + i \cos x \sin hy|$$

$$= \sqrt{\sin^2 x \cos h^2 y + \cos^2 x \sin h^2 y}$$

$$= \sqrt{\sin^2 x (1 + \sin h^2 y) + \cos^2 x \sin h^2 y}$$

$$= \sqrt{\sin^2 x + \sin h^2 y} \quad \text{...(1)}$$

Similarly we can show

$$|\cos z| = \sqrt{\cos^2 x + \sin h^2 y}. \quad \text{...(2)}$$

We know sinh$y$ is unbounded on a real line, therefore, from (1) and (2) we conclude that sin z and cos z are unbounded on the complex plane.

4.4.3 Zeroes of Trigonometric Functions

For real sine function, we know $\sin x = 0$ for all $x = n\pi$, $n \in$ I and $\cos x = 0$ for all $x = (2n+1)\frac{\pi}{2}$, $n \in I$. Similarly complex sine and cosine functions has zeroes at $n\pi$ and $(2n + 1)\pi/2$, $n \in$ I, respectively. This can be seen in the following way:

Consider $\quad \sin z = 0$

i.e., $$\frac{e^{iz} - e^{-iz}}{2i} = 0$$

$$\Rightarrow \quad e^{2iz} = 1$$

$$\Rightarrow \quad e^{2i(x+iy)} = 1 \quad (z = x + iy)$$

$$\Rightarrow \quad e^{2ix - 2y} = 1$$

$$\Rightarrow \quad e^{-2y} \cos 2x = 1, \qquad e^{-2y} \sin 2x = 0$$

Squaring and adding, we get

$$e^{4y} = 1 = e^{\circ} \Rightarrow y = 0.$$

Also, $\cos 2x = 1$, $\sin 2x = 0 \Rightarrow 2x = 2n\pi$, $n \in I$.

Thus, $\sin z = 0$ on $\{z : z = n\pi : n \in I\}$. Similarly $\cos z = 0$ on $\left\{z : z = (2n+1)\frac{\pi}{2}\right\}$. We can also conclude that $\tan z$ is defined for all z in $\subset\sim \{z : z = n\pi : n \in \pi\}$ and $\cot z$ is defined for all z in $\mathbf{C}\sim \left\{z : z = (2n+1)\frac{\pi}{2}, n \in \pi\right\}$.

4.4.4 Trigonometric Mappings

We discuss here the complex mapping w = $\sin z$ of z-plane onto w-plane. The complex sine function is periodic with period 2π, so we discuss the mapping in the infinite vertical strip $x_0 < \pi < x_0 + 2\pi$, $-\infty < y < \infty$. To study the mapping $w = \sin z$ on the entire complex plane, we shall study it on the strip $-\pi < x \le \pi$, $-\infty < y < \infty$. The function $\sin z$ is also one-one on this region.

Example 4.10

Find the images of the coordinate lines under the functions $z \to \sin z$.

Solution

Consider a line parallel to y-axis *i.e.*, $\{a + iy : y \in \mathbb{R}\}$, a is a constant real number. The image of this line under the map $z \to \sin z$ is $\{\sin(a + iy) : y \in \mathbb{R}\}$. We know,

$$\sin(a + iy) = \sin a \cosh y + i \cos a \sinh y = u + iv \text{ (say)}.$$

If $a \neq n\frac{\pi}{2}$ (so that neither sin *an* or cos *a* is zero) the image is hyperbola

$$\frac{u^2}{(\sin a)^2} - \frac{v^2}{(\cos a)^2} = 1$$

which intersects the x-axis at $u = \pm \sin a$. If $a = 2n\times\frac{\pi}{2}$, then $\sin a = 0$, the hyperbola degenerates to the imaginary axis.

If $a = (2n + 1)\pi/2$, then if $a = (4n+1)\frac{\pi}{2}$, $n \in I$, the image is the internal $[1, \infty[$ of the real axis and if $a = (4n+3)\frac{\pi}{2}$, $n \in I$, the image is the internal $[-\infty, -1]$ of the x-axis.

The line $\{x + ib \mid x \in \mathbb{R}\}$, b a constant real number is mapped to $\{\sin(x + ib) : x \in \mathbb{R}\}$. Now,

$\sin(x + ib) = \sin x \cosh b + i \cos x \sinh b = u + iv$ (say).

It's image is an ellipse $\dfrac{u^2}{(\cos h\, b)^2} + \dfrac{v^2}{(\sin h\, b)^2} = 1$, provided $b \neq 0$ (so that $\cosh b \neq 0$ and $\sinh b \neq 0$)

The ellipse intersects x-axis at $u = \pm \cosh b$ and y-axis at $v = \pm\sinh b$. The image of the real axis is $\{\sin x : x \in \mathbb{R}\}$, which is closed interval of the real axis -1 to 1.

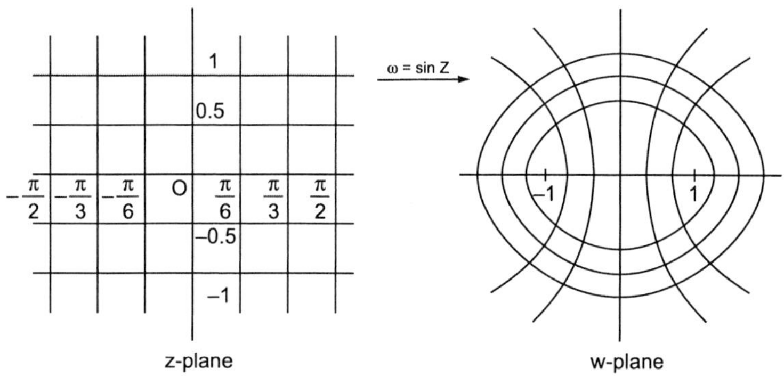

4.5 COMPLEX HYPERBOLIC FUNCTIONS

The definition of complex hyperbolic functions is similar to that of their real counterparts in terms of the exponential functions which are defined as follows:

Definition 4.4

The complex hyperbolic sine and hyperbolic cosine functions are defined by

$$\sinh z = \frac{e^z - e^{-z}}{2} \text{ and } \cosh z = \frac{e^z + e^{-z}}{2} \text{ respectively.}$$

The exponential functions are periodic, therefore $\sinh z$, $\cosh z$ are also periodic and has infinite number of zeroes.

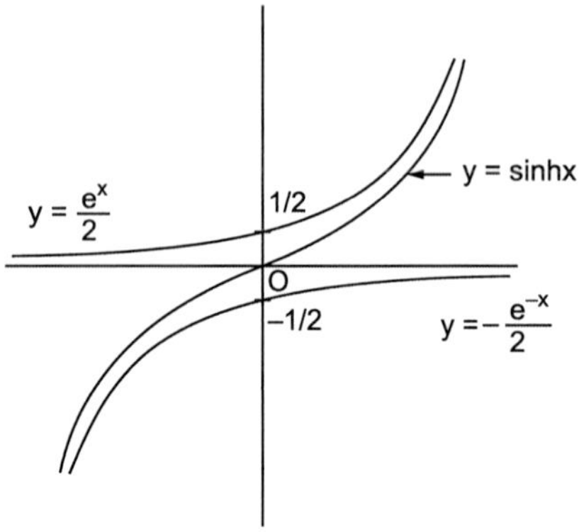

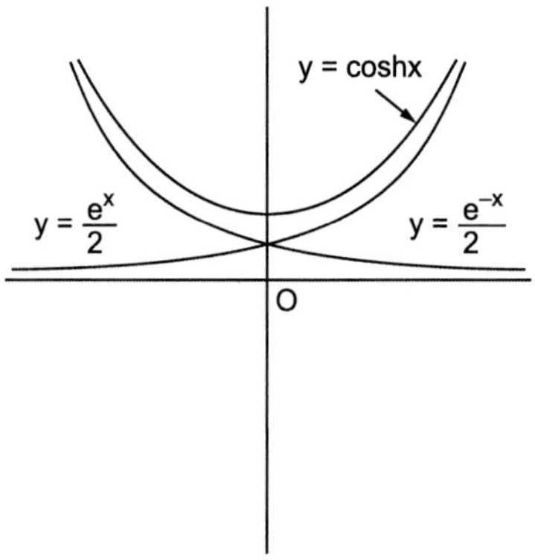

The complex hyperbolic tangent, cotangent, secant and cosecant are defined as

$$\tan h\,z = \frac{\sin h\,z}{\cos h\,z},\quad \cot h\,z = \frac{\cos h\,z}{\sin h\,z}, \sec h\,z = \frac{1}{\cos h\,z}, \operatorname{cosec} h\,z = \frac{1}{\sin h\,z}.$$

Since the exponential functions are entire, therefore hyperbolic sine and cosine functions are entire. We have

$$\begin{aligned}\frac{d}{dz}(\sin h\,z) &= \frac{d}{dz}\left(\frac{e^z - e^{-z}}{2}\right)\\ &= \frac{e^z + e^{-z}}{2}\\ &= \text{coshz}.\end{aligned}$$

Similarly, we can compute

$$\frac{d}{dz}(\cosh z) = -\sinh z$$

We can also establish the relationship between sin$h$ z and sin z. Consider

$$\sinh(iz) = \frac{e^{iz} - e^{-iz}}{2i} \times i$$
$$= i \sin z$$

and thus, $\sin z = -i \sinh(iz)$

Similarly, we can show that

$$\cos z = \cosh(iz), \quad \cos(iz) = \cosh z$$
$$\sin z = -i \sinh(iz), \quad \sin(iz) = i \sinh(iz).$$
$$\tan(iz) = i \tanh z.$$

We also deduce the properties of cos$h$ and sin$h$ from those of cos and sin. We list some of them in the following:

(*i*) $\sinh(-z) = -\sinh z, \quad \cosh(-z) = \cosh z$

(*ii*) $\cosh^2 z - \sinh^2 z = 1$

(*iii*) $\sinh(z_1 \pm z_2) = \sinh z_1 \cosh z_2 \pm \cosh z_1 \sinh z_2$

(*iv*) $\cosh(z_1 \pm z_2) = \cosh z_1 \cosh z_2 \pm \sinh z_1 \sinh z_2.$

4.5.1 Trigonometric Equations

The complex sine and cosine functions are periodic, therefore the trigonometric equations always have infinitely many solutions of the form $\sin z = w$ and $\cos z = w$.

Example 4.9

Find the solutions of the equation $\sin z = 2$.

Solution

$$\sin z = 2$$

i.e.,
$$\frac{e^{iz} - e^{-iz}}{2i} = 2$$

$$\Rightarrow \quad e^{2iz} - 1 = 4\, i\, e^{iz}$$

$$\Rightarrow \quad e^{2iz} - 4ie^{iz} - 1 = 0$$

Then, $$e^{iz} = \frac{4i \pm \sqrt{-16+4}}{2}$$

$$= \frac{4i \pm \sqrt{12}i}{2}$$

$$= 2i \pm \sqrt{3}i = (2 \pm \sqrt{3})i$$

$$iz = \log(2 \pm \sqrt{3})i$$

i.e., $$z = -i\log(2 \pm \sqrt{3})i$$

Since, $2 + \sqrt{3} > 0$ and $(2 + \sqrt{3})i$ is purely imaginary, so argument $((2 + \sqrt{3})i) = \frac{\pi}{2} + 2n\pi$. Thus,

$$z = -i[\log(2+\sqrt{3})i] = -i\left[\log_e(2+\sqrt{3}) + i\left(\frac{\pi}{2} + 2n\pi\right)\right]$$

$$z = \frac{(4n+1)\pi}{2} - i\log_e(2+\sqrt{3}) \text{ for } n = 0, \pm 1, \pm 2, \ldots$$

Similarly, if $e^{iz} = (2 - \sqrt{3})i$, then $z = (4n + 1)\frac{\pi}{2} - i\log_e(2 - \sqrt{3})$, $n = 0, \pm 1, \pm 2, \pm 3 \ldots$

Comparison with Real Analysis

(1) For all real numbers x, $|\sin x| \le 1$, $|\cos x| \le 1$, but complex trigonometric functions are not bounded for if $|\cos i| > 1$, $|\sin(2+i)| > 1$ since $|\cos i| \approx 1.45431$, $|\sin(2+i)| \approx 1.4859$.

(2) All real trigonometric functions are periodic with period 2π, but only complex trigonometric functions sine, cosine, secant and cosecant have periodicity 2π, whereas tangent and cotangent have periodicity π.

(3) As a function of a real variable x, sinh$x$ and cosh$x$ are not periodic, but the complex functions sinh$x$ and coshx are periodic. Moreover coshx has no zeroes and sinhx has a single zero at $x = 0$. On the other hand, the complex functions sinhz and cos$h$ z have infinitely many zeroes.

EXERCISE

1. Express the value of the given trigonometric function in the form $a + ib$.

(i) $\sin\left(\frac{\pi}{4}+i\right)$ (ii) $\cos i$

(iii) $\sin(2+i)$ (iv) $\tan(\pi - 2i)$

(v) $\sec\left(\frac{\pi}{2}-i\right)$ (vi) $\operatorname{cosec}(1+i)$.

2. Solve the following equations:

(i) $\cos z = 4$ (ii) $\sin z = \cos z$

(iii) $\cos z = i \sin z$ (iv) $\sin z = 2$

(v) $\sin z = -i$ (vi) $\sinh z = \cosh z$

(vii) $\sinh z = e^z$ (viii) $\cosh z = i$

(ix) $\sin z = 100$ (x) $\cos^2 z = 4$.

3. Find the derivative of the following functions:

(i) $z \tan \frac{1}{z}$ (ii) $\cos(i\, e^z)$

(iii) $\sin(z^2)$ (iv) $\sin z \sinh z$

(v) $\tanh z$ (vi) $\cosh(iz + e^{iz})$

(vii) $\tanh(iz - 2)$ (viii) $\sec z \cosh z$.

4. Find all zeroes of $\cos z$.

5. Find all z such that $|\tan z| = 1$.

6. Show that $\sin \bar{z}$ is nowhere analytic.

7. Find all the zeroes of the following:

(i) $(z^4 - 1)\sin \pi z$ (ii) $\cosh^2 z$

(iii) $\sin \frac{1}{z}$ (iv) $\cosh z$

(v) $\sinh z$.

ANSWERS

1. (*i*) $\frac{1}{\sqrt{2}}(\cosh 1 + i\sinh 1)$ (*ii*) $\frac{1+e^2}{2e}$

(*iii*) $\sin 2 \cosh 1 + i\cos 2 \sinh 1$

(*iv*) $\frac{-i\left(e^4-1\right)}{e^4+1}$ (*v*) $\frac{-2ie}{e^2-1}$

(*vi*) $\frac{1+i}{2}\sin 2$

2. (*i*) $2n\pi + i\log\left(4 \pm \sqrt{15}\right), n \in I$

(*ii*) $x = (4n+1)\frac{\pi}{2}, n \in I$

(*iii*) no solution

(*iv*) $(4n+1)\frac{\pi}{2} + i\log\left(2 \pm \sqrt{3}\right), n \in I$

(*v*) $2n\pi + i\log_e\left(\sqrt{2}-1\right)$ (*vi*) no solution

(*vii*) $(2n+1)\pi/2\, i$

(*viii*) $\log_e\left(-1+\sqrt{2}\right) + \frac{1}{2}(2n-1)\pi i, n \in I$

(*ix*) $(4n+1)\pi/2 - i\log_e(133), n \in I$

(*x*) $2n\pi - i\log\left(2 \pm \sqrt{3}\right), n \in I$

3. (*i*) $\tan\frac{1}{z} + \frac{1}{z}\sec^2\frac{1}{z}$ (*ii*) $-ie^z \sin\left(ie^z\right)$

(*iii*) $2z\sin(z^2)$ (*iv*) $\cos z \sinh z + h \sin z \cosh z$

(*v*) $h\sec^2 hz$ (*vi*) $(i + ie^{iz})\sinh(iz + e^{iz})$

(*vii*) $i\ \text{sech}^2(iz - 2)$

(*viii*) $\sec z \tan z \cosh z + h \sec z \sinh z$

4. $(2n+1)\pi/2\, i,\ n \in I$

7. (*i*) $\cos(4k+1)\dfrac{\pi}{8} + i\sin(4k+1)\dfrac{\pi}{8},\ k = 0, 1, 2, 3,\ n \in I$

(*ii*) $\dfrac{1}{4}\log_e{}^2 + \dfrac{(8n+3)\pi}{8}i,\ n \in I$

(*iii*) $\dfrac{1}{n\pi},\ n \in I$

(*iv*) $i\pi\left(\dfrac{2n+1}{2}\right),\ n \in I$

(*v*) $ni\pi,\ n \in I$

❑❑❑

5

Complex Integration

We begin this chapter with a study of complex valued function of a real variable and describe how to integrate such functions and develope some properties of the integral. The main aim of the chapter is to define an integral of a complex function f along some curve or contour in the complex plane. We shall observe that the properties and methods of evaluating such integrations are similar to those of real line integral in the cartesian plane.

5.1 COMPLEX FUNCTION OF A REAL VARIABLE

This section is concerned with the integration of functions whose domains are contained in $\mathbb{R}$ and whose ranges are contained in **C**. We call such functions as complex-valued functions of real variable. We examine functions of real variable because it is easy to develop a theory of integration for such functions. We restrict our attention to those functions whose domains are closed integrals $[a, b]$ of the real axis. A complex-valued function in terms of a real variable $t \in [a, b]$ is defined as

$$f(t) = u(t) + iv(t),\ t \in [a, b]$$

where $u(t)$ and $v(t)$ are real-valued functions. For example,

$$f_1(t) = t(1+i),\ t \in [0, 1],$$
$$f_2(t) = t^3(1-i),\ t \in [0, 1],$$
$$f_3(t) = 2e^{it},\quad t \in [0, 2\pi],$$

are complex-valued functions of real variable t. The concept of continuity can be studied for such functions in a similar manner to those which we have already studied in section 2.3. The usual rules for differentiating sums, products and quotients of functions of a real variable still apply but we need to be slightly careful while applying the chain rule. We state the chain rule in the following:

Theorem 5.1

If $\phi : [a, b] \to c$ is differentiable at t_0 and f is a complex function differentiable at $\phi(t_0)$ and its derivative is

$$(f o \phi)'(t_0) = f'(\phi(t_0)\ \phi'(t_0).$$

Suppose that f is a complex-valued function of a real variable and $Ref = U$ and Imf $f = V$ are both integrable on [a, b], in the sense of real analysis. Then, the integral $\int_a^b f$ can be defined as follows:

Definition 5.1

The complex-valued function f of a real variable $t \in [a, b]$ is integrable on $[a, b]$, if its real part U and imaginary part V are integrable on $[a, b]$ and

$$\int_a^b f(t)dt = \int_a^b U(t)dt + i\int_a^b V(t)dt.$$

Example 5.1

Evaluate $\int_0^1 f(t)dt$ where $f(t) = t^2 (1 + i)$, $t \in [0, 1]$.

Solution

If $f(t) = t^2 + it^2$, $t \in [0, 1]$, then

$$\begin{aligned}\int_0^1 f(t) &= \int_0^1 t^2 dt + i\int_0^1 t^2 dt \\ &= \frac{t^3}{3}\Big|_0^1 + i\frac{t^3}{3}\Big|_0^1 \\ &= \frac{1}{3} + \frac{i}{3} \\ &= \frac{1}{3}(1 + i).\end{aligned}$$

Example 5.2

Evaluate $\int_0^{2\pi} f(t)dt$, $f(t) = e^{it}$, $t \in [0, 2\pi]$.

Solution

Since, $f(t) = e^{it} = \cos t + i \sin t$, $t \in [0, 2\pi]$, therefore

$$\begin{aligned}\int_0^{2\pi} f(t)dt, &= \int_0^{2\pi} \cos t \; at + i\int_0^{2\pi} \sin t \; dt \\ &= \sin t \;\Big|_0^{2\pi} - i\cos t\Big|_0^{2\pi} \\ &= 0.\end{aligned}$$

Example 5.3

Evaluate $\int_0^1 f(t)dt$ where $f(t) = (2t + i)^2$, $t \in [0, 1]$.

Solution

$$\text{If} \qquad \begin{aligned} f(t) &= (2t + i)^2 \\ &= (4t^2 - 1) + i(4t)\end{aligned}$$

$$\text{then,} \qquad \begin{aligned}\int_0^1 f(t)dt &= \int_0^1 (4t^2 - 1)dt + i\int_0^1 (4t)dt \\ &= \left(\frac{4t^3}{3} - t\right)\Big|_0^1 + i\frac{4t^2}{2}\Big|_0^1 = \frac{1}{3} + 2i.\end{aligned}$$

All of the following familiar properties of integrals can be proved directly from the definition 5.1. If $f_1(t) = U_1(t) + iV_1(t)$ and $f_2(t) = U_2(t) + iV_2(t)$ are complex-valued functions of a real variable t continuous on the internal $a \le t \le b$, then

$$\int_a^b Kf_1(t)dt = K\int_a^b f_1(t)dt \text{, K is a complex constant}$$

$$\int_a^b f_1(t) + f_2(t)dt = \int_a^b f_1(t)dt + \int_a^b f_2(t)dt$$

$$\int_a^b f_1(t)dt = \int_a^c f_1(t)dt + \int_c^b f_1(t)dt \text{, } a < c < b,$$

$$\int_a^b f_1(t)dt = -\int_b^a f_1(t)dt .$$

The following theorem is an analogous of Fundamental Theorem of Calculus for real variables.

Theorem 5.2: Fundamental Theorem of Calculus

Let f be a complex-valued function of a real variable on $[a, b]$ such that f is integrable on $[a, b]$, then

$$\int_a^b f' = f(b) - f(a).$$

Proof

Let $U = Re\, f$ and $V = Im f$. Then $f' = U' + iV'$ and U' and V' are integrable on $[a, b]$. Then,

$$\int_a^b f' = \int_a^b U' + i\int_a^b V'. \qquad \text{... (1)}$$

Since, U and V are real-valued functions, therefore by Fundamental Theorem for real variables, we get

$$\int_a^b U' = U(b) - U(a)$$

and $$\int_a^b V' = V(b) - V(a)$$

Thus from (1), we get

$$\int_a^b f' = (U(b) - U(a)) + i\,(V(b) - V(a))$$

$$= f(b) - f(a).$$

This theorem gives us a technique for evaluating certain real integrals. Sometimes it is difficult to integrate a real-valued function which is a real part of a complex-valued function which is easy to integrate and we also use

$$\int_a^b Ref = Re\int_a^b f.$$

Example 5.4

Evaluate $\int_0^1 e^{at} \cos bt\, dt$, where a and b are non-zero real numbers.

Solution

Let $\alpha = a + ib$, then $e^{\alpha t} = e^{(a+ib)t}$

$$= e^{at}(\cos bt + i \sin bt)$$

Thus, $$\int_0^1 e^{at} \cos bt\, dt = Re\int_0^1 e^{\alpha t}\, dt.$$

Now, $$\int_0^1 e^{\alpha t}\, dt = \left.\frac{e^{\alpha t}}{\alpha}\right|_0^1$$

$$= \frac{1}{\alpha}(e^{\alpha} - 1)$$

$$= \frac{(a - ib)}{a^2 + b^2}\ [e^a (\cos b + i \sin b) - 1]$$

Thus, the equal part of the integral is

$$\int_0^1 e^{at} \cos bt\, dt = \frac{1}{a^2 + b^2} [e^a(a \cos b + b \sin b) - a]$$

EXERCISE

1. Let $f(t) = \sin \alpha t$, $t \in [-1, 1]$, where $\alpha = a + ib$ is a non-zero complex number.

(*i*) Find the real and imaginary part of f.

(*ii*) Show that f is continuous on $[-1, 1]$.

(*iii*) Find the derivative of f.

(*iv*) Find $\int_0^1 f(t)\, dt$ by using the Fundamental Theorem and hence evaluate the two integrals.

2. If f is a complex-valued function of a real variable which is integrable on $[-b, -a]$. Show that

$$\int_{-b}^{-a} f(t)\, dt = \int_a^b f(-t)\, dt .$$

3. Show that if ϕ is integrable on $[a, b]$ and $a < c < b$, then

$$\int_a^c \phi + \int_c^b \phi = \int_a^b \phi .$$

4. Evaluate $\int_0^{\pi/2} x \cos 2x\, dx$ and $\int_0^{\pi/2} x \sin 2x\, dx$.

5. Let ϕ be a continuous function of real variable defined on the internal $[a, b]$ of the real line and suppose that $\int_a^b \phi \neq 0$. Let $\int_a^b \phi = re^{i\theta}$. Show that

$$r = \int_a^b Re(e^{-i\theta}\phi(t))dt,$$

and
$$\left|\int_a^b \phi\right| \leq \int_a^b |\phi| .$$

ANSWERS

1. (*i*) Re $f(t)$ = sin at cos*h* bt, Imf (t) = Cos at sin*h* bt

(*ii*) Since Re $f(t)$ and Imf(t) are continuous, therefore $f(t)$ is continuous

(*iii*) $$\int_0^1 \sin \alpha t\, dt = -\frac{1}{2}\cos \alpha t \Big|_0^1$$

(using fundamental theorem of calculus)

$$\int_0^1 \sin at \cosh bt\, dt = \frac{1}{a^2+b^2}$$

$\{a(1 - \cos a \cosh b) + b \sin a \sinh b\}$

$$\int_0^1 \cos at \sin bt\, dt = \frac{-1}{a^2+b^2}$$

$\{a(1 - \cos a \cosh b) + a \sin a \sinh b\}$

2. Re $f = U$, Imf $= V$

$$\int_{-b}^{-a} f(x)dx = \int_{-b}^{-a} U(x)dx + i\int_{-b}^{-a} V(x)dx$$

Put $x = -t$ and find $\int_a^b f(-t)dt$.

3. Split ϕ into real and imaginary parts and apply the corresponding result for real integrads to each part.

$$\int_0^{\pi/2} x\cos 2x\, dx = \frac{-1}{2}, \int_0^{\pi/2} x\sin 2x\, dx = \frac{\pi}{4}$$

4. If $$re^{i\theta} = \int_a^b \phi(t)dt$$

$$\Rightarrow \quad r = \int_a^b e^{-i\theta}\phi(t)dt$$

$$= \int_a^b Re(e^{-i\theta}\phi(t))dt + i\int_a^b \text{Im}(e^{-i\theta}\phi(t)dt$$

Also $$\left|\int_a^b \phi\right| = \left|re^{i\theta}\right| = r$$

$$= \int_a^b \text{Re}(e^{-i\theta}\phi(t)dt$$

$$< \int_a^b \left|e^{-i\theta}\phi(t)\right| dt = \int_a^b |\phi(t)|\, dt$$

5.2 CONTOUR INTEGRATION

We consider a curve as subset of a plane, but for a complex-valued function of a real variable we consider curve as a trace of moving point. For example, a circle is the set of all those points which are equidistant from a fixed point, but $\gamma(t) = e^{it}$ travels anti-clockwise once round the unit circle as t increases from 0 to 2π. We now give the formal definition.

Definition 5.2 Curve

A curve $\gamma : [a, b] \to \mathbf{C}$ is a continuous function with parameter interval $[a, b]$. The set of points $\{\gamma(t) : t \in [a, b]\}$ is called trace (or path) of the curve γ. The point $\gamma(a)$ is called the initial point, and $\gamma(b)$ the final point of the path.

Example 5.5

(*i*) **Line segment:** $\gamma(t) = \dfrac{b-t}{b-a}\alpha + \dfrac{t-a}{b-a}\beta$ is a line joining α and β where $t \in [a, b]$. The initial point $\gamma(a) = \alpha$ and the final point $\gamma(b) = \beta$ (Fig. 5.1).

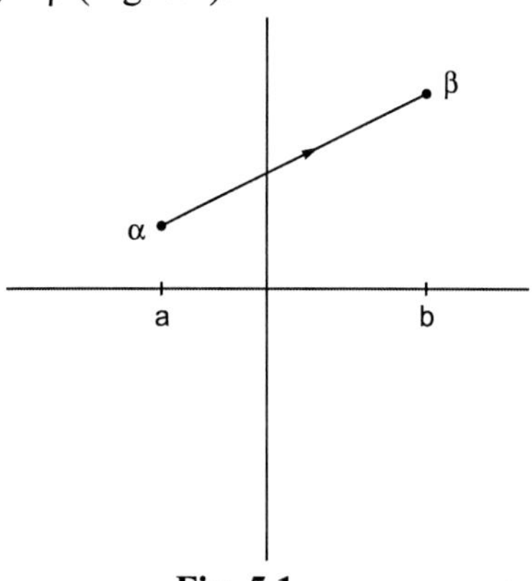

Fig. 5.1

(*ii*) **Circle:** If $\gamma(t) = a + b\,e^{it}$, $t \in [0, 2\pi]$, a is a complex number and b is a positive real number, then γ represents a circle with centre a and radius b. The initial and final points coincide at $a + b$. The trace of γ is the set $\{z : |z - a| = b\}$ (Fig. 5.2).

Suppose γ is a curve with parameter interval $[a, b]$, then the image set $\gamma([a, b]) := \{\gamma(t) : t \in [a, b]\}$ is denoted by γ^*. Since, $[a, b]$ is closed and bounded and therefore γ^* is compact. As a continuous image of a compact set, γ^* is a compact subset of $\mathbf{C}$.

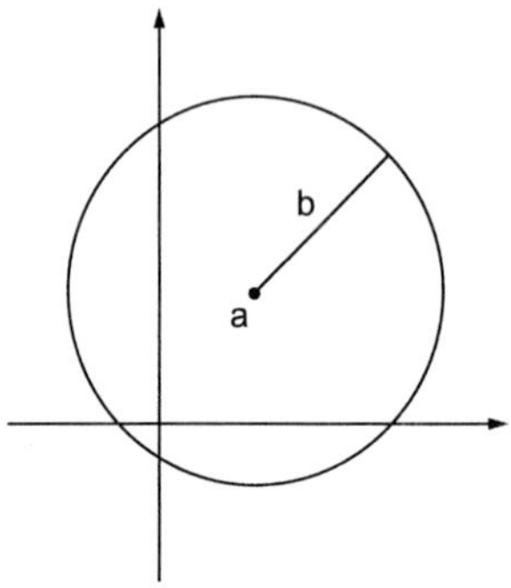

Fig. 5.2

Definition 5.3: Simple curve:

A curve $\gamma : [a, b] \to \mathbf{C}$ is simple if γ is one-one. In other words, γ is simple it does not cross itself except possibly at a and b.

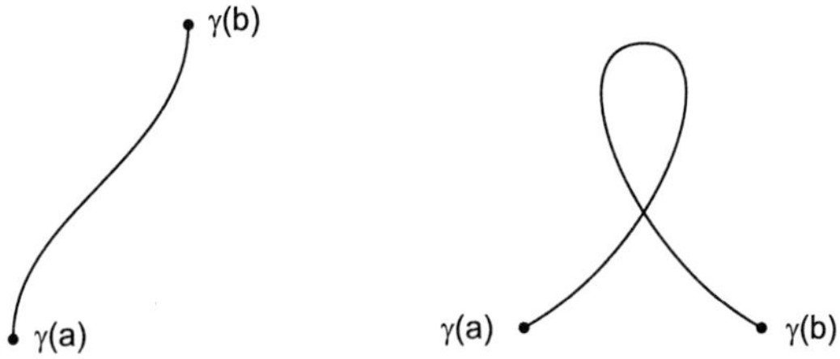

Simple curve Not simple curve

Fig. 5.3

Definition 5.4: Closed curve:

A curve $\gamma : [a, b] \to \mathbf{C}$ is closed if $\gamma(a) = \gamma(b)$.

Definition 5.5: Simple-closed curve:

A closed curve $\gamma : [a, b] \to \mathbf{C}$ such that γ is one-one on $[a, b]$ is said to be simple-closed curve.

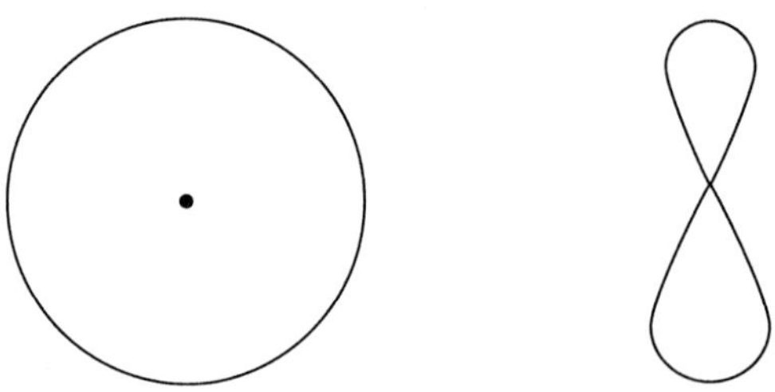

Simple-closed curve Closed but not simple curve

Fig. 5.4

A direction of a curve is determined by which $\gamma(t)$ traces out γ^* as t increases from a to b. Given a curve γ, there exists a curve $-\gamma$ with the same image set but in the opposite direction:

$$(-\gamma)(t) := \gamma(a + b - t),\ t \in [a, b].$$

Let $a \le a_1 < b_1 \le b$. If we restrict γ to $[a_1, b_1]$ then we obtain a new curve denoted by $\gamma\,|[a_1, b_1]$. If $a < c < b$ and let $\gamma_1|_{[a,\,c]}$ and $\gamma_2|_{[c,\,b]}$ such that final point of γ_1 is same as the initial point of γ_2. If $\gamma = \gamma_1 + \gamma_2$ and γ^* is obtained by tracing γ_1 followed by γ_2 with parameter intervals $[a_1, b_1]$ and $[a_2, b_2]$, respectively such that $\gamma_1(b_1) = \gamma_2(a_2)$, we say γ is the join of γ_1 and γ_2 defined as:

$$\gamma(t) = \begin{cases} \gamma_1(t), & a_1 \le t \le b_1 \\ \gamma_2(t + a_2 - b_1), & b_1 \le t \le b_1 + b_2 - a_2 \end{cases}.$$

The joining process can be iterated: the join of $\gamma_1, \gamma_2, \ldots, \gamma_3$ can be defined provided the final point of γ_k coincides with the initial point of γ_{k+1} (k = 1, 2 ... n–1) (Fig. 5.5).

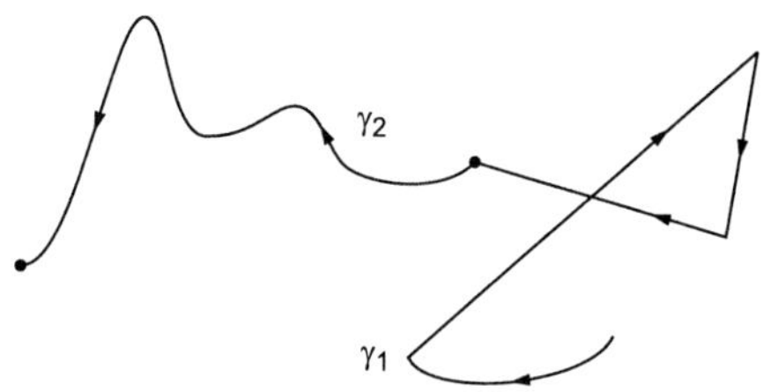

Join of γ_1 and γ_2

Fig. 5.5

Example 5.6

If $\gamma_1 : [0, 1] \to \mathbf{C}$ and $\gamma_2 : [0, 1] \to \mathbf{C}$ such that $\gamma_1(1) = \gamma_2(0)$. Define $\gamma = \gamma_1 + \gamma_2$ by

$$\gamma(t) := \begin{cases} \gamma_1(2t), & 0 \le t \le \dfrac{1}{2} \\ \gamma_2(2t-1), & \dfrac{1}{2} \le t \le 1. \end{cases}$$

Definition 5.6: Smooth Curve

If $\gamma : [a, b] \to \mathbf{C}$ is a curve and is parametrized by a set of equations $x = x(t)$ and $y = y(t)$, $a \le t \le b$ where $x(t)$ and $y(t)$ are continuous real-valued functions. Then,

$$\gamma(t) = x(t) + i\,y(t),\ a \le t \le b.$$

The curve γ is said to be smooth if $x' = \frac{dx}{dt}$ and $y' = \frac{dy}{dt}$ are continuous on the closed interval and not simultaneously zero on $]a, b[$ (Fig. 5.6).

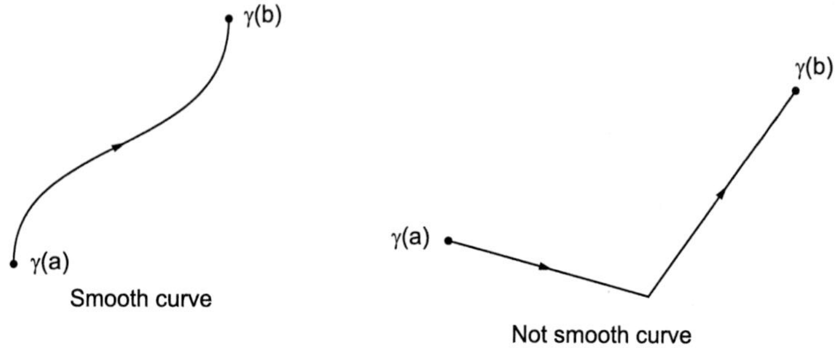

Fig. 5.6

We have

$$\gamma'(t) = x'(t) + iy'(t).$$

Definition 5.7: Piecewise Smooth.

Let p be a partition

$$a = x_0 < x_1 < x_2 \ldots\ldots\ldots < x_{n-1} < x_n = b$$

of $[a, b]$ into n-sub-intervals $[x_{k-1}, x_k]$. Then, $\gamma : [a, b] \to \mathbf{C}$ is piecewise smooth if γ is smooth in each of the sub-intervals $[x_{k-1}, x_k]$, $k = 1, 2, \ldots n$ (Fig. 5.7).

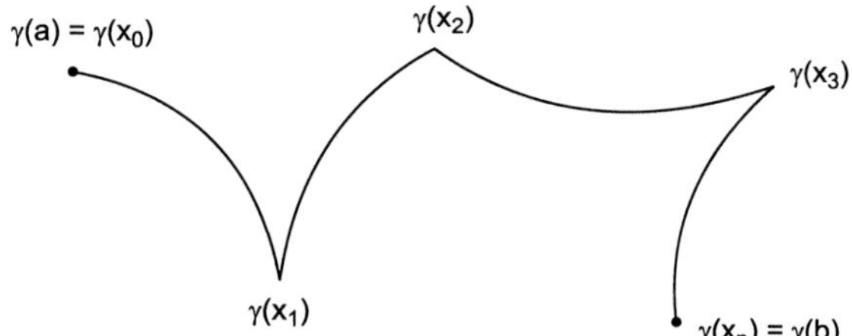

Piecewise Smooth Curve

Fig. 5.7

Example 5.7:

Define a curve as

$$\gamma(t) = \begin{cases} t^2, & -1 \le t \le 0 \\ it^2, & 0 \le t \le 1 \end{cases}$$

Then, γ is differentiable in $[-1, 1]$ and its derivative is continuous but $\gamma'(0) = 0$. So γ is not a smooth arc (Fig 5.8).

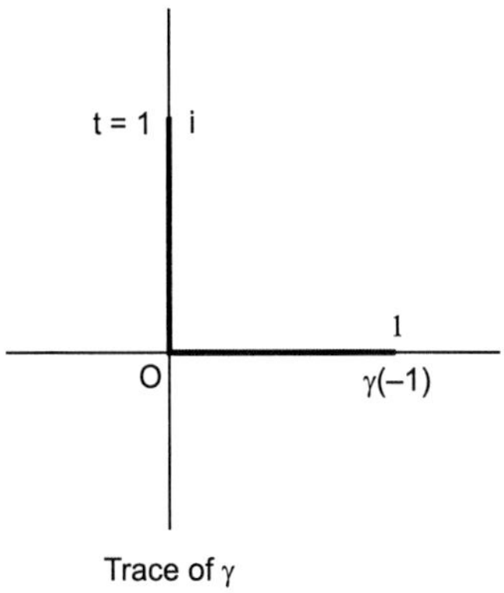

Fig. 5.8

5.2.1 Reparametrization

Suppose $\gamma : [c, d] \rightarrow \mathbf{C}$ and $\theta : [a, b] \rightarrow [c, d]$ is a continuous real function. Then, $\bar{\gamma} = \gamma o\, \theta : [a, b] \rightarrow \mathbf{C}$ is a curve with the same trace γ^*. This can be seen in the following way:

Let $\bar{\gamma}^*$ be the trace of $\bar{\gamma}$. Then,

$$\begin{aligned} \bar{\gamma}^* &= \{\bar{\gamma}(t) : a \le t \le b\} \\ &= \{\gamma\, 0\, \theta\, (t) : a \le t \le b\} \\ &= \{\gamma(s) : c \le s \le d\} \\ &= \gamma^*. \end{aligned}$$

Example 5.8

Consider $\gamma_1(t) = (1 - 2t^2) - it$, $t \in [-1, 1]$ and $\gamma_2(t) = \cos 2t - i \sin t$, $t \in [-\pi/2, \pi/2]$. Then, γ_2 is a reparametrization of the path of γ. As if we define $\theta : [-\pi/2, \pi/2] \rightarrow [-1, 1]$ as a continuous real function such that $\gamma_2 = \gamma_1 o\, \theta$. Now,

$$\begin{aligned} (\gamma_1 \text{ o } \theta)(t) &= \gamma_1(\sin t), \quad -\frac{\pi}{2} \le t \le \frac{\pi}{2} \\ &= (1 - 2\sin^2 t) - i \sin t \\ &= \cos 2t - i \sin t, \quad -\frac{\pi}{2} \le t \le \frac{\pi}{2}. \\ &= \gamma_2(t) \end{aligned}$$

Example 5.9

If $\gamma_1 = t(1 + i)$ for $t \in [0, 1]$ and $\gamma_2 = t^2 (1 + i)$, $t \in [0, 1]$. Then, γ_2 is a reparametrization of γ_1, if we define θ: $[0, 1] \to [0, 1]$ by $\theta(t) = t^2$ as a continuous function. Then,

$$\begin{aligned} \gamma_1 0\ \theta(t) &= \gamma_1(t^2) \\ &= t^2 (1 + i) \\ &= \gamma_2(t). \end{aligned}$$

The explanation given in examples can be summarized in the following definition:

Definition 5.8

Let $\gamma : [c, d] \to \mathbf{C}$ be a smooth curve and θ: $[a, b] \to [c, d]$ be an increasing, continuously differentiable function such that $\theta'(t) \neq 0\ (a \leq t \leq b)$. Then, $\gamma 0\ \theta$ is a reparametrization of the curve γ by θ.

Integration along Smooth Arcs

Let f be a complex-valued function of a real variable with domain containing the internal $[a, b]$ and $\gamma : [a, b] \to \mathbf{C}$ is a smooth curve, then we can define the line integral of f along γ in the following way:

Definition 5.9

Let $\gamma : [a, b] \to \mathbf{C}$ be a smooth curve and f is a continuous function on γ^* . Then, the integral of f along γ written as $\int_\gamma f$ or $\int_\gamma f(z)dz$, is defined by

$$\int_\gamma f(z)dz = \int_a^b f(\gamma(t))\ \gamma'(t)\ dt .$$

Example 5.10

Evaluate $\int_\gamma z^2\, dz$ where $\gamma(t) = t$, $t \in [0, 1]$.

Solution

Since $\gamma(t) = t$, therefore, $\gamma'(t) = 1$. Then,

$$\int_\gamma z^2\, dz = \int_0^1 t^2 \times 1\ dt = \frac{t^3}{3} \Big|_0^1 = \frac{1}{3}.$$

Example 5.11

Evaluate $\int_\gamma (z-a)^n$ where n is an integer and γ is a circle with centre a and radius r.

Solution

Let $\gamma(t) = a + r\,e^{it},\ 0 \le t \le 2\pi$, then

$\gamma'(t) = r\,i\,e^{it}$.

Then by the definition of complex integration along a curve, we get

$$\begin{aligned}
\int_\gamma (z-a)^n\,dz &= \int_0^{2\pi} (re^{it})^n \times r\,i\,e^{it}\,dt \\
&= i\,r^{n+1} \int_0^{2\pi} e^{(n+1)it}\,dt \\
&= i r^{n+1} \frac{e^{(n+1)it}}{(n+1)i}\Big|_0^{2\pi} \\
&= \frac{r^{n+1}}{n+1}\left[\cos(n+1)t + i\sin(n+1)t\right]\Big|_0^{2\pi} \\
&= \frac{r^{n+1}}{n+1} \times \begin{cases} 0 & \text{if} \quad n \neq -1 \\ 2\pi & \text{if} \quad n = -1 \end{cases}.
\end{aligned}$$

Example 5.12

Evaluate $\int_\gamma Re\,z\,dz$ where $\gamma(t) = t + it^2 (t \in [0, 1])$.

Solution

Since $\gamma(t) = t + it^2$, then $\gamma'(t) = 1 + 2\,it$.

Therefore,

$$\begin{aligned}
\int_\gamma Rez &= \int_0^1 t(1+2it)dt \\
&= \frac{t^2}{2} + 2i\frac{t^3}{3}\Big|_0^1 \\
&= \frac{1}{2} + \frac{2i}{3}.
\end{aligned}$$

Properties of Complex Integration along a Curve

The following properties of complex integration along a curve are analogous to the properties of real line integrals.

Proposition 5.3

Suppose γ: $[a, b] \to \mathbf{C}$ is a smooth curve and f is a continuous function on γ^*, then

$$\int_{-\gamma} f = -\int_{\gamma} f$$

Proof

We know $(-\gamma)(t) = \gamma(a + b - t),\ t \in [a, b]$, then

$$(-\gamma)'(t) = -\gamma^1(a + b - t).$$

Consider $\displaystyle\int_{-\gamma} f = \int_a^b f(\gamma(a+b-t)) \times (-\gamma'(a + b - t))dt$

Put $a + b - t = s \Rightarrow -dt = ds$, therefore

$$\int_{-\gamma} f = \int_b^a f(\gamma(s))\gamma'(s)ds$$

$$= -\int_a^b f(\gamma(s))\gamma'(s)ds$$

$$= -\int_{\gamma} f.$$

Proposition 5.4

Let $a < c < b$ and $\gamma_1 = \gamma\int_{[a,\,c]}$ $,\gamma_2 = \gamma\int_{[c,\,b]}$. If f is continuous on γ^* where $\gamma = \gamma_1 + \gamma_2$. Then,

$$\int_{\gamma} f = \int_{\gamma_1} f + \int_{\gamma_2} f.$$

Proof

Using the definition of join of two curve, we have

$$\gamma(t) = (\gamma_1 + \gamma_2)(t) = \begin{cases} \gamma_1(t) : a \le t \le c \\ \gamma_2(t) : c \le t \le b \end{cases}$$

Then,
$$\int_\gamma f = \int_a^c f(\gamma_1(t))\gamma_1'(t) + \int_c^b f(\gamma_2(t))\gamma_2'(t)$$
$$= \int_{\gamma_1} f + \int_{\gamma_2} f.$$

Proposition 5.5: The reparamerization theorem for integrals along curves.

Let γ_1 and γ_2 be two smooth curves (with parametric intervals $[a, b]$ and $[c, d]$ respectively) such that γ_1 is a proper reparametrization of the path of γ_2 by θ: $[a, b] \to [c, d]$. Let f be any function continuous on the path of γ_1. Then,

$$\int_{\gamma_1} f = \int_{\gamma_2} f.$$

Proof

By definition 5.8, $\gamma_2 = \gamma_1 \text{o}\, \theta$. Then,

$$\int_{\gamma_2} f = \int_c^d f(\gamma_2(t))\gamma_2'(t)dt$$
$$= \int_c^d f(\gamma_1 0\, \theta(t))(\gamma_1'(\theta(t)))\theta'(t)\, dt$$

Since, $\gamma_2(t) = \gamma_1(\theta(t))$ and $\gamma_2'(t) = \gamma_1'(\theta(t))\theta'(t)$

$$= \int_a^b f(\gamma_1(s))\ \gamma_1^1(s)ds$$ by substituting $\theta(t) = s$, $\theta'(t) = ds$ and $\theta(a) = c$, $\theta(\text{b}) = d$,
$$= \int_{\gamma_1} f.$$

The complex integration along a curve is a natural generalization of definite integral and thus they share many of the same properties.

Proposition 5.6

Let γ be smooth curve; f and g are continuous functions on γ and let c be any complex number. Then,

(*i*) $\int_\gamma [f(z)+g(z)]dz = \int_\gamma f(z)\,dz + \int_\gamma g(z)dz$

(*ii*) $\int_\gamma cf(z)\,dz = c\int_\gamma f(z)\,dz$

Example 5.13

If $f(z) = x^2 + iy^2$ where $z = x + iy$ and $\gamma(t) = t + it$, $0 \le t \le 1$. Evaluate $\int_\gamma f$.

Solution

Since $\gamma(t) = t + it$ then $\gamma^1(t) = 1 + i$. Then,

$$\begin{aligned}\int_\gamma f &= \int (t^2 + it^2)(1+i)dt \\ &= (1+i)^2 \int_0^1 t^2 dt \\ &= (1+i)^2 \frac{t^3}{3} \Big|_0^1 \\ &= \frac{2i}{3}.\end{aligned}$$

Example 5.14

Evaluate $\int_\gamma f$ where $f(z) = \dfrac{1}{z}$ and $\gamma(t) = \sin t + i\cos t$, $0 \le t \le 2\pi$.

Solution

Since, $$f(z) = \frac{1}{z} = \frac{1}{x+iy} = \frac{x}{x^2+y^2} - \frac{iy}{x^2+y^2},$$

and $\gamma(t) = \sin t + i\cos t$, $0 \le t \le 2\pi$

$\Rightarrow$ $\gamma^1(t) = \cos t - i\sin t$

then,
$$\begin{aligned}\int_\gamma f &= \int_0^{2\pi}\left(\frac{\sin t}{\cos^2 t + \sin^2 t} - \frac{i\cos t}{\cos^2 t + \sin^2 t}\right)(\cos t - i\sin t)dt \\ &= \frac{1}{i}\int_0^{2\pi}(\cos t + i\sin t)(\cos t - i\sin t)dt \\ &= \frac{1}{i}\int_0^{2\pi}\left(\cos^2 t + \sin^2 t\right)dt\end{aligned}$$

$$= \frac{t}{i} \Big|_0^{2\pi}$$

$$= \frac{2\pi}{i} = -2\pi i$$

Example 5.15

To compute $\int_\gamma z^2 dz$ where γ is the semi-circular closed curve formed by joining γ_1: $[-R_1 R]$ and γ_2 : = semi-circle with centre o and radius R.

Solution

We know $\gamma_1(t) = (1-t)(-R) + tR,\ o \le t \le 1;\ \gamma_1'(t) = 2R$

and $\gamma_2(t) = Re^{it},\ o \le t \le \pi;\ \gamma_2'(t) = Rie^{it}$

Since $\gamma = \gamma_1 + \gamma_2$. Then by proposition 5.4,

$$\int_\gamma z^2 = \int_{\gamma_1} z^2 + \int_{\gamma_2} z^2$$

$$= \int_0^1 (2tR - R)^2 (2R)dt + \int_0^\pi (\mathrm{R}e^{it})^2 (\mathrm{R}\, ie^{it})dt$$

$$= 2\mathrm{R}^2 \int_0^1 (2t-1)^2 dt + R^3 i \int_0^\pi e^{3it} dt$$

$$= 2\mathrm{R}^2 \left[\frac{4t^3}{3} + t - \frac{4t^2}{2}\right]_0^1 + \mathrm{R}^3\, i \times \frac{e^{3it}}{3i} \Big|_0^\pi$$

$$= 2\mathrm{R}^2 \left[\frac{4}{3} + 1 - 2\right] + \frac{R^3}{3}[-2]$$

$$= \frac{2R^2}{3} - \frac{2R^3}{3} = 0.$$

Example 5.16

If γ is piecewise smooth and $y = \gamma_1 + \gamma_2$ (as shown in Fig. 5.9). Evaluate $\int_\gamma (x^2 + iy^2)dz$ where $z = x + iy$.

Solution

In view of proposition 5.4, if $f(z) = x^2 + iy^2$, then

$$\int_{\gamma} f = \int_{\gamma_1} f + \int_{\gamma_2} f \qquad \dots (1)$$

We know f is a straight line joining o and $1 + i$, therefore,

$$\gamma_1(t) = (1 - t)\, o + t(1 + i),\ o \le t \le 1$$

then, $\gamma_1'(t) = 1 + i$

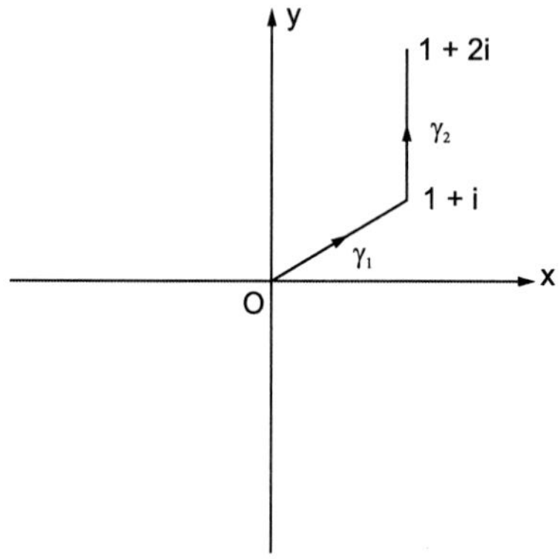

Also,
$$\int_{\gamma_1} f = \int_0^1 (t^2 + it^2)(1+i)dt$$

$$= (1 + i)^2 \frac{t^3}{3} \Big|_0^1$$

$$= \frac{(1+i)^2}{3} = \frac{2i}{3}$$

Similarly,
$$\gamma_2(t) = (1 - t)(1 + i) + t(1 + 2i),\ o \le t \le 1$$
$$= 1 + (1 + t)i$$

and $\gamma_2'(t) = i.$

Now,
$$\int_{\gamma_2} f = \int_0^1 (1 + i(1+t)^2)idt$$

$$= i\left[t + \frac{i(1+t)^3}{3}\right]_0^1$$

$$= i\left[1 + \frac{7i}{3}\right] = -\frac{7}{3} + i.$$

The Fundamental Theorem for complex integration (Theorem 5.2) can be transferred to integrals along a smooth curve.

Theorem 5.7: The Fundamental Theorem for integrals along curves

Let f be analytic in a region R and γ: $[a, b] \to R$ be a smooth curve in R. Suppose that f' is continuous on R. Then,

$$\int_\gamma f'(z)dz = f(\gamma(b)) - f(\gamma(a)).$$

Proof

By the definition 5.9

$$\begin{aligned}\int_\gamma f'(z)dz &= \int_a^b f'(\gamma(t))\gamma'(t)dt \\ &= \int_a^b (f \circ \gamma)'(t)dt \text{ (by chain rule)} \\ &= (f \circ \gamma)(b) - (f \circ \gamma)(a) \text{ (by Theorem 5.2)} \\ &= f(\gamma(b)) - f(\gamma(a)) \qquad \text{... (1)}\end{aligned}$$

Corollary 5.8

Let $\gamma : [a, b] \to R$ be a closed smooth curve in a region R and f be function analytic on R and f' is continuous on R. Then,

$$\int_\gamma f'dz = 0.$$

Proof

Since γ is a closed curve therefore $\gamma(a) = \gamma(b)$. Then by (1), we get

$$\int_\gamma f'(z)dz = 0.$$

The Fundamental Theorem can be used in evaluating certain integrals along curves as shown in the following examples:

Example 5.17

Evaluate $\int_\gamma (z - i)dz$ where γ is the parabolic segment $\gamma(t) = t + it^2$, $-1 \le t \le 1$

Solution

Let $g(z) = (z - i)$

$= f'(z)$

Then, $f(z) = \frac{z^2}{2} - iz$. The function $f(z)$ is analytic in **C** and $g(z)$ is continuous. Then by Theorem 5.7

$$\int_\gamma (z - i)dz = \left(\frac{z^2}{2} - iz\right)_{z=+1+i} - \left(\frac{z^2}{2} - iz\right)_{z=-1+i} = 0.$$

If γ is a closed smooth curve and f is continuous on γ, then we can find the absolute value of the integral $\int_\gamma f$ in the following way:

Theorem 5.9

Let f be a complex-valued function whose domain contains $[a, b]$, then

$$\left|\int_a^b f(t)dt\right| \leq \int_a^b |f(t)|dt.$$

Proof

Suppose $\int_a^b f(t)dt = Re^{i\theta}, R \geq o$ ... (1)

By proposition 5.6

$$\int_a^b e^{-i\theta} f(t)dt = R \quad \text{... (2)}$$

Let $e^{-i\theta} f(t) = A(t) + i B(t)$ where A and B are real valued functions.

Then, $R = \int_a^b A(t)dt = \int_a^b \text{Re}\, e^{-i\theta} f(t)dt$

We know Re z ≤ |Re z| ≤ |z|. Thus,

$$R \leq \int_a^b | f(t) | dt \quad \text{... (3)}$$

From (1) and (3) we get

$$\left|\int_a^b f(t)dt\right| \leq \int_a^b | f(t) | dt.$$

The above result can be applied to simple closed smooth curve and we get an estimation for complex integration along a curve.

Theorem 5.10: Esitmation Theorem

Let γ be a smooth curve of length L and f be continuous on γ such that $|f(z)| \leq M\ \forall\ z \in \gamma^*$. Then,

$$\left|\int_\gamma f(z)dz\right| \leq ML.$$

Proof

We know

$$\int_\gamma f(z)dz = \int_a^b f(\gamma(t))\gamma'(t)dt$$

Then applying theorem 5.9, we get

$$\begin{aligned}\left|\int_\gamma f(z)dz\right| &\leq \int_a^b |f(\gamma(t))||\gamma'(t)|\,dt \\ &\leq M\int_a^b |\gamma'(t)|\,dt \\ &\leq ML.\end{aligned}$$

(Because if $\gamma(t) = x(t) + y(t)$, then length of the curve γ is given by

$$\begin{aligned}L &= \int_a^b \sqrt{(x'(t))^2 + (y'(t))^2}\,dt \\ &= \int_a^b |\gamma'(t)|^2\,dt.\end{aligned}$$

Example 5.18

Find an upper bound for $\int_\gamma e^z dz$ where γ is the circle $|z| = 1$.

Solution

If $|z| = 1$, then

$$|e^z| = |e^{x+iy}| = e^x \leq e \qquad \text{(since } x \leq 1\text{)}$$

Let $M = e$ and $L = 2\pi$. Then by Theorem 5.10, we get

$$\left|\int_\gamma e^z dz\right| \leq 2\pi e.$$

Example 5.19

Find an upper bound for the absolute value of $\int_\gamma \frac{e^z}{z+1}dz$ where γ is the circle $|z| = 4$.

Solution

The length L of γ is the circumference of the circle $|z| = 4$, therefore, $L = 8\pi$. Also for all points z on the circle $|z + 1| \geq ||z| - 1| = 4 - 1 = 3$

Thus,
$$\left|\int_\gamma \frac{e^z}{z+1}dz\right| \leq \int_\gamma \left|\frac{e^z}{z+1}\right| dz$$
$$\leq \frac{1}{3}\int_\gamma \left|e^z\right| dz$$
$$\leq \frac{1}{3}\int_\gamma e^x dz \qquad \text{(where } z = x + iy\text{)}$$
$$\leq \frac{e^4}{3}\times 8\pi$$
$$= \frac{8\pi}{3}e^4.$$

Example 5.20

Show that, if f is a continuous real-valued function and $|f(z)| \leq 1$ on γ where γ is a unit circle, then

$$\left|\int_\gamma f(z)dz\right| \leq 4.$$

Solution

Let $\int_\gamma f(z)dz = Re^{i\theta}$, then

$$R = \left|\int_\gamma f(z)dz\right| = \int_\gamma e^{-i\theta} f(z)dz \qquad \text{... (1)}$$

Since γ is a unit circle therefore $\gamma(t) = e^{it}$, $0 \leq t \leq 2\pi$, then

$$R = \int_\gamma e^{-i\theta} f(z)dz = \int_0^{2\pi} f(e^{it})ie^{it}e^{-i\theta}dt$$

$$= i\int_0^{2\pi} f(e^{it})e^{i(t-\theta)}dt$$

$$= i\int_0^{2\pi} f(e^{it})(\cos(t-\theta)+i\sin(t-\theta))\,dt$$

$f(e^{it})$ is a real-valued function of t, then

$$R = \int_0^{2\pi} f(e^{it})\sin(\theta - t))\,dt \qquad \text{... (2)}$$

From (1) and (2), we get

$$R \le \int_0^{2\pi} |\sin(\theta - t)|dt$$

$$= \int_0^{2\pi} |\sin t|dt = 4.$$

Proposition 5.11

Suppose $\{f_n\}$ is a sequence of continuous functions and $f_n \to f$ uniformly. Then,

$$\int_\gamma f(z)dz = \lim_{n\to\infty} \int_\gamma f_n(z)dz$$

where γ is a smooth curve.

Proof

Consider

$$\left|\int_\gamma f(z)dz - \int_\gamma f_n(z)dz\right| = \left|\int_\gamma (f(z)-f_n(z))dz\right|$$

$$< \left|\int_\gamma |f(z)-f_n(z)|\,dz\right| \qquad \text{... (1)}$$

Let $\in > 0$ be given. Since $f_n \to f$ uniformly, therefore there exists an integer m such that

$$|f(z) - f_n(z)| < \frac{\varepsilon}{\text{length of } \gamma} \quad \forall\, n \ge m,\ \forall\, z \in \mathbf{C}. \qquad \text{... (2)}$$

From (1) and (2), we get

$$\left|\int_\gamma f(z)dz - \int_\gamma f_n(z)dz\right| \le \frac{\varepsilon}{\text{length of } \gamma}\ (\text{length of } \gamma)$$

$$= \in.$$

Thus, $\lim_{n\to\infty}\int_\gamma f_n(z)dz = \int_\gamma f(z)dz$

EXERCISE

1. Let $\gamma_1(t) = t(1 + i)$, $t \in [0, 1]$ and $\gamma_2(t) = t^2(1+ i)$, $t \in [0, 1]$.
   (*i*) Is γ_1 a smooth and simple curve?
   (*ii*) Is γ_2 a smooth and simple curve?
   (*iii*) What are traces of γ_1 and γ_2?
   (*iv*) Express γ_2 as a reparametrization of the path of γ_1. Is your reparametrization proper?

2. Let $\gamma_n(t) = e^{int}$, $t \in [0, 2\pi]$, n an integer.
   (*i*) Show that γ_n is a smooth closed curve for every $n \neq 0$.
   (*ii*) For which value of n is γ_n simple?
   (*iii*) For which value of n is γ_n simple and closed?
   (*iv*) For which values of n does γ_n is positively oriented?

3. Describe the image γ^* of the curve γ in the following cases:
   (*i*) $\gamma(t) = a \cos t + i\, b \sin t$, $t \in [0, 2\pi]$.
   (*ii*) $\gamma(t) = t + it^2$, $t \in [-a, a]$.
   (*iii*) γ is the join of $[-1, 1]$, $[1, 1 + i]$ and $[1 + i, -1 -i]$.
   (*iv*) γ is given by $\gamma(t) = e^{it}$, $t \in [0, \pi]$ and $\gamma(t) = e^{-it}$, $t \in [\pi, 2\pi]$.
   (*v*) $\gamma(t) = e^{it} \cos t$, $t \in [0, 2\pi]$.

In which cases is γ—(*a*) closed (*b*) simple (*c*) a path (*d*) smooth?

4. Define parametrically a path γ for which γ^* is
   (*i*) the closed semi-circle in the right half-plane with $[-Ri, Ri]$ as diameter.
   (*ii*) the pair of circles $|z - 1| = 1$ and $|z + 1| = 1$, one traced clockwise and other anticlockwise.
   (*iii*) A circle with radius 3 and centre -1.

5. Given a path γ, define length $(\gamma) = \int_a^b |\gamma'(t)|\, dt$, then prove the following:
   (*i*) length $(-\gamma)$ = length (γ)
   (*ii*) If γ is the join of paths γ_1 and γ_2, then length (γ) = length (γ_1) + length (γ_2).
   (*iii*) If $\bar{\gamma}$ is obtained by reparametrization γ in definition 5.8, then length $(\bar{\gamma})$ = length (γ).

6. Evaluate $\int_\gamma e^z dz$ where γ is the polygonal path consisting of the line segments $[0, 2]$ and $[2, 1 + \pi i]$.

7. Evaluate $\int_\gamma Im(z - i)dz$ where γ is the polygonal path consisting of the circular arc along $|z| = 1$ in the first quadrant and the line segment $[i, -1]$.

8. Find $\int_\gamma ze^z$ where γ is the square $[0, 1, 1 + i, i]$.

9. Define $\gamma(t) = e^{it}, 0 \le t \le 2\pi$ and find $\int z^n dz$ for every integer n.

10. Let γ be the closed polygon $[1 - i, 1 + i, - 1 + i, 1 - i]$. Find $\int_\gamma \frac{1}{z} dz$.

11. Find $\int_\gamma z^{-1/2} dz$ where

(*i*) γ is the upper-half of the unit circle from +1 to –1.
(*ii*) γ is the lower-half of the unit circle from +1 to –1.

12. Show that the relation in Definition 5.8 is an equivalence relation.

13. Let $\gamma(t) = 1 + e^{it}$ for $0 \le t \le 2\pi$ and find $\int_\gamma \frac{dz}{(z^2 - 1)}$.

14. Find the upper bound for the absolute value of the given interval along the indicated contour.

(*i*) $f(z) = \frac{1}{1+z^4}$, γ = semi-circle with radius R and centre at zero.

(*ii*) $f(z) = \frac{1}{z}$, $\gamma = e^{it}, 0 \le t \le 2\pi$.

(*iii*) $f(z) = \frac{1}{z^2 + 4}$, $\gamma = [0, 1 + i]$

(*iv*) $f(z) = \frac{1}{z^2 - 2i}$, γ = right half of the circle $|z| = 6$ and $z = -6i$ to $6i$.

(v) $f(z) = \frac{1}{z^3}$, γ = one quarter of the circle $|z| = 4$ from $z = 4i$ to 4.

15. Let Γ be the semi-circle $\{z : |z| = r, Im\, z \geq 0\}$ from $-r$ to r, and $a \in \mathbb{R}^+$.

(i) Prove that $\left|\int_\gamma \frac{dz}{z^2+a^2}\right| \leq \frac{\pi r}{r^2-a^2}$ if $r > a$, and find the corresponding result for $r < a$.

(ii) What can you say about $\lim_{r\to\infty}\left|\int_P \frac{dz}{z^2+a^2}\right|$?

ANSWERS

1. (i) γ_1 is smooth and simple.

(ii) γ_2 is not smooth and $\gamma_1'(0) = 0$, γ_2 is simple.

(iii) γ_1 is the line segment $[0, 1 + i]$.

γ_2 is the line segment $[0, 1 + i]$.

(iv) $\gamma_2 = \gamma_1\, o\theta$; $\theta:[0, 1] \to [0, 1]$, $\theta(t) = t^2$, $\theta'(0)$ = thus the reparametrization is not proper.

2. (i) Since γ_n has periodicty 2π, $\gamma_n(0) = \gamma_n(2\pi)$

Also $\gamma_n'(t) \neq 0$ if $n \neq 0$. γ_n is smooth and closed curve for every $n \neq 0$.

(ii) None

(iii) $n = -1, 1$

(iv) positive n.

3. (i) Elipse $\{(x, y)$: $\frac{x^2}{a^2}+\frac{y^2}{b^2} = 1\}$ – Simple, closed and smooth.

(ii) Pavabola $\{(x, y)\; y = x^2, -a < x < a\}$ – Simple, Smooth but not closed.

(iii) $\gamma_1(t) = \gamma_1(t) + \gamma_2(t) + \gamma_3(t)$ where

$\gamma_1(t) = (1 - t) - 1 + t,\;\; 0 \leq \text{t} \leq 1$

$\gamma_2(t) = (1 - t) + t(1 + i),\;\; 0 \leq \text{t} \leq 1$

$\gamma_3(t) = (1 - t)\,(1 + i) + t(-1 - i)$

It is neither simple nor closed.

(*iv*) $\gamma(t) = e^{it}$ is a positively directed upper half circle with center zero and radius 1–closed, smooth

(*v*) Circle with center 0 and radius cost – closed, smooth.

4. (*i*) $\gamma_1 = \gamma_1 + \gamma_2$ where $\gamma_1(t) = Re^{it}$, $t \in \left[\frac{-\pi}{2}, \frac{\pi}{2}\right]$ and $\gamma(t) = (1 - t) = (1 - t)\, Ri + t(-Ri)$, $0 \le t \le 1$.

(*ii*) $\gamma_1(t) = 1 + e^{it}$, $t \in [0, 2\pi]$, $\gamma_2(t) = -1 + e^{-it}$, $t \in [0, 2\pi]$

(*iii*) $\gamma(t) = -1 + 3e^{it}$, $t \in [0, 2\pi]$

6. $\frac{1}{2}(e^z - 3)$ **7.** i

8. $1 + (i - 1)e^i$ **9.** 0

10. $\log\left(\frac{1}{2} + \frac{5}{2}i\right)$ **11.** (*i*) $2(i - 1)$ (*ii*) $2(1 + i)$

13. 0

14. (*i*) 0 (*ii*) 1 (*iii*) $\frac{1}{\sqrt{2}}$ (*iv*) $6\sqrt{2}$ (*v*) $\frac{3}{35}$

(*vi*) $\frac{1}{16}$

15. $\lim\limits_{r \to \infty} \left| \int_\Gamma \frac{dz}{z^2 + a^2} \right| = 0$

5.3 THE CLOSED CURVE THEOREM FOR ENTIRE FUNCTIONS

In this section, we shall concentrate on contour integral where the contour γ is a simple closed curve with a positive (counter-clockwise) orientation. We observed in Example 5.15 that $\int_\gamma z^2 dz = 0$ where γ is a contour. Also, $\int_\gamma \frac{1}{z^2} = 0$ if γ is a unit circle. But $\int_\gamma \frac{1}{z} = 2\pi i$ if γ is a unit circle.

In all the examples mentioned above, γ is a contour, but in the first two cases $\int_\gamma f(z) = 0$ but in the third case $\int_\gamma f(z) \neq 0$. Therefore, in this section we shall discuss the entire functions for which $\int_\gamma f(z) = 0$ for a contour γ where γ is the boundary of a rectangle. We begin with the following:

Lemma 5.12

If f is a linear function and γ is the boundary of a rectangle R. Then $\int_\gamma f(z)dz = 0$.

Proof

Let $f(z) = a + bz$ and γ being boundary of a rectangle R is a simple closed curve. Since $f(z)$ is entire and is the derivative of the analytic function $F(z) = az + \frac{bz^2}{2}$. Then by fundamental theorem of calculus for complex integration along a closed curve.

$$\int_\gamma f(z)dz = \int_\gamma f'(z)dz = 0 \text{ (by Corollary 5.8)}$$

Theorem 5.13: Rectangle Theorem

Suppose f is entire and γ is the boundary of a rectangle R. Then, $\int_\gamma f(z)dz = 0$.

Proof

Let $I = \int_\gamma f(z)dz$. To show $I = 0$. Divide the rectangle R into four congruent substangles (join the mid points of the opposite sides). Let these rectangles be R_1, R_2, R_3, R_4 and γ_1, γ_2, γ_3 and γ_4 denote the boundaries of these rectangles. Since, the integrals along the interior lines appear in the opposite directions and thus cancel.

$(\therefore \int_{-\Gamma} f(z)dz = -\int_\Gamma f(z)dz)$. Hence

$$\int_\gamma f(z)dz = \sum_{i=1}^{4} \int_{\gamma_i} f(z)dz.$$

For some γ_k, $1 \le k \le 4$ we must have

$$\left|\int_{\gamma^{(1)}} f(z)dz\right| > \frac{I}{4} \quad \text{... (1)}$$

where $\gamma^{(1)}$ is the boundary of rectangle which satisfies (1) otherwise

if $\left|\int_{\gamma_i} f(z)dz\right| < \frac{I}{4}$ for $1 \le i \le 4$, then

$$|I| = \left|\int_I f(z)dz\right| \le \sum_{i=1}^{4} \left|\int_{\gamma_i} f(z)dz\right| < \frac{I}{4}.4 = I.$$

Let $R^{(1)}$ be the rectangle bounded by $\gamma^{(1)}$. Let $\Delta^{(1)}$ be the region bounded by $\gamma^{(1)}$. Repeating the argument with $\gamma^{(1)}$ in place of γ. Proceeding in this way, generate a sequence $\gamma^{(0)}, \gamma^{(1)}$.... of rectangles such that

(*i*) $\gamma^{(0)} = \gamma$

(*ii*) for each *n*, $\Delta^{(n+1)} \subseteq \Delta^{(n)}$,

(*iii*) length $(\gamma^{(n)}) = \dfrac{l}{2^n}$ where l = length (γ).

(*iv*) $\left|\int_{\gamma^{(n)}} f(z)dz\right| \ge \dfrac{|I|}{4^n}$ for all $n \ge 0$.

(*v*) $R^{(n+1)} = \dfrac{1}{2}\text{ diam } R^{(n)} = \dfrac{1}{2^{n+1}}(\text{diam } R)$.

The set $\bigcap_{n=0}^{\infty} \Delta^{(n)}$ contains a point z_0 common to all the rectangles $R^{(n)}$.

Let $\in > 0$ be given. Since f is analytic at z_0, therefore,

$$\frac{f(z) - f(z_0)}{z - z_0} \to f'(z_0)$$

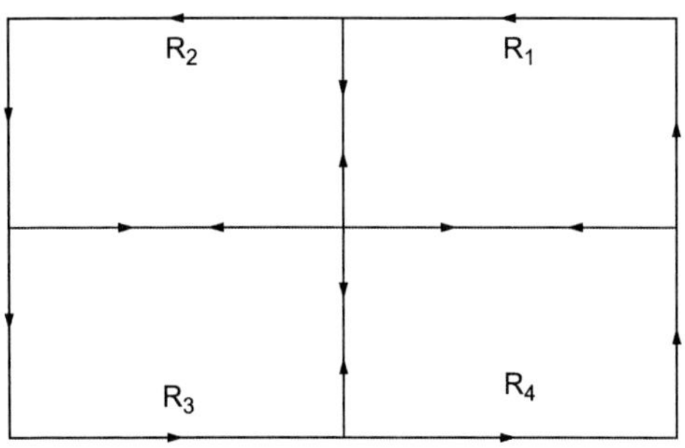

There exists $\delta > 0$ such that

$$\left|\frac{f(z) - f(z_0)}{z - z_0} - f'(z_0)\right| < \in \text{ whenever } 0 < |z - z_0| < \delta \qquad \text{... (2)}$$

we can write

$$f(z) = f(z) + f(z_0) + f'(z_0)(z - z_0) - f(z_0) - f'(z_0)(z - z_0) \quad \text{... (3)}$$

$$= f(z_0) + f'(z_0)(z - z_0) + \in (z - z_0).$$

Choose N such that $|z - z_0| \supseteq \Delta^N$. For such N

$$|z - z_0| \leq \frac{\varepsilon}{2^N} \text{ for all } z \in \Delta^N.$$

Integrating (3) along γ^N on both the sides, we get

$$\int_{\gamma^N} f(z)dz = \int_{\gamma^N} f(z_0)dz + f'(z_0)$$

$$\int_{\gamma^N} (z - z_0)dz + \in \int_{\gamma^N} (z - z_0)dz$$

$$= \varepsilon \int_{\gamma^N} (z - z_0)dz .$$

To estimate the integral, we take absolute value

$$\left|\int_{\gamma^N} f(z)dz\right| < \varepsilon \int_{\gamma^N} |z - z_0||dz|$$

$$= \varepsilon \frac{l}{2^N} \int_{\gamma^N} |dz| \quad \text{... (4)}$$

Also,

$$\int_{\gamma^N} |dz| = \text{length of } \gamma^N \leq \frac{l}{2^N}$$

From (4), we get

$$\frac{I}{4^N} < \frac{\varepsilon l^2}{4^{N+1}}$$

Thus,

$I < \in l^2$ for sufficiently large N. Thus, $\int_{\gamma} f = 0$.

Remark

We have taken orientation of γ in counter clockwise direction but the same result would hold with the opposite direction. Now, in this chapter and subsequent chapters unless mentioned otherwise, the integral around any convex curve will be taken in the counter clockwise direction.

Theorem 5.14 Integral theorem

If f is entire, then f is everywhere the derivative of an analytic function. That is there exists an entire function F such that $F'(z) = f(z)$ for all z.

Proof

Define

$$F(z) = \int_{[0,\,z]} f(s)ds$$

where $[0, z]$ is a straight line segment joining 0 and Rz and Rez to z. Then,

$$F(z+h) - F(z) = \int_{[0,\,z+h]} f(s)ds - \int_{[0,\,z]} f(s)ds$$

$$= \int_{[z,\,z+h]} f(s)ds\ .$$

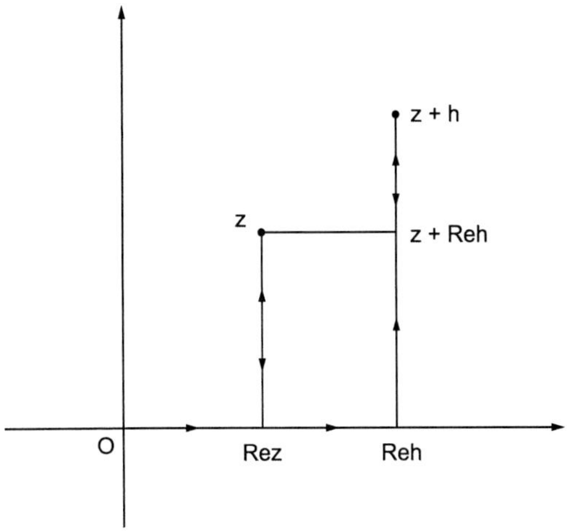

where $[z_1\ z + h]$ is a straight line segment joining z to $z + Re\ h$ and from $z + Re\ h$ to $z + h$. Consider

$$\frac{F(z+h)-F(z)}{h} - f(z) = \frac{1}{h}\int_{[z,\,z+h]} f(s)ds - f(z)$$

since, $\quad \frac{1}{h}\int_{z}^{z+h} dz = \frac{1}{h}[z+h-z] = 1$, therefore

$$\frac{F(z+h)-F(z)}{h}-f(z)=\frac{1}{h}\int_{[z,z+h]} f(s)ds-\frac{f(z)}{h}\int_{[z,z+h]} dS$$

$$=\frac{1}{h}\int_{z}^{z+h}[f(s)-f(z)]ds$$

Since f being centre is continuous, therefore for each $\in > 0$, there is $\delta > 0$ such that

$|f(s) - f(z)| < \in, 0 < |s - z| < \delta$

Thus by estimation theorem, if $0 < |h| < \delta$, then

$$\left|\frac{F(z+h)-F(z)}{h}-f(z)\right|<\frac{1}{|h|}\times\varepsilon|h| = \in.$$

Hence, $\lim\limits_{h\to 0}\left|\frac{F(z+h)-F(z)}{h}-f(z)\right| = 0$

In other words, F is differentiable at z and $F'(z) = f(z)$.

Theorem 5.15

If f is entire and γ is a smooth closed curve, then

$$\int_\gamma f(z)dz = 0.$$

Proof

Since f is entire, therefore these exists and entire function F such that $F^1(z) = f(z)$. Then by Fundamental Theorem of Calculus

$$\int_\gamma f(z)dz = \int_\gamma F'(z)dz = F(\gamma(b)) - f(\gamma(a) = 0.$$

Since, γ is closed therefore $\gamma(a) = \gamma(b)$.

Example 5.21

Given any rectangle with vertices (a, c), (b, c), (b, d) and (a, d), parameterize the boundary γ and prove that

$$\int_\gamma dz = \int_\gamma zdz = 0.$$

Solution

Let $\gamma = \gamma_1 + \gamma_2 + \gamma_3 + \gamma_4$ where

$$\gamma_1(t) = (1-t)\,a + tc,\ 0 < t < 1$$
$$\gamma_2(t) = (1-t)\,c + tb,\ 0 < t < 1$$
$$\gamma_3(t) = (1-t)b + td,\ 0 < t < 1$$
$$\gamma_4(t) = (1-t)d + ta,\ 0 < t < 1$$

Then,

$$\begin{aligned}\int_\gamma dz &= \int_0^1 \gamma_1'(t)dt + \int_0^1 \gamma_2'(t)dt + \int_0^1 \gamma_3'(t)dt + \int_0^1 \gamma_4'(t)dt \\ &= (c-a) + (b-c) + (d-b) + (a-d) \\ &= 0\end{aligned}$$

Also,

$$\begin{aligned}\int_\gamma zdz &= \int_0^1 (\gamma_1(t))\,\gamma_1'(t)dt + \int_0^1 (\gamma_2(t))\,\gamma_2'(t)dt \\ &\quad + \int_0^1 (\gamma_3(t))\,\gamma_3'(t)dt + \int_0^1 (\gamma_4(t))\,\gamma_4'(t)dt \\ &= \int_0^1 ((1-t)a + tc)(c-a)dt + \int_0^1 ((1-t)c + tb)(b-c)dt \\ &\quad + \int_0^1 ((1-t)b + td)(d-b)dt + \int_0^1 ((1-t)d + ta)(a-d)dt \\ &= (c-a)\left[-\frac{(1-t)^2 a}{2} + \frac{t^2}{2}C\right]_0^1 + \left[\frac{-(1-t)^2 c}{2} + \frac{t^2 b}{2}\right]_0^1 (b-c) \\ &= +(d-b)\left[\frac{-(1-t)^2 b}{2} + \frac{t^2}{2}d\right]_0^1 + (a-d)\left(\frac{-(1-t)^2 d}{2} + \frac{t^2}{2}a\right)_0^1 \\ &= (c-a)\left[\frac{c}{2} + \frac{a}{2}\right] + (b-c)\left[\frac{b}{2} + \frac{c}{2}\right] + (d-b)\left[\frac{d}{2} + \frac{b}{2}\right]\end{aligned}$$

$$+(a-d)\left(\frac{a}{2}+\frac{d}{2}\right)$$

$$= \frac{1}{2}\left\{c^2 - a^2 + b^2 - c^2 + d^2 - b^2 + a^2 - d^2\right\}$$

$$= 0.$$

EXERCISE

1. If $D = \{z : |z| < 1\}$ which of the following function f and contour γ shown in figure satisfy the hypothesis of Theorem 5.15 in D. In each case the circle is $|z| = 1$.

(i) 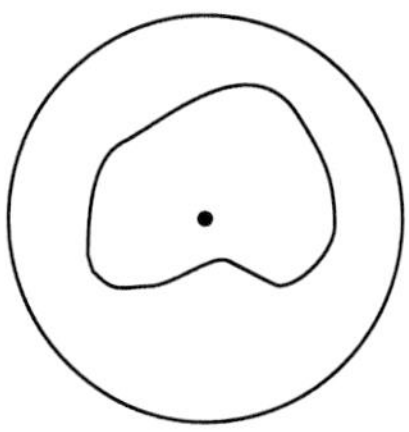 $f(z) = \frac{1}{z}$

(ii) 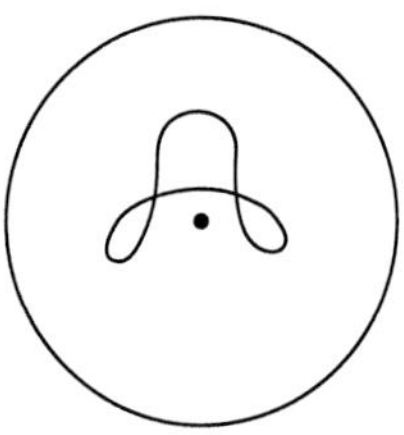 $f(z) = e^z$

(iii) 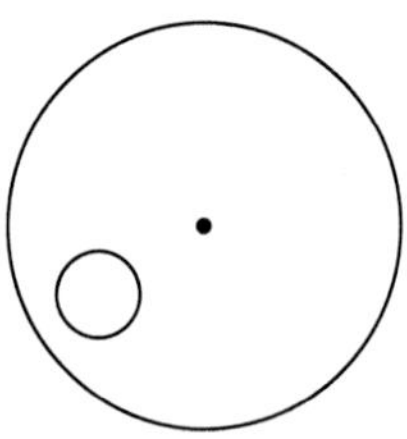 $f(z) = \log z$

(iv) 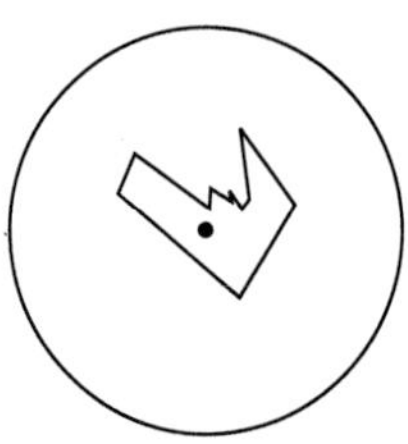 $f(z) = \frac{1}{z-3}$

(v) 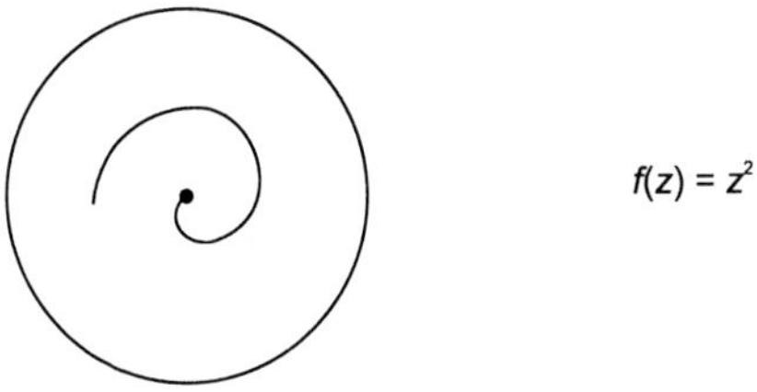

2. If f is analytic in a region R and γ_1 and γ_2 are two curves in R with the same initial and end points. Show that

$$\int_{\gamma_1} f = \int_{\gamma_2} f.$$

3. Each of the following integrals is zero. Give reason (or reasons) in each case and γ is a contour with $\gamma^* \subseteq D(0, 1)$.

(*i*) $\int_{\gamma} \frac{dz}{z-2}$ (*ii*) $\int_{\gamma(i;3)} \frac{1}{(z-2)^3} dz$

(*iii*) $\int_{\gamma(i;2)} \frac{\sin z}{z} dz$ (*iv*) $\int_{\gamma(0;1)} z|z|^4 \, dz$

(*v*) $\int_{\gamma(1;1)} \frac{1}{1+e^z} dz$.

ANSWERS

1. (*i*) No, f is not analytic in D

(*ii*) Yes, Γ is not simple

(*iii*) No, log is not analytic on all of D

(*iv*) Yes, f is analytic on D

(*v*) No, Γ is not closed.

2. $\gamma = \gamma_1 + \gamma_2$ is a closed curve, $\int_{\gamma} f(z)dz = 0 \Rightarrow \int_{\gamma_1} f = \int_{\gamma_2} f$.

3. (*i*) $\int_{\gamma} \frac{dz}{z-2} = 0$ because $f(z) = \frac{1}{z-2}$ is analytic in D(0, 1) (*ii*) $2\pi i\, f''(2) = 0$ when $f(z) = 1$ then $\int_{\gamma(i,3)} \frac{1}{(z-2)^3} dz = 0$

(*iii*) $\frac{\sin z}{z}$ is entire and $(i, 2)$ is closed.

(*iv*) $\int_{\gamma(0,1)} z|z|^4\, dz = 0$ because $z|z|^4$ is analytic in D(0, 1)

(*v*) $\int_{\gamma(1,1)} \frac{1}{1+e^z} dz = e^z = -1 \Rightarrow z = \pi i.$

❑❑❑

6

Cauchy's Integral Formulas and their Consequences

If f is analytic in a region R and z_0 is any point R then $\frac{f(z)}{z-z_0}$ is not defined at z_0 and hence not analytic in R. Then, we cannot talk about the integral of $\frac{f(z)}{z-z_0}$ around a simple closed contour γ. But Cauchy's integral formula says that we can talk about the integral and is equal to $2\pi i f(z_0)$. In this chapter we shall also discuss some of the consequences of Cauchy's integral formula such as Liouville's theorem, Fundamental theorem of algebra, Taylor's theorem etc.

6.1 CAUCHY'S INTEGRAL FORMULA

We begin with the principle of deformation of contours which states that if γ_1 is a continuous deformation of a contour γ and if the region between c and c_1 contains only points where f is analytic then the value of the integral of f does not change.

Theorem 6.1: Deformation Theorem

Suppose γ is a contour such that $\overline{D}\ (a; r) \subseteq I(\gamma)$ and f is analytic inside and on γ except at a. Then,

$$\int_{\gamma} f = \int_{\gamma(a;r)} f$$

where $\gamma(a; r)$ is a circle with radius r and centre a.

Proof

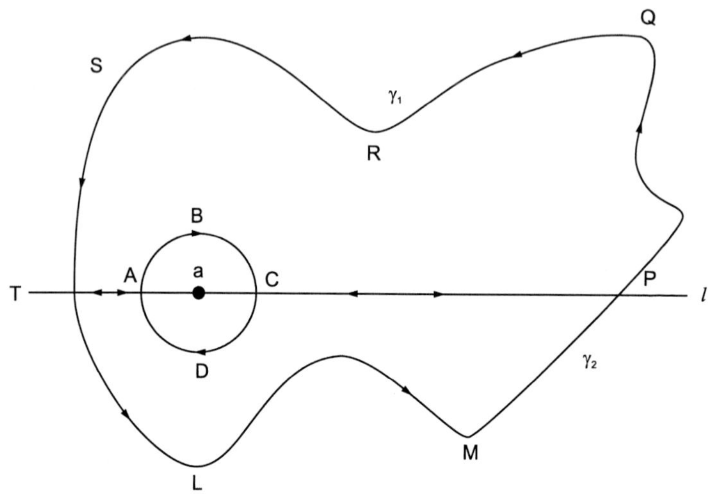

Fig. 6.1

Take a line l which passes through a but not from corner points of γ^*. Let A and C be the points where the line meets the circle $\gamma(a; r)$. Let γ_1 and γ_2 be the closed contour as shown in Fig. 6.1. Then by Theorem 5.15, we get

$$\int_{\gamma_1} f = \int_{\gamma_2} f = 0.$$

But, $$\int_{\gamma_1} f = \int_{PQRST} f + \int_{TA} f + \int_{ABC} f + \int_{CP} f$$

and $$\int_{\gamma_2} f = \int_{PC} f + \int_{CDA} f + \int_{AT} f + \int_{TLMP} f$$

then, $$\int_{\gamma_1} f + \int_{\gamma_2} f = \int_{PQRST} f + \int_{TLMP} f - \int_{CBA} f - \int_{ADC} f$$

$\Rightarrow$ $$0 = \int_{\gamma} f - \int_{\gamma(a;r)} f$$

then, $$\int_{\gamma} f = \int_{\gamma(a;r)} f.$$

Example 6.1

Let γ be a contour shown in the Fig 6.2, then evaluate $\int_\gamma \frac{dz}{z-i}$.

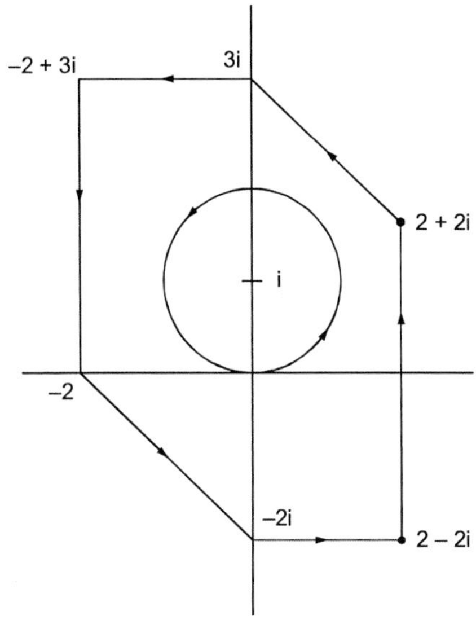

Fig 6.2

Solution

Let $f(z) = \dfrac{1}{z-i}$, then $f(z)$ is analytic in the complex plane except at $z = i$. Let $\gamma(i;\, 1)$ be a circle with radius 1 and centre at i, then by Theorem 6.1, we have

$$\int_\gamma \frac{dz}{z-i} = \int_{\gamma(i,1)} \frac{dz}{z-i}$$

Now $\gamma(t) = i + e^{it}$, $0 \le t \le 2\pi$, then $\gamma'(t) = ie^{it}$.

$$\int_{\gamma(i,1)} \frac{dz}{z-i} = \int_0^{2\pi} \frac{ie^{it}}{e^{it}}\, dt = 2\pi i$$

then, $$\int_\gamma \frac{dz}{z-i} = 2\pi i$$

Let γ be any simple closed curve and z_0 is any complex number in the interior of γ, then for any integer n, we get

$$\int_{\gamma} \frac{dz}{(z-z_0)^n} = \begin{cases} 2\pi i & \text{if } n = 1 \\ 0 & \text{if } n = -1 \end{cases}$$

Principle of deformation of contours can also be employed in proving the following Cauchy's Integral Formula.

Theorem 6.2: Cauchy's Integral Formula

Let f be analytic inside and on a positively oriented contour γ. Then, if a is in the interior of γ,

$$f(a) = \frac{1}{2\pi i}\int_{\gamma} \frac{f(z)}{z-a}\,dz \qquad ...(1)$$

Proof

There exists r such that $D(a; r) \subseteq I(\gamma)$, the interior of γ. For any $\varepsilon < r$, by deformation theorem

$$\int_{\gamma} \frac{f(z)}{z-a}\,dz = \int_{\gamma(a;\varepsilon)} \frac{f(z)}{z-a}\,dz$$

Consider

$$\left|\frac{1}{2\pi i}\int_{\gamma} \frac{f(z)}{z-a}dz - f(a)\right| = \left|\frac{1}{2\pi i}\left(\int_{\gamma(a;\in)} \frac{f(z)}{z-a}dz - \int_{\gamma(a;\in)} \frac{f(a)}{z-a}dz\right)\right|$$

$$= \frac{1}{2\pi}\left|\int_{\gamma(a;\in)} \frac{f(z)-f(a)}{z-a}dz\right|$$

$$= \frac{1}{2\pi}\left|\int_0^{2\pi} \frac{f\left(a+\in e^{i\theta}\right)-f(a)}{\in e^{i\theta}} \times \in ie^{i\theta}\,d\theta\right|$$

$$\leq \frac{1}{2\pi} \sup_{\theta\in[0,2\pi]}\left|f\left(a+\in e^{i\theta}\right)-f(a)\right|$$

$$\times 2\pi \to 0 \text{ as} \in \to 0$$

Since f is continuous at a, therefore

$$f(a) = \frac{1}{2\pi i}\int_{\gamma} \frac{f(z)}{z-a}\,dz\,.$$

Cauchy's Integral formula (1) can be used to evaluate contour integrals. It's applications are given in the following examples.

Example 6.2

Evaluate $\int_{\gamma} \frac{z^2 - 4z + 4}{z+i}$ where γ is the circle $|z| = 2$.

Solution

Let $f(z) = z^2 - 4z + 4$ and $a = -i$ lies inside the circle $|z| = 2$. Also $f(z)$ is analytic at all points within and on the contour γ. Then by Cauchy's Integral formula

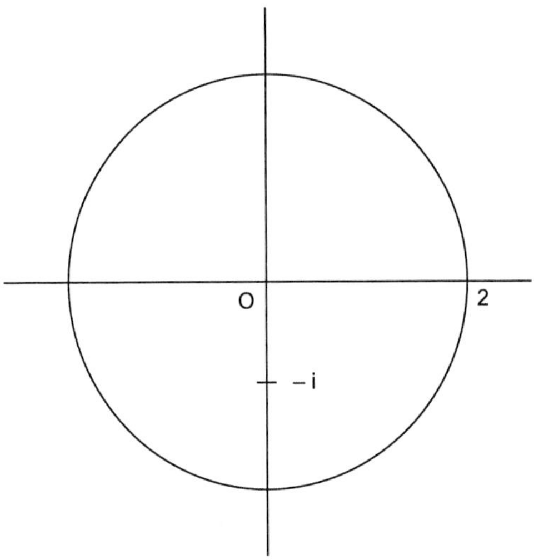

Fig. 6.3

$$\int_{\gamma} \frac{f(z)}{z+i} = 2\pi i\, f(-i)$$

$$= 2\pi i\,(3 + 4i)$$

$$= \pi\,(6i - 8).$$

Example 6.3

Let γ be a circle $|z - 2i| = 4$, evaluate $\int_\gamma \frac{z}{z^2+9} dz$.

Solution

We know $z^2 + 9 = (z + 3i)(z - 3i)$, then only $z = 3i$ lies inside γ (Fig 6.4).

Let $f(z) = \frac{z}{z+3i}$. The function $f(z)$ is analytic in γ. By Cauchy's Integral formula

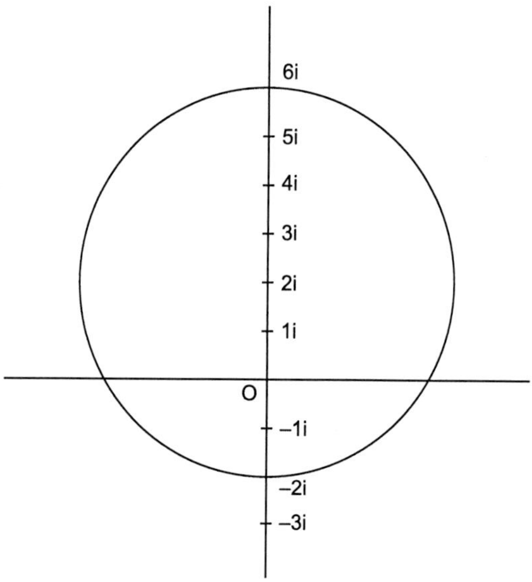

Fig. 6.4

$$\int_\gamma \frac{z}{z^2+9} dz = \int_\gamma \frac{f(z)}{z-3i}$$

$$= 2\pi i\, f(3i)$$

$$= 2\pi i \times \frac{1}{2}$$

$$= \pi i.$$

Example 6.4

Calculate $\int_\gamma \frac{\cos z}{z^3+z}\,dz$ where γ is the circle $|z| = 2$.

Solution

By the method of partial fractions

$$\begin{aligned}\frac{1}{z^3+z} &= \frac{1}{z(z-i)(z+i)} \\ &= \frac{1}{z} - \frac{1}{2(z+i)} - \frac{1}{2(z-i)}\end{aligned}$$

and so, $$\int_\gamma \frac{\cos z}{z^3+z}\,dz = \int_\gamma \frac{\cos z}{z}\,dz - \frac{1}{2}\int \frac{\cos z\,dz}{z+i} - \frac{1}{2}\int \frac{\cos z\,dz}{z-i}$$

Since θ, i and $-i$ lie inside γ, by Cauchy's Integral formula, we have

$$\begin{aligned}\int_\gamma \frac{\cos z}{z^3+z}\,dz &= 2\pi i\left(\cos 0 - \frac{1}{2}\cos(-i) - \frac{1}{2}\cos(i)\right) \\ &= 2\pi i\left(1 - \frac{1}{2}(\cos(-i) + \cos(i))\right) \\ &= 2\pi i\left(1 - \frac{1}{2}\cos(i) - \frac{1}{2}\cos(i)\right) \\ &= 2\pi i(1 - \cos i).\end{aligned}$$

The following Cauchy's formula for derivatives is used to evaluate contour integrals of the form $\int_\gamma \frac{f(z)}{p(z)}\,dz$ where γ is a positively oriented contour and $p(z)$ is a polynomial with repeated roots.

Theorem 6.3

Let f be analytic inside and on a positively oriented contour γ and a lie inside γ. Then $f^{(n)}(a)$ exists for all $n \geq 1$ and

$$f^{(n)}(a) = \frac{n!}{2\pi i}\int_\gamma \frac{f(z)}{(z-a)^{n+1}}\,dz \qquad \text{...(1)}$$

Proof

We shall prove the result by Mathematical induction. For $n = 0$, (1) is Cauchy's Integral formula. Suppose (1) holds for $n = k$. Consider $\gamma = \gamma(a; 2r)$ for some constant $r > 0$. Take $|h| < r$. Then (1) for $n = k$ is

$$f^{(k)}(a) = \frac{k!}{2\pi i}\int_\gamma \frac{f(z)}{(z-a)^{k+1}}dz$$

To prove
$$f^{k+1}(a) = \lim_{h\to 0}\frac{f^k(a+h)-f^k(a)}{h}$$
$$= \frac{(k+1)!}{2\pi i}\int_\gamma \frac{f(z)}{(z-a)^{k+1}}dz$$

Consider

$$f^{k+1}(a+h)-f^k(a) = \frac{k!}{2\pi i}\int_\gamma f(z)\left(\frac{1}{(z-a+h)^{k+2}}-\frac{1}{(z-a)^{k+1}}\right)dz$$
$$= \frac{(k+1)!}{2\pi i}\int_\gamma f(z)\left(\int_{(a,a+h)}\frac{1}{(z-\rho)^{k+2}}d\rho\right)dz$$

Now,

$$\left|\frac{f^{(k)}(a+h)-f^{(k)}(a)}{h}-\frac{(k+1)!}{2\pi i}\int_\gamma \frac{f(z)}{(z-a)^{k+z}}dz\right|$$
$$= \left|\frac{(k+1)!}{2\pi ih}\int_\gamma f(z)\left(\int_\gamma \frac{d\varsigma}{(z-\rho)^{k+2}}dz\right)-h\int_\gamma \frac{f(z)}{(z-a)^{k+1}}dz\right|$$
$$= \frac{(k+2)!}{2\pi|h|}\left|\int_\gamma f(z)\left(\left[\int_{[a,\rho]}\frac{1}{(z-M)^{k+3}}d\xi\right]d\rho\right)dz\right| \quad ...(2)$$

Since f is analytic and so continuous, it is bounded by M(say) on γ^*. For $\xi\in[a, \rho]$ $\rho\in[a, a+h]$ we have $|z-\xi| \geq r$ for all $z \in \gamma^*$. Also $|\rho - a| \leq |h|$ (Fig. 6.5). Hence from (2), we get

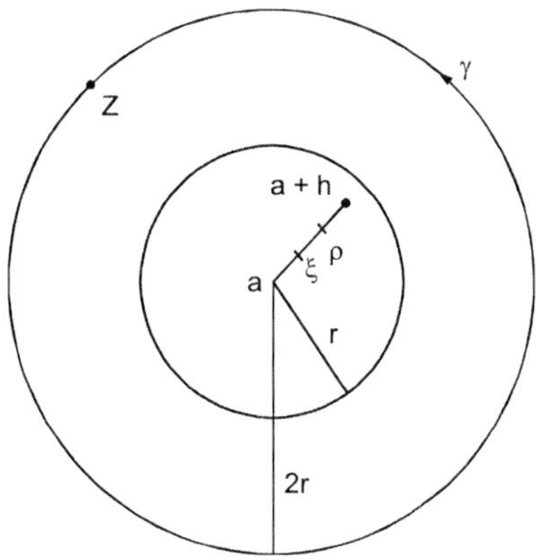

Fig. 6.5

$$\left|\frac{f^{(k)}(a+h)-f^{(k)}(a)}{h}-\frac{(k+1)!}{2\pi i}\int_{\gamma}\frac{f(z)}{(z-a)^{k+2}}dz\right|$$

$$\leq \frac{(k+2)!}{2\pi|h|}\times\frac{M|h|^2}{r^{k+3}}\times 4\pi r$$

$$= \frac{2(k+2)!M|h|}{r^{k+2}} \to 0 \text{ as } |h| \to 0.$$

Then, $$f^{(k+1)}(h) = \lim_{h\to 0}\frac{f^{(k)}(a+h)-f^{(k)}(a)}{h}$$

$$= \frac{(k+1)!}{2\pi i}\int_{\gamma}\frac{f(z)dz}{(z-a)^{k+2}}.$$

Example 6.5

Evaluate $\int_{\gamma}\frac{\sin z}{z^4}dz$ where γ is the circle $|z| = 2$.

Solution

Let $f(z) = \sin z$ and $a = 0$. Since a lies inside the circle $|z| = 2$ and f is analytic in and on γ, therefore by Cauchy's Integral formula

$$\int_{\gamma}\frac{\sin z}{z^4} = \frac{2\pi i}{3!}f^{(3)}(0)$$

$$\begin{aligned} f'(z) &= \cos z \\ f''(z) &= -\sin z \\ f'''(z) &= -\cos z \\ f'''(0) &= -1. \end{aligned}$$

Then, $$\int \frac{\sin z}{z^4} = \frac{-\pi i}{3}.$$

Example 6.1.6

If $\gamma = \gamma(0; 2)$ then evaluate $\int_\gamma \frac{e^{z^2}}{(z-1)^3} dz$.

Solution

Let $f(z) = e^{z^2}$. Being exponential $f(z)$ is entire and thus analytic within and on γ. The point $a = 1$ lies inside γ. Therefore, by Cauchy's Integral formula

$$\int_\gamma \frac{e^{z^2}}{(z-1)^3} = \frac{2\pi i}{2!} f^{(2)}(1)$$

Now, $$\begin{aligned} f'(z) &= 2ze^{z^2} \\ f''(z) &= 2\left\{2z^2 e^{z^2} + e^{z^2}\right\} \\ f''(1) &= 6e \end{aligned}$$

Hence, $$\int_\gamma \frac{e^{z^2}}{(z-1)^3} = 6\pi ie.$$

Example 6.7

Let $a, b \in \mathbf{C}$, with $|a| \neq 1,\ |b| \neq 1$. Evaluate $\int_{\gamma(0;1)} \frac{1}{(z-a)(z-b)} dz$.

Solution

Case (*i*) If $a, b \notin I(\gamma)$. Then,

$$\int_{\gamma(0;1)} \frac{1}{(z-a)(z-b)} = 0$$

($\because$ $\dfrac{1}{(z-a)(z-b)}$ is analytic and applying Theorem 5.15.)

Case (*ii*) If $a \notin I(\gamma)$, $b \in I(\gamma)$. Let $f(z) = \dfrac{1}{z-a}$. Then, f is analytic within and on γ. Then by Cauchy's Integral formula, we get

$$\int_{\gamma} \frac{1}{(z-a)(z-b)} = 2\pi i\, f(b) = \frac{2\pi i}{b-a}.$$

Case (*iii*) If $b \notin I(\gamma)$, $a \in I(\gamma)$ then taking $f(z) = \dfrac{1}{z-b}$, we get

$$\int_{\gamma} \frac{1}{(z-a)(z-b)} = \frac{2\pi i}{a-b}.$$

Case (*iv*) If $a, b \in I(\gamma)$, then by partial fraction, we get

$$\frac{1}{(z-a)(z-b)} = \frac{1}{a-b}\left[\frac{1}{z-a} - \frac{1}{z-b}\right]$$

By applying Cauchy's Integral formula, we get

$$\int_{\gamma} \frac{dz}{(z-a)(z-b)} = \frac{1}{a-b}[2\pi i - 2\pi i]$$

$$= 0.$$

Example 6.8

Using Cauchy's Integral formula for derivatives, evaluate $\displaystyle\int_{\gamma} \frac{z^3+3}{z(z-i)^2}dz$ where γ is a contour shown in Fig. 6.6.

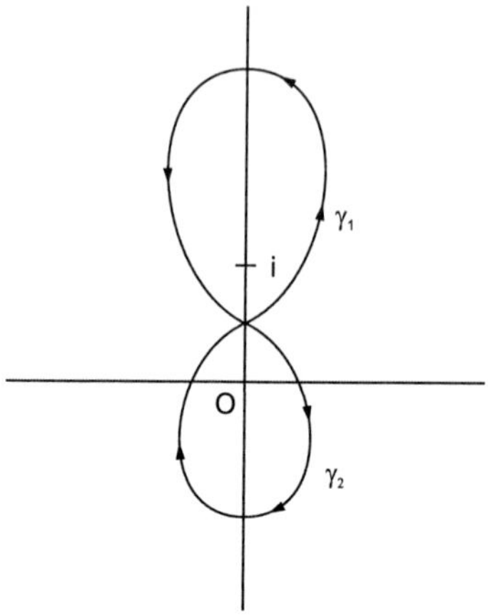

Fig. 6.6

Solution

The contour given in figure is not a simple closed contour, therefore we treat it as the union of two simple closed contours γ_1 and γ_2. But γ_2 is in the –ve direction. Hence, we write

$$\int_\gamma \frac{z^3+3}{z(z-i)^2}dz = \int_{\gamma_1} \frac{z^3+3}{z(z-i)^2}dz - \int_{\gamma_2} \frac{z^3+3}{z(z-i)^2}dz$$

$$= \int_{\gamma_1} \frac{\frac{z^3+3}{z}dz}{(z-i)^2} - \int_{\gamma_2} \frac{\frac{z^3+3}{(z-i)^2}dz}{z}$$

$$= I_1 - I_2.$$

To evaluate I_1, we consider $f(z) = \dfrac{z^3+3}{z}$ which is analytic in γ_1 and $a = i$ lies inside γ_1. By Cauchy's Integral formula

$$I_1 = \frac{2\pi i}{1!} f'(i)$$

But $$f'(z) = 2z - \frac{3}{z^2} \text{ and } f'(i) = 2i + 3. \text{ Then,}$$

$$I_1 = 2\pi i(2i+3) = -4\pi + 6\pi i$$

To evaluate I_2, we take $f(z) = \dfrac{z^3+3}{(z-i)^2}$. Then,

$$I_2 = 2\pi i f(0) = 2\pi i\,(-3) = -6\pi i$$

$$\text{Hence, } \int_{\gamma} \frac{z^3+3}{z(z-i)^2}dz = -4\pi + 12\pi i$$

Example 6.9

Evaluate $\displaystyle\int_{\gamma(0;1)} \frac{Rez}{z-\frac{1}{2}}dz$.

Solution

Rez is not analytic, therefore it cannot be integrated directly. $\gamma(0, 1) = e^{it}$, $t \in [0, 2\pi]$. Then, $z = e^{it}$ and $Rez = \cos t = \frac{1}{2}\left(e^{it} + e^{-it}\right) = \frac{z^2+1}{2z}$.

The integral becomes

$$\begin{aligned}
\int_{\gamma(0;1)} \frac{Rez}{z-\frac{1}{2}}dz &= \int_{\gamma(0;1)} \frac{z^2+1}{2z\left(z-\frac{1}{2}\right)} \\
&= \int_{\gamma(0;1)} \left(\frac{1}{2} - \frac{1}{z} + \frac{5}{2(2z-1)}\right)dz \\
&= 0 - 2\pi i + \frac{5}{2}\pi i \\
&= \frac{\pi i}{2}.
\end{aligned}$$

EXERCISE

1. Evaluate the following integrals along the indicated closed contour:

(*i*) $\displaystyle\int_{\gamma(0,5)} \frac{4}{z-3i}dz$ (*ii*) $\displaystyle\int_{\gamma(0,5)} \frac{z^2}{(z-3i)^2}dz$

(*iii*) $\displaystyle\int_{\gamma(0,1)} \frac{z^2}{z^2+1}dz$ (*iv*) $\displaystyle\int_{\gamma(0;1)} \frac{e^z}{z^3}dz$

(v) $\displaystyle\int_{\gamma(0;1)} \frac{1+e^z}{z}\,dz$

(vi) $\displaystyle\int_{\gamma} \frac{z}{z^2+9}\,dz$ where γ is the circle $|z-2i|=4$

(vii) $\displaystyle\int_{\gamma(0;1)} \frac{\cos 2z}{z^5}\,dz$ (viii) $\displaystyle\int_{\gamma\left(0;\frac{1}{2}\right)} \frac{z}{(z-1)(z-2)}\,dz$

(ix) $\displaystyle\int_{\gamma} \frac{1}{z^3(z-1)^2}\,dz$ where γ is the circle $|z-2|=5$

(x) $\displaystyle\int_{\gamma} \frac{dz}{z^2(z^2+1)}$ where γ is the circle $|z-i|=\frac{3}{2}$.

2. Evaluate $\displaystyle\int_{\gamma} \frac{3z+1}{z(z-2)^2}$ where γ is shown in the Fig. 6.7.

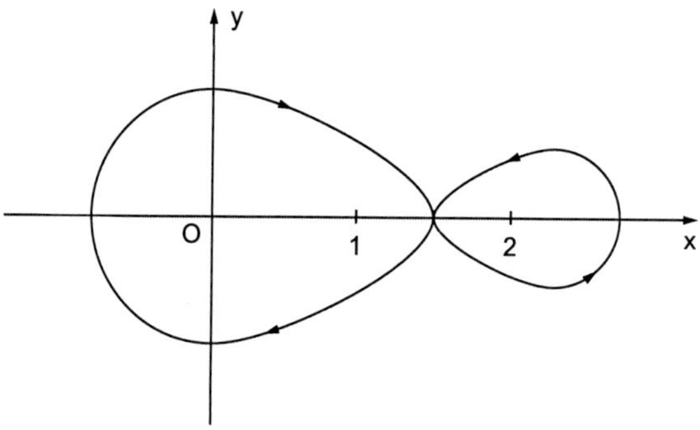

Fig. 6.7

3. Evaluate $\displaystyle\int_{\gamma(0;1)} \frac{e^{z^n}}{z}\,dz$, n is a positive integer. Hence, show that

$$\int_0^{2\pi} e^{\cos n\theta}\cos(\sin n\theta)\,d\theta = 2\pi$$

and

$$\int_0^{2\pi} e^{\cos n\theta}\sin(\sin n\theta)\,d\theta = 0.$$

ANSWERS

1. (*i*) $8\pi i$ (*ii*) -12π
   (*iii*) 0 (*iv*) $2\pi i$
   (*v*) $4\pi i$ (*vi*) $2\pi i$
   (*viii*) $-32\pi i$ (*viii*) 0
   (*ix*) 0 (*x*) πi.
2. 0
3. $2\pi i$.

6.2 CONSEQUENCES OF CAUCHY'S INTEGRAL FORMULA

This section deals with the immediate consequences of Cauchy's Integral formula such as Liouville's theorem, Fundamental theorem of algebra, Taylor's series etc.

We begin with Liouville's theorem which gives us severe limitation on the behaviour of analytic functions.

Theorem 6.4: Liouville's Theorem

If f is a bounded entire function, then f is constant.

Proof

Let $a, b \in \mathbf{C}$ $(a \neq b)$ and γ be a positively oriented circle centred at zero and radius $R > \max(|a|, |b|)$. Then, $|z-a| > |z| - |a| = R - |a|$ and $|z-b| > R - |b|$. By Cauchy's Integral formula, we get

$$f(b) - f(a) = \frac{1}{2\pi i}\int_\gamma \frac{f(z)}{z-b}\,dz - \frac{1}{2\pi i}\int \frac{f(z)}{z-a}\,dz$$

$$= \frac{1}{2\pi i}\int_\gamma \frac{f(z)(b-a)}{(z-a)(z-b)}.$$

Let M be the bound of f such that $|f(z)| < M$ for all z.

Therefore,

$$|f(b) - f(a)| < \frac{|a-b|\,M}{2\pi(R-|a|)(R-|b|)} \times 2\pi R$$

$$= \frac{M\,|a-b|\,R}{(R-|a|)(R-|b|)}$$

$$\to 0 \text{ as } R \to \infty.$$

Hence, $|f(b) - f(a)| < \in$ for all $\in > 0$. So $f(a) = f(b)$

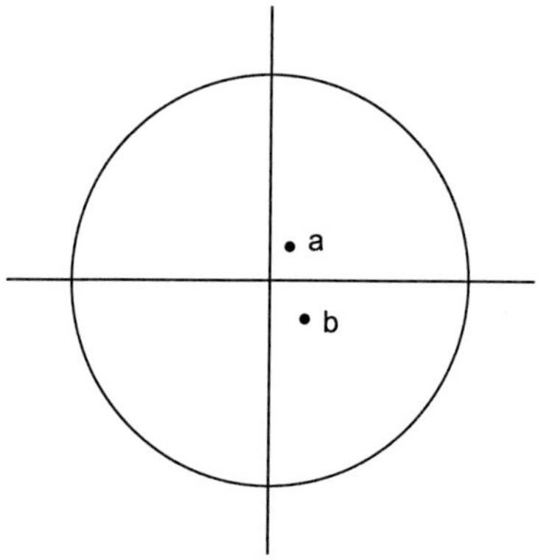

Fig. 6.8

Theorem 6.5: The Fundamental Theorem of Algebra

Let p be a polynomial function of degree at least 1. Then, $p(z) = 0$ for at least one z.

Proof

Let $p(z) = a_n z^n + a_{n-1} z^{n-1} + \ldots\ldots + a_1 z + a_0$ where $n > 1$ and $a_n \neq 0$. Since $p(z) = 0 \Leftrightarrow \frac{1}{a_n} p(z) = 0$. Suppose $p(z) \neq 0$ for all z. Let

$f(z) = \frac{1}{p(z)}$, then f is entire.

We shall show that $\lim\limits_{z \to \infty} f(z) = 0$. Since

$$\frac{p(z)}{z^n} = 1 + \frac{a_{n-1}}{z} + \ldots\ldots\ldots\ldots + \frac{a_1}{z^{n-1}} + \frac{a_0}{z^n}$$

$$\lim_{z\to 0}\frac{p(z)}{z^n} = 1 \text{ and so } \lim_{z\to\infty}\frac{z^n}{p(z)} = 1. \text{ Thus,}$$

$$\lim_{z\to\infty} f(z) = \lim_{z\to\infty}\frac{z^n}{p(z)} \times \lim_{z\to\infty}\frac{1}{z^n} = 1.0 = 0.$$

Thus, there is $r > 0$ such that $|f(z)| < 1$ if $|z| > r$. Since f is continuous on $D = \{z: |z| < r\}$ and thus bounded on D by some K. By Liouville's theorem, f is constant and so p is constant. This is a contradiction since p is not constant.

Our next result is an inequality desired from the Cauchy's Integral formula for derivatives and is known as Cauchy's Estimation Theorem.

Theorem 6.6: Cauchy's Estimation Theorem

Let D be the disc $|z - a| < R$. Suppose f is analytic on D such that $|f(z)| < M$, $z \in D$. Then,

$$|f^{(n)}(a)| < \frac{n!M}{R^n}.$$

Proof

Let $r < R$ and γ be the circle $\{z : |z - a| = r\}$. By Cauchy's Integral formula for derivatives, we have

$$f^{(n)}(a) = \frac{n!}{2\pi i}\int_\gamma \frac{f(z)}{(z-a)^{n+1}}dz.$$

$$\text{Hence,} \quad |f^{(n)}(a)| < \frac{n!}{2\pi r^{n+1}}\int_\gamma |f(z)||dz|$$

$$< \frac{n!}{2\pi r^{n+1}} M \cdot 2\pi r$$

$$= \frac{Mn!}{r^n}$$

Since, this holds for all $r < R$. Now taking limit as $r \to R$, we get

$$|f^{(n)}(a)| < \lim_{r\to R}\frac{Mn!}{r^n} = \frac{Mn!}{R^n}.$$

Example 6.10

If f is an centre function and k is a positive real number such that $|f(z)| > k$ for all z. Show that f is constant.

Solution

Let $g(z) = \dfrac{1}{f(z)}$. Since $f(z) \neq 0$, g is entire. Also $|g(z)| < \dfrac{1}{k}$. Thus, g is constant by Liouville's theorem. Hence f is constant.

We have seen that power series can be used to define analytic functions. Now, we show that an analytic function can be represented by power series, called Taylor's series of the function.

Theorem 6.7: Taylor Expansion of an Entire Function

If f is entire, then it has a power series representation. In fact, $f^{(k)}(0)$ exists for all $k > 1$, and

$$f(z) = \sum_{k=0}^{\infty} \frac{f^{(k)}(0)}{k!} z^k .$$

Proof

Suppose $a \neq 0$, $R = |a| + 1$ and let γ be the circle $\{w: |w| = R\}$. By Cauchy's Integral formula.

$$f(z) = \frac{1}{2\pi i} \int_{\gamma} \frac{f(w)}{w - z} dw \text{ for all } |z| < |a|$$

Now,
$$\frac{1}{w-z} = \frac{1}{w\left(1 - \dfrac{z}{w}\right)} = \frac{1}{w}\left(1 - \frac{z}{w}\right)^{-1}$$

$$= \frac{1}{w}\left(1 + \frac{z}{w} + \frac{z^2}{w^2} + \ldots\ldots\right)$$

$$= \frac{1}{w} + \frac{z}{w^2} + \frac{z^2}{w^3} + \ldots\ldots$$

Then, $$f(z) = \frac{1}{2\pi i}\int_{\gamma} f(w)\left[\frac{1}{w}+\frac{z}{w^2}+\frac{z^3}{w^3}+\ldots\ldots\right]dw$$

$$= \frac{1}{2\pi i}\int_{\gamma}\frac{f(w)}{w}dw+\left(\frac{1}{2\pi i}\int_{\gamma}\frac{f(w)}{w^2}dw\right)z$$

$$+\left(\frac{1}{2\pi i}\int_{\gamma}\frac{f(w)}{w^3}dw\right)z^2+\ldots\ldots$$

$$= \sum_{k=0}^{\infty} c_k z^k \qquad \ldots(1)$$

where $$c_k = \frac{1}{2\pi i}\int_{\gamma}\frac{f(w)}{w^{k+1}}dw. \qquad \ldots(2)$$

By Cauchy's Integral formula for higher derivatives, we have for $k > 1$

$$f^{(k)}(0) = \frac{n!}{2\pi i}\int_{\gamma}\frac{f(w)}{w^{k+1}}dw \qquad \ldots(3)$$

From (1) and (2), we have

$$c_k = \frac{f^{(k)}(0)}{n!}$$

Now, we shall show that the expression $f(z) = \sum_{k=0}^{\infty} c_k z^k$ is independent of the choice of γ. If we take $\gamma_1 = \{w : |w| = R_1 > R\}$. Then,

$$\int_{\gamma}\frac{f(w)}{w^{k+1}}dw = \int_{\gamma_1}\frac{f(w)}{w^{k+1}}dw$$

by deformation Theorem 6.1:

Note: The expansion (1) of $f(z)$ is called Taylor's series expansion and the coefficients $c'_k s$ given in (2) are called Taylor's coefficients.

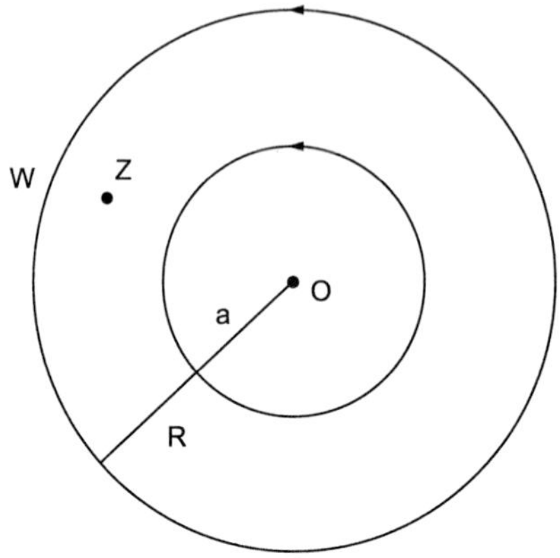

Fig. 6.9

We know if $f(z) = \sum_{k=0}^{\infty} c_k z^k$ then $f'(z) = \sum_{k=1}^{\infty} k\, c_k z^{k-1}$ have same radius of convergence. Thus, by induction we can see that $f^{(k)}(z)$ $(k > 1)$ has same radius of convergence as $f(z) = \sum_{k=0}^{\infty} c_k z^k$. By Taylor's theorem we can express an entire function as a power series thus we conclude the following:

Theorem. 6.8

An entire function is infinitely differentiable

Corollary 6.9

If f is entire and if a is any complex number then

$$f(z) = f(a) + f'(a)(z-a) + \frac{f''(a)}{2!}(z-a)^2 + \ldots\ldots$$

for all z.

Proof

Consider an entire function

$$g(\xi) = f(\xi + a)$$

By Taylor's expansion

$$g(\xi) = g(0) + g'(0)\xi + \frac{g''(0)\xi^2}{2!} + \ldots\ldots$$

so that

$$f(\xi + a) = f(a) + f'(a)\xi + \frac{f''(0)\xi^2}{2!} + \ldots\ldots$$

put $z = \xi + a$, then

$$f(z) = f(a) + f'(a)(z - a) + \frac{f''(a)(z-a)^2}{2!} + \ldots\ldots$$

Example 6.11

Expand $f(z) = \dfrac{1}{z+1}$ in a Taylor's series with centre $a = -i$.

Solution

We have $$\frac{1}{z+1} = \frac{1}{z+1+i-i} = \frac{1}{(1-i)+(z+i)}$$

$$= \frac{1}{1-i}\frac{1}{1+\left(\dfrac{z+i}{1-i}\right)} = \frac{1}{1-i}\left[1+\left(\frac{z+i}{1-i}\right)\right]^{-1}$$

$$= \frac{1}{1-i}\left[1-\left(\frac{z+i}{1-i}\right)+\left(\frac{z+i}{1-i}\right)^2 + \ldots\ldots\right]$$

$$= \sum_{n=1}^{\infty}\frac{(z+i)^n}{(1-i)^{n+1}}.$$

The following theorem is an extension of Liouville's theorem which is useful in knowing the structure of an entire function.

Theorem 6.10: The Extended Liouville's Theorem

If f is entire and if for some integer $k > 0$, there exist positive constants A and B such that

$$|f(z)| < A + B\,|z|^k$$

then f is a polynomial of degree at most k.

Proof

By Taylor's theorem, f has a power series expansion

$$f(z) = \sum_{n=0}^{\infty} c_n z^n \quad \text{for all } z \in D = \{z: |z| < R\}$$

where $$c_n = \frac{1}{2\pi i} \int_{\gamma(0;R)} \frac{f(z)}{z^{n+1}} dz$$

then, $$|c_n| < \frac{1}{2\pi R^{n+1}} \sup\{|f(z)| : |z| = R\} \times 2\pi R$$

$$< \frac{1}{R^n}\left(A + B R^K\right)$$

$$= \frac{A}{R^n} + \frac{B}{R^{n-k}} \to 0 \text{ as } R \to \infty \text{ if } n > k$$

Then, $|c_n| = 0 \quad \forall \quad n > k$, and

$f(z) = c_0 + c_1 z + \ldots\ldots + c_k z^k$, a polynomial of degree k.

Example 6.12

Suppose f is entire and $|f(z)| < A + B\,|z|^{3/2}$. Show that f is a linear polynomial.

Solution

Since f being entire has power series expansion as

$$f(z) = \sum_{n=0}^{\infty} c_n z^n \quad \text{for all } z \in D = \{z : |z| < R\}$$

where $$c_n = \frac{1}{2\pi i} \int_{\gamma(0;R)} \frac{f(z)}{z^{n+1}} dz$$

therefore, $$|c_n| < \frac{1}{2\pi R^{n+1}} \int_{\gamma(0;R)} |f(z)|\, dz$$

$$< \frac{1}{2\pi R^{n+1}} \times \left(A + B R^{3/2}\right) \times 2\pi R$$

$$= \frac{A}{R^n} + \frac{B}{R^{n-3/2}} \to 0 \text{ as } R \to \infty$$

$$\text{if } n > \frac{3}{2} \text{ or } n \geq 2.$$

Thus, $f(z) = C_0 + C_1 z$, a linear polynomial.

Example 6.13

Suppose f is entire and $|f'(z)| < |z|$ for all z. Show that $f(z) = a + bz^2$ with $|b| < \frac{1}{2}$.

Solution

Since $|f'(z)| < |z|$ for all z, therefore $f'(0) = 0$

By Liouville's theorem, $f'(z)$ is a linear function. So that

$$f(z) = f(0) + f'(0) + \frac{f''(0)}{2!} z^2$$
$$= a + b\,z^2$$

Now,
$$f''(0) = \frac{1}{2\pi i} \int_{\gamma(0;1)} \frac{f(w)}{w^2} dw$$

$$|f''(0)| < \frac{1}{2\pi} \times 2\pi = 1$$

Therefore,
$$|b| = \frac{|f''(0)|}{2} \leq \frac{1}{2}.$$

The following are the applications of the Fundamental theorem of algebra.

Example 6.14

A real polynomial is a polynomial whose coefficients are all real. Prove that a real polynomial of odd degree must have a real zero.

Solution

By Fundamental Theorem of Algebra, a polynomial of odd degree must have odd number of zeroes. Also from elementary algebra we know that complex zeroes occur in pairs, therefore a polynomial of odd degree must have a real root.

Example 6.15

Show that α is a zero of multiplicity k if and only if

$$P(\alpha) = P'(\alpha)....... = P^{(k-1)}(\alpha) = 0,\ P^{(k)}(\alpha) \neq 0.$$

Solution

Let α be a zero of $P(z)$ of multiplicity k, then

$$P(z) = (z-\alpha)^k Q(z),\ Q(\alpha) \neq 0$$

$$\Rightarrow \quad P'(z) = k(z-\alpha)^{k-1}Q(z) + (z-\alpha)^k Q'(z)$$

$$\Rightarrow \quad P''(z) = k(k-1)(z-\alpha)^{k-2} Q(z) + 2k(z-\alpha)^{k-1} \vdots\ Q'(z) + (z-\alpha)^k Q''(z)$$

$$P^k(z) = k!\ Q(z) + k(k-1)!\ (z-\alpha)\ Q'(z) \ldots\ldots + Q^k(z)\ (z-\alpha)^k$$

therefore, $P(\alpha) = O = P'(\alpha) = P'(\alpha) \ldots\ldots. P^{k-1(\alpha)}$

$$P^k(\alpha) = k!\ Q(\alpha) \neq 0$$

Conversely, let $P(\alpha) = 0 = P'(\alpha) \ldots\ldots\ldots = P^{k-1}(\alpha),\ P^k(\alpha) \neq 0$. Since, $P(z)$ being polynomial is an entire function and thus can be written as

$$P(z) = c_0 + c_1(z-\alpha) + c_2(z-\alpha)^2 + \ldots.. c_{k-1} (z-\alpha)^{k-1} + c_k (z-\alpha)^k + \ldots\ldots..$$

Since, $P(\alpha) = 0 = P'(\alpha) \ldots\ldots.. = P^{k-1}(\alpha) = 0$, where $c_n = \dfrac{p^n(\alpha)}{k!}$

therefore, $c_n = 0\ \forall\ n < k$ and $c_k \neq 0$

Thus,

$$P(z) = c_k(z-\alpha)^k + c_{k+1}(z-\alpha)^{k+1} \ldots\ldots\ldots$$

$$= (z-\alpha)^k \{c_k + c_{k+1}(z-\alpha)^{k+1} \ldots\ldots\}$$

$$= (z-\alpha)^k Q(z)$$

where $Q(z) = c_k + c_{k+1}(z-\alpha)^{k+1} \ldots\ldots.$ and $Q(\alpha) = c_k \neq 0$. Hence, $p(z)$ is a polynomial with α as a zero of multiplicity k.

Comparison with Real Analysis

(1) The Liouville's theorem does not hold in real analysis because there are infinitely differentiable bounded real function which are vary far from being constant. For example, e^{-x^2} and arc tan x are bounded and everywhere differentiable but are not constant.

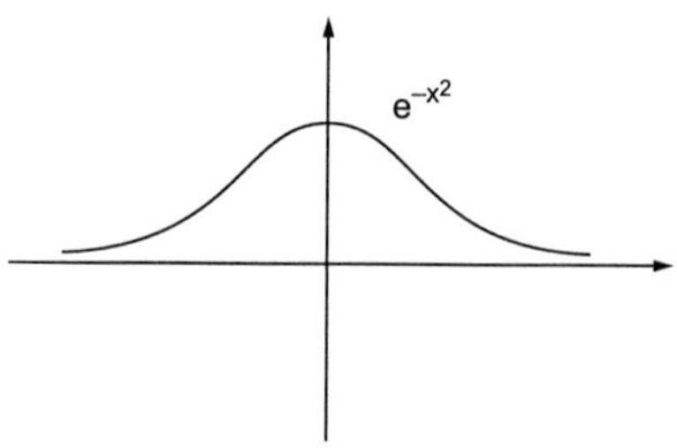

Fig. 6.10 (*i*)

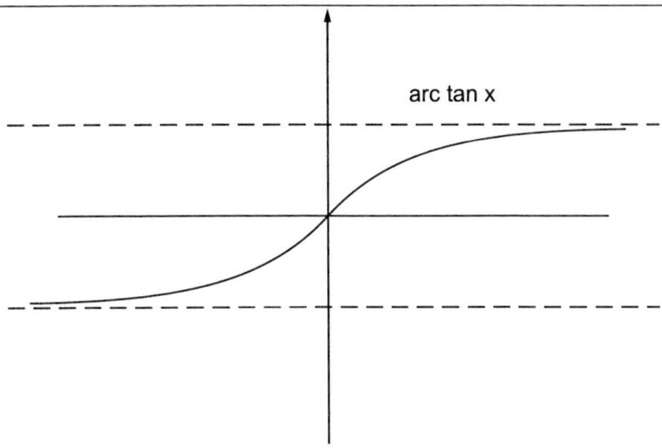

Fig. 6.10 (*ii*)

(2) We know $|\sin x| < 1$ for all real x and $y = \sin x$ is infinitely differentiable but it is not a constant function. But in case of complex analysis $|\sin z|$ is not bounded, therefore complex trigonometric functions are non-constant functions, using Liouville's theorem.

(3) Given any analytic complex function f and a point z in its domain, we can final a Taylor series which converges to $f(z)$, but given a real function which is infinitely differentiable although we can calculate a Taylor series, there is no guarantee that the series converges. For example, $f(x) = \dfrac{1}{1+x^2}$, the Taylor polynomial of f does not converge if $|x| > 1$.

(4) We know that an analytic function f is infinitely differentiable and it can be expanded in a power series with a non-zero radius R of convergence. In real analysis, a function f can be infinitely differentiable, but it may be impossible to represent it by a power series. For example,

$$f(x) = \begin{cases} e^{-1/x^2} & x \neq 0 \\ 0 & x = 0 \end{cases}$$

is infinitely differentiable, but cannot be expanded in power series.

EXERCISE

1. Let f be an entire function such that f' is bounded show that f is linear.
2. Let f be analytic in a region R and suppose that $z \to e^{f(z)}$ is constant on R. Show that f is constant on R.
3. Let f be an entire function such that $Re f$ is bounded above. Show that f is constant.
4. Suppose that f is an entire function, α is a complex number and $k > 0$ is a real number such that $|f(z) - \alpha| > k$ for all z. Show that f is constant.
5. Why $z \to e^{i|z|}$ is not entire.
6. Write the Taylor series for f at a for each of the following function f. Also find the radius of convergence of each of the Taylor series.

   (*i*) $f(z) = \dfrac{1}{z}$; $a = 1$

   (*ii*) $f(z) = e^{1+z}$; $a = 2$

   (*iii*) $f(z) = \dfrac{1}{(1-z)^2}$; $a = 0$

   (*iv*) $f(z) = \dfrac{1}{(1-z)^2}$; $a = -1$

   (*v*) $f(z) = \dfrac{1}{1+z}$; $a = 1$

   (*vi*) $f(z) = z^2$, $a = 2$

   (*viii*) $f(z) = \cot z$, $a = \pi i$.

ANSWERS

1. f' is entire and bounded. By Liousille's theorem f' is constant. Thus $f'(z) = az + b$.
2. Suppose $e^{f(z)} = k$. Let $z_0 \in R$, $\alpha = f(z_0)$. Then $e^{\alpha} = k$. $\alpha, \beta \in \mathbf{C}$ $(\alpha \neq \beta)$ such that $|\alpha - \beta| \geq 2\alpha$. By connectedness $f(z) = \alpha$ for all $z \in R$.

3. Let $g(z) = e^{f(z)}$, then g is entire. Suppose $Re f(z) \le k \; \forall \; z$. Then

$|g(z)| = |e^{\operatorname{Re} f(z)}||e^{i \operatorname{Im} f(z)}| = e^{\operatorname{Re} f(z)} \le e^k$.

Thus g is bounded and entire and hence constant f is also constant.

4. Let $g(z) = f(z) - \alpha$, $h(z) = \dfrac{1}{g(z)}$. Also $|h(z)| \le \dfrac{1}{k}$. Thus, f is constant.

5. $|e^{i(z)}| = 1$ and $z \to e^{i|z|}$ is not constant. It cannot be entire.

6. (*i*) $\sum_{n=0}^{\infty} (-1)^n (z-1)^n, R = 1$

(*ii*) $e^3 \sum_{n=0}^{\infty} \dfrac{(z-2)^n}{n!}, R = \infty$

(*iii*) $\sum_{n=0}^{\infty} (n+1)\, z^n, R = 1$

(*iv*) $\sum_{n=0}^{\infty} \dfrac{n+1}{2^{n+2}} (z+1)^n, R = 2$

(*v*) $\sum_{n=0}^{\infty} \dfrac{(-1)^n (z-1)^n}{2^{n+1}}, R = 2$

(*vi*) $4 + 4\,(z-2) + (z-2)^2, R = \dfrac{1}{4}$

(*viii*) $\cot\,(z - i\pi) = \dfrac{1}{(z-i\pi)} - \dfrac{(z-i\pi)}{3} + 0((z-i\pi)^3)$

❑❑❑

7

Analytic Functions in a Disc

In this chapter, we focus our attention to the relationship between power series and analytic functions on a disc.

In Theorem 3.9 we proved that every power series represents an analytic function inside the circle of convergence. In this chapter, we want to prove the converse of this theorem, *i.e.*, an analytic function in a disc can be represented there by a power series.

7.1 POWER SERIES REPRESENTATION OF AN ANALYTIC FUNCTION IN A DISC

Theorem 7.1

If f is analytic in a disc $D(z_0, r)$ and $a \in D(z_0, r)$ then there exist functions F and G analytic in D and

$$F'(z) = f(z), \;\; G'(z) = \frac{f(z) - f(a)}{z - a}$$

Proof

Define

$$F(z) = \int_{z_0}^{z} f(\varsigma)\,d\varsigma \;\; \text{and} \;\; G(z) = \int_{z_0}^{z} \frac{f(\varsigma) - f(a)}{\varsigma - a}\,d\varsigma$$

where the path of integration is from z_0 to z firstly horizontally and then along vertical line segment. For any $z \in D(z_0, r)$ and h small enough, $z + h \in D(z_0, r)$. Then,

$$\frac{F(z+h)-F(z)}{h} - f(z) = \frac{1}{h}\int_{[z,\, z+h]} f(\varsigma)\,d\varsigma - \frac{f(z)}{h}\int_{[z,\, z+h]} d\varsigma$$

$$= \frac{1}{h}\int_{z}^{z+h}\left[f(\varsigma)-f(z)\right]d\varsigma$$

Since f is analytic in $D(z_0, r)$ therefore for $\in > 0$ there exists $\delta > 0$ such that $\left|f(\varsigma) - f(z)\right| < \in$, $0 < |\zeta - z| < \delta$. Thus, if $0 < |h| < \delta$

$$\left|\frac{F(z+h)-F(z)}{h} - f(z)\right| < \frac{1}{|h|} \in |h| = \in$$

Thus, $f(z)$ is differentiable at $z \in D(z_0, r)$ and $F'(z) = f(z)$ similarly we can show that $G'(z) = \dfrac{f(z)-f(a)}{z-a}$.

Theorem 7.2

If f is analytic in $D(z_0, r)$ and $a \in D(z_0, r)$ and γ is any closed curve contained in $D(z_0, r)$ then

$$\int_{\gamma} f(z)\,dz = \int_{\gamma} \frac{f(z)-f(a)}{z-a}\,dz = 0$$

Proof

From Theorem 7.1, there exists an analytic function G in $D(z_0, r)$ such that

$$G'(z) = \frac{f(z)-f(a)}{z-a}$$

By fundamental theorem of calculus for closed curves

$$\int_{\gamma} \frac{f(z)-f(a)}{z-a}\,dz = \int_{\gamma} G'(z)\,dz = 0$$

Similarly there is an analytic function F in $D(z_0, r)$ such that $F'(z) = f(z)$, then

$$\int_{\gamma} f(z)\,dz = \int_{\gamma} F'(z)\,dz = 0.$$

Theorem 7.3: Cauchy's Integral Formula

Suppose f is analytic in a disc $D(z_0, r)$, $0 < \rho < r$ and $|a - z_0| < \rho$, then

$$f(a) = \frac{1}{2\pi i}\int_\gamma \frac{f(z)}{z-a}dz$$

where $\gamma(z_0, \rho)$ is a circle $z_0 + \rho e^{i\theta}$, $0 < \theta < 2\pi$.

Proof

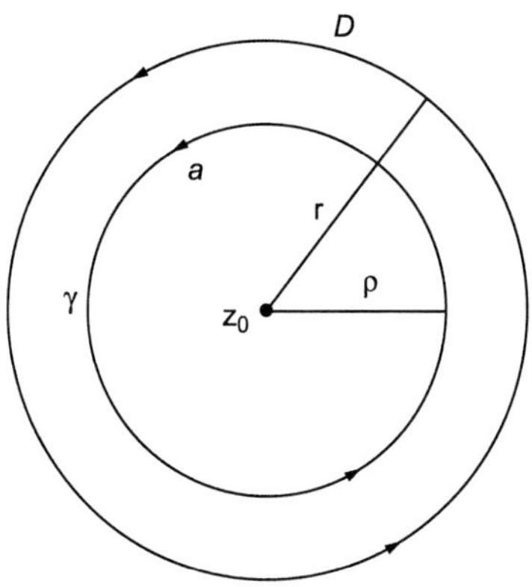

Fig. 7.1.1

From Theorem 7.2, we have

$$\int_\gamma \frac{f(z)-f(a)}{z-a}dz = 0$$

$$\Rightarrow \quad \int_\gamma \frac{f(z)}{z-a}dz = \int_\gamma \frac{f(a)}{z-a}dz$$

$$= f(a)\int_\gamma \frac{dz}{z-a} \qquad \text{...(1)}$$

Write

$$\frac{1}{z-a} = \frac{1}{(z-z_0)-(a-z_0)}$$

$$= \frac{1}{(z-z_0)\left[1-\left(\frac{a-z_0}{z-z_0}\right)\right]} \qquad \text{...(2)}$$

$$= \frac{1}{(z-z_0)(1-w)}$$

where
$$w = \frac{a - z_0}{z - z_0} = \frac{a - z_0}{\rho}$$

Also
$$|w| = \frac{|a - z_0|}{\rho} < 1 \text{ through } \gamma.$$

Also from (2)

$$\frac{1}{z-a} = \frac{1}{z-z_0}(1-w)^{-1}$$

$$= \frac{1}{z-z_0}\left[1+\left(\frac{a-z_0}{z-z_0}\right)+\left(\frac{a-z_0}{z-z_0}\right)^2+\ldots\ldots\right]$$

$$= \frac{1}{z-z_0}+\frac{a-z_0}{(z-z_0)^2}+\frac{(a-z_0)^2}{(z-z_0)^3}+\ldots\ldots$$

Then, $$\int_\gamma \frac{dz}{z-a} = \int_\gamma \frac{dz}{z-z_0}+\int_\gamma \frac{a-z_0}{(z-z_0)^2}+\int_\gamma \frac{(a-z_0)^2}{(z-z_0)^3}+\ldots\ldots$$

$$= 2\pi i + 0 + 0 \ldots\ldots$$

$$= 2\pi i$$

From (1), we get

$$\int_\gamma \frac{f(z)}{z-a}dz = 2\pi i\, f(a).$$

Theorem 7.4

Power series representation for functions analytic in a disc

If f is analytic in $D(z_0, r)$ there exist constants c_k such that

$$f(z) = \sum_{k=0}^{\infty} c_k (z-a)^k$$

for all $z \in D(z_0, r)$.

Proof

Choose $a \in D(z_0, r)$ and $\rho > 0$ such that $|a - z_0| < \rho < r$. (See Fig. 7.1). If $|z - z_0| < |a - z_0|$, then by Cauchy's Integral Formula

$$f(z) = \frac{1}{2\pi i}\int_{\gamma}\frac{f(w)}{w-z}dw$$

Consider

$$\frac{1}{w-z} = \frac{1}{(w-z_0)-(z-z_0)} = \frac{1}{w-z_0}\left[1-\frac{z-z_0}{w-z_0}\right]^{-1}$$

$$= \frac{1}{w-z_0}\left[1+\frac{z-z_0}{w-z_0}+\left(\frac{z-z_0}{w-z_0}\right)^2+........\right]$$

$$= \frac{1}{w-z_0}+\frac{z-z_0}{(w-z_0)^2}+\frac{(z-z_0)^2}{(w-z_0)^3}+........$$

$$= \sum_{n=0}^{\infty}\frac{(z-z_0)^n}{(w-z_0)^{n+1}}$$

Now $$\left|\frac{1}{w-z}\right| \le \sum_{n=0}^{\infty}\frac{1}{|w-z_0|}\left|\frac{z-z_0}{w-z_0}\right|^n$$

Since $\left|\dfrac{z-z_0}{w-z_0}\right| < 1$

$\therefore \sum\left(\dfrac{z-z_0}{w-z_0}\right)^n$ is uniformly convergent to $\dfrac{1}{w-z}$ throughout γ

$$f(z) = \frac{1}{2\pi i}\int_{\gamma}f(w)\left[\frac{1}{w-z_0}+\frac{z-z_0}{(w-z_0)^2}+\frac{(z-z_0)^2}{(w-z_0)^3}+........\right]dw$$

$$= c_0 + c_1(z-z_0) + c_2(z-z_0)^2 \qquad ...(1)$$

where $$c_k = \int_{\gamma}\frac{f(w)}{(w-z_0)^{n+1}}dw$$

and these coefficients are independent of the choice of γ. Also from (1) f is infinitely differentiable at z_0 and

$$c_k = \frac{f^{(k)}(z_0)}{\eta!}$$ for each ρ, $0 < \rho < r$ and for all k.

Hence $$f(z) = \sum_{k=0}^{\infty} c_k (z-a)^k \text{ for all } z \in D(a; r) \text{ with}$$

$$c_k = \frac{f^{(k)}(a)}{k!} = \frac{1}{2\pi i}\int_{\gamma} \frac{f(z)}{(z-z_0)^{k+1}}dz$$

Example 7.1

Find the power series representation of $f(z) = \dfrac{1}{z-1}$ in the disc $D(2; 1)$.

Solution

Since $\dfrac{1}{z-1}$ is analytic in $D(2; 1)$. Therefore,

$$\frac{1}{z-1} = \frac{1}{1+(z-2)} = 1-(z-2)+(z-2)^2-(z-2)^3+\ldots\ldots\ldots$$

which convergence in $|z-2| < 1$. This series diverges throughout $|z-2| > 1$ despite the fact that $f(z) = \dfrac{1}{z-1}$ is analytic everywhere except at the single point $z = 1$.

Example 7.2

Find a power series for $\dfrac{1}{z}$ around $z = 1 + i$.

Solution

We write $$\frac{1}{z} = \frac{1}{(1+i)+z-(1+i)}$$

$$= \frac{1}{(1+i)\left(1+\dfrac{z-(1+i)}{1+i}\right)}$$

$$= \frac{1}{1+i}\left[1+\left(\frac{z-(1+i)}{1+i}\right)\right]^{-1}$$

$$= \frac{1}{1+i}\left[1-\frac{z-(1+i)}{1+i}+\frac{(z-(1+i))^2}{1+i}.........\right]$$

$$= \sum_{k=0}^{\infty}\frac{(-1)^k(z-(1+i))^k}{(1+i)^{k+1}}.$$

Example 7.3

Using the identity $\frac{1}{1-z} = 1 + z + z^2 + ...$ for $|z| < 1$, find closed forms of the sums $\sum nz^n$ and $\sum n^2 z^n$.

Solution

$$\text{Let } f(z) = \frac{1}{1-z} = 1 + z + z^2 + ... = \sum_{n=0}^{\infty} z^n$$

$$\text{Now } \sum nz^{n-1} = \frac{d}{dz}\left(\sum_{n=0}^{\infty} z^n\right) = \frac{d}{dz}\left(\frac{1}{1-z}\right) = \frac{1}{(1-z)^2}$$

$$\text{Also } \sum_{n=1}^{\infty} nz^n = \frac{z}{(1-z)^2} \text{ and}$$

$$\sum_{n=1}^{\infty} n^2 z^{n-1} = \frac{d}{dz}\left(\sum_{n=1}^{\infty} nz^n\right)$$

$$= \frac{d}{dz}\left(\frac{z}{1-z}\right)^2 = \frac{1+z}{(1-z)^3} \text{ and therefore } \sum_{n=1}^{\infty} n^2 z^n = \frac{z(1+z)}{(1-z)^3}.$$

Example 7.4

Find a power series representation for $\frac{1}{z^2}$ near $z = 3$. Also find its radius of convergence.

Solution

Let $$\frac{1}{z^2} = \left[\frac{1}{3+(z-3)}\right]^2 = \frac{1}{9}\left(1+\frac{(z-3)}{3}\right)^{-2}$$

$$= \frac{1}{9}\left[1-\left(\frac{z-3}{3}\right)+\left(\frac{z-3}{3}\right)^2+\dots\dots\right]^2$$

$$= \frac{1}{9}\left[1-\frac{2(z-3)}{3}+\frac{3(z-3)^2}{9}-4\frac{(z-3)^3}{27}+\dots\dots\dots\right]$$

$$= \sum_{k=0}^{\infty}\frac{(-1)^k}{9}\frac{(k+1)}{3^k}(z-3)^k$$

It's radius of convergence is

$$R = \frac{1}{\limsup\limits_{k\to\infty}|c_k|^{1/k}} = \lim_{k\to\infty}\left(\frac{9\times 3^k}{k+1}\right)^{1/k} = 3$$

Thus, $\frac{1}{z^2}$ is analytic in $\{z : |z-3| < 3\}$.

Theorem 7.5

Suppose f is analytic in a disc $D = D(z_0, r)$. Let γ be the boundary of the closed rectangle R contained in D and the point $a \in D$.

Then,

$$\int_{\gamma} f(z)\,dz = \int_{\gamma}\frac{f(z)-f(a)}{z-a}\,dz = 0$$

Proof

Define a function $g(z)$ as

$$g(z) = \begin{cases}\dfrac{f(z)-f(a)}{z-a} & z \neq a \\ f'(a) & z = a\end{cases}$$

To show g is analytic in $D(z_0, r)$. By power series representations of $f(z)$, we get

$$f(z) = f(z_0) + f'(z_0)(z - z_0) + \frac{f''(z_0)}{2!}(z - z_0)^2 + \ldots\ldots\ldots$$

Then, $$g(z) = \frac{f(z) - f(z_0)}{z - z_0} = f'(z_0) + \frac{f''(z_0)}{2!}(z - z_0) + \ldots\ldots$$

which is a power series in $D(z_0; r)$. Then by theorem 3.9, $g(z)$ is analytic in $D(z_0; r)$. Now we want to show $\int_\gamma g(z)\,dz = 0$. We consider the following three cases:

Case (*i*) $a \in Ext\ (R)$, then g is analytic in γ and by Rectangle Theorem 5.13, $\int_\gamma g(z)\,dz = 0$.

Case (*ii*) $a \in \gamma$

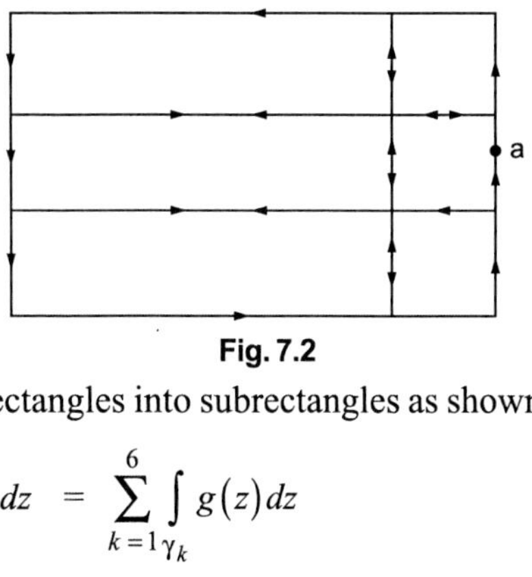

Fig. 7.2

Divide the rectangles into subrectangles as shown in Fig. 7.2, then

$$\int_\gamma g(z)\,dz = \sum_{k=1}^{6} \int_{\gamma_k} g(z)\,dz \qquad \ldots(1)$$

Let γ_1 be the boundary of the subrectangle containing a. Let $l(\gamma_1) < \in$. Since g is continuous on R, therefore it is bounded by M (say). Then

$$\left|\int_{\gamma_1} g(z)\,dz\right| < M \int_{\gamma_1} |dz| = M \in$$

Also $$\int_{\gamma_k} g(z)\,dz = 0,\ k \neq 1 \text{ (by Case (}i\text{))}$$

Then from (1), we get

$$\int_{\gamma} g(z)\,dz = \int_{\gamma_1} g(z)\,dz \leq M \in$$

Since $\in > 0$ be arbitrary therefore the proof is complete

Case (*iii*) $a \in \text{int } R$

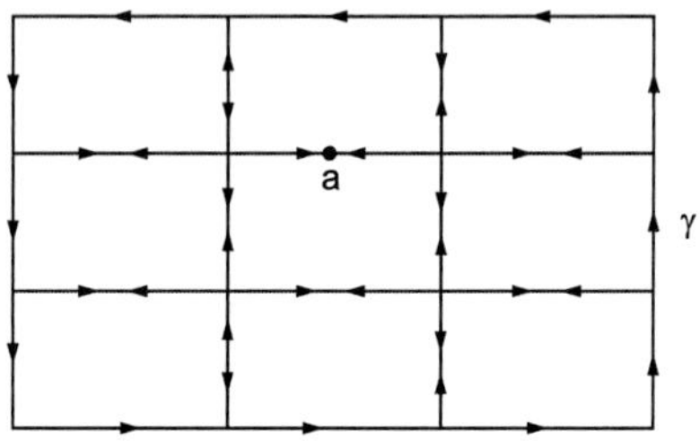

Fig. 7.3

We divide the rectangle R into 9 subractangle and then applying Case (*ii*), we get

$$\int_{\gamma} g(z)\,dz = 0$$

Also f is analytic in R as it is analytic in $D(z_0; r)$ which contains R. By Rectangle Theorem 5.13, we get

$$\int_{\gamma} f(z)\,dz = 0.$$

In Rectangle Theorem we proved that if f is analytic within and on a rectangle R then the integral of f along the boundary of R is zero. The following theorem gives us the converse of the Rectangle Theorem.

Theorem 7.6: Morera's Theorem

Let f be a continuous functions on an open set D. If

$$\int_{\gamma} f(z)\,dz = 0$$

where γ is the boundary of a closed rectangle in D, then f is analytic in D.

Proof

Let $z_0 \in D$. Since D is open there exists $r > 0$ such that $D(z_0, r) \subseteq D$.

Define

$$F(z) = \int_{z_0}^{z} f(\varsigma)d\varsigma$$

Then, $$\frac{F(z+h)-F(z)}{h} = \frac{1}{h}\int_{z}^{z+h} f(\varsigma)d\varsigma$$

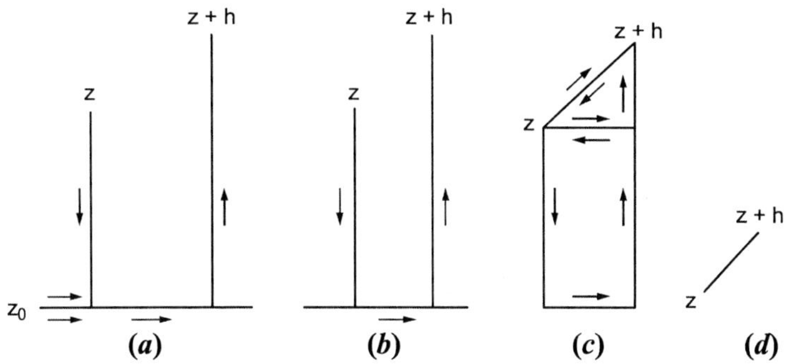

Fig. 7.4

The function f is first integrated along z_0 to $z + h$ with the original orientation and then along z_0 to z with the reverse orientation (because of the minus sign in front of the second integral). This corresponds to (*a*) in Fig. 7.4. Since we integrate f over the line segment starting at the origin in two opposite directions, it cancels, leaving us with the contour in (*b*). Then we complete the square and triangle as shown in (*c*). Since $\int_{\gamma} f(z)dz = 0$, where γ is a rectangular path then we are left with the segment from z to $z + h$ as shown in (*d*). Now

$$\left|\frac{F(z+h)-F(z)}{h} - f(z)\right| = \frac{1}{|h|}\left|\int_{z}^{z+h} f(\varsigma)d\varsigma - f(z)\int_{z}^{z+h} d\varsigma\right|$$

$$< \frac{1}{|h|}\int_{z}^{z+h} |f(\varsigma)-f(z)|\, d\rho$$

Since f is continuous at ζ, therefore given $\in > 0$, there exists $\delta > 0$ such that

$$|f(\zeta) - f(z)| < \in, \quad 0 < |\zeta - z) < \delta$$

In particular if $0 < |h| < \delta$, then

$$\left|\frac{F(z+h)-F(z)}{h} - f(z)\right| < \frac{1}{h}\times\in\times h$$

$$= \in, 0 < |h| < \delta$$

$$\text{Then, } \lim_{h \to 0} \frac{F(z+h) - F(z)}{h} = f(z)$$

$$\text{i.e.,} \quad F'(z) = f(z)$$

7.2 UNIQUENESS THEOREM, MAXIMUM-MODULUS THEOREM

In this section, we prove that if $\{z_n\}$ is a sequence of points in a region R that converges to $\alpha \in R$, and f and g are analytic on R with $f(z_n) = g(z_n)$ for all n then $f(z) = g(z)$ for all z in R. Also, if f and g agree on any line segment in R, or any non-empty open subset in R then they are equal throughout R.

These results provide a method of defining complex functions that reduce to known real functions on the real axis and extending real Taylor series to complex Taylor series. Our aim in this section is also to generalize the result that if f is analytic on an open disc D and is continuous on $\overline{D}$ then f is uniquely determined by its values on the boundary of R.

Theorem 7.7: Uniqueness Theorem

Suppose f is a function analytic in a region R and $f(z_n) = 0$ where $\{z_n\}$ is a sequence of distinct points and $z_n \to z_0 \in R$. Then $f \equiv 0$ in R.

Proof

Since f has a power series representation around z_0, by the uniqueness theorem for power series (Theorem 3.12), $f = 0$ throughout some disc containing z_0. To show $f \equiv 0$ in the whole domain R. Let $R = A \cup B$ where

$A = \{z \in R: z \text{ is a limit of zeroes of } f\}$

$B = \{z \in R: z \notin A\}$

By the definition, $A \cap B = \phi$. We prove the result in the following steps.

Step-I. A is open: Let $z_0 \in A$ then by Theorem 3.12 $f = 0$ in some $D(z_0, r)$ $(r > 0)$. Then $D(z_0, r) \subseteq A$. Thus, A is open.

Step-II. B is open: Let $z_1 \in B$. Since z_1 is not a limit point of zeroes of f, there exists a disc $D(z_1; r)$ such that f is never zero. Thus, $D(z_1, r) \subseteq B$.

Since R is connected, therefore either $A = \phi$ or $B = \phi$.

By the hypothesis $z_0 \in A$. Thus $B = \phi$ and $A = R$. Thus, every $z \in R$ in a limit of zeroes of f. By continuity of f, $f \equiv 0$ on R.

Theorem 7.8

Suppose R is a region, f and g are two functions analytic in G and $f(z) = g(z)$ for all $z \in s \subseteq R$ where s has a limit point in G. Then $f \equiv g$ on R.

Proof

Define $h : R \to \mathbf{C}$ by

$$h(z) = f(z) - g(z) \text{ for all } z \in R$$

Since f and g are analytic on R, therefore, h is analytic on D. Also $h(z) = 0$ on s. Then applying Theorem 7.7, we get $h(z) \equiv 0$ on R. Thus, $f \equiv g$ on R.

As a corollary to this theorem we have the following:

Corollary 7.9

If f and g are analytic on a region R and if $f = g$ on a line segment or a non-empty open set in R then $f = g$ on R.

Proof

Since f and g are analytic in a region R and $f = g$ on $[a, b]$, therefore by Taylor's Theorem,

$$f(z) = \sum a_n (z-a)^n, \ a_n = \frac{f^n(a)}{n!}$$

$$g(z) = \sum b_n (z-a)^n, \ b_n = \frac{g^n(a)}{n!}$$

Since $f(a) = f(b)$, therefore $a_0 = b_0$.

$$\text{Let } z_0 \in [a, b], \text{ then } f'(z_0) = \lim_{z \to z_0} \frac{f(z) - f(z_0)}{z - z_0}$$

$$= \lim_{z \to z_0} \frac{g(z) - g(z_0)}{z - z_0}$$

$$= g'(z_0)$$

i.e., $a_1 = b_1$ proceeding in this way, we get $f^n(z_0) = g^n(z_0) \ \forall \ n > 1$. Since $z_0 \in [a, b]$ is arbitrary $\therefore \ a_n = b_n \ \forall \ n$. Thus $f(z) = g(z)$ for all $z \in R$.

Example 7.5

The function $z \to \sin \frac{1}{z}$ is not defined at $z = 0$, but this function is analytic on a neighbourhood of zero. $\sin\frac{1}{z} = 0$ if $z = \frac{1}{n\pi}, n = \pm 1, \pm 2, ...$ and 0 is a cluster point of the set $s = \{z : z = \frac{1}{n\pi}\}$.
If f is a function that is known real-valued function on the real axis for which we know the Taylor series, then the Taylor series of the complex function can be obtained using Theorem 7.8. Thus, because

$$\sin x = x - \frac{x^3}{3!} + ..., x \in R$$

We can deduce that

$$\sin z = z - \frac{z^3}{3!} + ... z \in \mathbf{C}$$

Similarly

$$\cos z = 1 - \frac{z^2}{2!} + \frac{z^4}{4!} .... z \in \mathbf{C}$$

$$e^z = 1 + \frac{z^2}{2!} + \frac{z^3}{3!} .... z \in \mathbf{C}$$

Theorem 7.8 is useful to extend some important identities of trigonometry for real numbers to complex numbers. Some of the important identities are listed below:

(*i*) $\sin^2 z + \cos^2 z = 1 \quad \forall z \in \mathbf{C}$

(*ii*) $\sin (z_1 + z_2) = \sin z_1 \cos z_2 - \cos z_1 \sin z_2$

(*iii*) $e^{z_1 + z_2} = e^{z_1} e^{z_2}$

(*iv*) $\cos 2z = 2\cos^2 z - 1$

(*v*) $\cos 2z = 1 - 2\sin^2 z$.

A real-valued function ϕ has a maximum on a set s at a point $a \in S$ if $\phi(a)$ is the maximum of ϕ on S, that is if $\phi(a) > \phi(z)$ for all $z \in S$. Then ϕ has a local maximum on S at $a \in S$ if there is some neighbourhood D of a such that ϕ has a maximum on $D \cap S$ at a. We say that f is constant on a set S if there is some constant a such that $f(z) = a$ for all $z \in S$.

Theorem 7.10: The Local Maximum Principle

Let f be analytic on a region R. If f is not constant on R, then $|f|$ has no local maximum at any point in R.

Proof

We shall prove the result by contradiction. Suppose f is not constant on R, but $|f|$ has a local maximum at a point $\alpha \in R$.

Since R is open, there is $\in > 0$ such that $|f(z)| < |f(\alpha)$ whenever $|z - \alpha| < \in$

By Cauchy's Integral Formula, we have

$$f(\alpha) = \frac{1}{2\pi i} \int_{\gamma(\alpha, r)} \frac{f(z)}{z - \alpha} dz$$

where $\gamma(\alpha, r)$ is the circle with centre α and radius r.

$$= \frac{1}{2\pi} \int_0^{2\pi} \frac{f\left(\alpha + re^{i\theta}\right)}{re^{i\theta}} \times rie^{i\theta} d\theta$$

$$= \frac{1}{2\pi} \int_0^{2\pi} f\left(\alpha + re^{i\theta}\right) d\theta$$

Therefore,

$$|f(\alpha)| = \frac{1}{2\pi} \left| \int_0^{2\pi} f\left(\alpha + re^{i\theta}\right) d\theta \right|$$

$$< \frac{1}{2\pi} \int_0^{2\pi} \left| f\left(\alpha + re^{i\theta}\right) d\theta \right|$$

$$< \frac{1}{2\pi} \int_0^{2\pi} |f(\alpha)| d\theta,$$

(Since $\left| f\left(\alpha + ie^{i\theta}\right) \right| < |f(\alpha)|$)

$$= |f(\alpha)|$$

and so $$|f(\alpha)| = \frac{1}{2\pi} \int_0^{2\pi} \left| f\left(\alpha + re^{i\theta}\right) \right| d\theta,$$

i.e., $$\int_0^{2\pi}\left(|f(\alpha)| - \left|f\left(\alpha + re^{i\theta}\right)\right|\right)d\theta = 0$$

Since $$\left(\left|f(\alpha) - f\left(\alpha + re^{i\theta}\right)\right|\right) \geq 0 \text{ and real}$$

Thus, $$|f(\alpha)| = \left|f\left(\alpha + re^{i\theta}\right)\right| \text{ whenever } 0 < \theta \leq 2\pi.$$

Since r is arbitrary, therefore $|f|$ is constant on $D = \{z : |z - \alpha| < \in\}$. By uniqueness theorem f is constant on D and hence constant on R. This is a contradiction.

Now we want to discuss the geometrical significance of Theorem 7.10. Suppose f is non-constant entire function, then by Liouville's theorem $|f|$ is unbounded and since the image of **C** under $|f|$ is an interval, $|f|$ takes all sufficiently large real values. Ironically the Maximum Modulus Theorem actually asserts that an analytic function has no relative maximum. There is a corollary to Theorem 7.10, which is actually in the form in which it is applied. To prove this we require the following lemma:

Lemma 7.11

Let S be a set and f, g be continuous functions on $\overline{S}$, such that $f = g$ on S. Then $f = g$ on $\overline{S}$.

Proof

Define a function h on S by

$$h(z) = f(z) - g(z)$$

then $h(z) = 0$ on S. To show that $h(z) = 0$ on $\overline{S}$.

Suppose $a \in \overline{S} - S$, $h(a) \neq 0$. There is a $\delta > 0$ such that if $z \in S$ and $|z - a| < \delta$ then $h(z) \neq 0$. Since a is a limit point of S, there is $z_0 \in S$ such that $0 < |z_0 - a| < \delta$ and $h(z_0) \neq 0$. But $h(z_0) = 0$ since $z_0 \in S$. This is a contradiction and so $h(a) = 0$.

Corollary 7.12: The Maximum Principle

Let f be analytic on a bounded region R, and continuous on $\overline{R}$. Then $|f|$ has a maximum on $\overline{R}$ at a point on the boundary of R.

Proof

Since R is bounded, it is contained in some closed disc and so $\overline{R}$ is also bounded. Now $|f|$ has a maximum on $\overline{R}$ at some point $a \in \overline{R}$ (since f is continuous on $\overline{R}$, an $\overline{R}$ is closed and bounded) if $a \notin R$ then the proof is complete. Suppose $a \in R$, by Theorem 7.10, f is constant on R, *i.e.*, there is some k such that $f(z) = K$, $z \in R$. By the Lemma 7.11, $f(z) = K, z \in \overline{R}$. So $|f|$ has a maximum at every point of the boundary of R.

Theorem 7.13

Let f and g be analytic on a bounded region R and continuous on $\overline{R}$. Suppose $f = g$ on the boundary of R. Then $f = g$ on R.

Proof

Define $h(z) = f(z) - g(z)$ on R. Since f and g are analytic on R, Therefore h is analytic on R and continuous on $\overline{R}$. Also $|h|$ attains its maximum on $\overline{R}$ at the boundary of R. Since $f = g$ on the boundary, this maximum value is zero. Hence

$$|h(z)| = |f(z) - g(z)| \leq 0 \text{ for all } z \in R$$

Then, $$f(z) = g(z) \text{ on } R.$$

Example 7.5

Let $S = \{z : 0 < Re\ z < \pi, 0 < Im\ z < \pi\}$ be a closed square. Find the maximum value of $|\sin z|$ for $z \in S$.

Solution

Let $f(z) = \sin z$. By Cordlary $|f|$ attains its maximum on S at the boundary of S. We shall discuss the behaviour of $|f|$ on the four sides of the square.

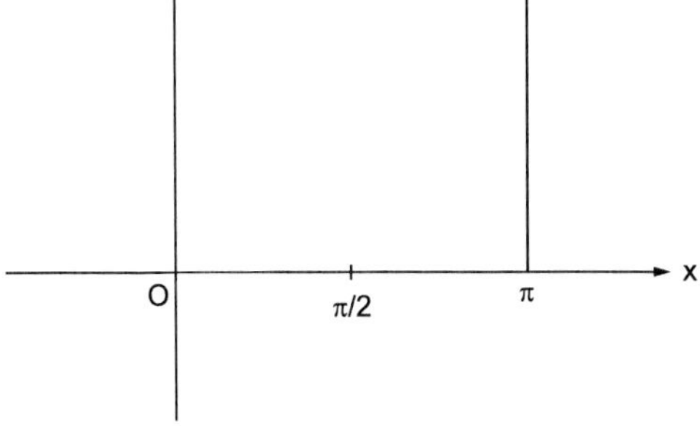

Fig. 7.5

(*i*) On side $[0, \pi]$

If $0 < x < \pi$, $|\sin x| < 1$ and $|\sin \pi/2| = 1$

(*ii*) On side $[0, \pi i]$

If $0 < y < \pi$, $|\sin i\, y| = \sin h\, y < \sin h\, \pi$

If $z = x + iy$, then

$$\sin z = \sin x \cosh y + i \cos x \sinh y$$

$$\Rightarrow \quad |\sin z|^2 = \sin^2 x \cosh^2 y + \cos^2 x \sinh^2 y$$
$$= \sin^2 x\,(1 + \sinh^2 y) + \cos^2 x \sinh^2 y$$
$$= \sin^2 x + (\sin^2 x + \cos^2 x) \sinh^2 y$$
$$= \sin^2 x + \sinh^2 y. \quad ...(1)$$

(*iii*) On side $[\pi, \pi + \pi i]$

If $x = \pi$, $0 < y < \pi$

$$|\sin z|^2 < \sinh^2 y \text{ (From (1))}$$
$$< \sinh^2 \pi$$
$$\Rightarrow \quad |\sin z| < \sinh \pi$$

(*iv*) On side $[\pi i, \pi + \pi i]$

If $y = \pi$ and $0 < x < \pi$

$$|\sin z|^2 = \sin^2 x + \sinh^2 \pi$$
$$< 1 + \sinh^2 \pi \text{ (equallity at } x = \pi/2)$$
$$= \cosh^2 \pi$$

and so $\quad |\sin z| < \cosh \pi$

Since $1 < \sin h\, \pi < \cosh \pi$, then the maximum of $|f|$ on S is $\cosh \pi$ and occurs at the point $\frac{\pi}{2} + \pi i$.

Example 7.6

Suppose f is analytic in $D(0; 1) = \{z : |z| < 1\}$, $|f(z)| < 2$ for $|z| = 1$ if $Im\, z > 0$ and $|f(z)| < 3$ for $|z| = 1$ if $Im\, z < 0$. Show that $|f|(0)| < \sqrt{6}$.

Solution

Consider the function

$$g(z) = f(z)\, f(-z)$$

Then, $|g(z)| < 6$ throughout $|z| = 1$.

Since f is analytic in D, therefore g is analytic in D and continuous on $\overline{D}$. By Theorem 7.13, $|g(0)| < 6$. Then,

$$|g(0)\, f(0)| < 6$$

i.e.,
$$|f(0)|^2 < 6$$

or
$$|f(0)| < \sqrt{6}$$

Theorem 7.14: Minimum Modulus Theorem

If f is non-constant analytic function in a region D, then no point $z \in D$ can be a relative minimum of f unless $f(z) = 0$.

Proof

Suppose that $f(z) \neq 0$ and consider $g(z) = \dfrac{1}{f(z)}$. A minimum point of f would be a maximum point for g. Then if g has a maximum at any point of D, g becomes constant, which gives f a constant function, contradiction to the hypothesis. Thus, $f(z) = 0$.

Remark

The Maximum Modulus Theorem can be studied by analyzing the power series representation of an analytic function. Consider a power series of $f(z)$ about $z = \alpha$,

$$f(z) = c_0 + c_1 (z - \alpha) + c_2 (z - \alpha)^2 + \ldots\ldots\ldots$$

which is convergent in $D = \{z : |z - \alpha| < r\}$. Let us assume $c_1 \neq 0$ and $z = \alpha + re^{i\theta}$, $r > 0$ and θ is chosen such that c_0 and $c_1\, \delta\, e^{i\theta}$ have the same argument. Then,

$$|f(\alpha)| = |c_0|$$

$$|f(z)| > |c_0 + c_1(z - \alpha)| - |c_2(z - \alpha)^2 + c_3 (z - \alpha)^3 + \ldots\ldots|$$

$$> |c_0| + |c_1\delta| - \delta^2|\, c_2 + c_3(z - \alpha) + \ldots\ldots|$$

$$> |c_0| + |c_1\delta| - A\delta^2$$

$$> |c_0| + \frac{1}{2}\, |c_1\delta|$$

$$> |\, f(\alpha)| \qquad \text{if } \frac{c_1}{2A} > \delta$$

$\Rightarrow \alpha$ cannot be a maximum point.

This technique of studying the local behaviour of an analytic function by considering the first term of its power series can be employed in proving an anti-calculus proposition. In calculus, we know relative maximum exists at the critical points of a differentiable function. But the following result by Erdos is a contrast in the behaviour of an analytic function.

Theorem 7.15

Suppose f is analytic throughout a closed disc and assumes its maximum modulus at the boundary point α. Then $f'(\alpha) \neq 0$ unless f is constant

Proof

Since f is analytic at α, therefore it has power series expansion at α.

$f(z) = c_0 + c_1(z - \alpha) + c_2(z - \alpha)^2 + c_3(z - \alpha)^3 + \ldots\ldots$

We assumes that $c_1 = f'(\alpha) = 0$ and $c_2 \neq 0$. Choose $z = \alpha + \delta e^{i\theta}$ inside the disc such that c_0 and $c_2\delta^2 e^{2i\theta}$ have same argument.

Now

$$|c_0 + c_1(z - \alpha)^2| = |c_0 + c_2\, \delta^2\, e^{2i\theta}|$$

$$> |c_0| + \frac{1}{2}|\, c_2\, \delta^2\, |$$

Thus, for sufficiently small δ,

$$|f(z)| > |c_0| + \frac{1}{4}|\, c_2\, \delta^2\, | > |\, f(\alpha)\, |$$

Thus, $f(z)$ does not attain its maximum at α. This is a contradiction. Thus, $c_1 \neq 0$.

Example 7.7

Show that the maximum and minimum moduli of e^z are always assumed on the boundary of a compact domain.

Solution

Consider the unit disc $D(0; 1)$ as the compact domain,

let $z = e^{i\theta}$. Then, $e^z = e^{\cos\theta + i\sin\theta}$

$$\Rightarrow \qquad |e^z| = e^{\cos\theta} < e$$

The maximum values of $z \to e^z$ on D is e at $\theta = 0$ and $z = 1$ and minimum value of $z \to e^z$ on D is $\frac{1}{e}$ at $\theta = \pi$ and $z = -1$.

Example 7.8

Find the maximum and minimum moduli of $(z^2 - z)$ in the disc $|z| < 1$.

Solution

Let $f(z) = z^2 - z$ for all $|z| < 1$

Now $|f(z)| = |z|\,|z - 1|$

At $z = -1$, $|f(z)| = |-1||-2| = 2$

and at $z = 1$, $|f(z)| = |1| \times 0 = 0$

Thus, the maximum value is 2 at $z = -1$ and minimum value 0 at $z = 1$.

Example 7.9

Suppose f and g are both analytic in a compact domain D. Show that $|f(z)| + |g(z)|$ takes maximum on the boundary.

Solution

Suppose $|f(z)| + |g(z)|$ assumed its maximum at the interior point z_0 in D.

Let $f(z_0) = A\,e^{-i\alpha}$ and $g(z_0) = B\,e^{-i\beta}$

Suppose $h(z) = f(z)\,e^{i\alpha} + g(z)\,e^{i\beta}$, then

$$
\begin{aligned}
h(z_0) &= f(z_0)\,e^{i\alpha} + g(z_0)\,e^{i\beta} \\
&= A\,e^{-i\alpha}\,e^{i\alpha} + B\,e^{-i\beta}\,e^{i\beta} \\
&= A + B \\
&= |f(z_0)| + |g(z_0)|
\end{aligned}
$$

Also $|h(z)| < |f(z)| + |g(z)| < |h(z_0)|$

Thus, the analytic function $h(z)$ assumes its maximum value at an interior point but not on the boundary. It is a contradiction hence, $|f(z)| + |g(z)|$ takes its maximum on the boundary.

EXERCISE

1. Show that if f is analytic in $|z| < 1$, there must be some positive integer n such that $f\left(\frac{1}{n}\right) \neq f\left(\frac{1}{n+1}\right)$.
2. Prove that $\sin(z_1 + z_2) = \sin z_1 \cos z_2 + \cos z_1 \sin z_2$.
3. Suppose that f is entire and that $|f(z)| > |z|^n$ for sufficiently large z. Show that f must be a polynomial of degree at least N.

4. Suppose an analytic function f agrees with tan x, $0 < x < 1$. Show that $f(z) = i$ has no solution. Could f be entire?

5. Suppose G is an open set, $f : G \to \subset$ is continuous and f is anlaytic in $G \sim [a, b]$, where $[a, b]$ is the line segment lying in G. Use Morera's theorem to prove that f is analytic in G.

6. Is it possible to construct a function f analytic in $D(0; 1)$ such that $f\left(\frac{1}{n}\right) = z_n$ $(n = 1, 2......)$ when (i) $z_n = (-1)^n$, (ii) $z_n = \frac{n}{n+1}$, (iii) $z_n = 0$ (n even), $z_n = \frac{1}{n}$ (n odd)?

7. Let f be analytic in a region G. By considering e^f show that $Re\, f$ attain a maximum value at any point of G. Can $Re\, f$ attain a minimum value?

8. If f is analytic on $\{z : |z| < 1\}$ and $f\left(1 - \frac{1}{n}\right) = 0$ for all $n = 1, 2, 3, ...$ then f is zero throughout $\{z : |z| < 1\}$. It this statements true?

9. Let f be analytic on a region R containing the point zero and let $f\left(\frac{1}{n}\right)$ be real and $f\left(\frac{1}{n}\right) < \frac{1}{2^n}$ for $n = 1, 2, 3, ...$ Prove that $f = 0$ on R.

10. Let f be analytic on **C** and real-valued on the internal $(-\in, \in)$ of the real axis. Prove that f is real-valued on the whole real axis and $f(\bar{z}) = \overline{f(z)}$ for all $z \in$ **C**.

11. Let f be a function which is real on the real axis and imaginary on the imaginary axis. Show that f is an odd function. Find a similar condition which guarantees that f is even function.

12. Let f be analytic on the open disc $\{z : |z| < 1\}$ and continuous on the closed disc $\{z : |z| < 1\}$. What can you say about the set S of points at which $|f|$ has a maximum?

13. Let f be analytic and non-constant on the bounded region R, and continuous on $\overline{R}$. Let $M = \max \{|f(z)| : z \in \overline{R} - R\}$. Show that $|f(z)| < M$ for all $z \in R$.

ANSWERS

1. If $f\left(\frac{1}{n}\right) = f\left(\frac{1}{n+1}\right)$. Then for all $z_n = \frac{1}{n}$. $f(z_n) = f\left(\frac{1}{\frac{1}{z_n}+1}\right)$

$= f\left(\frac{z_n}{z_n+1}\right)$. Since $\{z_n\} \to 0$, therefore, $f(z) = f\left(\frac{z}{z+1}\right)$ f is not analytic at $z = 1$, a contradiction.

2. Let $f(z) = \sin (z_1 + z_2)$, $g(z) = \sin z_1 \cos z_2 + \cos z_1 \sin z_2$. Apply uniquents theorem.

3. Since $|f(z)| > |z|^N$ for large N, $f(z) \to \infty$ as $z \to \infty$ & hence f is a polynomial and f has degree at least N.

4. If $\tan z = i$, $e^{iz} = 0$ which is not possible.

5. By taking different cases that $[a, b]$ is a part of rectangle γ, using continuity at $[a, b]$ and Morera's theorem, the result can by proved.

6. (*i*) Not possible (*ii*) Possible (*iii*) Not possible.

7. f is bounded in G, Ref is odd, Re $f \leq K$. $| e^{f(z)} | = e\text{Re} f \leq e^k$, $z \leq G$.

8. False, the sequence $\left\{1-\frac{1}{n}\right\}$ has a limit which is not in the open disc.

9. $f(0) = 0$ then either $f \equiv 0$ on R or $\exists$ g and $m \in I^+$ such that

$$f(z) = z^m g(z) \Rightarrow f\left(\frac{1}{n}\right) = \frac{1}{n^m} g\left(\frac{1}{n}\right) < \frac{1}{2^n}$$

$$\Rightarrow \quad g\left(\frac{1}{n}\right) = \frac{n^m}{2^n} \to 0$$

as $n \to \infty$, a contradiction,

10. Let z be fixed, $f_N(z) = \sum_{0}^{\infty} a_N z^N$ and $f_N(\overline{z}) = \overline{f_N(z)}$ $\forall$ N. $f_N(z)$ $= U_N + iV_N$, $f_N(\overline{z}) = U_N - iV_N$. If $\lim_{n\to\infty} U_N = u$, $\lim_{n\to\infty} V_N = V$.

Then $f(z) = u + iv$ and $f(\overline{z}) = u - iv = \overline{f(z)}$.

11. By Taylor's series $f(iy) = \sum_{n=0}^{\infty} a_n (iy)^n = \sum_{n=0}^{\infty} (-1)^n a_{2n}\, y^{2n} +$

$i \sum_{n=0}^{\infty} (-1)^n a_{2n+1}\, y^{2n+1}$, $f(iy)$ = Imaginary, $a_{2n} = 0 \;\forall\; n$. Thus,

$f(z) = \sum_{n=0}^{\infty} a_{2n+1}\, y^{2n+1}$, $f(-z) = -f(z)$.

12. Every point of $\{z : |z| \leq 1\}$ belongs to S or S is contained in the unit circle.

13. Let $|f(z)| \leq M$ for $z \in R$. By Local Maximum principle $|f(z)| \neq M$.

❑❑❑

8

Simply-Connected Regions

We have observed that if a function f is analytic on a closed curve and yet $\int_C f(z)\,dz \neq 0$. For example $\int_{\gamma(0,1)} \frac{1}{z}\,dz = 2\pi i$. But on the other hand, the closed curve theorem showed that if f is analytic in a disc D then $\int_D f(z)\,dz = 0$. In this chapter, we want to find the most general domain in which the closed curve theorem holds. In the above mentioned example there is 'hole' inside the curve along which f is analytic. But if there is a domain in which there is no 'hole', is called simply-connected region. In this chapter Cauchy's theorem for simply-connected region is given, we also have proofs of antiderivative theorem, closed curve theorem for the simply-connected region. We also find a branch of log in a simply-connected region.

8.1 SIMPLY-CONNECTED REGION

We begin the section with the formal definition of simply-connected region.

Definition 8.1

A region R is said to be simply-connected if its complement $\mathbf{C} \sim R$ is connected. That is, if for any $z_0 \in \bar{R}$ and $\in > 0$, there is a continuous curve $\gamma(t)$, $0 < t < \infty$ such that

(*i*) $d(\gamma(t), \bar{R}) < \in$ for all $t > 0$

(*ii*) $\gamma(0) = z_0$

(*iii*) $\lim_{t \to \infty} \gamma(t) = \infty$

Example 8.1

The annulus $A = \{z : | < | z | < 3\}$ is not simply-connected as if $\mathbf{C} \sim A = \{z : | z | < 1\} \cup \{z : | z | > 3\}$ is not connected (Fig. 8.1)

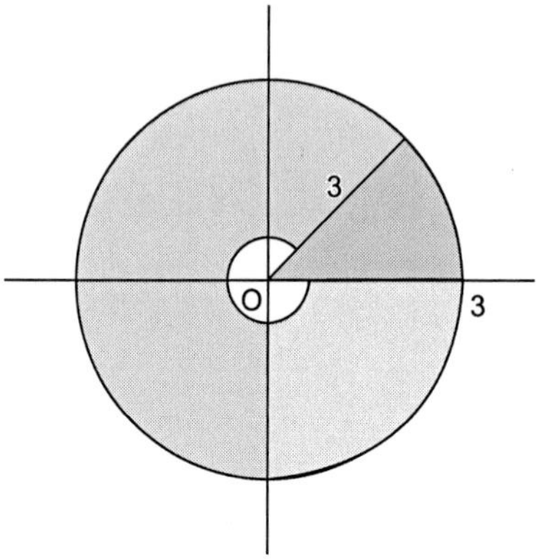

Fig. 8.1

Example 8.2

The unit disc minus the positive real axis is simply-connected since for any z_0 in the complement a curve

$$\gamma(t) = (t + 1)\, z_0$$

Connects z_0 to ∞ and is contained in the complement (Fig. 8.2).

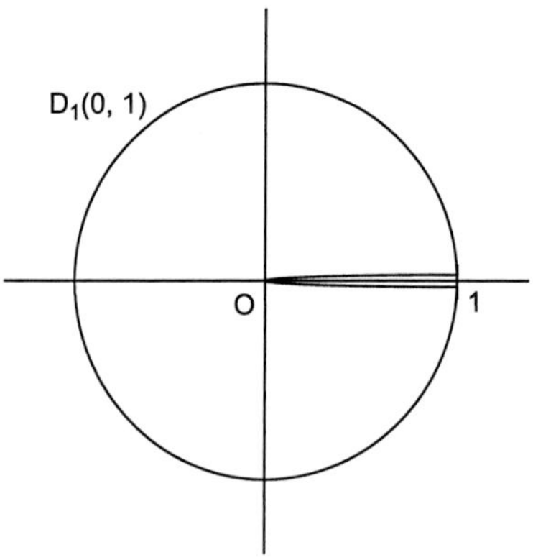

Fig. 8.2

i.e., $D_1(0, 1) = D(0, 1) \sim (z\text{: } Re\, z > 0]$ is simply-connected region.

Example 8.3

Every open convex set is simply connected.

Example 8.4

$G = C_\infty \sim \{z : Re\, z \le 0\}$ is simply connected. As its complement $\mathbf{C}_\infty \sim G$ $= \{z : Re\, z \le 0\}$ is connected (Fig. 8.3).

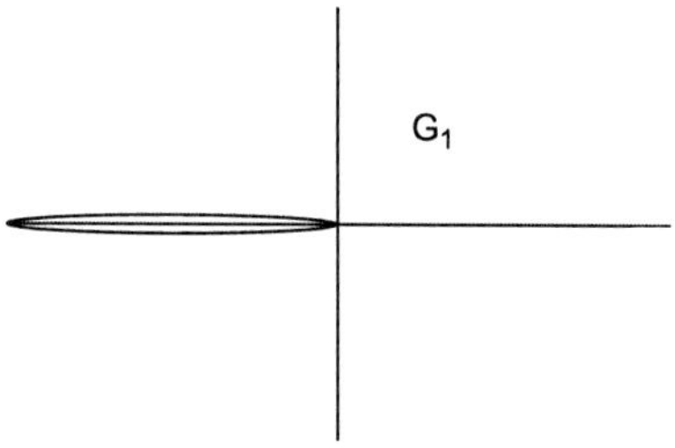

Fig. 8.3

Example 8.5

The infinite strip $S = \{z : -1 < Im\, z < 1\}$ is simply connected. But in this case, the complement $\tilde{S}$ is not connected. (Fig. 8.4).

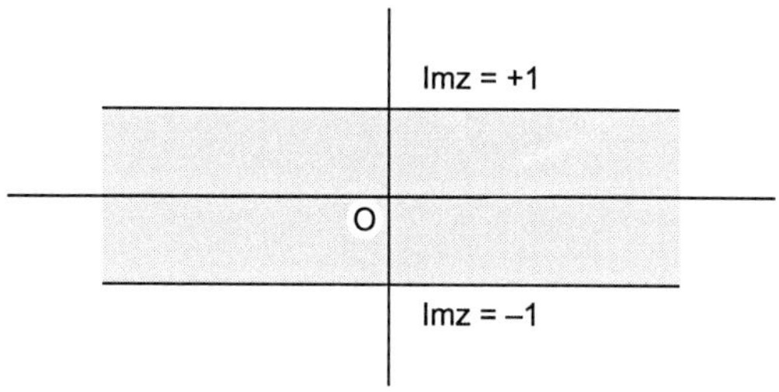

Fig 8.4

The definition 8.1 needs more clarification as in Example 8.5. S is simply connected but $\mathbf{C} \sim s$ is not connected. We say a simply connected region contains, along with any closed curve, all the points inside the curve. Now we want to define 'inside' of a general closed curve from the elementary geometry, it is easy to see that inside of the circle $C = \{z: |z| = 1\}$ is the disc $\{z : |z| < 1\}$ and the outside is $\{z : |z| > 1\}$. Note that the inside and the outside are regions, disjoint from each other, whose union is the complement of C, and each having boundary C. Also the inside region in bounded and outside is unbounded. The Jordan Curve Theorem gives specifications about these regions:

Theorem 8.1: The Jordan Curve Theorem

If γ is a simple closed arc, then the set of points in the plane which do not lie on the path of γ is the union of two disjoint regions. One of these regions is bounded, called inside of γ. Other, the outside, is unbounded. Each point of the path of γ is a boundary point of either region.

Intuitively speaking, a region is simply-connected if it has no holes, cracks or pinpricks contained in its midst. The following regions are simply connected (Fig. 8.5).

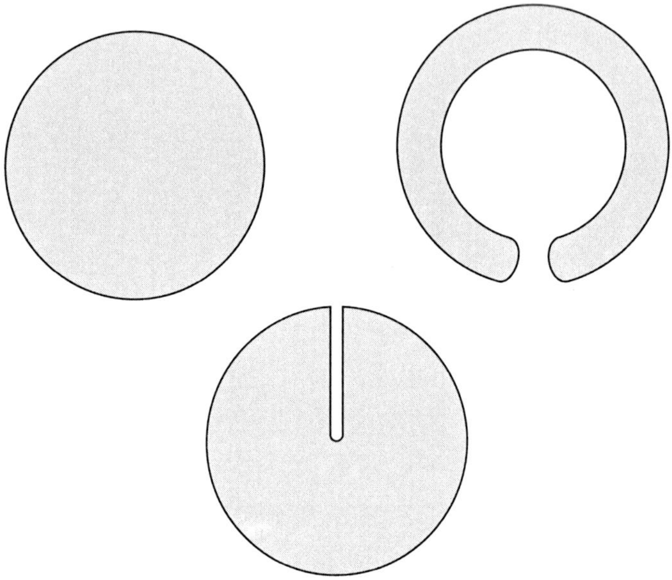

Fig. 8.5

The following are not simply-connected (Fig. 8.6).

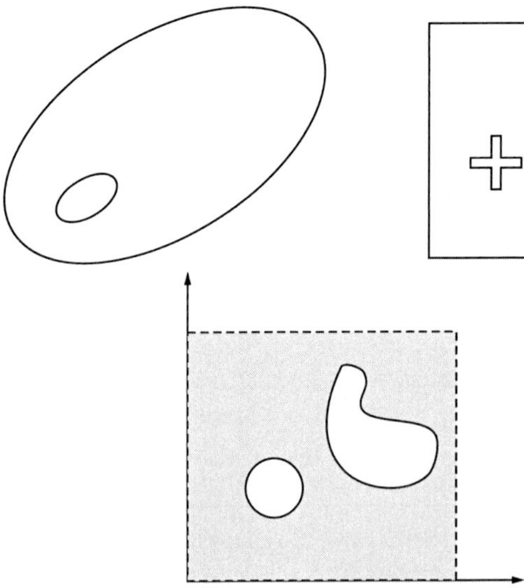

Fig. 8.6

Before moving towards the proof of closed curve theorem for simply connected region we first prove the same for a simple closed polygon. We define the following:

Definition 8.2: Polygonal path

A polygonal path is a finite chain of horizontal and vertical line segments. A simple closed polygonal path γ is a polygonal path which is simple and $\gamma(a) = \gamma(b)$ if $[a, b]$ is the parameter interval.

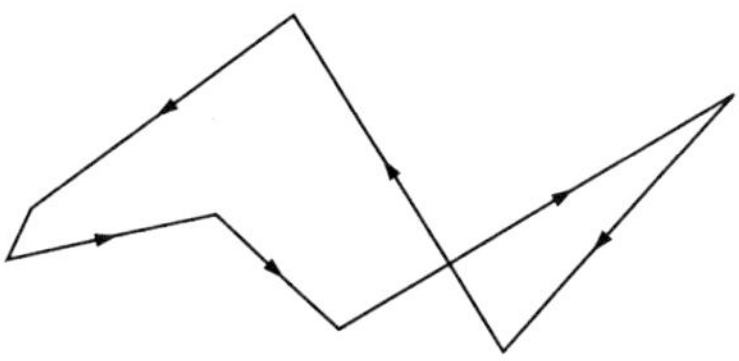

Closed polygonal path but not simple

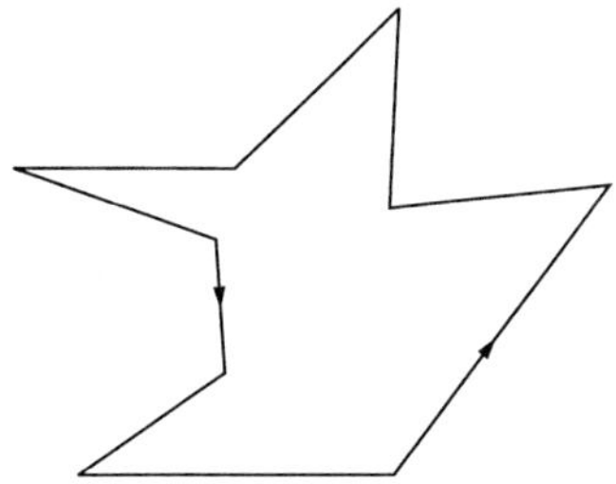

Simple closed polygonal path

Fig. 8.7

We can decompose a simple closed polygonal path with more than three sides into triangles by joining the vertices by lines not crossing any side. We know a simple closed polygon is a simple closed contour having orientation. If we take into account this and orientating triangles appropriately, we end up with the following lemma:

Lemma 8.2

Let Γ be a simple closed polygon with n sides ($n > 3$). Then there are $n - 2$ triangles $T_1, \ldots T_{n-2}$ with the following properties:

(*i*) each point inside a T_j is inside Γ,

(*ii*) each point inside Γ is inside or on the edge of some T_j,

(*iii*) each edge of Γ is an edge of some T_j, with the same orientation.

Such a system of triangles $T_1, T_2 \ldots T_{n-2}$ is called a triangularization of Γ. The triangularization of a simple closed contour is not unique (Fig. 8.8)

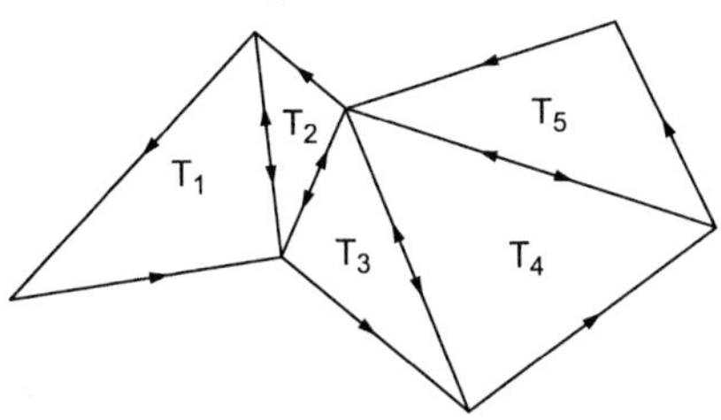

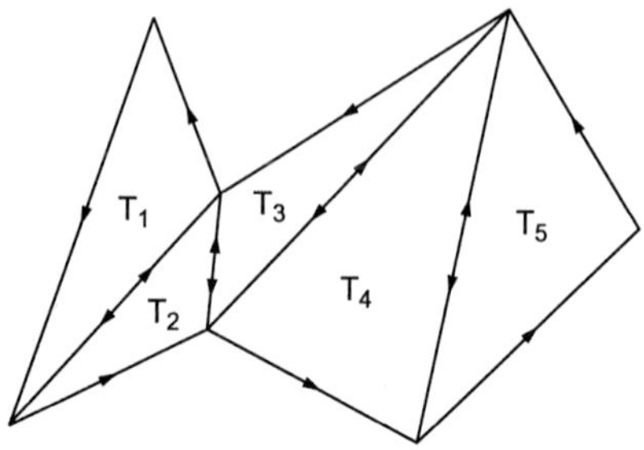

Fig. 8.8

With the aid of Lemma 8.2 we can prove the following Closed Curve Theorem for a simple polygon.

Theorem 8.3

Let R be a simply connected region and f be a function analytic on R, Γ a simple polygon in R. Then,

$$\int_{\Gamma} f = 0$$

Proof

We can assume that Γ is a polygonal path with n sides ($n > 3$). Then by Lemma 8.2, $T_1, T_2 \ldots T_{n-2}$ be the triangularization of Γ. Since R is simply connected, therefore inside of Γ is contained in R and so each T_j and its inside is contained in R. Thus, f is analytic within and on each T_j. Thus, using closed curve theorem for smooth curves, we get

$$\int_{T_j} f = 0$$

Now

$$\int_{\Gamma} f = \int_{T_1} f + \int_{T_2} f + \ldots\ldots\ldots\ldots \int_{T_{n-2}} f$$
$$= 0 + 0 + \ldots + 0$$
$$= 0.$$

Now we are in a position to prove the antiderivative theorem for simply connected region.

Theorem 8.4

Let f be analytic on a simply-connected region. Then f has an antiderivative on R; *i.e.*, there exists an analytic F on R such that

$$F'(z) = f(z), \quad z \in R.$$

Proof

Let z_0 be a fixed point of R. Define

$$F(z) = \int_{\Gamma} f(w)\, dw$$

where Γ is a polygonal line in R from z_0 to z. There is at least one such Γ. Let Γ^* is another polygonal line joining z_0 to z, then $\Gamma + (-\Gamma^*)$ is a simple polygonal. Then,

$$\int_{\Gamma+(-\Gamma^*)} f = 0$$

$$\Rightarrow \qquad \int_{\Gamma} f - \int_{\Gamma^*} f = 0$$

$$\Rightarrow \qquad \int_{\Gamma} f = \int_{\Gamma^*} f$$

Thus, $F(z)$ is independent of Γ. For $|h|$ sufficiently small

$$\frac{F(z+h)-F(z)}{h} = \frac{1}{h}\int_{[z,\, z+h]} f$$

Also

$$\left|\frac{F(z+h)-F(z)}{h} - f(z)\right| = \frac{1}{|h|}\left|\int_{[z+h]} f(w)\, dw - \int_{[z,\, z+h]} f(z)\, dw\right|$$

$$= \frac{1}{|h|}\left|\int_{[z,\, z+h]} (f(w)-f(z))\, dw\right|$$

$$\leq \frac{1}{|h|}\int_{[z,\, z+h]} |f(w)-f(z)|\,|dw|$$

Since f is continuous at z, therefore for $\in > 0$ there exist $\delta > 0$ such that

$$|f(w) - f(z)| < \in, \quad 0 < |w - z| < \delta$$

In particular if $0 < |h| < \delta$, then

$$\left|\frac{F(z+h)-F(z)}{h} - f(z)\right| < \frac{\in}{|h|}.|h| = \in$$

i.e., $\qquad F'(z) = f(z).$

Theorem 8.5

Let R be a simply-connected region, f analytic on R and Γ any closed contour in R, then $\int_\Gamma f = 0$.

Proof

Since f is analytic in R therefore, there exists an analytic function F on R such that $F' = f$. Γ is a closed contour, therefore by Theorem 8.4.

$$\int_\Gamma f = \int_\Gamma f' = 0$$

using Fundamental Theorem of calculus.

Theorem 8.5 is stated for simply-connected regions, but it has implications for other domains as well. For example, if f is analytic in $\mathbf{C} \sim \{0\}$ and γ is a closed curve in the upper half plane then $\int_\gamma f = 0$ (Fig. 8.9), because γ is a closed curve in

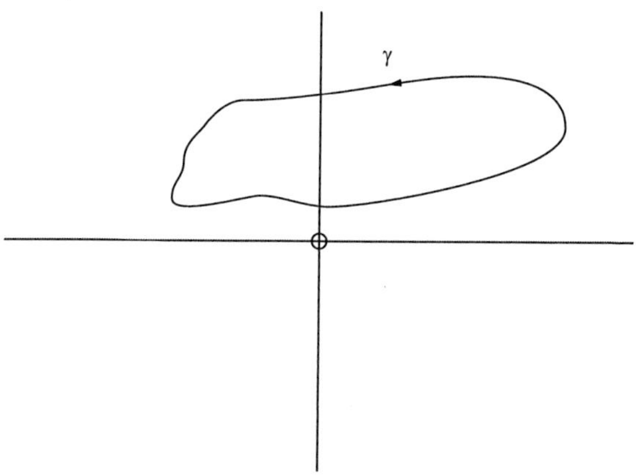

Fig. 8.9

the simply-connected region $\{z : Im\, z > 0\}$.

Example 8.6

Let R be a simply-connected region, Γ is a closed contour in R, and $\alpha \notin R$, then $\int_\Gamma \frac{dz}{z-\alpha} = 0$. Since $\frac{1}{z-\alpha}$ is analytic in simply-connected region R.

Example 8.7

Suppose f is analytic in the annulus $1 \leq |z| \leq 4$. Then,

$$\int_{|z|=2} f(z)\,dz = \int_{|z|=3} f(z)\,dz$$

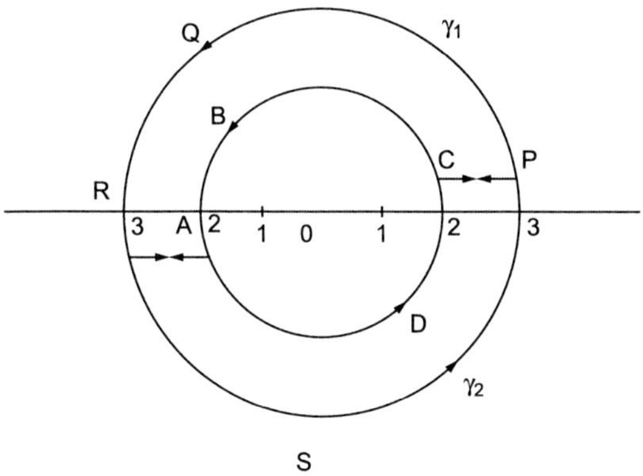

Proof

Let γ_1 and γ_2 be two closed contours in simply-connected portion of the annulus.

$$\int_{\gamma_1} f = 0 = \int_{\gamma_2} f$$

Then,

$$\int_{PQR} f + \int_{RA} f + \int_{ABC} f + \int_{CP} f + \int_{PC} f + \int_{CDA} f + \int_{AR} f + \int_{RSP} f = 0$$

$$\Rightarrow \int_{|z|=3} f - \int_{|z|=2} f = 0$$

$$\Rightarrow \qquad \int_{|z|=3} f = \int_{|z|=2} f.$$

Example 8.8

Show that if

$$\tilde{S} = \left\{\begin{matrix} x+iy:\ 0<x\leq 1, \\ y=\sin\frac{1}{x} \end{matrix}\right\} \cup \{iy: -1 \leq y < \infty\}$$

then S is simply-connected.

Proof

Since,

$$\begin{aligned} \tilde{S} &= \left\{\begin{matrix} x+iy:\ 0<x\leq 1, \\ y=\sin\frac{1}{x} \end{matrix}\right\} \cup \{iy: -1 \leq y < \infty\} \\ &= A \cup B \end{aligned}$$

Then,

$$\begin{aligned} S &= \subset \sim \tilde{S} \\ &= \subset \sim (A \cup B) \\ &= (\subset \sim A) \cap (\subset \sim B) \\ &= \left\{\begin{matrix} x+iy:\ -\infty < x \leq 0, 1 < x < \infty, \\ y = \sin\frac{1}{x} \end{matrix}\right\} \cap \{iy: -\infty \leq y < -1\} \end{aligned}$$

Moreover any point $z_0 = \left(x_0, \sin\frac{1}{x_0}\right)$ can be connected by the curve $y = \sin\frac{1}{x}$ to $\left(\frac{1}{k\pi}, 0\right)$ if $k > \frac{1}{\pi \in}$. The positive y-axis in $\tilde{S}$, connects the origin to ∞. Thus, S is simply-connected.

Example 8.9

Show that a polygonal line γ connecting z to ∞ intersects the boundary of every rectangle R containing z.

Solution

Let $z_0 \in R$ and γ is a polygonal line connecting z_0 to ∞. Let $t_0 = \text{Sup } \{t : \gamma(t) \in R\}$.

Case (*i*): If $\gamma(t_0)$ is inside R and γ is continuous and also $d(z_0, \partial R) < \delta$ implies $\gamma(t_0 + \delta)$ is also inside R for some $\delta > 0$.

Case (*ii*): If $\gamma(t_0)$ is outside R then $\gamma(t_0 - h)$, $0 \le h \le \delta$ would also lie outside R. But by the definition of t_0, $\gamma(t_0)$ lies on the boundary of R.

EXERCISE

1. Prove that every convex region is simply-connected.
2. Let f be analytic and non-zero on a simply-connected region R. Show that there is a function g analytic on R such that $e^{g(z)} = f(z)$, $z \in R$.
3. Let R be the complement of the non-negative real axis. Prove that R is simply-connected.
4. Let γ: $[0, \infty] \to \mathbf{C}$ be a one-one continuous function such that $\lim_{t \to \infty} |\gamma(t)| = \infty$. Show that the complement of range of γ is simply-connected.

ANSWERS

2. If such a exists, then $g'(z) = \dfrac{f'(z)}{f(z)}$, $\exists\, F' = \dfrac{f'}{f}$ such that $(e^{-f}f)'(z) = 0$. Thus, $f(z) = ke^{f(z)}$. $g(z) = f(z) + \alpha \Rightarrow e^{g(z)} = f(z)$.
3. Let $G = \{t \in R : [t_0, t]$ lies inside Γ, α is least upper bound of Γ, $\alpha > 0$, If $\alpha \in G$, then α lies inside Γ, but inside of Γ is open, a contradiction.
4. Let Γ be any closed contour in $\mathbf{C} \sim R(\gamma)$. Suppose $\gamma(t_0)$ lies inside Γ, for some $t_0 > 0$. Let $G = \{t \in R, \gamma(s)$ lies inside Γ for all $s \in [t_0, t]\}$. Also $|z| < k$ for all $z \in \Gamma$. Also $|\gamma(t)| > k$ for all $t > t_1$. Let α be the least upper bound of G. Suppose $\alpha \in G$ then $\gamma(\alpha)$ lies inside Γ. Since γ is continous, $\delta > 0$ such that $|t - \alpha| < \delta$, $|\gamma(t) - \gamma(\alpha)| < \in$. $\gamma(t)$ lies inside Γ. Hence $\alpha + \dfrac{\delta}{2} \in G$ and so a is not an upper bound. If $\alpha \notin G$ then α is not an upper bound, the outside of Γ being open.

8.2 PROPERTIES OF THE ANALYTIC FUNCTION LOG Z

Definition 8.3

A continuous function f is an analytic branch of log z in a domain D if

(*i*) f is analytic in D

(*ii*) $e^{f(z)} = z$.

We prove that following important properties of the branch of log z

1. If f is an analytic branch of log z iff there exists an analytic function, $g(z)$ such that

$$g(z) = f(z) + 2\pi ki$$

for any fixed integer k, then $g(z)$ is a branch of log z.

Proof

Let $g(z) = f(z) + 2\pi ki$ for some fixed integral k. Since f is analytic, therefore $g(z)$ is also analytic

Also $$e^{g(z)} = e^{f(z) + 2\pi Ki}$$

$$\{\because 2\pi ki \text{ is the periodicity of } e^z, e^z = e^{z + 2k\pi i})$$

$$= e^{f(z)} = z$$

Conversely, let g is an analytic branch of log z, then

$$e^{g(z)} = e^{f(z)}$$

So $$e^{g(z) - f(z)} = 1$$

and $$g(z) - f(z) = 2k\pi i \text{ for some fixed integer } k.$$

2. We know $e^w \neq 0$ for any w, so log 0 is not defined.

But for any $z = Re^{i\theta}$, $R > 0$ if

$$f(z) = u(z) + iv(z) = \log z \qquad ...(i)$$

Then, $$e^{f(z)} = e^{\log z} = e^{u(z)}\, e^{iv(z)}$$

which is possible iff

$$e^{u(z)} = |\, z\,| = R$$

and $$v(z) = \text{Arg } z = i\theta + 2k\pi \text{ for an integer } k.$$

Now from (*i*) $f(z) = R + i \text{ Arg } z$. ...(*ii*)

However, Arg z is not a well-defined function and even if we adopt a convention for Arg z, then the function in (*ii*) is analytic. We prove in the following that a branch of log can always be defined if D is a simply-connected region.

3. Suppose D is simply-connected and $0 \notin D$. Choose $z_0 \in D$, fix a value of $\log z_0$ and set

$$f(z) = \int_{z_0}^{z} \frac{d\zeta}{\zeta} + \log z_0 .$$

Then f is an analytic branch of $\log z$ in D.

Proof

Since $\frac{1}{\zeta}$ is analytic in domain $D(0 \notin D)$, therefore, f is well-defined because integral along any path from z_0 to z yield the same value. Also $f'(z) = \frac{1}{z}$, so f is analytic in D.

To show: $e^{f(z)} = z$.

Consider a function

$$\begin{aligned} g(z) &= ze^{-f(z)} \text{ on } D \\ g'(z) &= -ze^{-f(z)} f'(z) + ze^{-f(z)} \\ &= -e^{-f(z)} + ze^{-f(z)} \\ &= 0 \end{aligned}$$

Then, g is analytic, $g'(z) = 0$ thus g is constant and

$$\begin{aligned} g(z) &= g(z_0) \\ &= z_0 e^{-f(z_0)} \\ &= 1 \end{aligned}$$

Hence, $$e^{f(z)} = z.$$

In an analogous manner, we can define an analytic branch of log $f(z)$ in any simply-connected domain where f is analytic and unequal to zero. For this we fix $z_0 \in D$ and a value of $\log f(z_0)$. Set

$$\log f(z) = \int_{z_0}^{z} \frac{f'(\zeta)}{f(\zeta)} d\zeta + \log f(z_0).$$

Now we discuss a typical situation in which $D = \mathbf{C} \sim \{z : Re\, z \le 0\}$ then, the branch of log can be defined with Arg $z \in\,]-\pi, \pi[$.

4. Let $D = \mathbf{C} \sim \{z : Re\, z \le 0\}$. If $z = Re^{i\theta}$, $R > 0$, $-\pi < \theta < \pi$. Then, $f(z) = \log R + i\theta$ is an analytic branch of $\log z$ in D.

Proof

Let $\{z_n\}$ be a sequence such that $z_n \to z$. Let $z_n = R_n e^{i\theta_n}$. Then, $R_n \to R$ and $\theta_n \to \theta$. Also, $\log R_n + i\theta_n \to \log R + i\theta$.

Also, $f(z_n) \to f(z)$, f is continuous in D and analytic in D. Now $e^{f(z)} = e^{\log R + i\theta} = Re^{i\theta} = z$. Thus, f is an analytic branch of $\log z$.

5. If we slit the plane $G = \mathbf{C} \sim \{(-\infty, 0]$, then the principal branch of the logarithm is defined as

$$\log z = \log r + i\theta$$

where $z = re^{i\theta}$ with $|\theta| < \pi$. To prove this we use the path of integration shown in Fig. 8.10. If $z = re^{i\theta}$ with $|\theta| < \pi$, the path consists of the line segment from 1 to r and the arc η from r to z.

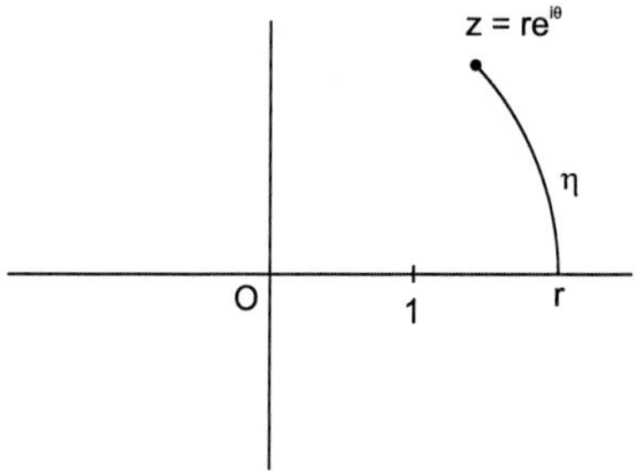

Fig. 8.10

Then,

$$\log z = \int_1^r \frac{dx}{x} + \int_\eta \frac{dw}{w}$$

$$= \log r + \int_0^\theta \frac{ire^{it}}{re^{it}}\,dt$$

$$= \log r + i\theta.$$

8.3 STAR REGIONS

Definition 8.4

A set S is called a star like if there is a point $z_0 \in s$ such that for all $z \in S$, the line segment $[z_0, z]$ is contained in S. The point z_0 is called a star for S. (Fig. 8.11)

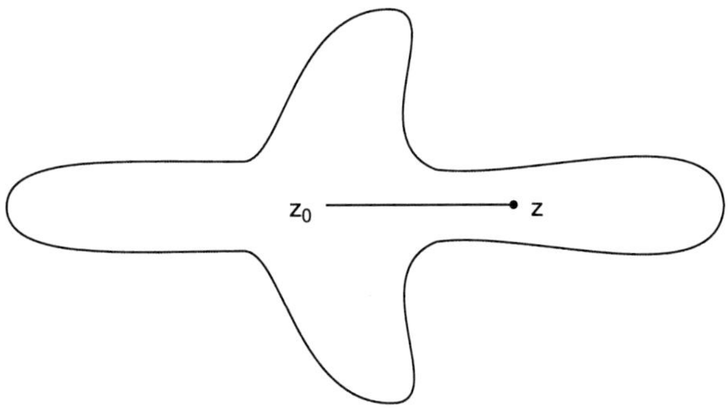

Fig. 8.11

We can think of z_0 as a source of light, then z_0 is a star of S if every point of S is illuminated by z_0.

A region which is star-like is called a star region.

We have some important facts about a star, like set.

1. An open set which is a star-like is a star region.

Proof

Let z_0 be a star of a set S. Let $z, z' \in S$, then $[z_0, z]$ and $[z_0, z']$ lie in S (Fig. 8.12). Then $[z, z_0, z']$ lies in S. Thus, S is polygonally connected and hence S is a region.

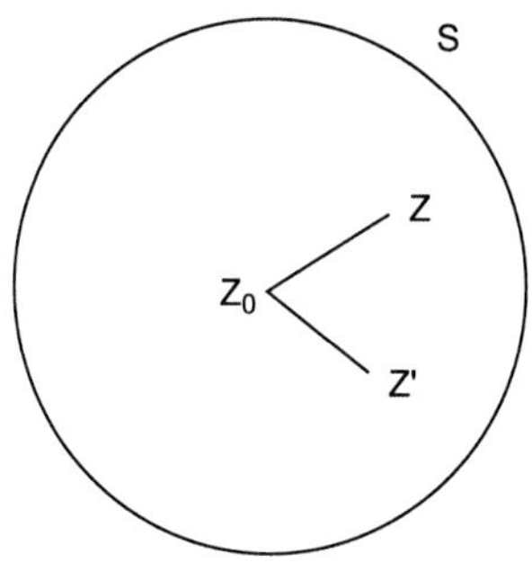

Fig. 8.12

2. Every convex set is star-like.

Proof

Let S be a convex set, then for $z, z' \in S$ the line segment $[z, z'] \subseteq S$. If we fix z as star of S then $[z, z'] \subseteq S$ for every $z' \in S$. Thus, S is star-like.

Note: Every point of a convex set is a star of the set.

3. Every star-like set is a convex set.

Proof

Let S be a star-like set such that every point of S is a star then S is a convex set.

4. Every star-like set is simply-connected.

Proof

Since every star-like set is a convex set and every convex set is simply connected.

5. Every open disc is a star region.

Proof

Let $D = \{z : |z - \alpha| < r\}$. If $z_1, z_2 \in D$ and $z \in [z_1, z_2]$ (Fig. 8.13) then

$$|z - \alpha| \le \max \{|z_1 - \alpha|, |z_2 - \alpha|) < r.$$

and thus $z \in D$.

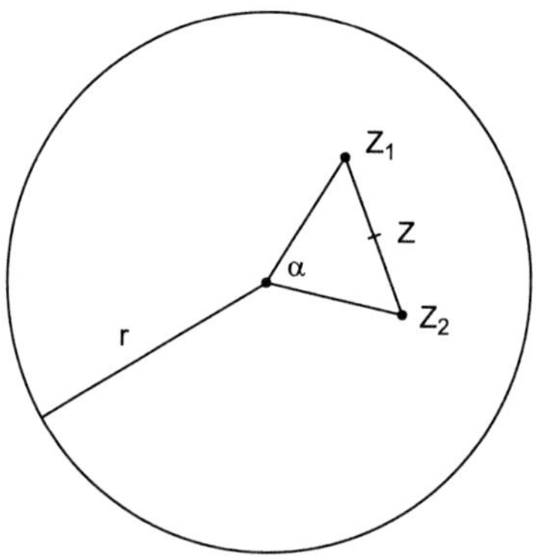

Fig. 8.13

EXERCISE

1. Prove that any punctured disc $D' = \{z : 0 < |z| < 1\}$ is not a star region.
2. Let R be a star region, a be a point not in R. Show that there is a ray from a not meeting R.

3. Which of the following sets are star-like

(*i*) $\{z : 1 < | z | < 2\}$

(*ii*) $\{z : | z - 2 | > 3, z | < 2\}$

(*iii*) $\{z : Im\, z > 0, 1 < | z | < 2\}$

(*iv*) $C \sim \{-1, 1\}$

(*v*) $C \sim \{z : | z | = 1, Re\, z \geq 0\}$.

Give reasons?

ANSWERS

1. Let z be a star in D', $-z \in D'$. Then $[-z, z]$ contains 0 but $0 \notin D'$. Thus D' is not a star region.

2. Let b be a star of R. Thus the ray from a with direction opposite to $[a, b]$ contains a point $\mathbf{C} \in R$. Thus $[b, c] \subseteq R$ and so $a \in R$, which is a contradiction.

3. (*i*) Not a star (*ii*) Not a star

(*iii*) Not a region (*iv*) Star region

(*v*) Star region

❑❑❑

9

Isolated Singularities

In the previous chapters, we have been concentrating on the properties which follow from the fact that a function is analytic on a region, but in this chapter we shall examine functions which failed to be analytic at certain points of a region (for example $\frac{1}{z}$ at $z = 0$). Laurent's theorem provides a satisfactory substitute for Taylor's theorem for functions holomorphic except at isolated singular points. It leads to the classification of singularities which proves valuable in the next three chapters. Our focus is now on the special behaviour of an analytic function in the neighbourhood of an isolated singularity.

9.1 SINGULARITIES

Consider the following functions

$$z \to \frac{\sin z}{z},\ z \neq 0$$

$$z \to \frac{\cos z}{z},\ z \neq 0$$

$$z \to e^{\frac{1}{z}},\ z \neq 0$$

Each function is analytic on its domain $\subset \sim \{0\}$, but not at zero. This point zero is called singularity of each of these functions. We define singularity of a function *f* properly in the following definition:

Definition 9.1

Let $D' = \{z : 0 < |z - a| < r\}$ be a punctured disc. If a function f is analytic in D' but not on the disc. $D = \{z : |z - a| < r\}$, then a is called isolated singularity of f. (Note that the function f does not have to be defined at a).

We can observe that the function is discontinuous at an isolated singularity. For example,

(*i*) The function $f(z) = \begin{cases} \sin z & z \neq 2 \\ 0 & z = 2 \end{cases}$ has an isolated singularity at $z = 2$.

(*ii*) $g(z) = \dfrac{1}{(z-3)^2}$ has an isolated singularity at $z = 3$

(*iii*) $e^{\frac{1}{z}}$ has an isolated singularity at $z = 0$.

In the above examples, all the three functions have isolated singularity but these singularities are of different types. We classify the singularities into three categories:

1. Definition 9.2

Removable Singularity: If f has a singularity at a but there is a complex number α such that the function

$$z \to \begin{cases} f(z), & z \neq a \\ \alpha, & z = a \end{cases}$$

is analytic on a neighbourhood of a, then a is said to be removable singularity and we remove the singularity by setting.

$$f(a) = \alpha$$

2. Definition 9.3

Pole: If a function f be written in the form $f(z) = \dfrac{A(z)}{B(z)}$ (for $z \neq a$) where A and B are analytic at a, A(a) $\neq 0$ and B(a) $= 0$ we say f has a pole at a. If B has a zero of order k at a, then f has a pole of order k. A pole of order one is called simple pole.

Definition 9.4 Essential Singularity

If f has neither a removable singularity nor a pole at a, we say f has on essential singularity at a.

In the following theorem, we develop some methods for identifying the type of a given singularity— in other words whether it is removable, a pole or essential. We begin with removable singularity.

Theorem 9.1

If f has an isolated singularity at $z = a$ then $\lim_{z \to a} (z - a) f(z) = 0$, iff a is a removable singularity of f.

Proof

Suppose f is analytic in $D' = \{z : 0 < |z - a| < R\}$. Define a function g such that

$$g(z) = \begin{cases} (z-a)f(z) & z \neq a \\ 0 & z = a \end{cases}$$

Since $\lim_{z \to a} g(z) = \lim_{z \to a} (z - a) f(z) = 0 = g(a)$, therefore, g is a continuous function at $z = a$. We want to show that g is analytic in D, let R be the rectangle in $D = \{z : |z - a| < R\}$.

Then, following three cases arise:

Case (*i*). If $a \notin R$ (Fig. 9.1) then $g(z)$ is analytic in R, therefore

$$\int_R g(z)dz = 0$$

By Morera's theorem, g is analytic in D.

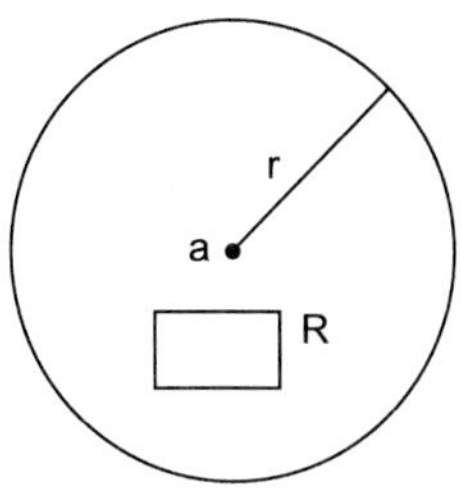

Fig. 9.1

Case (*ii*). If $a \in R$ (Fig. 9.2). Divide the rectangle into subrectangles, then

$$\int_R g(z)dz = \sum_{k=1}^{6} g(z)dz$$

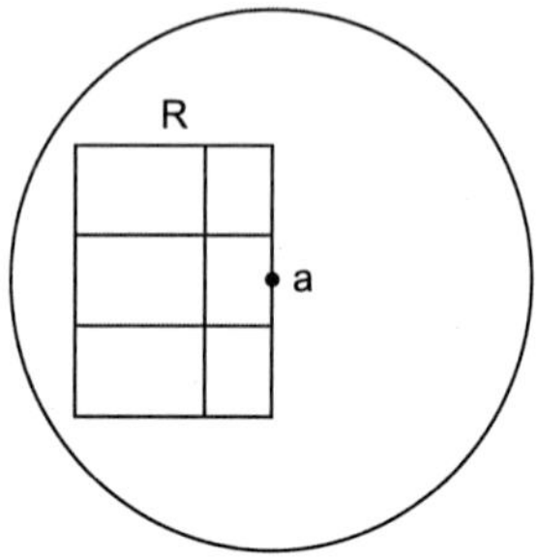

Fig. 9.2

Let R_1 be the boundary of the subrectangle containing a. Let $l(R_1) = l$. Since g is continuous at a_0, therefore given $\in > 0$, there exists $\delta > 0$ such that

$$|g(z) - g(a)| = |g(z)| < \frac{\in}{l}, \; 0 < |z - a| < \delta$$

Then,

$$\left|\int_R g(z)dz\right| \le \int_{R_1} |g(z)||dz|$$

$$< \frac{\in}{l} \times l = \in$$

Since $\in > 0$ be arbitrary, therefore $\int_R g = 0$.

Case (*iii*) If $a \in$ int R (Fig. 9.3).

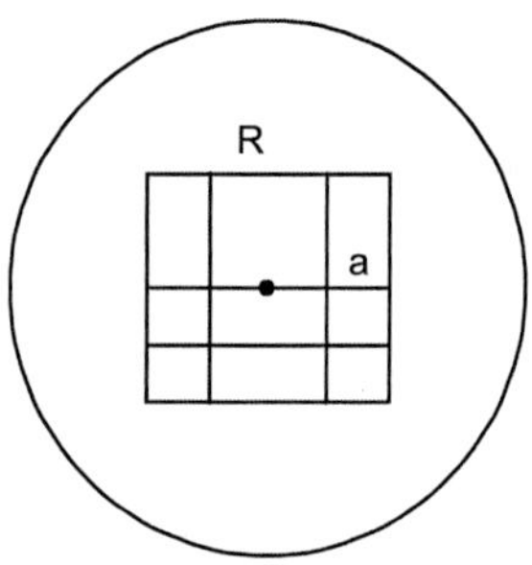

Fig. 9.3

We divide the rectangle R into nine rectangles and then by applying case (*ii*), we get

$$\int_R g(z)dz = 0$$

Thus, by using Morera's theorem $g(z)$ is analytic in D. Also $g(a) = 0$, it means a is zero of g, there is function $h(z)$ analytic in D such that

$$g(z) = (z - a)\, h(z),\ h(a) \neq 0$$

But $$g(z) = (z - a)\, f(z)$$

Then, $$f(z) = h(z),\ 0 < |z - a| < R.$$

Thus, $z = a$ is a removable singularity of f.

Conversely, if $z = a$ is a removable singularity of f, then the function

$$g(z) = \begin{cases} f(z), & z \neq a \\ a, & z = a \end{cases}$$

is analytic on the disc $D = \{z : |z - a| < r\}$ and

$$\lim_{z\to a} (z - a)\, f(z) = \lim_{z\to a} (z - a)\, g(z) = \lim_{z\to a} (z - a)\, .\, a = 0.$$

Examples 9.1

(*i*) The function $f(z) = \dfrac{\sin z}{z}$ has a removable singularity at 0 as if

$$\lim_{z\to 0} (z - 0)\, \frac{\sin z}{z} = 0$$

(*ii*) The function $g(z) = \dfrac{\cos z}{z}$ has a singularity at zero, but it is not removable because

$$\lim_{z\to 0} z\, g(z) = \lim_{z\to 0} z\, \frac{\cos z}{z} = \cos 0 = 1 \neq 0$$

(*iii*) The function $h(z) = \dfrac{z+i}{z^2+1}$ has two isolated singularities i and $-i$. But $z = -i$ is removable singularity.

Since $$\lim_{z\to -i} (z + i)\frac{z+i}{z^2+1} = \lim_{z\to -i} \frac{z+i}{z-i} = 0.$$

Now we want to move on to poles of a function. If a is a pole of f of order m then we can write

$$f(z) = (z - a)^{-m}\, g(z) \text{ for } z \neq a \tag{1}$$

where g is analytic on the disc $\{z : |z - a| < r\}$ and $g(a) \neq 0$. The following theorem gives us necessary as well as sufficient condition for a pole of order m.

Theorem 9.2

If $z = a$ is an isolated singularity of f, then $z = a$ is a pole of f of order m if and only if $\lim\limits_{z\to a} (z-a) f(z)$ exists and is non zero.

Proof

Let $z = a$ be a pole of $f(z)$ of order m, then from (1)

$$\lim_{z\to a}(z-a)^m f(z) = \lim_{z\to a} g(z) = g(a) \neq 0.$$

Conversely, let $\lim\limits_{z\to a}(z-a)^m f(z) \neq 0$. The function $z \to (z-a)^m$ $f(z)$ has a singularity at a. Since $\lim\limits_{z\to a}(z-a)^m f(z)$ exists, therefore the singularity is removable. Thus, if

$$g(z) = \begin{cases} (z-a)^m f(z), & z \neq a \\ \lim\limits_{z\to a}(z-a)^m f(z), & z = a \end{cases}$$

Then, g is analytic on the disc $|z-a| < r$, $g(a) \neq 0$ and $f(z) = \dfrac{g(z)}{(z-a)^m}$ for $0 < |z-a| < r$. Thus, $z = a$ is a pole of f of order m.

There is a relationship between zeros and isolated singularities of an analytic function. We observe that if an analytic function has an isolated zero at the point a, then its reciprocal has an isolated singularity at a. To exploit this we need some preliminary facts about zeros.

Definition 9.5

Zeros of an analytic function: Suppose f is analytic in $D(a; r)$, for some $r > 0$ and that $f(a) = 0$. Assume that $f \neq 0$ in $D(a; r)$. By Taylor's theorem

$$f(z) = \sum_{n=m}^{\infty} c_n (z-a)^n \quad \text{where } m \geq 1,\ C_m \neq 0$$

We define the order of the zero of f at a to be m. We know

$$c_n = \frac{f^{(n)}(a)}{n!}$$

Then, f has a zero of order m at a if and only if

$$f(a) = f'(a) = \ldots\ldots\ldots\ldots = f^{m-1}(a) = 0,\, f^{m}(a) \neq 0$$

(see Example 6.9)

From Theorem 9.2, we can conclude that if $z = a$ is a zero of an analytic function f in $D(a; r)$. Then,

$$\lim_{z \to a} (z - a)^{-m} f(z) \neq 0. \tag{2}$$

Theorem 9.2 also has an important corollary, which shows that there is a simple relationship between poles and zeros.

Corollary 9.3

Suppose that function f is analytic on a disc with centre a and has a zero of order m at a. Then, $\dfrac{1}{f}$ has a pole of order m at a.

Proof

Since $z = a$ is a zero of order m of $f(z)$, therefore from (2), we get

$$\lim_{z \to a} (z - a)^{-m} f(z) = D \neq 0$$

$$\Rightarrow \qquad \lim_{z \to a} \frac{(z-a)^m}{f(z)} = \frac{1}{D} \neq 0$$

$$\text{i.e.,} \qquad \lim_{z \to a} (z-a)^m \frac{1}{f(z)} \neq 0$$

Then, by Theorem 9.2, $z = a$ is a pole of $\dfrac{1}{f(z)}$ of order m.

Example 9.2

1. The function $f(z) = \dfrac{z+i}{z^2+1}$ has removable singularity at $z = -i$ (Example 9.1 (*iii*)), but $z = i$ is also an isolated singularity of $f(z)$. Also $f(z) = \dfrac{z+i}{z^2+1} = \dfrac{1}{z-i}$ in a punctured disc centred at i, therefore, the singularity is a simple pole.

2. The function $g(z) = \dfrac{\sin z}{z^m}$, where m is an integer and $m > 2$, has a singularity at 0 which is not removable. Now

$$\lim_{z \to 0} z^{m-1} \frac{\sin z}{z^m} = \lim_{z \to 0} \frac{\sin z}{z} = 1$$

so that singularity is a pole of order $m - 1$.

3. The function $h(z) = \dfrac{\cos z}{z^2}$ has isolated singularity at $z = 0$.

$\lim_{z \to 0} z^2 h(z) = \lim_{z \to 0} \cos z = 1 \neq 0$. Thus, $z = 0$ is a pole of order 2.

Theorem 9.4

If $z = a$ is an isolated singularity of $f(z)$ such that $\lim_{z \to a} |f(z)| = \infty$ then $z = a$ is a pole of f.

Proof

Since $z = a$ is an isolated singularity there exists $R_1 > 0$ such that f is analytic in the disc

$D' = \{z : 0 < z - a| < R_1\}$. Also $\lim_{z \to a} |f(z)| = \infty$, therefore for k > 0 there exists $R_2 > 0$ such that

$|f(z)| \geq k$, $0 < |z - a| < R_2$.

Let $R = \min \{R_1, R_2\}$ and $D = \{z : |z - a| < R\}$. Since f is analytic in D'. Therefore, $| f(z) | > 0$. Define a function

$$g(z) = \begin{cases} \dfrac{1}{f(z)}, & z \neq a \\ 0 & z = a \end{cases}$$

Then, $$\lim_{z \to a} |g(z)| = \lim_{z \to a} \frac{1}{| f(z) |} = 0 = g\,(a).$$

Therefore g is continuous at $z = a$. Also $\lim_{z \to a} (z - a)\dfrac{1}{f(z)} = 0$. The function g is analytic in D.

Also $g(a) = 0$. Thus, $z = a$ is a zero of analytic function g of order m (say). Then,

$$g(z) = (z-a)^m h(z),\ h(a) \neq 0 \text{ and } h \text{ is analytic}$$

$$\Rightarrow \quad \frac{1}{f(z)} = (z-a)^m h(z)$$

$$\Rightarrow \quad (z-a)^m f(z) = \frac{1}{h(z)}$$

$$\Rightarrow \quad \lim_{z \to a} (z-a)^m f(z) = \frac{1}{h(a)} \neq 0$$

By Theorem 9.2. $z = a$ is a pole of order m.

Corollary 9.5

Suppose f is analytic in some disc $D(a; r)$ and f has a pole of order m at a. Suppose g is analytic in $D(a; r)$ for some r. Then, the function fg has

(*i*) a pole of order m if $g(a) \neq 0$

(*ii*) a pole of order $m - n$ if g has a zero of order n at a and $n < m$.

(*iii*) a removable singularity if g has a zero of order at least m.

Proof

Since f has a pole of order m at a. Then by Theorem 9.2.

$$\lim_{z\to a} (z-a)^m f(z) \neq 0.$$

(*i*) If $g(a) \neq 0$. Consider

$$\lim_{z\to a} (z-a)^m (fg(z)) = \lim_{z\to a} (z-a)^{\mathrm{m}} f(z) \lim_{z\to a} g(z)$$
$$= 0.\ g(a)$$
$$= 0$$

Thus, fg has a pole of order m.

(*ii*) If g has a zero of order n at a and $n < m$, then

$$\lim_{z\to a} (z-a)^{-n} g(z) \neq 0.$$

Consider

$$\lim_{z\to a} (z-a)^{m-n}(fg(z)) = \lim_{z\to a} (z-a)^m f(z) \lim_{z\to a} (z-a)^{-n} g(z)$$
$$\neq 0$$

This gives that fg has pole of order $m - n$ if $n < m$.

(*iii*) If g has zero of order at least m, then

$$\lim_{z \to a} (z - a)^{-m} g(z) \neq 0$$

Then,

$$\lim_{z \to a} (z - a)(fg)(z) = \lim_{z \to a} (z - a)(z - a)^m f(z)(z - a)^{-m} g(z)$$

$$= \lim_{z \to a} (z - a) \lim_{z \to a} (z - a)^m f(z)$$

$$\lim_{z \to a} (z - a)^{-m} g(z)$$

$$= 0$$

Then by Theorem 9.1 (fg) has a removable singularity at $z = a$.

Example 9.3

Suppose f and g are analytic in $D'(a\,;r)$ and $z = a$ is a pole of f and g of order m and n, respectively. Find the singularities of $f + g, f. g$ and $\frac{f}{g}$ at a.

Solution

Since f has a pole of order m.

$$\lim_{z \to a} (z - a)^m f(z) \neq 0$$

and g has a pole of order n

$$\lim_{z \to a} (z - a)^n g(z) \neq 0$$

Also $f(z) = (z - a)^{-m} h(z)$ and $g(z) = (z - a)^{-n} h_1(z)$. Then $h(a) \neq 0$, $h_1(a) \neq 0$ where $h(z)$ and $h(z)$ are analytic

(*i*) $$f(z) + g(z) = \frac{h(z)}{(z-a)^m} + \frac{h_1(z)}{(z-a)^n}$$

If $m = n$, then

$$f(z) + g(z) = \frac{h(z) + h_1(z)}{(z-a)^m}$$

Thus $f + g$ has a pole of order m.

If $m > n$, then

$$f(z) + g(z) = \frac{h(z)+(z-a)^{m-n}h_1(z)}{(z-a)^m}$$

Then, $f + g$ has pole of order m.

(*ii*) Consider $\lim_{z\to a} (z-a)^{m+n} fg(z)$

$$= \lim_{z\to a} (z-a)^m f(z) \lim_{z\to a} (z-a)^n g(z)$$

$$\neq 0$$

Thus, $z = a$ is a pole of order $(m + n)$ of (fg).

(*iii*) Since g has a pole of order n at $z = a$, therefore $z = a$ is a zero of g of order n, thus

$$\lim_{z\to a} (z-a)^{-n} \frac{1}{g(z)} \neq 0.$$

Consider $\lim_{z\to a} (z-a)^{m-n} \left(\frac{f(z)}{g}\right) = \lim_{z\to a} (z-a)^m f(z)$

$$\lim_{z\to a} (z-a)^{-n} \frac{1}{g(z)}$$

$$\neq 0$$

Then, $\frac{f}{g}$ has a pole of order m–n at $z = a$.

An essential singularity is a singularity which is neither removable nor a pole. Now we shall see drastic difference in the behaviour of a function near a non-removable singularity between the cases of a pole and an essential singularity. Near a pole the modulus of the function gets large. On the other hand, a function approximates every complex value in a disc centred at the singularity; if it is an essential singularity.

Theorem 9.6: The Casorati-Weierstrass Theorem

Suppose f is analytic in $D' = \{z : 0 < |z - a| < r\}$ and $z = a$ is an essential singularity of f. Given any complex number w, and any positive real numbers $\in$ and δ with $\delta < r$, there is a complex number z such that $0 < |z - a| < \delta$ for which $|f(z) - w| < \in$.

Proof

We shall prove the theorem by contradiction. Suppose the assertions are false, that is there is a complex number w and positive real numbers $\in$ and δ with $\delta < r$ such that whenever $0 < |z - a| < \delta$ then $|f(z) - w| \geq \in$. We shall show $z = a$ cannot be an essential singularity.

Since $f(z) - w \neq 0$ on the disc $D'' = \{z : 0 < |z - a| < \delta\}$. Consider the function

$$g(z) = \frac{1}{f(z) - w}$$

analytic in D''. Also $|g(z)| \leq \frac{1}{\in}$ on D'' and $\lim_{z \to a} (z - a)\, g(z) = 0$

So by Theorem 9.1, $z = a$ is a removable singularity of g. By appropriate defining of $g(z)$ we could remove the singularity and extend g to become analytic on the disc $|z - a| < \delta$.

Now $$f(z) = w + \frac{1}{g(z)} \text{ on } D''.$$

If $g(a) \neq 0$ then f has a removable singularity at a.

If g has a zero of order m at a, then

$$g(z) = (z - a)^m\, h(z), \;\; h(a) \neq 0.$$

Then, $$\lim_{z \to a} (z - a)^m f(z) = \lim_{z \to a} (z - a)^m w + \lim_{z \to a} \frac{1}{g(z)}$$

$$= \frac{1}{g(a)} \neq 0$$

Thus, $z = a$ is a pole of order m. $z = a$ is not an essential singularity of f. We conclude that if a is an essential singularity of f then the assertion of the theorem is correct.

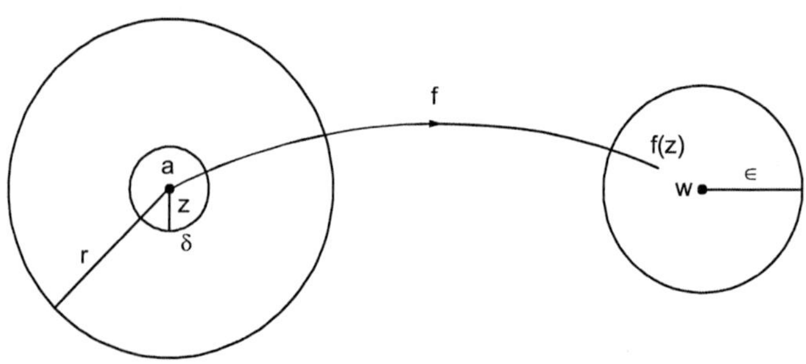

Fig. 9.4

A strong consequence of Casorati-Weierstrass theorem is the following corollary:

Corollary 9.7

Suppose that f has an essential singularity at a. If D is any punctured disc at $z = a$, then $\overline{\{f(z) : z \in D\}} = \mathbf{C}$.

Proof

Suppose the conclusion of the Casorati-Weierstrass theorem holds. Then, if $w \in \mathbf{C}$ and $\in > 0$ is any number, there is $z \in D$ such that $|f(z) - w| < \in$. This implies that w is a limit point of the set $\{f(z) : z \in D\}$. Thus, $\overline{\{f(z) : z \in D\}} = \mathbf{C}$.

Example 9.4

Classify the singularities of the following functions:

(*i*) $\dfrac{1}{z^4 + z^2}$ (*ii*) $\cot z$ (*iii*) $\operatorname{cosec} z$ (*iv*) $\dfrac{e^{\frac{1}{z^2}}}{z-1}$.

Solution

(*i*) Let
$$f(z) = \frac{1}{z^4 + z^2} = \frac{1}{z^2(z^2+1)} = \frac{1}{z^2(z+i)(z-i)}$$

$z = 0, i, -i$ are isolated singularities of $f(z)$.

Also $$\lim_{z\to 0} z^2 f(z) = \lim_{z\to 0} \frac{1}{(z+i)(z-i)} = 1 \neq 0$$

Therefore, $z = 0$ is a double pole of $f(z)$.

Now $$\lim_{z\to i} (z-i) f(z) = \lim_{z\to i} \frac{1}{z^2(z+i)} = \frac{1}{-2i} \neq 0.$$

and $$\lim_{z\to -i} (z+i) f(z) = \lim_{z\to -i} \frac{1}{z^2(z-i)} = \frac{1}{2i} \neq 0.$$

Thus, we conclude $z = 0$ is a double pole and $z = i, -i$ are simple poles of $f(z)$.

(*ii*) $\cot z = \dfrac{\cos z}{\sin z}$

We know $\sin z = 0$ at $z = n\pi$, $n \in \pi$. Thus, at the points $n\pi (n \in \pi)$, sin z has simple zeros and $\cos z \neq 0$. Hence, cot z has simple poles at $z = n\pi$ $(n \in \pi)$.

(*iii*) $\operatorname{cosec} z = \dfrac{1}{\sin z}$.

Same as (*ii*) cosec z has simple poles at $z = n\pi$ $(n \in \pi)$

(*iv*) Let $$g(z) = \frac{e^{\frac{1}{z^2}}}{z-1}.$$

$z = 0$ and $z = 1$ are isolated singularities of g.

Also $\lim\limits_{z\to 1} (z - 1)\, g(z) = \lim\limits_{z\to 1} e^{\frac{1}{z^2}} = e \neq 0$

Thus, $z = 1$ is a simple pole of $g(z)$. $z = 0$ is an essential singularity of $g(z)$.

EXERCISE

1. Find the singularities of the functions, and classify them as removable singularities, poles, or essential singularities.

(*i*) $z \to \dfrac{1}{(1-z)(2-z)}$

(*ii*) $z \to \dfrac{z^5 - 2z^4 + z - 2}{z-2}$

(*iii*) $z \to \tan z$

(*iv*) $z \to e^{(z+\frac{1}{z})}$

(*v*) $z \to \dfrac{1}{z^2(z^2+1)}$

2. Show that if f is analytic on the punctured disc $0 < |z - a| < r$, and is bounded on the disc $|z - a| < r$, then f has a removable singularity at a.

3. Show that the singularities of a rational function are either removable, or poles.

4. The function $z \to \tan \frac{1}{z}$ is defined on **C** except at the points,

$\frac{1}{n\pi + \frac{\pi}{2}}$ $n = \pm 1, \pm 2, ...$ and at 0. Where are the singularities?

5. Does there exist a function f with an isolated singularity at 0 and such that $|f(z)| \sim \exp\left(\frac{1}{|z|}\right)$ near $z = 0$?

6. Show that the image of the unit disc minus the origin under $f(z) = \text{cosec}\ \frac{1}{z}$ is dense in the complex plane.

ANSWERS

1. (*i*) Simple poles at $z = 1, 2$
   (*ii*) Removable singularities $z = 2$.
   (*iii*) Simple poles at $\pi/2 + n\pi$, $n = 0, \pm 1, \pm 2,.......$
   (*iv*) Essential singularty at $z = 0$
   (*v*) Removable singularity at 0, simple pole at $2n\pi i$, $n = \pm 1, \pm 2,...$

2. If $|f(z)| < k$, $|z - \alpha| < r$. Then $|(z - \alpha)f(z)| < k|z - \alpha|$. So $\lim_{z \to \alpha} |(z - \alpha) f(z)| = 0 \Rightarrow f$ has removable singularity at z = a.

3. Singularities of a rational function occur at the zeroes of its denominator. If $f(z) = \frac{p(z)}{q(z)}$, $q(\alpha) = 0$. Then $q(\alpha) = (z - \alpha)^m$ $\phi(z)$, $\phi(\alpha) \neq 0$. If $p(\alpha) = 0$, then $p(z) = (z - \alpha)^n p(z)$, $p(\alpha) \neq 0$.

If $n > m$, the singularities is removable. If $m > n$ the singularity is a pole of order $m - n$.

4. The function $f(z) = \tan\frac{1}{z}$ has singularity at the points $\frac{1}{n\pi + \pi/2}$ $n = +1, +2, \ldots\ldots$ But $\{0\}$ is not an isolated point, therefore it is not a point of singularity.

5. No, f has a pole at $z = 0$, but $|f(z)| \sim \frac{A}{|z|^k}$ near $z = 0$.

6. Since range of $\sin\left(\frac{1}{z}\right)$ is dense in **C**, therefore $\operatorname{cosec}\frac{1}{z}$ is dense in **C**.

9.2 LAURENT EXPANSIONS

In chapter 6, we found a power series expansion for a function analytic in a disc. A similar type of two-sided expansion of the form $\sum_{n=-\infty}^{\infty} c_n(z-a)^n$ can be derived for functions analytic in an annulus $R_1 < |z-a| < R_2$. These power series are known as Laurent expansion and are valuable tools in the classification of isolated singularities.

Theorem 9.8

If $f(z) = \sum_{-\infty}^{\infty} c_k z^k$ is convergent in the domain $D = \{z : R_1 < |z| < R_2\}$

where
$$R_2 = \frac{1}{\limsup_{k\to\infty} |c_k|^{\frac{1}{k}}}$$

$$R_1 = \limsup_{k\to\infty} |c_{-k}|^{\frac{1}{k}}$$

If $R_1 < R_2$, D is an annulus and f is analytic in D.

Proof

Let $f_1(z) = \sum_{k=0}^{\infty} c_k z^k$, then $f_1(z)$ converges for $|z| < R_2$ (by Theorem 2.14). If $f_2(z) = \sum_{k=-\infty}^{-1} c_k z^k = \sum_{1}^{\infty} c_{-k}\left(\frac{1}{z}\right)^k$, then it converges for $\left|\frac{1}{z}\right| < \frac{1}{R_1}$ or $|z| > R_1$. Thus $\sum_{-\infty}^{\infty} c_k z^k$ converges for all z in the intersection.

Since $f_1(z)$ and $f_2(z) = g(\frac{1}{z})$ are power series, f_1 and f_2 are both analytic in their respective domains of convergence. Hence, f is analytic in the intersection of these domains (Fig. 9.5).

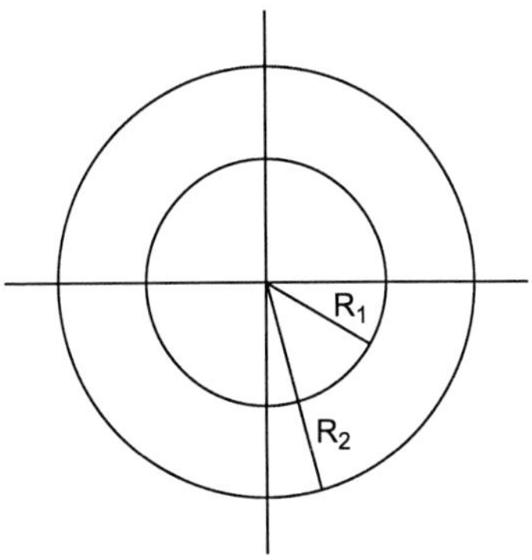

Fig. 9.5

Theorem 9.9: Laurent's Theorem

Let f be analytic within the annulus $A = \{z : R_1 < |z - a| < R_2\}$. Then f has the series representation

$$f(z) = \sum_{k=-\infty}^{\infty} c_k (z-a)^k$$

valid for $z \in A$. The coefficients c_k are given by

$$c_k = \frac{1}{2\pi i}\int_c \frac{f(w)}{(w-a)^{k+1}}\, dw,\ k = 0, \pm 1, \pm 2 \,.....$$

where c is a simple closed curve that lies entirely within A and has a in its interior (Fig. 9.6).

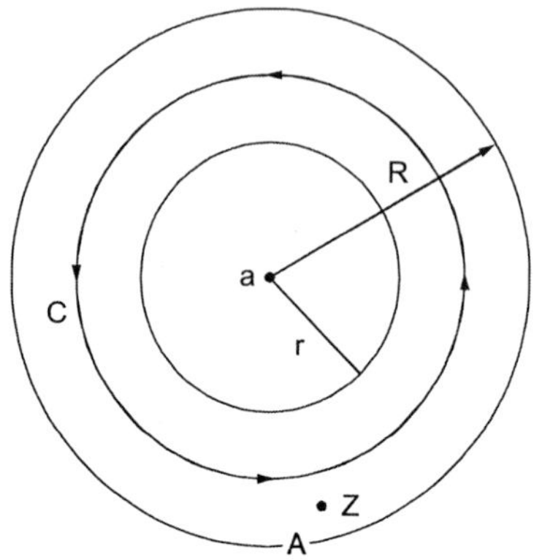

Fig. 9.6

Proof

Without loss of generality we can assume $a = 0$. Then, the annulus $A = \{z : R_1 < |z| < R_2\}$. Let C_1 and C_2 be two concentric circles with centre zero and radii r_1 and r_2 where $0 < R_1 < r_1 < r_2 < R_2$. Let z be a fixed point in A that also satisfies the inequality $r_1 < |z| < r_2$ (Fig. 9.7).

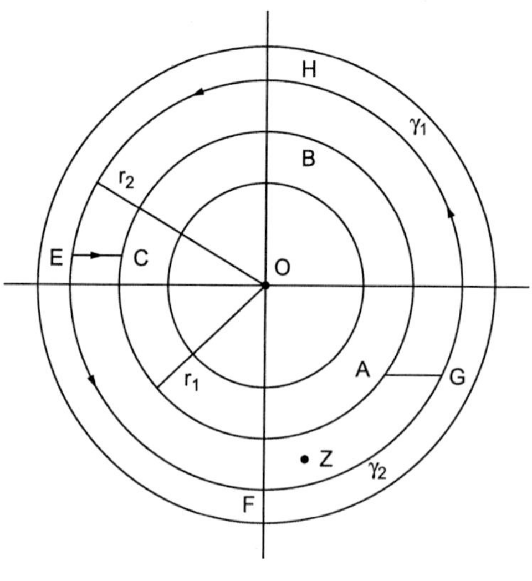

Fig. 9.7

Let γ_2 = EFGADCE and γ_1 = GHECBAG be two closed curves in A. By Cauchy's Integral formula on γ_1, we get

$$0 = f(z) = \frac{1}{2\pi i}\int_{\gamma_1}\frac{f(w)}{w-z}dw \qquad ...(1)$$

Also applying Cauchy's Integral formula on γ_2, we get

$$f(z) = \frac{1}{2\pi i}\int_{\gamma_2}\frac{f(w)}{w-z}dw \qquad ...(2)$$

Adding (1) and (2), we get

$$f(z) = \frac{1}{2\pi i}\int_{\gamma_1}\frac{f(w)}{w-z}dw + \frac{1}{2\pi i}\int_{\gamma_2}\frac{f(w)}{w-z}dw$$

$$= \frac{1}{2\pi i}\int_{EFGHE}\frac{f(w)}{w-z}dz - \frac{1}{2\pi i}\int_{ABCDA}\frac{f(w)}{w-z}dw$$

$$= \frac{1}{2\pi i}\int_{\gamma(0,\,r_2)}\frac{f(w)}{w-z}dz - \frac{1}{2\pi i}\int_{\gamma(0,\,r_1)}\frac{f(w)}{w-z}dw \qquad ...(3)$$

If $w \in \gamma(0, r_2)$, then $|w| = r_2 > |z|$, therefore

$$\therefore \qquad \left|\frac{z}{w}\right| = \frac{|z|}{|w|} < 1$$

Now $$\frac{1}{w-z} = \frac{1}{w\left(1-\dfrac{z}{w}\right)} = \frac{1}{w}\left(1-\frac{z}{w}\right)^{-1}$$

$$= \frac{1}{w}\sum_{n=0}^{\infty}\frac{z^n}{w^n} = \sum_{n=0}^{\infty}\frac{z^n}{w^{n+1}}$$

If $w \in \gamma(0, r_1)$, then $|w| < |z|$, therefore $\left|\dfrac{w}{z}\right| < 1$ and

$$\frac{1}{w-z} = -\sum_{n=0}^{\infty}\frac{w^n}{z^{n+1}}.$$

From (3)

$$f(z) = \frac{1}{2\pi i}\int_{\gamma(0,\,r_2)}\sum_{n=0}^{\infty}\frac{f(w)z^n}{w^{n+1}}dw + \frac{1}{2\pi i}\int_{\gamma(0,\,r_1)}\sum_{n=0}^{\infty}\frac{f(w)w^n}{z^{n+1}}dw \qquad ...(4)$$

Since f is analytic on $\gamma(0; r_2)$ and hence bounded therefore, there exists $m_1 > 0$ such that $|f(w)| \le m_1$ for all $w \in \gamma(0, r_2)$.

Then, $\left|\frac{f(w)z^n}{w^{n+1}}\right| \le \frac{m_1\zeta^n}{|w|}$ where $\zeta = \left|\frac{z}{w}\right| < 1$.

Thus, $\sum_{n=0}^{\infty} \frac{m_1\zeta^n}{|w|}$ is convergent and hence $\sum \frac{f(w)z^n}{w^{n+1}}$ is uniformaly convergent. Similarly $\sum_{n=0}^{\infty} \frac{f(w)w^n}{z^{n+1}}$ is uniformaly convergent. Thus,

$$f(z) = \frac{1}{2\pi i}\sum_{n=0}^{\infty}\left(\int_{\gamma(0,r_2)} \frac{f(w)dw}{w^{n+1}}\right)z^n + \sum_{n=0}^{\infty}\left(\frac{1}{2\pi i}\int_{\gamma(0,r_1)} f(w)w^n dw\right)\frac{1}{z^{n+1}}$$

Since $r_1 < r < r_2$ then $\int_{\gamma(0,\, r_2)} \frac{f(w)}{w^{n+1}}dw = \int_{\gamma(0,\, r)} \frac{f(w)}{w^{n+1}}dw$

and $\int_{\gamma(0,\, r_1)} f(w)w^n dw = \int_{\gamma(0,\, r)} f(w)w^n dw$.

Consider

$$\left(\frac{1}{2\pi i}\int_{\gamma(0,\, r)} f(w)w^n dw\right)\frac{1}{z^{n+1}} = \left(\frac{1}{2\pi i}\int_{\gamma(0,\, r)} \frac{f(w)dw}{w^{m+1}}\right)z^m$$

Put $n = -m - 1$ and if n varies from 0 to ∞ then m varies from -1 to $-\infty$. Thus,

$$f(z) = \sum_{n=\infty}^{\infty}\left(\frac{1}{2\pi i}\int_{\gamma(0,\, r)} \frac{f(w)}{w^{n+1}}dw\right)z^n + \sum_{n=-1}^{-\infty}\left(\frac{1}{2\pi i}\int_{\gamma} \frac{f(w)}{w^{n+1}}dw\right)z^n$$

$$= \sum_{n=-\infty}^{\infty}\left(\frac{1}{2\pi i}\int_{\gamma(0,r)} \frac{f(w)}{w^{n+1}}dw\right)z^n$$

$$= \sum_{n=-\infty}^{\infty} c_n z^n$$

where $c_n = \frac{1}{2\pi i}\int_{\gamma(0,r)} \frac{f(w)}{w^{n+1}}dw$

Note: The coefficients c_n's are called Laurent's Coefficients. The expansion $\sum_{-\infty}^{\infty} c_n (z-a)^n$ is called Laurent Expansion of $f(z)$.

Corollary 9.10

If f is analytic in $A = \{z : R_1 < |z - a| < R_2\}$ then f has unique representation

$$f(z) = \sum_{-\infty}^{\infty} c_k (z-a)^k$$

where $$c_k = \frac{1}{2\pi i}\int_\gamma \frac{f(z)}{(z-a)^{k+1}}\,dz$$

and $\gamma = \gamma(a; r)$ with $R_1 < r < R_2$.

Proof

Let if possible f has two representations

$$f(z) = \sum_{-\infty}^{\infty} c_k (z-a)^k$$

and $$f(z) = \sum_{-\infty}^{\infty} d_k (z-a)^k$$

in the annulus $A = \{z : R_1 < |z| < R_2\}$. Now

$$c_n = \frac{1}{2\pi i}\int_\gamma \frac{f(w)}{(w-a)^{n+1}}\,dw \text{ where } \gamma = \gamma(a; r),\ R_1 < r < R_2.$$

$$= \frac{1}{2\pi i}\int_\gamma \frac{1}{(w-a)^{n+1}}\left(\sum_{m=-\infty}^{\infty} d_m (w-a)^m\right)dw$$

$$= \frac{1}{2\pi i}\int_\gamma \sum_{-\infty}^{\infty} d_m (w-a)^{m-n-1}\,dw$$

$$= \frac{1}{2\pi i}\sum_{-\infty}^{\infty} d_m \int_\gamma (w-a)^{m-n-1}\,dw \qquad (1)$$

We know

$$\int_\gamma \frac{dw}{(w-a)^p}dw = \begin{cases} 0 & if \quad p \neq 1 \\ 2\pi i & if \quad p = 1 \end{cases}$$

Then,

$$\int_\gamma (w-a)^{m-n-1}dw = \int_{2\pi i}^{0} \begin{matrix} if & n-m+1 \neq 1 \\ if & n-m+1 = 1 \\ & i.e.,\ n = m. \end{matrix}$$

Thus from (1), we get

$$c_n = \frac{1}{2\pi i} d_n \times 2\pi i$$

$$= d_n \text{ for all } n.$$

Hence, we conclude that $f(z)$ has a unique representation in $A = \{z : R_1 < |z-a| < R_2\}$.

If we set $R_1 = 0$, we obtain the following:

Corollary 9.11

If f has an isolated singularity at z_0, then for some $\delta > 0$ and $0 < |z-a| < \delta$

$$f(z) = \sum_{-\infty}^{\infty} c_k (z-a)^k,$$

the c_k are defined in Corollary 9.10.

Example 9.4

Expand $f(z) = \dfrac{1}{z(z-1)}$ in a Laurent series valid for the following annular domains:

(*i*) $0 < |z| < 1$ (*ii*) $1 < |z|$ (*iii*) $0 < |z-1| < 1$ (*iv*) $1 < |z-1|$

Solution

(*i*) If $0 < |z| < 1$ then by writing

$$f(z) = \frac{-1}{z(1-z)}$$

$$= \frac{-1}{z}(1-z)^{-1}$$

$$= \frac{-1}{z}(1 + z + z^2 + z^3 + ...)$$

$$= \frac{-1}{z} - 1 - z - z^2 - z^3 ....$$

Converges for $0 < |z| < 1$

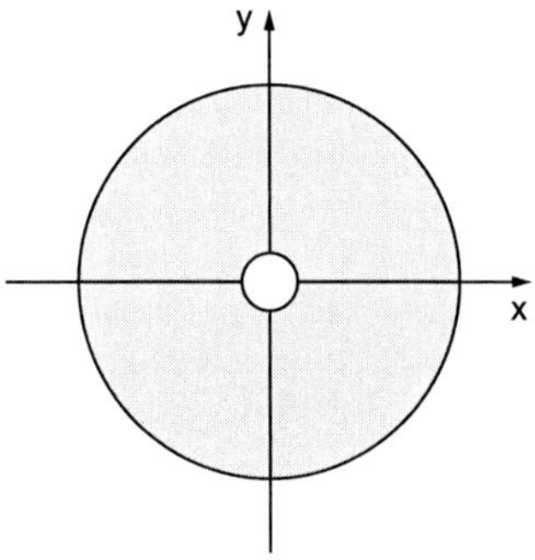

Fig. 9.8

(*ii*) If $1 < |z|$ then $\frac{1}{|z|} < 1$. We write the given function f as

$$f(z) = \frac{1}{z^2\left(1-\frac{1}{z}\right)}$$

$$= \frac{1}{z^2}\left(1-\frac{1}{z}\right)^{-1}$$

$$= \frac{1}{z^2}\left[1+\frac{1}{z}+\frac{1}{z^2}+\frac{1}{z^3}+...\right]$$

$$= \frac{1}{z^2}+\frac{1}{z^3}+\frac{1}{z^4}+\frac{1}{z^5}+...$$

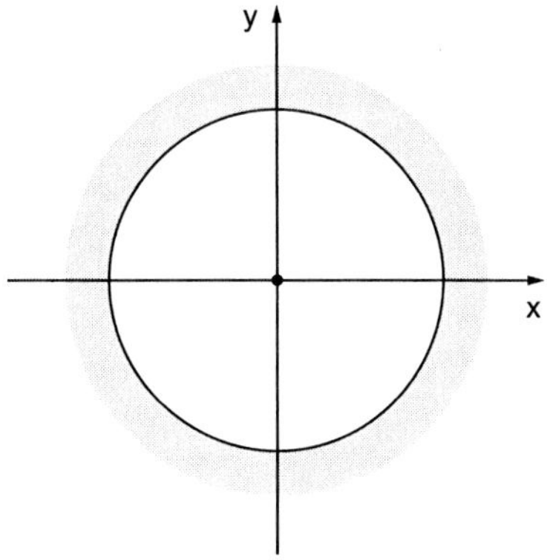

Fig. 9.9

The series converges for $\frac{1}{|z|} < 1$ or $1 < |z|$ (Fig. 9.9).

(*iii*) Let $0 < |z - 1| < 1$, then

$$f(z) = \frac{1}{(1-1+z)(1-z)}$$

$$= \frac{1}{1-z}\ \frac{1}{1+(z-1)}$$

$$= \frac{1}{1-z}(1+(z-1))^{-1}$$

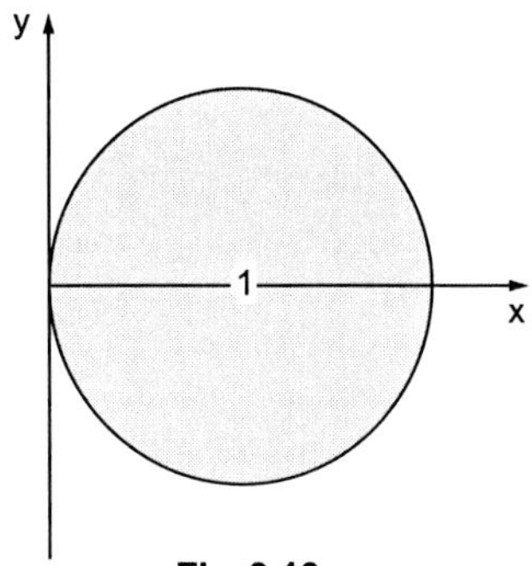

Fig. 9.10

$$= \frac{1}{1-z}\left[1-(z-1)+(z-1)^2+...\right]$$

$$= \frac{1}{1-z}-1+(z-1)-(z-1)^2+...$$

Also $z \neq 1$ because $0 < |z-1|$. Thus, the series is convergent if $0 < |1-z|$ and $|1-z| < 1$ and hence, if $0 < |z-1| < 1$ (Fig. 9.10)

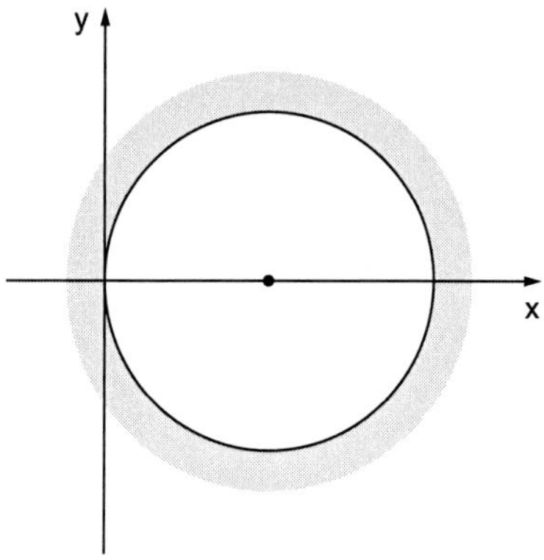

Fig. 9.11

(*iv*) We write

$$f(z) = \frac{1}{z-1}\frac{1}{1+z-1}$$

$$= \frac{1}{(z-1)^2}\frac{1}{1+\frac{1}{z-1}}$$

$$= \frac{1}{(z-1)^2}\left[1-\frac{1}{z-1}+\frac{1}{(z-1)^2}-\frac{1}{(z-1)^3}+...\right]$$

$$= \frac{1}{(z-1)^2}-\frac{1}{(z-)^3}+\frac{1}{(z-1)^4}-\frac{1}{(z-1)^5}+...$$

The series converges if $|z-1| > 1$

Example 9.5

Expand $f(z) = \dfrac{1}{(z-1)^2(z-3)}$ in a Laurent series valid for

(*i*) $0 < |z-1| < 2$ (*ii*) $0 < |z-3| < 2$.

Solution

(*i*) If $0 < |z-1| < 2$, then

$$f(z) = \frac{1}{(z-1)^2(z-3)} = \frac{1}{(z-1)^2(-2+(z-1))}$$

$$= \frac{-1}{2(z-1)^2}\frac{1}{1-\frac{z-1}{2}}$$

$$= \frac{-1}{2(z-1)^2}\left[1+\frac{z-1}{2}+\frac{(z-1)^2}{2^2}+\frac{(z-1)^3}{2^3}+....\right]$$

$$= \frac{-1}{2(z-1)^2}-\frac{1}{4(z-1)}-\frac{1}{8}-\frac{1}{16}(z-1)...$$

(*ii*) Let $0 < |z-3| < z$, then

$$f(z) = \frac{1}{(z-3)(z-3+2)^2}$$

$$= \frac{1}{4(z-3)}\left[1+\frac{z-3}{2}\right]^{-2}$$

$$= \frac{1}{4(z-3)}\left[1+\frac{(-2)}{1!}\left(\frac{z-3}{2}\right)+\frac{(-2)(-3)}{2!}\left(\frac{z-3}{2}\right)^2\right.$$

$$\left.+\frac{(-2)(-3)(-4)}{3!}\left(\frac{z-3}{2}\right)^3+.....\right]$$

The binomial series in the brackets is valid for $\dfrac{|z-3|}{2} < 1$. Then, the Laurent series is given by

$$f(z) = \frac{1}{4(z-3)} - \frac{1}{4} + \frac{3}{16}(z-3) - \frac{1}{8}(z-3)^2 + ...$$

Example 9.6

Expand $f(z) = e^{\frac{3}{z}}$ in a Laurent series valid for $0 < |z| < \infty$.

Solution

We know for all $|z| < \infty$,

$$e^z = 1 + z + \frac{z^2}{2!} + \frac{z^3}{3!} + ... \qquad (1)$$

Now if we replace z by $\frac{3}{z}$ in (1), we get

$$e^{\frac{3}{z}} = 1 + \frac{3}{z} + \frac{3^2}{z^2 2!} + \frac{3^3}{3! z^3} + ...$$

This series is valid for $z \neq 0$, that is $0 < |z| < \infty$.

Example 9.7

Find the Laurent expansion for $\frac{1}{z^4 + z^2}$ about $z = 0$.

Solution

Let
$$f(z) = \frac{1}{z^4 + z^2}$$

$$= \frac{1}{z^2\left(1+z^2\right)}$$

$$= \frac{1}{z^2}\left(1+z^2\right)^{-1}$$

$$= \frac{1}{z^2}\left[1 - z^2 + z^4 - z^6 ......\right]$$

$$= \frac{1}{z^2} - 1 + z^2 - z^4 + z^6 .....$$

$$= \sum_{k=-1}^{\infty} (-1)^{k+1} z^{2k} .$$

Example 9.8

Expand $\dfrac{\exp\left(\frac{1}{z^2}\right)}{z-1}$ about $z = 0$ using Laurent expansion.

Solution

Let $$f(z) = \frac{\exp\left(\frac{1}{z^2}\right)}{z-1} = -\exp\left(\frac{1}{z^2}\right)(1-z)^{-1}$$

$$= -\left(1 + z + z^2 + z^3 + z^4 ....\right)\left(1 + \frac{1}{z^2} + \frac{1}{2!z^4} + \frac{1}{3!z^6} + ...\right)$$

$$= -\left\{\left[1 + \frac{1}{z^2} + \frac{1}{2!z^4} + ...\right] + \left[z + \frac{1}{z} + \frac{1}{2!z^3} + \frac{1}{z^5 \times 3!} + ...\right]\right.$$

$$+ \left[z^2 + 1 + \frac{1}{2!z^2} + \frac{1}{3!z^4} + ...\right] + \left[z^3 + z + \frac{1}{2!z} + \frac{1}{3!z^3} + ...\right]$$

$$\left. + \left[z^4 + \frac{1}{z^2} + \frac{1}{2!} + \frac{1}{3!z^2} + ...\right] ....\right\}$$

$$= -\left[1 + 1 + \frac{1}{2!} + \frac{1}{3!} + ...\right] - z\left[1 + 1 + \frac{1}{2!} + \frac{1}{3!} + ...\right]$$

$$- z^2\left[1 + 1 + \frac{1}{2!} + ...\right]$$

$$= -\frac{1}{z}\left[1 + \frac{1}{2!} + \frac{1}{3!} + ...\right] - \frac{1}{z^2}\left[1 + \frac{1}{2!} + \frac{1}{3!}....\right]....$$

$$= \sum_{k=-\infty}^{\infty} c_k z^k$$

$$\text{Where } c_k = \begin{cases} -e & \text{if } k \geq 0 \\ -\left(1+\dfrac{1}{2!}+\dfrac{1}{3!}+...\right) & \text{if } k = -2j \text{ or } -2j+1, \quad j = 1, 2 ... \end{cases}$$

Example 9.9

Show that if f is analytic in $z \neq 0$ and odd then all the even terms in its Laurent expansion about 0 are 0.

Solution

Since f is analytic in **C** ~ {0}, therefore its Laurent expansion is in the form

$$f(z) = \sum_{k=-\infty}^{\infty} c_k z^k$$

Since $f(z) = -f(-z)$

$$= -\sum_{k=-\infty}^{\infty} c_k (-z)^k$$

Now $f(z) = \dfrac{2f(z)}{2} = \dfrac{f(z)-f(-z)}{2}$

$$= \sum_{k=-\infty}^{\infty} c_k z^k - \sum_{k=-\infty}^{\infty} c_k (-z)^k$$

$$= \sum_{k=-\infty}^{\infty} c_{2k+1} z^{2k+1}$$

Thus, all even terms are zero in the Laurent expansion.

Use of Laurent Series

The classification of singularities discussed in Section 9.1 may be simplified using Laurent series about a singularity, which converges on a punctured disc. If $f(z) = \sum_{-\infty}^{\infty} c_k (z-a)^k$ is the Laurent expansion of f

about an isolated singularity a, $\sum_{-\infty}^{-1} c_k (z-a)^k$ is called the Principal part of f at a and $\sum_{0}^{\infty} c_k (z-a)^k$ is called the analytic part. Since the Laurent expansion is unique, we can derive the following characterization of the principal parts around the different types of singularities.

Theorem 9.12

Suppose that f is analytic on the punctured disc $0 < |z-a| < r$, and that its Laurent series about a is $\sum_{-\infty}^{\infty} c_n (z-a)^n$. Then,

(*i*) If $c_n = 0$ for all $n < 0$ or, if the principal part of the function is the zero function, then a is a removable singularity.

(*ii*) If $c_n = 0$ for all $n < -m$, $m > 0$, but $a_{-m} \neq 0$. In other words, if the principal part contains only finitely many terms, then a is a pole of order m.

(*iii*) If the principal part contains infinitely many terms, then a is an essential singularity.

Proof

(*i*) Since $f(z) = g(z)$ for $z \neq a$, the Laurent expansion for f must agree with the Taylor expansion for g around z_0.

(*ii*) Since $f(z) = \dfrac{A(z)}{B(z)}$ where $A(a) \neq 0$ and B has zero of order k at $z = a$, therefore

$$f(z) = \frac{Q(z)}{(z-a)^k}$$

where $Q(z)$ is analytic and non-zero at a. If $Q(z) = \sum_{n=0}^{\infty} c_n (z-a)^n$

then,
$$f(z) = \sum_{n=0}^{\infty} c_n \frac{(z-a)^n}{(z-a)^k} = \sum_{n=0}^{\infty} c_n (z-a)^{n-k}$$

$$= \sum_{j=-k}^{\infty} a_j (z-a)^j$$

where $a_j = c_{j+k}$. Thus, $a_{-k} = a_0 = Q(a) \neq 0$.

(*iii*) A singularity which is neither removable nor a pole is an essential singularity. The Laurent series for a function about a removable singularity is in fact a Taylor series, so its principal part is a zero function; the principal part of Laurent series of a function about a pole contains only finitely many terms. Then, if the function *f* has a principal part at *a* containing infinitely many terms, *a* must be an essential singularity of *f*.

Note: (*i*) If $f(z)$ has removable singularity at $z = a$, then $f(z)$ has Taylor expansion and we can consider $f(z)$ to be analytic in the disc $D = \{z: |z-a| < r\}$ instead of $D' = \{z: 0 < |z-a| < r\}$.

(*ii*) The above theorem applies only to the Laurent series for a function about a singularity, convergent on a punctured disc; it does not apply to Laurent series convergent on an annulus. For example, if we expand $z \to \dfrac{z}{(1-z)(2-z)}$ about 0, we get

$$\cdots\cdots \frac{-1}{z^2} - \frac{1}{z} - 1 - \frac{z}{2} - \frac{z^2}{2^2} - \frac{z^3}{2^3} \cdots\cdots$$

which is convergent on the annulus $1 < |z| < 2$. This series contains infinitely many negative powers of z, but it does not follow that the function has an essential singularity at 0.

On the other hand, the Laurent series about 0 for the function $z \to \sin\dfrac{1}{z}$, $z \neq 0$ is

$$\frac{1}{z} - \frac{1}{3!}\frac{1}{z^3} + \frac{1}{5!}\frac{1}{z^5} \cdots\cdots$$

It contains infinitely many negative powers of *z* and converge on a punctured disc, so 0 is an essential singularity.

Example 9.10

The function $f(z) = \dfrac{\sin z}{z}$ expansion

$$\frac{\sin z}{z} = 1 - \frac{z^2}{3!} + \frac{z^4}{5!} - \cdots\cdots$$

Since $c_n = 0$ for all $n < 0$. Thus, $z = 0$ is a removable singularity.

Example 9.11

The function $f(z) = \dfrac{1}{z^4 + z^2}$ about $z = 0$, has Laurent expansion.

$$f(z) = \frac{1}{z^2} - 1 + z^2 - z^4 + z^6 \ldots\ldots$$

Since $c_n = 0$ for all $n < -2$, $c_{-2} = 1 \neq 0$. Thus, it has a pole of order 2 at $z = 0$.

The partial fraction decomposition of proper rational functions can be desired as a corollary to the theory of Laurent expansion.

Corollary 9.13

Any proper rational function

$$R(z) = \frac{P(z)}{Q(z)} = \frac{P(z)}{(z-z_1)^{k_1}(z-z_2)^{k_2}\ldots\ldots(z-z_n)^{k_n}}$$

where P and Q are polynomials with $\deg P < \deg Q$ can be expanded as a sum of polynomials in $\dfrac{1}{z - z_k}$, $k = 1, 2, \ldots.., n$.

Proof

Since $R(z)$ has a pole at z_1 of order at most k_1, therefore

$$R(z) = P_1\left(\frac{1}{z-z_1}\right) + A_1(z)$$

where $P_1\left(\dfrac{1}{z-z_1}\right)$ is the principal part of R around z_1 and A_1 is the analytic part. Further more

$$A_1(z) = R(z) - P_1\left(\frac{1}{z-z_1}\right)$$

has a removable singularity at z_1. Similarly $P_j\left(\dfrac{1}{z-z_j}\right)$, $j = 2, 3, \ldots\ldots., n$ be the principal part of R at $z_2, z_3, \ldots\ldots.., z_n$. We get

$$A_n(z) = R(z) - \sum_{j=1}^{n} P_j\left(\frac{1}{z - z_j}\right)$$

is an entire function. Also A_n is bounded since R and all its principal parts approach 0 as $z \to \infty$. Thus, by Liouville's theorem, A_n is constant, indeed $A_n = 0$. Hence,

$$R(z) = \sum_{j=1}^{n} P_j\left(\frac{1}{z - z_j}\right)$$

Example 9.11

Find the partial fraction decomposition for

$$f(z) = \frac{1}{z^4 + z^2}$$

Solution

$f(z)$ has a double pole at $z = 0$ and simple poles at $z = i$ and $-i$. The principal part of $f(z)$ about $z = 0$, $z = i$ and $z = -i$ are $\frac{1}{z^2}, \frac{-1}{2i(z-i)}, \frac{1}{2i(z+i)}$. Thus, the partial fraction decomposition is

$$f(z) = \frac{1}{z^2} - \frac{1}{2i(z-i)} + \frac{1}{2i(z+i)}.$$

EXERCISE

1. Find the Laurent expansion of $(z^2 - 1)$ valid for
   (*i*) $0 < |z - 1| < 2$ (*ii*) $|z + 1| > 2$.
2. Find the principal part of the Laurent expansion about the indicated point a of

   (*i*) $\dfrac{1}{z^2 \sin z}(a = 0)$ (*ii*) $(e^z - 1)^{-2}$ $(a = 0)$

   (*iii*) $e^{-1/z^4}(a = 0)$ (*iv*) $\dfrac{e^z - 1}{e^z + 1}(a = \pi i)$

   (*v*) $\dfrac{e^{iz}}{\left(z^2 + b^2\right)^3}(a = ib)$ (*vi*) $\cot z$ $(a = 0)$.

3. Find the Principal part of the Laurent expansion $f(z) = \dfrac{e^{-2z}}{(z+1)^2}$ about $a = -1$ that is valid on the annulus $0 < |z + 1| < \infty$.

4. Show that if f is entire and $z \to f\left(\dfrac{1}{z}\right)$ has a pole at 0, then f is a polynomial. Deduce that $z \to \sin\dfrac{1}{z}$ has an essential singularity at 0.

5. Show that if f has a finite number of poles, and no other singularities, and if $z \to f\left(\dfrac{1}{z}\right)$ has a pole at 0, then f is a rational function.

6. Find partial fraction decomposition for

(i) $\dfrac{1}{z^2+1}$ (ii) $\dfrac{z^2+1}{(z^2+z+1)(z-1)^2}$.

ANSWERS

1. (i) $\dfrac{1}{4(z-1)^2} - \dfrac{1}{4(z-1)^2} + \dfrac{1}{8} + \dfrac{(z-1)^3}{32} + \ldots\ldots$

(ii) $\dfrac{1}{(z-1)^4} - \dfrac{4}{(z-1)^5} + \dfrac{6}{(z-1)^6} + \ldots\ldots$

2. (i) $\dfrac{1}{z^3}$ (ii) $\dfrac{1}{z}$

(iii) $1 - \dfrac{1}{z^4} + \dfrac{1}{z^8} - \dfrac{1}{z^{12}} + \ldots\ldots$ (iv) $\dfrac{1}{z\pi i}$

(v) 0 (vi) $\dfrac{1}{z}$

3. $\dfrac{e^2}{(z+1)^2} - \dfrac{2e^2}{z+1}$

4. $f\left(\dfrac{1}{z}\right) = \dfrac{a-m}{z^m} + ... + \dfrac{a-1}{z} + a_0 + z\,\phi(z)$, $\phi(z)$ is entire

$f(z) = a_m z^m + a_m z^{m-1} + ... + a_{-1}z + a_0 + \dfrac{1}{z}\phi\left(\dfrac{1}{z}\right)$ $\phi(z)$ is

bounded for $|z| > 1$, $\lim\limits_{z\to\infty} \dfrac{1}{z}\phi\left(\dfrac{1}{z}\right) = 0$. Thus $\dfrac{1}{z}\phi\left(\dfrac{1}{z}\right) = 0$. Thus

$f(z) = a_{-m}z^m + a_{-m_1}z^{m-1} + ... + a_{-1}z + a_0$ is a polynomial

and $f\left(\dfrac{1}{z}\right)$ has essential singularity at $z = 0$.

5. Suppose f has poles α_1, α_2, ..., α_n and ϕ_1, ϕ_2,......., ϕ_n are singular parts of f at α_1, α_2,...., α_n respectively.

Then $f(z) - \phi_1(z) - \phi_2(z)$..... $\phi_n(z)$ has removable singularity and then is entire. Since ϕ_1, ϕ_2, ..., ϕ_n are rational function therefore $f(z)$ is rational.

6. (*i*) $\dfrac{1}{2i(z-i)} - \dfrac{1}{2i(z+i)}$

(*ii*) $\dfrac{2}{3(z-1)^2} - \dfrac{\left(1-\sqrt{3i}\right)^2}{12(z-w)} - \dfrac{\left(1+\sqrt{3i}\right)^2}{12(z-w)^2}$, $w = \dfrac{-1+\sqrt{3i}}{2}$, w^2

$= \dfrac{-1-\sqrt{3i}}{2}$.

❑❑❑

10

The Calculus of Residues

Up to this point in the course, our study of the integration of functions of a complex variable has led us in two different directions. On the one hand, we have been concerned with the theory of the integration of functions along contours and on the other hand, we have been developing techniques which can be used when we actually want to evaluate a particular integral. As far as theory in concerned, we introduced the idea of integration along a contour in chapter 5 and Cauchy's Closed Theorem in chapter 6 and in chapter 8 Cauchy Closed Theorem for simply-connected region. In this chapter, we generalize the Cauchy Closed Curve Theorem to functions which have isolated singularities and also prove Residue Theorem using winding number of a closed contour.

10.1 EVALUATION OF RESIDUES

In this section, we shall look at various methods of calculating residues. Many of the residues we calculate in this section will be needed in the next chapter.

Let f be an analytic function in the punctured disc $D' = \{z : 0 < |z - a| < r\}$. Then, it has Laurent expansion about the isolated singularity a.

$$f(z) = \ldots\ldots\frac{c_{-2}}{(z-a)^2} + \frac{c_{-1}}{(z-a)} + c_0 + c_1(z-a) + c_2(z-a)^2 + \ldots\ldots$$

Then, the residue of f at a is the coefficient c_{-1} in the Laurent expansion of $\frac{1}{z-a}$.

i.e., $$Res\ (f;\ a) = \frac{1}{z-a}.$$

For example, the Laurent expansion of $f(z) = \frac{\sin z}{z^4}$ at the isolated singularity 0 is

$$\frac{\sin z}{z^4} = \frac{1}{z^3} - \frac{1}{6z} + \frac{z}{5!} - \ldots\ldots\ldots$$

The residue is therefore $= Res(f; 0) = \frac{-1}{6}$.

If γ is a circle in D' surrounding a single isolated singularity 'a' and $f(z) = \sum_{-\infty}^{\infty} c_k (z-a)^k$ in a deleted neighbourhood of 'a' that contains γ, then,

$$\int_\gamma f = 2\pi i\ c_{-1}.$$

Thus, the coefficient c_{-1} is of special significance in this context.

Definition 10.1

If $f(z) = \sum_{-\infty}^{\infty} c_k (z-a)^k$ in a deleted neighbourhood of a, c_{-1} is called the residue of f at a, denoted by $Res\ (f;\ a) = c_{-1}$.

We use the following methods in calculating residue of a function at an isolated singularity.

Method I: Using the Laurent Series

We can find the residue of a function by looking at the Laurent expansion of a function about an isolated singularity.

Example 10.1

Find the residue of $f(z) = \dfrac{1}{z(z-1)^2}$ at 1.

Solution

We can write

$$f(z) = \frac{1}{(z-1)^2(z-1+1)}$$

$$= \frac{1}{(z-1)^2}(1+(z-1))^{-1}$$

$$= \frac{1}{(z-1)^2}\left[1-(z-1)+(z-1)^2-(z-1)^3+....\right]$$

$$= \frac{1}{(z-1)^2} - \frac{1}{(z-1)} + 1 - (z-1) + ...$$

Therefore, *Res* (*f*; 1) = coefficient of $\dfrac{1}{(z-1)} = -1$.

Example 10.1.2

Find the residue of $f(z) = e^{3/z}$ at 0.

Solution

We know

$$e^z = 1 + z + \frac{z^2}{2!} + \frac{z^3}{3!}......$$

Therefore, $0 < |z| < \infty$

$$e^{\frac{3}{z}} = 1 + \frac{3}{z} + \frac{1}{2!}\left(\frac{3}{z}\right)^2 + \frac{1}{3!}\left(\frac{3}{z}\right)^3 + ...$$

Then, the coefficient of $\dfrac{1}{z}$ is C_{-1}= *Res* (*f*; 0) = 3.

Method II: (i) Residue of Simple Pole at '*a*'.

Theorem 10.1

If f has a simple pole at a, then

$$Res(f;\, a) = \lim_{z \to a} (z-a)\, f(z)$$

Proof

Since f has a simple pole at a, therefore the Laurent expansion about a is

$$f(z) = \frac{c_{-1}}{(z-a)} + c_0 + c_1(z-a) + c_2(z-a)^2 + \ldots$$

then, $(z-a)\, f(z) = c_{-1} + c_0(z-a) + c_1(z-a)^2 + c_2(z-a)^3 + \ldots$

and $\lim\limits_{z \to a} (z-a)\, f(z) = c_{-1} = Res\,(f;\, a)$

(*ii*) If $f(z) = \dfrac{A(z)}{B(z)}$ such that $A(a) \neq 0$, $B(a) = 0$.

$$\text{then, } \lim_{z \to a} (z-a)\, f(z) = \lim_{z \to a} (z-a) \frac{A(z)}{B(z)}$$

$$= \lim_{z \to a} \frac{A(z)}{\dfrac{B(z) - B(a)}{z-a}}$$

$$= \frac{\lim\limits_{z \to a} A(z)}{\lim\limits_{z \to a} \dfrac{B(z) - B(a)}{z-a}}$$

$$= \frac{A(a)}{B'(a)}.$$

Example 10.3

$f(z) = \dfrac{1}{(2-z)(z^2+4)}$ has a simple poles at 2 and at + 2*i*. Then,

$$\begin{aligned} Res\,(f(z);\,2) &= \lim_{z\to 2}(z-2)f(z) \\ &= \lim_{z\to 2}\frac{-1}{z^2+4} = \frac{-1}{2^2+4} = \frac{-1}{8} \\ Res\,(f;\,2i) &= \lim_{z\to 2i}(z-2i)f(z) \\ &= \lim_{z\to 2i}\frac{1}{(2-z)(z+2i)} \\ &= \frac{1}{(2-2i)(4i)} = \frac{1}{8(1+i)} = \frac{1-i}{16} \end{aligned}$$

Similarly, $Res\,(f;\,-2i) = \dfrac{1+i}{16}$.

Example 10.4

$f(z) = \dfrac{1}{1+z^4}$ has simple poles at $z_k = e^{(2k+1)\frac{\pi i}{4}}$, ($k = 0, 1, 2, 3$). Then,

$$\begin{aligned} Res(f(z);\,z_k) &= \left[\frac{1}{4z^3}\right]_{z=z_k} = \frac{z_k}{4z_k^4} = \frac{-z_k}{4} \\ &= -\frac{1}{4}e^{(2k+1)\frac{\pi i}{4}} \end{aligned}$$

Method III: Residue of Poles of Order *k*.

Theorem 10.2

If *f* has a pole of order *k* at *a,* then

$$Res\,(f;\,a) = \frac{1}{(k-1)!}\frac{d^{k-1}}{dz^{k-1}}\left[(z-a)^k f(z)\right]_{z=a}$$

Proof

Since f has a pole of order k at a, then f can be written as

$$f(z) = \frac{c_{-k}}{(z-a)^k} + \frac{c_{-k+1}}{(z-a)^{k-1}} \cdots + \frac{c_{-1}}{z-a} + c_0 + c_1(z-a) + \ldots, \; C_{-m} \neq 0.$$

and $(z-a)^k f(z) = c_{-k} + c_{-k+1}(z-a) + c_{-k+2}(z-a)^2$
$+ \ldots + c_{-1}(z-a)^{k-1} + c_0(z-a)^k + c_1(z-a)^{k+1} + \ldots$

Differentiating $(k-1)$ times gives

$$\frac{d^{k-1}}{dz^{k-1}}\left[(z-a)^k f(z)\right] = (k-1)!\, c_{-1} + k!\, c_0(z-a) + \frac{(k+1)!}{2!} c_1(z-a)^2 + \ldots$$

$$\Rightarrow \left[\frac{d^{k-1}}{dz^{k-1}}\left((z-a)^k f(z)\right)\right]_{z=a} = (k-1)!\, c_{-1}$$

$$\Rightarrow \quad Res(f;\, a) = c_{-1}$$

$$= \frac{1}{(k-1)!}\left[\frac{d^{k-1}}{dz^{k-1}}\left((z-a)^k f(z)\right)\right]_{z=a}.$$

Example 10.5

$f(z) = \dfrac{e^{iz}}{z^4}$ has a pole of order 4 at 0. Therefore, by Theorem 10.2, we get

$$Res\{f(z), 0\} = \frac{1}{3!}\left[\frac{d^3}{dz^3}\left(z^4 f(z)\right)\right]_{z=0}$$

$$= \frac{1}{3!}\left[\frac{d^3}{dz^3}\left(e^{iz}\right)\right]_{z=0}$$

$$= \frac{1}{3!}\left[-ie^{iz}\right]_{z=0}$$

$$= \frac{-i}{6}.$$

Method IV: Residue of Essential Singularity.

If a function f has essential singularity at a, then the most convenient way to determine the residue is directly from the Laurent expansion.

Example 10.6

Find the $Res\ (f(z);\ 1)$ where $f(z) = \sin\dfrac{1}{z-1}$.

Solution

We know $$\sin\frac{1}{z-1} = \frac{1}{z-1} - \frac{1}{3!(z-1)^3} + \frac{1}{5!(z-1)^5} \cdots\cdots$$

Then, $$Res\left(\sin\frac{1}{z-1};1\right) = \text{coefficient of } \frac{1}{z-1} = 1.$$

Winding Number

The winding number counts how many times the closed arc winds round the point α. For example,

$$\int_{\gamma(0;\,r)} \frac{1}{z}dz = 4\pi i = 2.2\pi i, \text{ where } \gamma(0;\,r)$$

$$= \{re^{i\theta} : \theta \in [0, 4\pi]\}$$

$$\Rightarrow \quad \frac{1}{2\pi i}\int_{\gamma} \frac{1}{z}dz = 2.$$

It means the curve $\gamma(0;\,r)$ rotates twice around the point 0.

For curves which are difficult to draw accurately, it is hard to determine the number geometrically. So we give an abstract definition in the following.

Definition 10.2

Given a smooth arc γ and a point α not on the path of γ, the winding number of γ about α, written as $\eta(\gamma;\,\alpha)$, is defined as

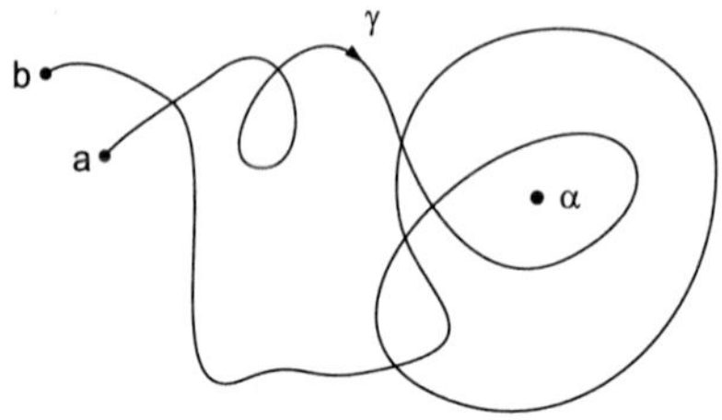

Fig. 10.1

$$\eta(\gamma;\,\alpha) = \frac{1}{2\pi i}\int_{\gamma}\frac{dz}{z-\alpha}$$

$$= \frac{1}{2\pi i}\int_{a}^{b}\frac{\gamma'(t)\,dt}{\gamma(t)-\alpha}$$

if γ has domain $[a, b]$.

Note: If γ represents the boundary of a circle, then

$$\eta(\gamma;\,\alpha) = \begin{cases} 1 & \text{if } \alpha \text{ lies inside the circle and circle} \\ & \text{is traversed counter clockwise} \\ 0 & \text{if } \alpha \text{ is outside the circle} \\ -1 & \text{if } \alpha \text{ lies inside the circle and circle} \\ & \text{is traversed clockwise} \end{cases}$$

Theorem 10.3

If γ is any closed curve and $\alpha \notin \gamma$ then $\eta(\gamma;\,\alpha)$ is an integer.

Proof

Suppose $\gamma = \{\gamma(t) : 0 < t < 1\}$ and set

$$F(s) = \int_{0}^{s}\frac{\gamma'(t)}{\gamma(t)-\alpha}dt,\ 0 \le s \le 1$$

Then, $$F'(s) = \frac{\gamma'(s)}{\gamma(s)-\alpha}$$

Define a function $h\ R \to \mathbf{C}$ by

$$h(s) = (\gamma(s) - a)\, e^{-F(s)}$$

h is continuous and differentiable, therefore

$$\begin{aligned} h'(s) &= \gamma'(s)\, e^{-F(s)} - (\gamma(s) - a)\, F'(s)\, e^{-F(s)} \\ &= \gamma'(s)\, e^{-F(s)} - \gamma'(s)\, e^{-F(s)} \\ &= 0 \end{aligned}$$

By Lagrange's Mean-Value Theorem h is constant. Then,

$$\begin{aligned} h(0) &= h(1) \\ \text{i.e.,}\quad (\gamma(0) - a)\, e^{-F(0)} &= (\gamma(1) - a)\, e^{-F(1)} \\ \Rightarrow \quad e^{F(1)} &= e^{F(0) + 2\pi i \times n},\ n \in I \end{aligned}$$

(because γ is closed and exponential has periodicity $2\pi i$)

$$\Rightarrow \quad F(1) = F(0) + 2\pi i n,\ n \in \mathrm{I}$$

$$\Rightarrow \quad \int_0^1 \frac{\gamma'(t)}{\gamma(t) - \alpha}\, dt = 2\pi i n$$

$$\Rightarrow \quad \frac{1}{2\pi i} \int_\gamma \frac{dz}{z - \alpha} = n = \text{an integer.}$$

The Jordan Curve Theorem asserts that any simple closed curve divide the plane into exactly two components—one bounded and the other unbounded. So if γ is a Jordan Curve,

$$\eta(\gamma;\, \alpha) = \begin{cases} k & \text{if } \alpha \in \text{bounded component} \\ 0 & \text{if } \alpha \in \text{unbounded component} \end{cases}$$

But in this course we shall deal with simple closed contour and we will prove that $\eta(\gamma;\, \alpha) = 0$ or $+ 1$ for all $\alpha \notin \gamma$.

Theorem 10.4

If Γ is a simple closed contour, $\alpha \notin \Gamma$. Then, the winding number of Γ about α satisfies

$$\eta(\Gamma;\, \alpha) = \begin{cases} \pm 1, & \text{if } \alpha \text{ lies inside } \Gamma \\ 0, & \text{if } \alpha \text{ lies outside } \Gamma \end{cases}$$

Proof

Let R_2 be the unbounded component of the plane with respect to Γ.

Then, $\displaystyle\int_\Gamma \frac{dz}{z - \alpha} = 0$. If $\alpha \in R_2$ because $\dfrac{1}{z - \alpha}$ is analytic and Γ is simple closed contour. Then $\eta(\Gamma; \alpha) = 0$. Let R_1 be the inside of Γ and let $\alpha \in R_1$. Let C be a circle with centre α such that C and its inside lie in R_1. Let L be any line through α (Fig. 10.2). Let Γ_1 and Γ_2 be two contours as shown in Fig. 10.2. Since α lies outside Γ_1. Therefore,

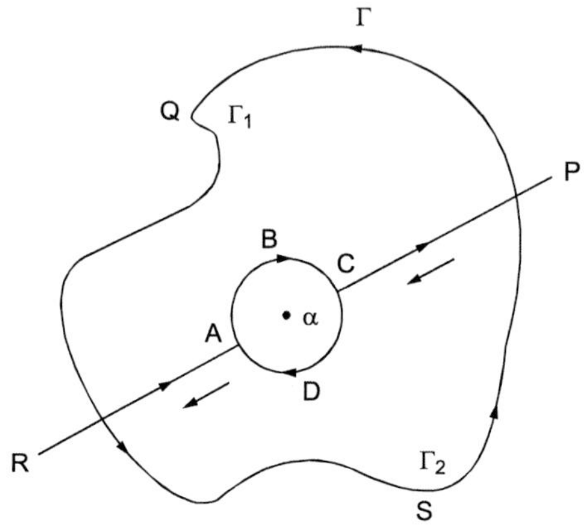

Fig. 10.2

$$\int_{\Gamma_1} \frac{dz}{z-\alpha} = 0$$

Similarly $$\int_{\Gamma_2} \frac{dz}{z-\alpha} = 0$$

Now $$\int_{\Gamma} \frac{dz}{z-\alpha} - \int_{C} \frac{dz}{z-\alpha} = \int_{\Gamma_1} \frac{dz}{z-\alpha} + \int_{\Gamma_2} \frac{dz}{z-\alpha}$$

$$= 0$$

Then, $$\frac{1}{2\pi i}\int_{\Gamma} \frac{dz}{z-\alpha} = \frac{1}{2\pi i}\int_{C} \frac{dz}{z-\alpha} = 1$$

where C is the circle with the counter clockwise orientation. If C traverses in the negative direction, then

$$\frac{1}{2\pi i}\int_{\Gamma} \frac{dz}{z-\alpha} = -1.$$

Proposition 10.5

If γ is a smooth closed curve $\alpha \notin \gamma$, then

(*i*) $\eta(-\gamma; \alpha) = -\eta(\gamma; \alpha)$

(*ii*) If $\gamma = \gamma_1 + \gamma_2$, then

$$\eta(\gamma; \alpha) = \eta(\gamma_1; \alpha) + \eta(\gamma_2; \alpha)$$

Proof

(*i*) If γ: $[0, 1] \to \subset$ is a closed curve, then

$$(-\gamma)(t) = \gamma(1-t), 0 < t < 1.$$

Consider $$\eta(-\gamma; \alpha) = \frac{1}{2\pi i}\int_{-\gamma}\frac{dz}{z-\alpha} = \frac{-1}{2\pi i}\int_0^1 \frac{\gamma'(1-t)}{\gamma(1-t)-\alpha}dt$$

Put $1 - t = s$ then $-dt = ds$

$$\begin{aligned}\eta(-\gamma, \alpha) &= \frac{1}{2\pi i}\int_1^0 \frac{\gamma'(s)ds}{\gamma(s)-\alpha} \\ &= \frac{-1}{2\pi i}\int_0^1 \frac{\gamma'(s)ds}{\gamma(s)-\alpha} \\ &= -\int_\gamma \frac{dz}{z-\alpha} \\ &= -\eta(\gamma; \alpha)\end{aligned}$$

(*ii*) If γ_1: $[0, 1] \to \subset$ and γ_2: $[0, 1] \to \subset$ such that

$$\gamma = \gamma_1 + \gamma_2 = \begin{cases}\gamma_1(2t); & 0 \le t \le ½ \\ \gamma_2(2t-1); & ½ \le t \le 1\end{cases}$$

Consider

$$\begin{aligned}\eta(\gamma; \alpha) &= \frac{1}{2\pi i}\int_\gamma \frac{dz}{z-\alpha} \\ &= \frac{1}{2\pi i}\int_0^{1/2}\frac{\gamma_1'(2t)}{\gamma_1(2t)-\alpha}2dt + \\ &\quad \frac{1}{2\pi i}\int_{1/2}^1 \frac{\gamma_2'(2t-1)}{\gamma_2(2t-1)-\alpha}2dt\end{aligned}$$

Now $$\frac{1}{2\pi i}\int_0^{1/2}\frac{2\gamma_1'(2t)dt}{\gamma_1(2t)-\alpha)} = \frac{1}{2\pi i}\int_0^1\frac{\gamma_1'(s)ds}{\gamma_1(s)-\alpha}, \qquad \text{(Put } 2t = s\text{)}$$

$$\frac{1}{2\pi i}\int_{1/2}^{1}\frac{2\gamma_2'(2t-1)dt}{\gamma_2(2t-1)-\alpha} = \frac{1}{2\pi i}\int_0^1\frac{\gamma_2'(s')\,ds'}{\gamma_2(s)-\alpha} \qquad \text{(Put } 2t-1 \neq s'\text{)}$$

Thus, $$\eta(\gamma_1; a) = \eta(\gamma_1; \alpha) + \eta(\gamma_2; \alpha).$$

Example 10.7

Let γ be a semicircle traversed clockwise.

Then, $$\eta(\gamma; \alpha) = \begin{cases} -1 & \text{if } a \text{ is inside the semicircle} \\ 0 & \text{if } a \text{ is outside} \end{cases}$$

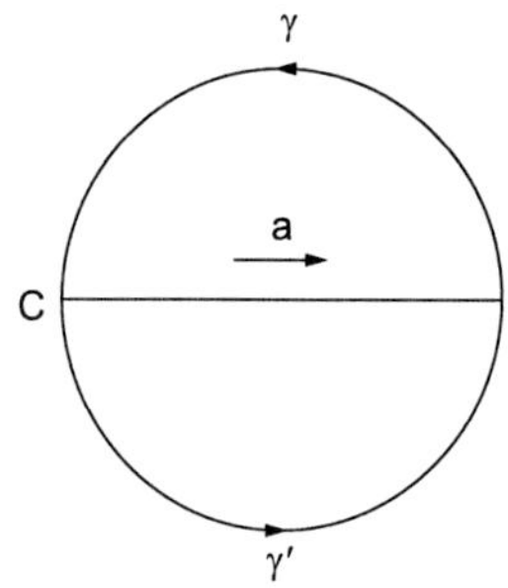

Fig. 10.3

Solution

We know from Fig. 10.3 that

$$\int_C \frac{dz}{z-a} = \int_{-\gamma}\frac{dz}{z-a} + \int_{\gamma'}\frac{dz}{z-a}$$

Since $\alpha \notin \gamma'$, therefore $\frac{1}{z-a}$ is analytic in the closed curve γ' and

$\int_{\gamma'}\frac{dz}{z-a} = 0$, and $\int_C \frac{dz}{z-a} = 1$. Then, $\int_{\gamma}\frac{dz}{z-a} = -\int_{-\gamma}\frac{dz}{z-a} = -1$

We proved Cauchy's Integral formula for a circle, which stated that for a circle Γ

$$f(\alpha) = \frac{1}{2\pi i}\int_{\Gamma}\frac{f(z)}{z-\alpha}dz.$$

If α lies inside Γ under certain condition on f. We shall prove the analogous of this for a general closed curve in terms of winding numbers.

Theorem 10.6

Let f be analytic on a simply- connected region R, γ a closed contour on R and α a point in R not on γ. Then,

$$\frac{1}{2\pi i}\int_{\gamma}\frac{f(z)}{z-\alpha}dz = N f(\alpha) \text{ where } N = \eta(\gamma; a)$$

Proof

We know $$N = \eta(\gamma; \alpha) = \frac{1}{2\pi i}\int_{\gamma}\frac{dz}{z-\alpha},$$

$$\frac{1}{2\pi i}\int_{\gamma}\frac{f(z)}{z-\alpha}dz - N f(\alpha) = \frac{1}{2\pi i}\left(\int_{\Gamma}\frac{f(z)}{z-\alpha}dz - \int_{\Gamma}\frac{f(\alpha)}{z-\alpha}dz\right)$$

$$= \frac{1}{2\pi i}\int_{\Gamma}\frac{f(z)-f(\alpha)}{z-\alpha}dz$$

Now α is a removable singularity of the function $z \to \dfrac{f(z)-f(\alpha)}{z-\alpha}$.

Define a function $g(z)$ by

$$g(z) = \begin{cases} \dfrac{f(z)-f(\alpha)}{z-\alpha}, & z \neq \alpha \\ f'(\alpha), & z = \alpha \end{cases}$$

is analytic on R. Thus,

$$\frac{1}{2\pi i}\int_{\Gamma}\frac{f(z)-f(\alpha)}{z-\alpha}dz = \frac{1}{2\pi i}\int_{\Gamma}g(z)\,dz$$

$$= 0 \text{ (by Theorem 8.5)}$$

The result follows immediately.

Definition 10.3

A closed curve γ is said to be regular if γ is a simple closed curve with $\eta(\gamma; a) = 0$ or 1 for all $a \notin \gamma$. If $s = \{a : \eta(\gamma; a) = 1\}$, then s is inside of γ and $s' = \{a : \eta(\gamma; a) = 0\}$ is called outside of γ.

The concept of residue is very useful in evaluating contour integrals of the form $\int_C f(z)\,dz$, by summing the residue at the isolated singularities of f within the closed contour C.

Theorem 10.7: Cauchy's Residue Theorem

Suppose D is a simply connected domain and γ is a simple closed contour lying entirely within D. If a function f is analytic on and within γ, except at a finite number of isolated singularities $z_1, z_2, \ldots, z_n$ within γ, then

$$\int_C f(z)\,dz = 2\pi i \sum_{k=1}^{n} \eta(\gamma; z_k)\, Res(f; z_k).$$

Proof

Let $P_1\left(\frac{1}{z-z_1}\right) \ldots\ldots\ldots P_n\left(\frac{1}{z-z_n}\right)$ be the principal parts of Laurent expansion of f about $z_1, z_2 \ldots\ldots, z_n$ (see Corollary 9.13), then the difference

$$g(z) = f(z) - P_1\left(\frac{1}{z-z_1}\right) - P_2\left(\frac{1}{z-z_2}\right) \ldots\ldots P_n\left(\frac{1}{z-z_n}\right)$$

is an analytic function in D. By Closed Curve Theorem

$$\int_\gamma g = 0$$

and

$$\int_\gamma f = \sum_{k=1}^{n} \int_\gamma P_k\left(\frac{1}{z-z_k}\right) dz \qquad \ldots(1)$$

Also

$$\int_\gamma P_k\left(\frac{1}{z-z_k}\right) dz = \int_\gamma \frac{c_{-1}}{(z-z_k)}\,dz + \int \frac{c_{-2}}{(z-z_k)^2}\,dz + \ldots.$$

for $k = 1, 2, \ldots, n$. Furthermore, for any k

$$\int_{\gamma} \frac{1}{(z - z_k)^n} = 0 \text{ if } n \neq 1.$$

Hence,

$$\int_{\gamma} P_k\left(\frac{1}{z - z_k}\right)dz = \int \frac{c_{-1}}{z - z_k}dz = c_{-1} \times 2\pi i \eta\,(\gamma; z_k)$$

From (1), we get

$$\int_{\gamma} f(z)\,dz = 2\pi i \sum_{k=1}^{n} \eta(\gamma; z_k) Res\,(f, z_k). \qquad \ldots(2)$$

Corollary 10.8

If f is analytic in a simply-connected domain except isolated singularity $z_1, z_2, \ldots, z_n$ and γ is a regular closed curve in the domain of analyticity of f, then

$$\int_{\gamma} f = 2\pi i \sum_{k=1}^{n} Res\,(f, z_k).$$

Proof

Since γ is regular, therefore $\eta(\gamma; z_k) = 1$. Then, from (2) we get the result.

Example 10.8

Prove that for any positive integer n, $Res((1 - e^{-z})^{-n}; 0) = 1$.

Proof

Let $f(z) = \dfrac{1}{(1 - e^{-z})^n}$, then $f(z)$ has singularities at $z = 2\pi k i$, $k = 0, +1, +2, \ldots$ Let C be any regular closed curve enclosing only $z = 0$ and the other singularities $z = 2\pi i k$, $k = +1, +2, \ldots$ lie outside C. Then

by Corollary 10.8, $\displaystyle\int_{C} \frac{1}{(1 - e^{-z})^n} = 2\pi i\, Res(f; 0)$

Let $w = 1 - e^{-z}$, then $dz = \dfrac{dw}{1-w}$ and

$$Res(f(z);\ 0) = Res\left(\frac{1}{w^n(1-w)};0\right), \text{ therefore}$$

$$\frac{1}{2\pi i}\int_C \frac{dz}{\left(1-e^{-z}\right)^n} = \frac{1}{2\pi i}\int_{C^*} \frac{dw}{w^n(1-w)}$$

Where C^* is the curve in w-plane that surrounds 0 and not 1. Thus,

$$Res\left(\frac{1}{\left(1-e^{-z}\right)^n};0\right) = Res\left(\frac{1}{w^n(1-w)};0\right) = 1$$

$$\text{Because}\quad \frac{1}{w^n(1-w)} = \frac{1}{w^n}(1-w)^{-1}$$

$$= \frac{1}{w^n}\left(1+w+w^2 \ldots\ldots\right)$$

$$Res\left(\frac{1}{w^n(1-w)},0\right) = 1 \text{ for all } n.$$

Example 10.9

Use the Residue Theorem to evaluate

(*i*) $\displaystyle\int_{|z|=2} \frac{dz}{(z-4)\left(z^3-1\right)}$ (*ii*) $\displaystyle\int_{|z|=1} \sin\frac{1}{z}\,dz$ (*iii*) $\displaystyle\int_{|z|=2} ze^{3/z}\,dz$.

Solution

Let $f(z) = \dfrac{1}{(z-4)\left(z^3-1\right)}$. $z = 4, 1, \omega, \omega^2$ $\left(\omega = \dfrac{-1+\sqrt{3}}{2}\right)$ are the isolated singularities of $f(z)$. But $z = 4$ lies outside $|z| = 2$ and $1, \omega, \omega^2$ are simple poles of $f(z)$. Therefore

$$Res(f;\ 1) = \lim_{z\to 1}(z-1)\frac{1}{(z-4)\left(z^3-1\right)}$$

$$= \lim_{z\to 1}\frac{1}{(z-4)(z-\omega)\left(z-\omega^2\right)}$$

$$= \frac{1}{(-3)\left(\frac{3-\sqrt{3}}{2}\right)\left(\frac{3+\sqrt{3}}{2}\right)} = \frac{4}{(-3)(9-3)}$$

$$= \frac{2}{-9}$$

$$Res(f;\ \omega) = \lim_{z \to w} \frac{(z-\omega)}{(z-4)(z-1)(z-\omega)(z-\omega^2)}$$

$$= \frac{1}{(\omega-4)(\omega-1)(\omega-\omega^2)}$$

$$= \frac{2}{3(-6+5\sqrt{3})} = \frac{-2}{9}\left(\frac{-6-5\sqrt{3}}{13}\right)$$

$$Res(f;\ \omega^2) = \lim_{z \to w^2} \frac{(z-\omega^2)}{(z-4)(z^3-1)}$$

$$= \frac{1}{(\omega^2-4)(\omega-1)(\omega^2-\omega)}$$

$$= \frac{-2}{3(6+5\sqrt{3})} = \frac{2}{9}\left(\frac{6-5\sqrt{3}}{13}\right)$$

$$Res(f;\ 1) + Res(f,\ \omega) + Res(f,\ \omega^2) = \frac{-2}{9} - \frac{2}{9}\left(\frac{-6-5\sqrt{3}}{13}\right) + \frac{2}{9}\left(\frac{6-5\sqrt{3}}{13}\right)$$

$$= \frac{-2}{9}\left[\frac{13-(6+5\sqrt{3})-(6-5\sqrt{3})}{13}\right]$$

$$= \frac{-2 \times 1}{9 \times 13}$$

$$= \frac{-2}{117}$$

Then, $$\int_{|z|=2} \frac{dz}{(z-4)(z^3-1)} = 2\pi i \times \frac{-2}{117} = \frac{-4\pi i}{117}$$

(*ii*) Let $g(z) = \sin\frac{1}{z}$

$z = 0$ is an essential singularity of $g(z)$. By Laurent expansion

$$\sin\frac{1}{z} = \frac{1}{z} - \frac{1}{3!\,z^3} + \frac{1}{5!\,z^5} \ldots\ldots$$

$$Res(g;\ 0) = \text{Coefficient of } \frac{1}{z} = 1$$

Therefore, by Cauchy's Residue theorem

$$\int_{|z|=1} \sin\frac{1}{z} = 2\pi i$$

(*iii*) Let $h(z) = ze^{3/z}$, $z = 0$ is an essential singularity of $h(z)$. Then,

$$ze^{3/z} = z\left[1 + \frac{3}{z} + \frac{1}{2!}\left(\frac{3}{z}\right)^2 + \frac{1}{3!}\left(\frac{3}{z}\right)^3 + \ldots\ldots\right]$$

$$= z + 3 + \frac{9}{2z^2} + \frac{9}{2z^3} + \ldots\ldots$$

$$Res(h;\ 0) = \frac{9}{2}$$

Then,. $$\int_{|z|=2} ze^{3/z}\,dz = 2\pi i \times \frac{9}{2} = 9\pi i$$

Example 10.10

Evaluate $\int_\gamma \frac{e^z}{z^4 + 5z^3}\,dz$, where the contour γ is the circle $|z| = 2$.

Solution

We know $z^4 + 5z^3 = z^3(z + 5)$ has pole of order 3 at $z = 0$ and simple pole at $z = -5$. But $z = -5$ lies outside $|z| = 2$.

$$Res\left(\frac{e^z}{z^4 + 5z^3},\ 0\right) = \frac{1}{2!}\frac{d^2}{dz^2}\left[z^3 \frac{e^z}{(z+5)z^3}\right]_{z=0}$$

$$= \frac{1}{2!}\left[\frac{\left(z^2+8z+17\right)e^z}{(z+5)^3}\right]_{z=0}$$

$$= \frac{17}{2\times 125}$$

Then, $$\int\limits_{|z|=2} \frac{e^z}{z^4+5z^3} = 2\pi i \times \frac{17}{2\times 125} = \frac{17\pi i}{125}$$

EXERCISE

1. Find the residue at each pole of the given function

(*i*) $f(z) = \dfrac{z}{z^2+16}$ (*ii*) $f(z) = \dfrac{1}{\left(z^2-2z+2\right)^2}$

(*iii*) $f(z) = \dfrac{e^z}{e^z-1}$ (*iv*) $f(z) = \dfrac{\cos z}{z^2(z-\pi)^3}$

(*v*) $f(z) = \dfrac{1}{z\sin z}$ (*vi*) $f(z) = \dfrac{e^z}{\sin z}$

(*vii*) $f(z) = \dfrac{z^2-z+9}{\left(z^2+1\right)\left(z^2+9\right)}$ (*viii*) $f(z) = \dfrac{z^2}{z^4-1}$.

2. Find the residue of the function $f(z) = \dfrac{z^2}{z^4+1}$ at the points $e^{i\pi/4}$ and $e^{-i\pi/4}$.

3. Calculate the residues of the following functions at the points α indicated

(*i*) $f(z) = \dfrac{ze^{iz}}{(z-\pi)^2}, \alpha = \pi$ (*ii*) $f(z) = \dfrac{1+e^z}{z^4}, \alpha = 0$

(*iii*) $f(z) = \dfrac{\left(z^2+1\right)^n}{z^{n+1}}$ where n is a positive integer, $\alpha = 0$.

4. Prove that the function $f(\alpha) = \eta(\gamma; \alpha)$ is continuous on the complement of γ.

5. Prove that $\eta(\gamma; \alpha) = 0$ for fixed γ and sufficiently lary $|\alpha|$.

6. Compute

(*i*) $\displaystyle\int_{|z|=2} \frac{1}{(z-1)^2(z^2+1)}dz$ (*ii*) $\displaystyle\int_{|z|=8} \frac{dz}{1+e^z}$

(*iii*) $\displaystyle\int_{|z|=1} \cot z\, dz$

7. Evaluate $\displaystyle\int_\gamma \frac{\sin z}{z^2-1}dz$ where γ is

(*i*) the ellipse $x^2 + 4y^2 = 4$.

(*ii*) the square with vertices $\pm\frac{1}{2}, \pm\frac{1}{2}i$.

8. By considering the integral

$$\int_{|z|=1} \frac{z\, dz}{(2z^4+5z^2+2)}$$

prove that

$$\int_0^{2\pi} \frac{1}{1+8\cos^2\theta}d\theta = \frac{2\pi}{3}.$$

9. Evaluate $\displaystyle\int_0^{2\pi} (\cos^4\theta + \sin^4\theta)d\theta$ by converting it into an integral around $\gamma(0; 1)$ and applying the Residue Theorem.

10. Evaluate $\displaystyle\int_\gamma \frac{z^3}{z^4+1}dz$ where γ is the closed semi-circular contour with radius 2 and centre 0.

11. Evaluate $\displaystyle\int_0^{2\pi} \frac{d\theta}{2+\sin\theta}$.

12. Evaluate $\displaystyle\int_\gamma \frac{1+z}{\sin z}dz$ where γ is the square whose vertices are the points $4 + 4i, -4 + 4i, -4 - 4i, 4 - 4i$.

13. Find an analytic functions f in **C** except for simple poles at the cube roots of unity, where it has residues 1, α and β respectively. Such that $\alpha\beta = 1$ and there exists a constant k such that

$$|z^2 f(z)| < k \text{ for } |z| > 2.$$

ANSWERS

1. (*i*) $\text{Res}\,(f, +4i) = \frac{1}{2}$ (*ii*) $\text{Res}\,(f; -1 + i) = \frac{1}{4}$

(*iii*) $\text{Res}\,(f; 2n\pi i) = 1$

(*iv*) $\text{Res}\,(f, 0) = \frac{-3}{\pi^4}$, $\text{Res}\,(f, \pi) = \frac{\pi^2 - 6}{2\pi^4}$

(*v*) $\text{Res}(f, 0) = 1$, $\text{Res}\,(f, n\pi) = \frac{(-1)^n}{n\pi}$

(*vi*) $\text{Res}\,(f; 1) = 1$, $\text{Res}\,(f; n\pi) = (-1)^n e^{n\pi}$

(*viii*) $\text{Res}\,(f; i) = \frac{1+8i}{16}$, $\text{Res}\,(f; i) = \frac{-1+8i}{16}$

$\text{Res}\,(f; +3i) = \frac{1}{16}$

(*viiii*) $\text{Res}(f; +1) = \pm\frac{1}{4}$, $\text{Res}(f; +i) = \pm\frac{i}{4}$

2. $\text{Res}\left(f; e^{i\pi/4}\right) = \frac{1-i}{4\sqrt{2}}$, $\text{Res}\left(f; e^{-\pi/4}\right) = \frac{1+i}{4\sqrt{2}}$

3. (*i*) $-1 - i\pi$ (*ii*) $\frac{1}{6}$

(*iii*) 0 if n is odd and $\begin{pmatrix} n \\ \frac{1}{2}n \end{pmatrix}$, if n even

6. (*i*) $-\pi i$ (*ii*) $-2i$

(*iii*) $2\pi i$

7. (*i*) $2\pi i \sin 1$ (*ii*) 0

8. Put $z = e^{i\theta}$ and $\cos\theta = \frac{1}{2}\left(z+\frac{1}{z}\right)$ and $\int_0^{2\pi} \frac{1}{1+8\cos^2\theta} =$

$$\int_{|z|=1} \frac{zdz}{2z^4+5z^2+2}$$

9. $24\pi i$ **10.** πi

11. $2\pi/\sqrt{3}$ **12.** $-2\pi i$

13. $3(z^3-1)^{-1}$, $3z(z^3-1)^{-1}$

10.2. APPLICATIONS OF RESIDUE THEOREM

In this section, we shall show that the theory of residue can be used to know the information about the number of zeros and poles of a function inside a given closed contour. The result is known as the Principle of the Argument. We shall also prove Rouche's Theorem which tells us about the similarity between number of zeros of f and $f+g$ where f and g are analytic functions.

We begin special type of functions whose only singularities are poles.

Definition 10.4

A function f is called meromorphic on a bounded region R if the only singularities of f lying in R are poles.

We need the following lemma to prove the Principle of the Argument.

Lemma 10.9

If f is meromorphic function on a bounded region R, then the poles of f'/f in R, all occur at points which are either zeros or poles of f.

Proof

Let f be a function with zeros $\alpha_1, \alpha_2, ..., \alpha_n$ and poles $\beta_1, \beta_2, ..., \beta_m$, then we can write

$$f(z) = \frac{(z-\alpha_1)^{l_1}(z-\alpha_2)^{l_2}........(z-\alpha_1)^{l_n}}{(z-\beta_1)^{k_1}(z-\beta_2)^{k_2}........(z-\beta_n)^{k_m}} g(z)$$

where $g(z)$ is an analytic function.

Then, $$\frac{f'(z)}{f(z)} = \sum_{j=1}^{n} \frac{l_j}{z-\alpha_j} - \sum_{j=1}^{m} \frac{k_j}{z-\beta_j} + \frac{g'(z)}{g(z)}$$

where $\frac{g'(z)}{g(z)}$ is an analytic and non-zero in R. Thus, the poles of $\frac{f'(z)}{f(z)}$ occurs at the points $\alpha_1, \alpha_2, \ldots\ldots, \alpha_n, \beta_1, \beta_2, \ldots\ldots, \beta_m$ and that they all are simple poles.

Principle of the Argument

Theorem 10.10

Let f be a function, meromorphic on a simply-connected bounded region R and let Γ be a simple closed contour contained in R. Assume that f has no zeros or poles on Γ. If N is the number of zeros and P is the number of poles of f inside Γ, each counted according to its order, then

$$\frac{1}{2\pi i}\int_{\gamma} \frac{f'}{f} = N - P.$$

Proof

By the lemma the singularities of $\frac{f'}{f}$ can occur only at poles or the zeros of f.

Suppose f has a pole of order k inside Γ at α. Then,

$$f(z) = \frac{g(z)}{(z-\alpha)k} \qquad \ldots(1)$$

where g is analytic and non-zero in the neighbourhood of α. Differentiating (1) we get

$$f'(z) = \frac{g'(z)}{(z-\alpha)k} - \frac{k\,g(z)}{(z-\alpha)^{k+1}} \; (z \neq \alpha)$$

so that

$$\frac{f'(z)}{f(z)} = \frac{g'(z)}{g(z)} - \frac{k}{(z-\alpha)}.$$

Then, f'/f has simple pole at α. Since g'/g is analytic in a neighbourhood of α, therefore $\int_\gamma \frac{g'(z)}{g(z)} = 0$. Hence,

$$\frac{1}{2\pi i}\int_\gamma \frac{f'(z)}{f(z)} = Res(\frac{f'}{f}, \alpha) = -k.$$

Now, if f has a zero of order k at $z = \alpha$, then

$$f(z) = (z-\alpha)^k g(z), g(z) \neq 0 \text{ and } g \text{ is analytic}$$

on some neighbourhood of α. Then,

$$f'(z) = k(z-\alpha)^{k-1} g(z) + (z-\alpha)^k g'(z).$$

and $$\frac{f'(z)}{f(z)} = \frac{k}{(z-\alpha)} + \frac{g'(z)}{g(z)}.$$

Hence at zeros of f, f'/f has a simple pole with residue k. Then,

$$\frac{1}{2\pi i}\int_\gamma \frac{f'}{f} = Res(\frac{f'}{f}, \alpha) = \text{k}$$

If f has zeros $\alpha_1, \alpha_2 \ldots \alpha_n$ of multiplicity $k_1, k_2 \ldots k_n$ and poles β_1, $\beta_2 .. \beta_m$ of order $n_1, n_2 \ldots n_m$. Then f'/f has simple poles at $\alpha_1\alpha_2 \ldots \alpha_n$ with residues $k_1, k_2 \ldots k_n$ respectively and at $\beta_1, \beta_2 \ldots \beta_m$ of residues $-n_1, -n_2 \ldots -n_m$. By Cauchy's Residues Theorem

$$\begin{aligned}\frac{1}{2\pi i}\int_\gamma \frac{f'}{f} &= \Sigma\, Res(\frac{f'}{f}) \\ &= k_1 + k_2 \ldots + k_n - (n_1 + n_2 \ldots + n_m) \\ &= \text{No. of zeros} - \text{No. of poles} \\ &= N - P.\end{aligned}$$

Example 10.11

Let f be the function defined by

$$f(z) = \frac{(z+3)(z+1)}{z^2}$$

Then, show that $\frac{1}{2\pi i}\int_\gamma \frac{f'}{f} = -1$ where $\gamma = \{z : |z| = 2\}$.

Proof

f has zeros at 3 and -1 of multiplicity 1, but $z = 3$ lies outside γ. f has poles at $z = 0$ of order 2. Therefore, by Theorem 10.10.

$$\begin{aligned}\frac{1}{2\pi i}\int_\gamma \frac{f'}{f} &= \text{No. of zeros inside } \gamma - \text{No. of poles}\\ &= 1-2\\ &= -1.\end{aligned}$$

Example 10.12

Using the Argument Principle, evaluate $\int_C \frac{2z+1}{z^2+z}$, where C is $|z| = 2$.

Solution

If $f(z) = z^2 + z$, then the given integral is of the form $\int_C \frac{f'}{f}$. By Argument Principle,

$$\int_C \frac{f'}{f} = \text{No. of zeros} - \text{No. of poles.}$$

But $f(z)$ has zero at $z = 0$ and $z = -1$ of multiplicity 1. Therefore,

$$\int_C \frac{2z+1}{z^2+z} = 2 - 0 = 2.$$

Remark

1. Why is Theorem 10.2 called the Argument principle? The point of fact is that there is a relationship between $N - P$ and the argument of $f(z)$. More precisely

$$N - P = \frac{1}{2\pi}[\text{change in } \arg f(z) \text{ as } z \text{ traverses } C \text{ once in the positive direction}]$$

Consider

$$\int_\Gamma \frac{f'(z)}{f(z)}dz = \int_{f(\Gamma)} \frac{dw}{w} \text{ if we put } w = f(z)$$

$$= \log|w|_{f(\Gamma)} + i/\text{Arg}(w)/_{f(\Gamma)}$$
$$= i/\text{Arg}(w)/_{f(\Gamma)} \text{ (because } \Gamma \text{ to closed)}$$
$$= i\,[\text{Arg } f(z)]_{\Gamma}.$$

Let $\Gamma = \{\gamma(t) : 0 \le t \le 1\}$. Then, z travels around Γ from starting point $\gamma(0)$ to the terminal point $\gamma(1)$ and $\gamma(0) = \gamma(1)$.

Let $P = \{0 = t_0 < t_1 < t_2 \ldots. < t_n = 1\}$ be the partition of [0, 1] such that

$$\gamma_1 : = \gamma_1(t),\ 0 = t_0 \le t \le t_1$$
$$\gamma_2 : = \gamma_2(t),\ t_1 \le t \le t_2$$
$$\vdots$$
$$\gamma_n : = \gamma_n(t),\ t_{n-1} \le t \le t_n = 1 \text{ (Fig. 10.3)}$$

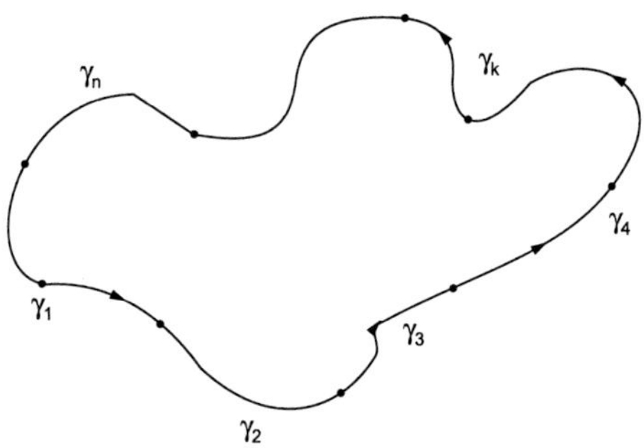

Fig. 10.3

Since an analytic branch of log f can be defined in a simply-connected domain containing γ_1, therefore

$$\int_{\gamma_1} \frac{f'}{f} = i[\text{Arg } f(\gamma(t_1)) - \text{Arg } f(\gamma(t_0)]$$

Similarly
$$\int_{\gamma_k} \frac{f'}{f} = i[\text{Arg } f(\gamma(t_k)) - \text{Arg } f(\gamma(t_{k-1}))]$$

We know

$$\int_{\gamma} = \int_{\gamma_1} + \int_{\gamma_2} + \ldots\ldots. + \int_{\gamma_n}$$

Thus,
$$\int_{\gamma} \frac{f'}{f} = i[\text{Arg } f(\gamma(t_1)) - \text{Arg } (f(\gamma(t_0)) + [\text{Arg } f(\gamma(t_2) - \text{Arg } f(\gamma(t_1) \ldots.. \text{Arg}(f(\gamma(t_n)) - \text{Arg } f(\gamma(t_{n-1}))]$$

$$= i[\text{Arg}\,(f(\gamma(t_n)) - \text{Arg}\,(f(\gamma(t_0))]$$
$$= i[\text{Arg}\,f(\gamma(1)) - \text{Arg}\,f(\gamma(0))].$$

Thus,
$$N - P = \frac{1}{2\pi i}\int \frac{f'}{f}dz$$
$$= \frac{1}{2\pi}[\text{Arg}\,f(\gamma(1)) - \text{Arg}\,f(\gamma(0))].$$

2. The Argument Principle can be restated in terms of the winding number of Γ. If Γ is closed contour and $0 \notin \Gamma$, then

$$\eta(\Gamma\,;0) = \frac{1}{2\pi i}\int_{\Gamma}\frac{dw}{w}$$

If f is meromorphic then the image contour $f(\Gamma)$ is a closed contour (not necessarily simple) and (Fig. 10.4)

$$\eta(f(\Gamma)\,;0) = \frac{1}{2\pi i}\int_{f(\Gamma)}\frac{dw}{w} = \frac{1}{2\pi i}\int_{\Gamma}\frac{f'(z)}{f(z)}dz$$

by using the substitution $w = f(z)$, $dw = f'(z)\,dz$. Therefore, the Theorem 10.10 can be restated as follows:

If f is a function, meromorphic on a simply-connected bounded region R and Γ is a simple closed contour contained in R, f has zeros or poles in Γ. If N is the number of zeros and P is the number of poles of f inside Γ, then

$$\eta(f(\Gamma), 0) = N - P.$$

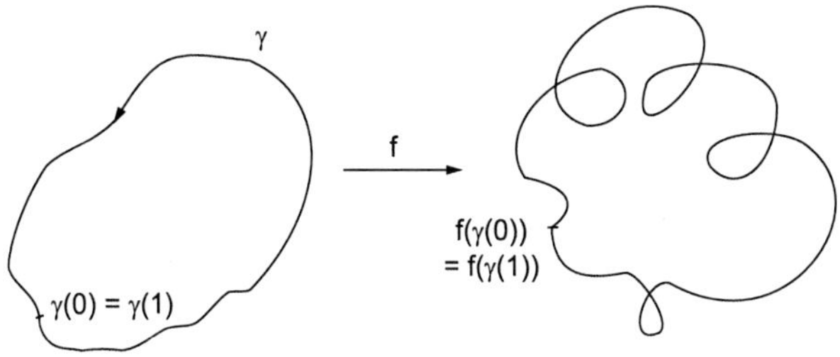

Fig. 10.4

Example 10.12

Suppose that f is entire and that $f(z)$ is real if and only if z is real. Use the Argument Principle to show that f can have at most one zero.

Solution

Consider the image of the circle $|z| = R$ under the mapping $w = f(z)$. Since $f(z)$ is real if and only if, f maps the entire upper semi-circle $|z| = R$, $y > 0$ into either the upper half-plane or the lower half-plane. Similarly the lower semi-circle $|z| = R$, $\gamma < 0$ is mapped by f into either the upper half-plane or the lower half-plane.

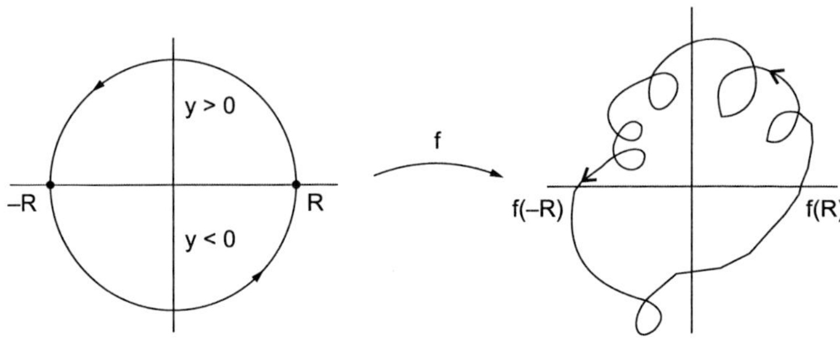

Fig. 10.5

The change in the argument of $f(z)$ in either upper or lower half-plane is at most π as z traverses either $|z| = R_1$ y > 0 or $|z| = R, y <$ 0. Thus, change in Arg $f(z)$ is at most 2π if it traverses $|z| = R$.

$$\text{No. of zeros of } f \text{ (in } |z| \leq R) = \frac{1}{2\pi} \text{ (change in the arg } f(z))$$

$$< \frac{1}{2\pi} \times \pi = \frac{1}{2} \leq 1$$

Thus, f can have at most one zero.

Example 10.14

If $\log(z^2 - 1) = \int_{\sqrt{2}}^{z} \frac{2\zeta}{\zeta^2 - 1} d\zeta$ is analytic in the plane minus the internal $(-\infty, 1]$. Hence, so is

$$\sqrt{z^2 - 1} = exp(\frac{1}{2} \log(z^2 - 1))$$

Show that $\sqrt{z^2 - 1}$ is analytic in the entire plane minus $[-1, 1]$.

Solution

Let $$f(z) = \sqrt{z^2 - 1}$$

$$= e^{\frac{1}{2}\log(z^2-1)}$$

$$= e^{\frac{1}{2}\int_{\sqrt{2}}^{z}\frac{2\zeta}{\zeta^2-1}d\zeta}$$

There is no loss of generality if we assume that the path of integration is upper half-plane if *Im z* > 0 and lower half-plane if *Im z* < 0. Since exponential is continuous, therefore we need to show that

$$\lim_{\substack{z\to x\\(\operatorname{Im} z>0)}} \int_{\sqrt{2}}^{z}\frac{2\zeta}{\zeta^2-1}d\zeta = \lim_{\substack{z\to x\\(\operatorname{Im} z<0)}} \int_{\sqrt{2}}^{z}\frac{2\zeta}{\zeta^2-1}d\zeta$$

Let $$A = \lim_{\substack{z\to x\\(\operatorname{Im} z<0)}} \int_{\sqrt{2}}^{z}\frac{2\zeta}{\zeta^2-1}d\zeta \text{ and}$$

$$B = \lim_{\substack{z\to x\\(\operatorname{Im} z<0)}} \int_{\sqrt{2}}^{z}\frac{2\zeta}{\zeta^2-1}d\zeta$$

But $A-B = \int_C \frac{2\zeta}{\zeta^2-1}d\zeta$ where C is a regular closed curve surrounding $\zeta = \pm 1$. By Argument Principle

$$\int_C \frac{2\zeta}{\zeta^2-1}d\zeta = 2\pi i \ \Sigma\ Res\left(\frac{2\zeta}{\zeta^2-1}, \pm 1\right)$$

$$Res\left(\frac{2\zeta}{\zeta^2-1}, 1\right) = \lim_{z\to 1}\frac{2\zeta}{\zeta+1} = 1$$

and $$Res\left(\frac{2\zeta}{\zeta^2-1}, -1\right) = \lim_{z\to -1}\frac{2\zeta}{\zeta+1} = 1$$

Thus, $$\int_C \frac{2\zeta}{\zeta^2-1}d\zeta = 2\pi i\,(1+1) = 4\pi\, i.$$ Hence,

$$\lim_{\substack{z\to x\\(\operatorname{Im} z>0)}} f(z) = e^A \text{ and } \lim_{\substack{z\to x\\(\operatorname{Im} z<0)}} f(z) = e^{B+4\pi i} = e^B$$

Then, $\lim_{z\to x}\sqrt{z^2-1}$ exists Thus, f is analytic in $\mathbf{C} \sim V[-1, 1]$.

The following theorem known as Rouche's Theorem, is a consequence of the Argument Principle. The theorem is helpful in determining the number of zeros of an analytic function.

Theorem 10.11: Rouche's Theorem

Let C be a simple closed contour lying entirely within a domain. Suppose f an g are analytic in If $|f(z) - g(z)| < |f(z)|$ for all z in γ, then f and g have same number of zeros (counted according to their order or multiplicities) inside γ.

Proof

Since $|f(z) - g(z)| < |f(z)|$ for all z on γ, therefore f and g have no zeros on the contour γ. Also we know

$$|f(z) - g(z)| = |g(z) - f(z)| < |f(z)|$$

then,
$$\left|\frac{g(z)}{f(z)} - 1\right| < 1$$

Let
$$F(z) = \frac{g(z)}{f(z)}, \text{ then } |F(z) - 1| < 1 \tag{1}$$

From (1), we get that the image γ' in w-plane of the curve γ under the mapping $w = F(z)$ is closed path and must be within the unit open disc $D(1; 1)$.

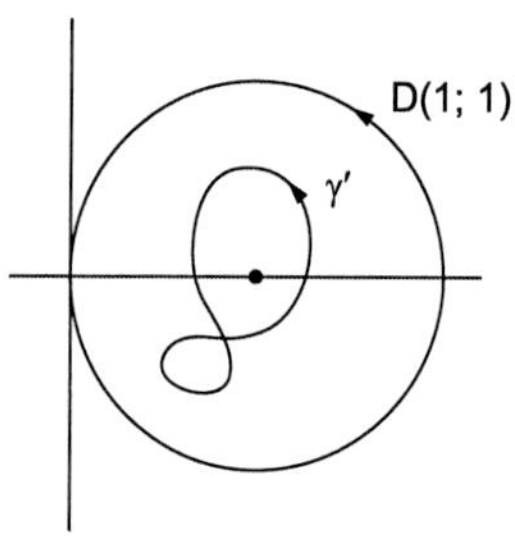

Fig. 10.6

Since γ' does not enclose $w = 0$, therefore $\frac{1}{w}$ is analytic in γ'. By Cauchy's theorem

$$0 = \int_{\gamma'} \frac{1}{w} dw = \int \frac{F'(z)}{F(z)} dz = 0 \qquad ...(2)$$

Since $w = F(z)$ and $dw = F'(z)\, dz$.

Now
$$F'(z) = \frac{d}{dz}\left(\frac{g(z)}{f(z)}\right)$$

$$= \frac{f(z)g'(z) - g(z)f'(z)}{[f(z)]^2}$$

and $$\frac{F'(z)}{F(z)} = \frac{g'(z)}{g(z)} - \frac{f'(z)}{f(z)} \quad ...(3)$$

From (2) and (3), we get

$$\int_\gamma \left[\frac{g'(z)}{g(z)} - \frac{f'(z)}{f(z)}\right] dz = 0$$

or $$\int_\gamma \frac{g'(z)}{g(z)} dz = \int_\gamma \frac{f'(z)}{f(z)} dz$$

Then, the number of zeros of g inside γ is same as the number of zero of f inside γ.

Example 10.15

Locate the zeros of the polynomial function

$$z^9 - 8z^2 + 5.$$

Solution

Let γ be the circle $|z| = 1$. Assume that $g(z) = z^9 - 8z^2 + 5$ and $f(z) = -8z^2 + 5$. Then for all z on $|z| = 1$

$$|f(z) - g(z)| = |-8z^2 + 5 - z^9 + 8z^5 - 5| = |-z^9| = |z|^9 = 1 \quad ...(1)$$

Also for all z on $|z| = 1$

$$|f(z)| = |-8z^2 + 5| = |8z^2 - 5| > |8|z|^2 - |5|| = |8 - 5| = 3 \quad ...(2)$$

From (1) and (2), we have

$|f(z) - g(z)| < |f(z)|$ for all z on $|z| = 1$.

By Rouche's Theorem f and g have the same no. of zeros inside the unit circle. Since $f(z)$ has two zeros therefore g has two zeros inside $|z| = 1$.

Example 10.16

Find the number of zeros of $3e^{-z} - z$ in $|z| < 1$.

Solution

Let $g(z) = 3e^{-z} - z$ and $f(z) = 3e^{-z}$

Then, $|f(z) - g(z)| = |z| = 1$ on $|z| = 1$

and $|f(z)| = |3e^{-z}| > \frac{3}{e} > 1$

Thus, $g(z)$ has no zero inside $|z| < 1$. Because $e^{-z} \neq 0, z \in \mathbf{C}$.

Example 10.17

Find the number of zeros of $z^4 - 5z + 1$ in $1 <| z |< 2$.

Solution

Let $g(z) = z^4 - 5z + 1$ on $|z| = 2$, let $f(z) = z^4$

Then, $|f(z) - g(z)| = |+5z - 1| = 9$ on $|z| = 2$

and $|f(z)| = |z|^4 = 16$ on $|z| = 2$

Thus, $|f(z) - g(z)| < |f(z)|$

Since $f(z)$ has four zeros inside $|z| = 2$, therefore $g(z)$ has four zeros inside $|z| = 2$.

Now on $|z| = 1$, assume $f(z) = -5z$, then

$$|f(z) - g(z)| = |z^4 + 1| = 2$$

and $|f(z)| = |-5z| = 5$

This gives $|f(z) - g(z)| < |f(z)|$ on $|z| = 1$. By Rouche's Theorem $g(z)$ has only one zero inside $|z| = 1$ as f has only one.

We calculate that inside the annulus $1 <| z | < 2$, $g(z) = z^4 - 5z + 1$ has precisely 3 zeros.

Example 10.18

The Fundamental Theorem of Algebra

Solution

Let $f(z) = a_n z^n$, $q(z) = a_0 + a_1 z + ... + a_{n-1} z^{n-1}$ and $p = q + f$. Let γ be the circle $|z| = R$.

$|q(z)| < |a_0| + |a_1| R + ...|a_{n-1}| R^{n-1}$

and $|f(z)| = |a_n| R^n$

$$\text{But } \lim_{R \to \infty} \frac{|a_0| + |a_1| R + ...|a_{n-1}| R^{n-1}}{|a_n| R^n} = 0$$

Choosing R sufficiently large, we get

$$|q(z)| < |f(z)| \text{ if } |z| = R.$$

Since $a_n z^n = f(z)$ has a zero in the disc $|z| < R$ (in fact, it has n) and so $p = q + f$ has a zero in the disc $|z| < R$, by Rouche's Theorem.

We have proved Cauchy Integral formula for higher order derivatives as

$$f^k(z) = \frac{k!}{2\pi i}\int_\gamma \frac{f(w)}{(w-z)^{k+1}}$$

Where γ is a circle containing z. As an application of the Residue Theorem, we have the same result in the following form:

Theorem 10.12: Cauchy Integral Formula

Suppose D is a simply-connected region and γ is a regular closed curve contained in D. If f is analytic in D, then for each z inside γ and $k = 0, 1, 2, \ldots\ldots$

$$f^{(k)}(z) = \frac{k!}{2\pi i}\int_\gamma \frac{f(w)}{(w-z)^{k+1}}dw.$$

Proof

Since f is analytic in D, therefore by Taylor's series

$$f(w) = f(z) + f'(z)(w-z) + \ldots\ldots + \frac{f^{(k)}(z)}{k!}(w-z)^k + \ldots\ldots\ldots \text{ in the}$$

neighbourhood of z. Then,

$$\frac{f(w)}{(w-z)^{k+1}} = \frac{f(z)}{(w-z)^{k+1}} + \frac{f'(z)}{(w-z)^k}$$

$$+ \ldots + \frac{f^{(k)}(z)}{k!(w-z)} + \frac{f^{(k+1)}(z)}{(k+1)!} + \ldots$$

$$Res\left(\frac{f(w)}{(w-z)^{k+1}}; z\right) = \text{coefficient of } \frac{1}{w-z}$$

$$= \frac{f^{(k)}(z)}{k!}$$

By Cauchy's Residue Theorem

$$\int_\gamma \frac{f(w)}{(w-z)^{k+1}}dz = 2\pi i\frac{f^{(k)}(z)}{k!}$$

$$f^{(k)}(z) = \frac{k!}{2\pi i}\int_\gamma \frac{f(w)}{(w-z)^{k+1}}dz.$$

Theorem 10.13

Suppose $\{f_n\}$ is a sequence of functions analytic in a region D such that $f_n \to f$ uniformly on $\overline{D}$. Then f is analytic, $f_n' \to f'$ on D and the convergence is uniform in $\overline{D}$.

Proof

Using Theorem 10.12, if $z_0 \in D$ and $\gamma = \gamma(z_0; r)$ for some $r < 1$, then

$$f_n'(z) - f'(z) = \frac{1}{2\pi i}\int_\gamma \frac{f_n(w) - f(w)}{(w-z)^2}dw$$

for all $z \in D(z_0; r)$. Since $f_n \to f$ uniformly in $\overline{D}$, therefore

$$|f_n - f(z)| < \frac{\in r}{4} \quad \forall\, n > m$$

$$\text{Thus, } |f_n'(z) - f'(z)| < \frac{1}{2\pi}\frac{\in r}{4r^2} \times 2\pi r$$

$$< \frac{\in}{4} \qquad \forall\, n > m,\ z \in D(z_0; r/2)$$

Since any compact subset of D can be covered by finitely many discs of the form $D_0(z_0; r/2)$. Then, the convergence is uniform.

Theorem 10.14

Suppose $\{f_n\}$ is a sequence of non-vanishing analytic functions in a region D and suppose $f_n \to f$ uniformly on $\overline{D}$. Then, $f \equiv 0$ in D or $f(z) \neq 0$ for all $z \in D$.

Proof

Suppose $f(z) \neq 0$ for some $z \in D$. If $f \neq 0$, there is some circle C centred at z and such that $f(z) \neq 0$ on **C**;

$$\frac{f_n'}{f_n} \to \frac{f'}{f} \text{ uniformly on } \mathbf{C}.$$

But $\frac{1}{2\pi i}\int_C \frac{f'}{f}$ = no. of zeros of $f > 1$ (because $f(z) = 0$ for some $z \in D$)

and $\frac{1}{2\pi i}\int_C \frac{f'_n}{f_n}$ = no. of zeros of $f_n = 0$ (because $f_n \neq 0$ in D)

which is not possible. Thus, $f \equiv 0$.

Corollary 10.15

If $\{f_n\}$ is a sequence of analytic function in a region D such that $f_n \to f$ uniformly on $\overline{D}$ and that $f_n \neq a$, Then, either $f \equiv a$ or $f \not\leq a$ in D.

Proof

Applying Theorem 10.14 to the function $g_n(z) = f_n(z) - a$. We get the result.

Theorem 10.16

If $f_n \to f$ uniformly on $\overline{D}$ where D is a region. If f_n is one-one in D for all n, then either f is one-one in D or f is constant.

Proof

Let $f(z_1) = f(z_2) = a$. Let D_1 and D_2 be two disjoint discs enclosing z_1 and z_2 respectively. Then, $f_n(z) = a$ must have a solution in D_1 once n is large enough. since f_n is one-one, $f_n(z) \neq a$ throughout D_2 for all large n and hence $f(z_2) \neq a$ contradicting the assumption. Thus f is one-one.

Example 10.19

Let f and γ be analytic on a contour γ and $|f(z)| > |g(z)|$ for all $z \in \gamma^*$. Set

$$J(\lambda) = \frac{1}{2\pi i}\int_\gamma \frac{(f+\lambda g)'}{f+\lambda g},\ 0 < \lambda < 1, \text{ then}$$

$J(\lambda)$ is continuous function of λ and is always integer-valued. Also show that J is constant and the number of zeros of f is equal to the number of zeros of $f + g$.

Proof

Since $f(z)$ and $g(z)$ are analytic within γ, therefore $\dfrac{1}{2\pi i}\displaystyle\int_\gamma \frac{f'(z)+\lambda g'(z)}{f(z)+\lambda g(z)}$ is an integer by Argument Principle. Thus, J: $[0, 1] \to \mathbf{C}$ is a well-defined.

To Prove: J is continuous function

Let $t, s \in [0, 1]$, then

$$|\phi(t)-\phi(s)| = \left|\frac{1}{2\pi i}\int_\gamma \left[\frac{f'(z)+tg'(z)}{f(z)+tg(z)} - \frac{f'(z)+sg'(z)}{f(z)+sg(z)}\right]dz\right|$$

$$< \frac{1}{2\pi}\int_\gamma \left|\frac{(f'(z)+tg'(z))(f(z)+sg(z))-(f'(z)+sg'(z))(f(z)+tg(z))}{|f(z)+tg(z)||f(z)+sg(z)|}\right| |dz|$$

$$< \frac{|t-s|}{2\pi}\int_\gamma \frac{|g'(z)f(z)-f'(z)g(z)|}{|f(z)+tg(z)||f(z)+sg(z)|}|dz|$$

Let t be fixed. Consider $|f(z) + tg(z)|$

If at some point $|f(z) + tg(z)| = 0 \Rightarrow f(z) = -tg(z)$, $|f(z) = t|g(z)| \leq |g(z)|$ which is a contradiction to the given hypothesis, then $|f(z) + tg(z)| > 0 \; \forall \; z \in \gamma^*$.

Since γ^* is compact, $\inf|f(z) + tg(z)| = m > 0 \; \forall \; z \in \gamma^*$

i.e., $\quad |f(z) + tg(z)| \geq m \; \forall \; z \in \gamma^*$

Since f and g being continuous are bounded on γ^*, therefore

$|g'(z)f(z) - f'(z)\, g(z)| < M$ and $|g(z)| < m \; \forall \; z \in \gamma^*$

$$\text{Then,} \quad |\phi(t)-\phi(s)| < \frac{|t-s|M}{2\pi m}\int \frac{|dz|}{|f(z)+sg(z)|}$$

$$\begin{aligned}\text{Now} \quad |f(z) + s\, g(z)| &= |f(z) + tg(z) - (t-s)\, g(z)| \\ &> |f(z) + tg(z)| - |t-s|\, |g(z)| \\ &> |m - |t-s|\, M|\end{aligned}$$

Then, $|\phi(t) - \phi(s)| < \dfrac{|t-s|M}{2\pi m} \times \dfrac{l(\gamma)}{|m-(t-s)M|}$

Let $\in > 0$ be any real number. Choose $\delta > 0$ such that

$$0 < \delta < \left(\frac{\pi m^2}{m\,l(\gamma)}\in, \frac{m}{2M}\right)$$

then, if $|t - s| < \delta$, then $|t - s| < \dfrac{m}{2M}$

Also $|m - M|t - s|| > \dfrac{m}{2}$

Hence, $|\phi(t) - \phi(s)| < \dfrac{\not{2}\,|t-s|\,M\,l(\gamma)}{\not{2}\pi m^2}$

Since $|t - s| < \delta < \dfrac{\pi m^2}{l(\gamma)\,M}\in$. Therefore

$$|\phi(t) - \phi(s)| < \in$$

and ϕ is continuous and $\phi(\lambda)$ is an integer. Hence, ϕ is a constant *i.e.*, $\phi(0) = \phi(1)$ (because $\phi\,[0, 1]$ is connected)

or $$\frac{1}{2\pi i}\int_\gamma \frac{f'}{f} = \frac{1}{2\pi i}\int \frac{f'+g'}{f+g} = N - P$$

Thus, f and $f + g$ have the same number of zeros.

EXERCISE

1. Evaluate the given integral along the indicated contour:

(*i*) $\displaystyle\int_\gamma \frac{dz}{(z-1)(z-2)^2}, |z| = \frac{3}{2}$ (*ii*) $\displaystyle\int_\gamma \frac{(z+1)dz}{z^2(z-2i)}, |z-2i| = 1$

(*iii*) $\displaystyle\int_\gamma \frac{1}{z\sin z}dz, |z| = 5$ (*iv*) $\displaystyle\int_\gamma \frac{dz}{z^2+4z+13}, |z-3i| = 3$

(*v*) $\displaystyle\int_\gamma \cot z\,dz, |z| = 1$ (*vi*) $\displaystyle\int_{|z|=2} z\,e^{3/z}dz.$

2. Prove that $n = 3, 4,......$ the polynomial $z^n + nz - 1$ has n zeros inside the circle with centre at 0 and radius $1+\sqrt{2/(n-1)}$.

3. For the function $f(z) = z + \frac{1}{z}$, verify $\eta\ (\Gamma; 0) = N - P$ where N = number of zeros; P = number of poles where

(*i*) $\Gamma = \{z: |z| = r > 1\}$ (*ii*) $\Gamma = \{z: |z| = r < 1\}$.

4. Let γ be a closed semi-circular contour of radius $r(>3)$. By applying Rouche's Theorem with $f(z) = z + 2$ and $g(z) = -e^z$. Show that the function $z \to z + 2 - e^z$ has exactly one zero inside Γ. Deduce that the equation $e^z = z + 2$ has exactly one root in the half plane $\{z: Re z < 0\}$.

5. Find the number of zeros of

(*i*) $f_1(z) = z^6 - 5z^4 + 3z^2 - 1$ in $|z| < 1$

(*ii*) $f_2(z) = \frac{1}{3}e^z - z$ in $|z| \le 1$

(*iii*) $f_3(z) = 2z^5 + 8z - 1$ in $\{z : 1 < |z| < | < 2\}$.

6. Suppose f is analytic inside and on a regular closed curve γ and has no zeros on γ. Show that if m is a positive integer, then

$$\frac{1}{2\pi i}\int_\gamma z^m \frac{f'(z)}{f(z)}dz = \sum_k (z_k)^m$$

where the sum is taken over all the zeros of f inside γ.

7. If $R > 0$, n is large enough, show that

$$P_n(z) = 1 + z + \frac{z^2}{2!} + \frac{z^3}{3!} + ... + \frac{z^n}{n!} \text{ has no zero in } |z| < R.$$

ANSWERS

1. (*i*) $2\pi i$ (*ii*) $\frac{-\pi i}{2} \times (2i + 1)$

(*iii*) $\begin{cases} \dfrac{-2i}{n} & \text{if } n \text{ is odd} \\ \dfrac{2i}{n} & \text{if } n \text{ is even} \end{cases}$ (*iv*) $\dfrac{\pi}{3}$

(*v*) $2\pi i$ (*vi*) $9\pi i$

2. Consider $f(z) = z^n$, $g(z) = n\,z - 1$ and $|f(z)| > |g(z)|\ \forall\ z \in \gamma$

$$\left(0, 1 + \sqrt{\frac{2}{(n-1)}}\right)$$

3. (*i*) $\Gamma = \{z: |z| = r > 1\}, N = 2, P = 1\ \eta(\Gamma; 0) = 1$

(*ii*) $\Gamma = \{z: |z| = r < 1\}, N = 0, P = 1, \eta(\Gamma; 0) = -1$

5. (*i*) 4 zeroes in $|z| < 1$ (*ii*) $1, |z| > \left|\frac{1}{3}e^z\right|$

(*iii*) 4 zeroes in $\{z: |<| z| < 2\}$

6. $\text{Res}\left(\dfrac{z^m f'(z)}{f(z)}, z_k\right) = p{z_k}^m$ where p is the order of the zero at z_k.

7. The convergence of the series is uniform in $|z| < R$. Also $1 + z + \dfrac{z^2}{2!} + \dfrac{z^3}{3!} + \ldots\ldots\ldots \to e^z$ which has no zero anywhere.

❑❑❑

11

Contour Integration and Summation of Series

In this chapter, we shall show how the Residue Theorem can be used to evaluate various types of contour integrals and to sum certain series of the form.

$$\sum_{n=1}^{\infty} \phi(n) \text{ and } \sum_{n=1}^{\infty} (-1)^n \phi(n).$$

11.1 EVALUATION OF DEFINITE INTEGRAL BY CONTOUR INTEGRAL TECHNIQUES

Type I

Integrals of the form $\int_{-\infty}^{\infty} \frac{P(x)}{Q(x)} dx$ where $P(x)$ and $Q(x)$ are polynomials.

We know from real variable calculus that an integral of this type will converge if $Q(x) \neq 0$ and $\deg P < \deg Q$. With the assumption we have

$$\int_{-\infty}^{\infty} \frac{P(x)}{Q(x)} dx = \lim_{R \to \infty} \int_{-R}^{R} \frac{P(x)}{Q(x)} dx.$$

Let γ_R be the closed contour consisting of the real line segment from $-R$ to R and upper semi-circle Γ_R centred at the origin and of radius R such that it consist of all the zeros of Q lying in the upper half-plane. Then by Residue Theorem

$$\int_{\gamma_R} \frac{P(z)}{Q(z)}dz = 2\pi i \sum_{-k} Res\left(\frac{P}{Q}, Z_k\right) \quad ...(1)$$

where Z_k are the poles of $\frac{P}{Q}$.

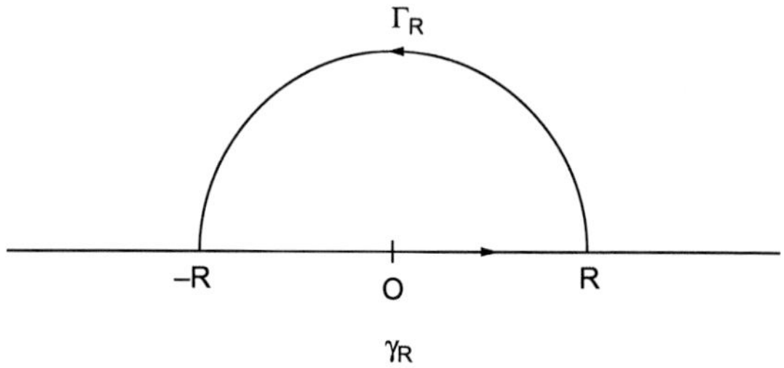

Fig. 11.1

From Fig. 11.1,

$$\int_{\gamma_R} \frac{P(z)}{Q(z)}dz = \int_{-R}^{R} \frac{P(x)}{Q(x)}dx + \int_{\Gamma_R} \frac{P(z)}{Q(z)}dz \quad ...(2)$$

From (1) and (2), we get

$$\int_{-R}^{R} \frac{P(x)}{Q(x)}dx + \int_{\Gamma_R} \frac{P(z)}{Q(z)}dz = 2\pi i \sum_{k} Res\left(\frac{P}{Q}, Z_k\right) \quad ...(3)$$

To evaluate $\int_{\Gamma_R} \frac{P}{Q}$ we shall use Estimation Theorem and prove

$$\int_{\Gamma_R} \frac{P}{Q} = 0 \text{ if } R \to \infty. \quad ...(4)$$

Combining (3) and (4)

$$\int_{-\infty}^{\infty} \frac{P(x)}{Q(x)}dx = 2\pi i \sum_{k} Res\left(\frac{P}{Q}, Z_k\right).$$

Example 11.1

Evaluate $\int_0^{\infty} \frac{x^2\, dx}{\left(x^2+4\right)^2\left(x^2+9\right)}$.

Solution

We know

$$\int_0^{\infty} \frac{x^2\,dx}{\left(x^2+4\right)^2\left(x^2+9\right)} = \frac{1}{2}\int_{-\infty}^{\infty} \frac{x^2\,dx}{\left(x^2+4\right)^2\left(x^2+9\right)}$$

Consider the contour γ_R as shown in Fig 11.1, then

$$\int_{\gamma_R} \frac{z^2}{\left(z^2+4\right)^2\left(z^2+9\right)}dz = \int_{-R}^{R} \frac{x^2\,dx}{\left(x^2+4\right)^2\left(x^2+9\right)} + \int_{\Gamma_R} \frac{z^2\,dz}{\left(z^2+4\right)^2\left(z^2+9\right)} \quad ...(1)$$

Let $f(z) = \dfrac{z^2}{\left(z^2+4\right)^2\left(z^2+9\right)}$. The function $f(z)$ has a double poles at + 4i and simple poles at + 3i. But only $z = 4i$ and $z = 3i$ lie inside γ_R.

$$\text{Res}(f;\ 3i) = \lim_{z\to 3i}(z-3i)f(z)$$

$$= \lim_{z\to 3i}\frac{z^2}{\left(z^2+4\right)^2(z+3i)}$$

$$= \frac{-9}{25\times 6i} = \frac{3i}{50}$$

$$\text{Res}(f;\ 2i) = \left[\frac{d}{dz}\left((z-2i)^2 f(z)\right)\right]_{z=2i}$$

$$= \left[\frac{d}{dz}\left(\frac{z^2}{(z+2i)^2\left(z^2+9\right)}\right)\right]_{z=2i}$$

$$= \frac{-13}{200}i$$

By Cauchy Residue Theorem

$$\int_{\gamma_R}\frac{z^2}{\left(z^2+4\right)^2\left(z^2+9\right)} = 2\pi i\left(\frac{-13}{200}+\frac{3}{50}\right)i$$

$$= \frac{2\pi}{200} = \frac{\pi}{100} \qquad ...(2)$$

Now

$$\left|\int_{\Gamma_R} \frac{z^2\,dz}{\left(z^2+4\right)^2\left(z^2+9\right)}\right| = \left|\int_0^{\pi} \frac{R^2e^{2i\theta}\,Rie^{i\theta}d\theta}{\left(R^2e^{2i\theta}+4\right)^2\left(R^2e^{2i\theta}+9\right)}\right|$$

$$< R^3\int_0^{\pi} \frac{d\theta}{\left|R^2e^{2i\theta}+4\right|\left|R^2e^{2i\theta}+9\right|}$$

($\Gamma_R = z(t) = Re^{i\theta}$, $0 < \theta < \pi$, then $dz = Rie^{i\theta}d\theta$)

$$< \frac{R^3\pi}{\left(R^2-4\right)\left(R^2-9\right)} \to 0 \text{ as } R \to \infty \qquad ...(3)$$

From (1), (2) and (3), we get

$$\int_{-\infty}^{\infty} \frac{x^2dx}{\left(x^2+4\right)^2\left(x^2+9\right)} = \frac{\pi}{100}$$

But $$\int_0^{\infty} \frac{x^2dx}{\left(x^2+4\right)^2\left(x^2+9\right)} = \frac{\pi}{200}.$$

Type II

Integrals of the form $\int_{\Gamma} \frac{P(z)}{Q(z)}dz$.

The basic method for this type of integral is given below:

(1) Set up the integral of f along suitable contour;

(2) Identify the poles of f which lie inside Γ;

(3) Calculate the Residue of f at these poles.

Then, using Residue Theorem

$$\int_{\Gamma} \frac{P(z)}{Q(z)}dz = 2\pi i\sum_k Res\left(\frac{P}{Q}, z_k\right)$$

where z_k are the poles of f. In this unit, we are concerned with those functions whose only singularity are poles.

Example 11.2

Evaluate $\int_{\Gamma} \frac{z+3}{(z-1)(z-2)(z+4)} dz$

where Γ is the ellipse $\frac{x^2}{9} + \frac{y^2}{4} = 1$.

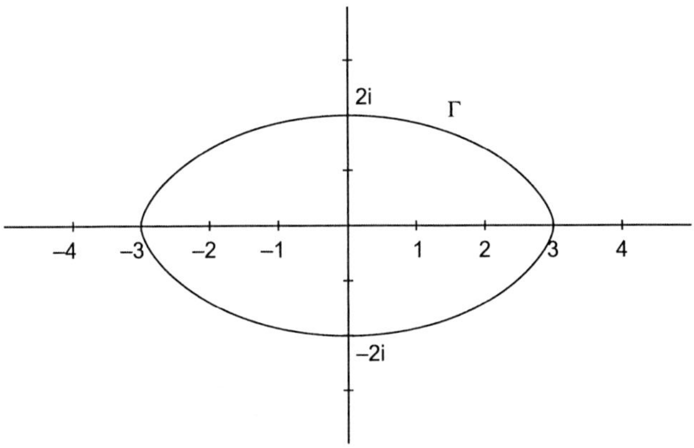

Fig. 11.2

Solution

Let $$f(z) = \frac{z+3}{(z-1)(z-2)(z+4)}$$

This function has poles at $z = 1, 2, -4$ but $z = -4$ does not lie inside Γ.

$$Res(f;\ 1) = \lim_{z \to 1} \frac{z+3}{(z-2)(z+4)} = \frac{4}{-5}$$

$$Res(f;\ 2) = \lim_{z \to 2} \frac{z+3}{(z-1)(z+4)} = \frac{5}{6}$$

By Residue Theorem

$$\int_{\Gamma} \frac{z+3}{(z-1)(z-2)(z+4)} dz = 2\pi i \left(\frac{-4}{5} + \frac{5}{6} \right) = \frac{\pi i}{15}.$$

Type III

Integrals of the form $\int_0^{2\pi} F(\cos\theta, \sin\theta)\, d\theta$.

To convert this real trigonometric integral of this form into a complex integral, we use the contour C, the unit circle $|z| = 1$ centred at the origin. We parametrize the contour C by $z = e^{i\theta}$, $0 < \theta < 2\pi$. We write

$$dz = ie^{i\theta} d\theta, \qquad \cos\theta = \frac{e^{i\theta} + e^{-i\theta}}{2}, \qquad \sin\theta = \frac{e^{i\theta} - e^{-i\theta}}{2i}$$

$$\text{then, } z^{-1} = \frac{1}{z} = e^{-i\theta}, \ \cos\theta = \frac{z + \frac{1}{z}}{2}, \qquad \sin\theta = \frac{z - \frac{1}{z}}{2i} \qquad \ldots(1)$$

$$\text{Thus, } \int_0^{2\pi i} F(\cos\theta, \sin\theta)\, d\theta = \int_\gamma F\left(\frac{1}{2}\left(z + z^{-1}\right), \frac{1}{2i}\left(z - z^{-1}\right)\right)\frac{dz}{iz}$$

where γ is the unit circle $|z| = 1$.

Example 11.3

Evaluate $\displaystyle\int_0^{2\pi} \frac{dx}{(2 + \cos x)^2}$

Solution

Substituting from (1) in the given integral

$$\int_C \frac{1}{\left(2 + \frac{1}{2}\left(z + z^{-1}\right)\right)^2} \frac{dz}{iz} = \int_C \frac{1}{\left(2 + \frac{z^2 + 1}{2z}\right)^2} \frac{dz}{iz}$$

$$= \frac{4}{i} \int_C \frac{z}{\left(z^2 + 4z + 1\right)^2} dz .$$

The zeros of the polynomial $z^2 + 4z + 1 = 0$ are $z_1 = -2 - \sqrt{3}$, $z_2 = -2 + \sqrt{3}$.

Thus, $$f(z) = \frac{z}{\left(z^2+4z+1\right)^2} = \frac{z}{\left(z-z_1\right)^2\left(z-z_2\right)^2}$$

But only z_2 lies inside the unit circle C. Therefore,

$$\begin{aligned} Res(f(z);\, z_2) &= \lim_{z\to z_2}\frac{d}{dz}\left[\left(z-z_2\right)^2 f(z)\right]_{z=z_2} \\ &= \lim_{z\to z_2}\frac{d}{dz}\left(\frac{z}{\left(z-z_1\right)^2}\right)_{z=z_2} \\ &= \lim_{z\to z_2}\frac{-z-z_1}{\left(z-z_1\right)^3} = \frac{1}{6\sqrt{3}} \end{aligned}$$

Hence,

$$\begin{aligned} \frac{4}{i}\int_C \frac{z}{z^2+4z+1}\,dz &= \frac{4}{i}\times 2\pi i\times\frac{1}{6\sqrt{3}} \\ &= \frac{4\pi}{3\sqrt{3}}. \end{aligned}$$

Type IV

An integration of the form $\int_{-\infty}^{\infty} R(x)\cos x\,dx$ or $\int_{-\infty}^{\infty} R(x)\sin x\,dx$

where $R(x) = \dfrac{P(x)}{Q(x)}$ where P and Q are polynomial and $Q(x) \neq 0$,

then the integral converges if deg $Q >$ deg P. In type I integrals, the functions was continuous in $(-\infty, \infty)$ and poles are inside the contour γ_R. But if the poles of f lie on the real axis we must modify the procedure. If $f(z)$ has pole at $x = c$ (real axis), then we indent the contour at c. The symbol γ_r denotes semi-circular contour centred at $z = c$ and radius r oriented in the positive direction.

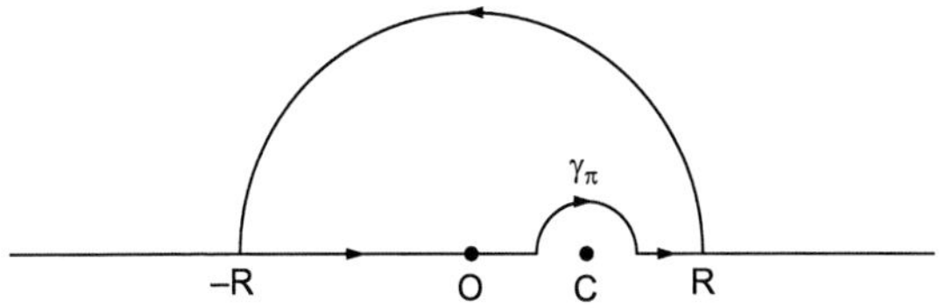

Fig. 11.3

We shall make use of the following inequality in the evaluation of contour integrals.

Jordan's inequality: Suppose $0 < \theta < \pi/2$. Then,

$$\frac{2}{\pi} < \frac{\sin\theta}{\theta} \leq 1.$$

Example 11.4

Evaluate $\int\limits_{-\infty}^{\infty} \frac{\sin x}{x} dx$.

Solution

We write $\int\limits_{-\infty}^{\infty} \frac{\sin x}{x} dx = \text{Im} \int\limits_{-\infty}^{\infty} \frac{e^{ix}}{x} dx$

The function $f(z) = \frac{e^{iz}}{z}$ has a simple pole at $z = 0$. If $0 < r < R$ and Γ_R be the closed curve (Fig. 11.4). By Cauchy's Theorem $\int\limits_{\gamma} f = 0$

(because $\frac{e^{iz}}{z}$ is analytic in Γ_R).

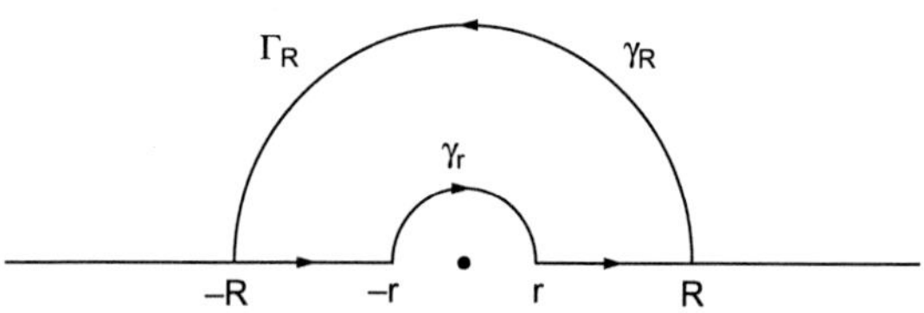

Fig. 11.4

Breaking the contour Γ_R into pieces

$$0 = \int\limits_{r}^{R} \frac{e^{ix}}{x} dx + \int\limits_{\gamma_R} \frac{e^{iz}}{z} dz + \int\limits_{-R}^{-r} \frac{e^{ix}}{x} dx + \int\limits_{\gamma_r} \frac{e^{iz}}{z} dz \qquad \text{...(1)}$$

Where γ_R and γ_r are semi-circles from $-R$ to R and $-r$ to r respectively. But

$$\int\limits_{r}^{R} \frac{\sin x}{x} = \frac{1}{2i} \int\limits_{r}^{R} \frac{e^{ix} - e^{-ix}}{x} dx$$

$$= \frac{1}{2i}\int_{r}^{R}\frac{e^{ix}}{x} + \frac{1}{2i}\int_{-R}^{-r}\frac{e^{ix}}{x}dx.$$

Also
$$\left|\int_{\gamma_R}\frac{e^{iz}}{z}dz\right| = \left|i\int_0^{\pi}\frac{e^{iRe^{i\theta}}}{Re^{i\theta}}iRe^{i\theta}\,d\theta\right|$$

$$< \int_0^{\pi}\left|e^{iRe^{i\theta}}\right|d\theta$$

$$= \int_0^{\pi}e^{-R\sin\theta}d\theta = \frac{1}{2}\int_0^{\pi/2}e^{-R\sin\theta}d\theta \quad ...(2)$$

$(iRe^{i\theta} = iR(\cos\theta + i\sin\theta) = -R\sin\theta + iR\cos\theta,\ \left|e^{iRe^{i\theta}}\right| = \left|e^{-R\sin\theta}\right|\left|e^{iR\cos\theta}\right| = e^{-R\sin\theta})$

By Jordan's inequality:

$$\frac{2\theta}{\pi} < \sin\theta < \theta$$

$$\Rightarrow \quad e^{\frac{-2R\theta}{\pi}} > e^{-R\sin\theta} \ge e^{-R\theta}$$

From (2)

$$\left|\int_{\gamma_R}\frac{e^{iz}}{z}dz\right| < \frac{1}{2}\int_0^{\pi/2}e^{\frac{-2R\theta}{\pi}}d\theta$$

$$= \frac{\pi}{2}\left.\frac{e^{\frac{-2R\theta}{\pi}}}{-2R}\right|_0^{\pi/2}$$

$$= \frac{\pi}{4R}\left[1-e^{-R}\right] \to 0 \text{ as } R\to\infty \quad ...(3)$$

Since $\frac{e^{iz}-1}{2}$ has a removable singularity at $z = 0$, there is a constant $M > 0$ such that $\left|\frac{e^{z}-1}{z}\right| \le M$ for $|z| < 1$. Hence,

$$\left|\int_{\gamma_r} \frac{e^{iz}-1}{z} dz\right| < \pi rM$$

$$\text{i.e.,} \quad \lim_{r \to 0} \int_{\gamma_r} \frac{e^{iz}-1}{z} dz = 0.$$

$$\text{But} \quad \int_{\gamma_r} \frac{1}{z} dz = -\pi i \text{ for each } r \text{ so that}$$

$$\int_{\gamma_r} \frac{e^{iz}-1}{z} = \int_{\gamma_r} \frac{e^{iz}}{z} dz - \int_{\gamma_r} \frac{1}{z} dz$$

$$\Rightarrow \quad 0 = \int_{\gamma_r} \frac{e^{iz}}{z} dz + \pi i$$

$$\text{i.e.,} \quad \int_{\gamma_r} \frac{e^{iz}}{z} dz = -\pi i \qquad \text{...(4)}$$

Thus, if we take $r \to 0$ and $R \to \infty$ and using (2), (3) and (4) in (1), we get

$$\int_0^\infty \frac{\sin x}{x} = \frac{\pi}{2}.$$

Type V: Integration along a branch cut.

We examine integrals of the form $\int_0^\infty f(x)\,dx$, where the integrand $f(x)$ is algebraic. These are special type of integrals in the sense that when $f(x)$ is converted to a complex function the resulting integrand $f(z)$ has, in addition to poles, a non-isolated singularity at $z = 0$.

In such cases we use branch cut method. In general, a branch cut for a branch f_1 of multivalued function is a portion of a curve that is excluded from a domain of F so that f_1 is continuous on the remaining points.

Example 11.5

Evaluate $\int_0^{\infty} \frac{1}{x^{1/2}(x+1)} dx$.

Solution

The real integral is improper for two reasons (*i*) It has infinite discontinuity at $x = 0$ and (*ii*) the infinite limit of integration. To evaluate the integral we shall use branch cut method. The point $z = 0$ is called a branch point of z^{-2}. Let $G = \{z: z \neq 0, 0 < \arg z < 2\pi\}$ define a branch of the logarithm on G by putting $\log(re^{i\theta}) = \log(r + i\theta), 0 < \theta < 2\pi$.

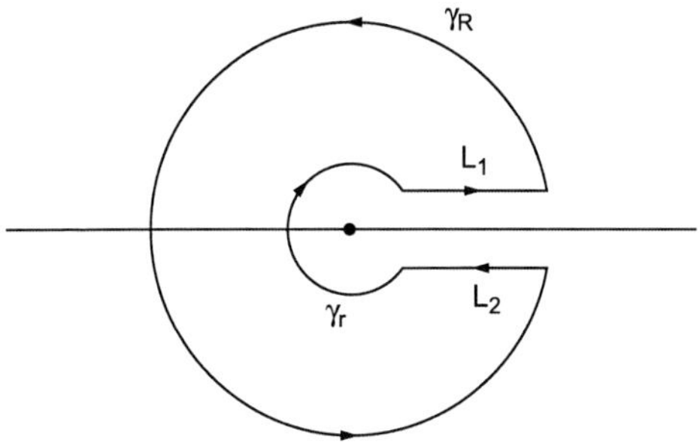

Fig. 11.5

For $z \in G$ put $f(z) = e^{-\frac{1}{2}\log z}$; f is a branch of $z^{-1/2}$.

Let γ be an appropriate curve in G. Let $0 < r < 1 < R$ and let $\delta > 0$. Let L_1 be the line segment $[r + \delta i, R + \delta i]$; γ_R is the part of the circle $|z| = R$ from $R + \delta i$ counter clockwise to $R - \delta i$; L_2 the line segment $[R - \delta i, r - \delta_i]$ and γ_r the part of the circle $|z| = r$ from $r - \delta i$ clockwise. Then $\gamma = L_1 + \gamma_R + L_2 + \gamma_r$. Since $z = -1$ is a simple pole of $\frac{1}{z^{1/2}(z+1)}$, therefore,

$Res(f(z).(1 + z)^{-1}; -1) = f(-1) = \frac{1}{e^{-2i\pi}}$. By Residue Theorem

$$\int_{\gamma} \frac{f(z)}{1+z} dz = 2\pi i \frac{1}{e^{-2i\pi}} \quad ...(1)$$

The lines L_1 and L_2 are parallel to the positive real axis; L_1 coincides with the upper side of the positive real axis for which $\theta = 0$ and L_2 coincide with lower side of the positive real axis for which $\theta = 2\pi$. On L_1; $z = xe^{0i}$ and on L_2; $z = xe^{(0+2\pi)i} = xe^{2\pi i}$, so that

$$\int_{L_2} \frac{f(z)}{1+z} dz = \int_R^r \frac{\left(xe^{2\pi i}\right)^{-1/2}}{xe^{2\pi i}+1}\left(e^{2\pi i}dx\right)$$

$$= -\int_R^r \frac{x^{-1/2}}{x+1} dx$$

$$= \int_r^R \frac{x^{-1/2}}{x+1} dx \qquad ...(2)$$

and

$$\int_{L_1} \frac{f(z)}{1+z} dz = \int_r^R \frac{\left(xe^{oi}\right)^{-1/2}\left(e^{oi}dx\right)}{xe^{oi}+1}$$

$$= \int_r^R \frac{x^{-1/2}}{x+1} dx \qquad ...(3)$$

Now

$$\left|\int_{\gamma_r} \frac{f(z)}{1+z} dz\right| < \int_{2\pi}^{0} \frac{\left|r^{-1/2}\, e^{\frac{-1}{2}i\theta}\right|}{\left|re^{i\theta}+1\right|}\left|rie^{i\theta}\right| d\theta$$

$$(\gamma_r = re^{i\theta}, -2\pi < \theta < 0)$$

$$< \frac{-r}{\sqrt{r}} \int_0^{2\pi} \frac{d\theta}{r-1}$$

$$= \frac{-2\sqrt{r}\pi}{r-1} \to 0 \text{ as } r \to 0 \qquad ...(4)$$

Similarly $\displaystyle\int_{\gamma_R} \frac{f(z)}{1+z} dz \to 0$ as $R \to \infty$ where $\gamma_R = Re^{i\theta}$, $0 < \theta < 2\pi$

...(5)

Thus, from (1), (2), (3), (4) and (5)

$$2\int_r^R \frac{1}{\sqrt{x}(x+1)}dx = 2\pi i\, e^{\frac{-i\pi}{2}}$$

$$= 2\pi i\left(\cos \pi/2 - i\sin \pi/2\right)$$

$$= 2\pi$$

Thus, taking limit as $r \to 0$ and $R \to \infty$

$$\int_0^\infty \frac{1}{\sqrt{x}(x+1)}dx = \pi$$

Type VI:

Integration involving functions with infinitely many poles: Integrals of the type.

$$\int_{-\infty}^{\infty} \phi(x)\begin{Bmatrix}\cos m\,x\\ \sin m\,x\end{Bmatrix}dx \text{ and } \int_{-\infty}^{\infty} \phi(x)\,e^{imx}\,dx$$

where $\phi(z)$ denotes a function which has an infinite number of poles.

Example 11.6

To evaluate $\int_{-\infty}^{\infty} \frac{e^{ax}}{\cos h\,x}dx\,(-1<a<1)$.

Solution

The function $f(z) = e^{az}$ sech z has simple poles at $z = \frac{1}{2}(2n+1)\pi i$, $n \in$ I. It is analytic inside and on the contour (Fig. 11.6) γ except for a simple pole inside γ.

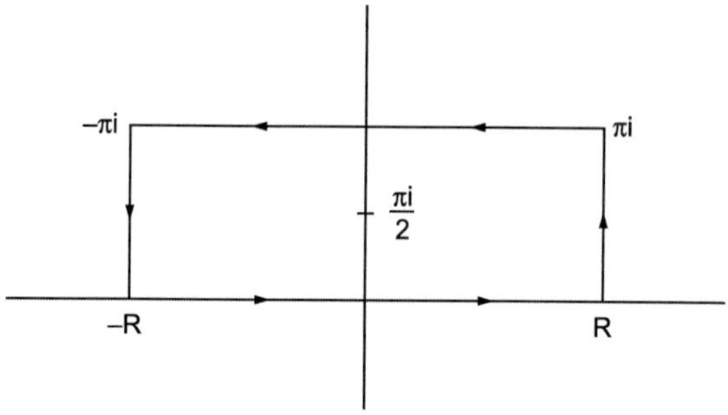

Fig 11.6

$$Res(f;\ \pi/2i) = \lim_{z\to\pi/2i} \frac{e^{az}}{\sin h\, z} = \frac{e^{\frac{a\pi}{2}i}}{i} = -\, ie^{a\pi/2i}$$

By Residue Theorem

$$\int_{\gamma} \frac{e^{ax}}{\cos h\, x}dx \;=\; 2\pi i \times -ie^{\frac{a\pi}{2}i} = 2\pi e^{\frac{a\pi}{2}i}$$

$$\int_{-R}^{R} \frac{e^{ax}}{\cos hx}dx + \int_{0}^{\pi} \frac{e^{a(R+iy)}}{\cos h(R+iy)}idy + \int_{R}^{-R} \frac{e^{a\pi i}\, e^{ax}}{\cos h(x+\pi i)}dx$$

$$+\int_{\pi}^{0} \frac{e^{a(-R+iy)}}{\cos h(-R+iy)}idy = 2\pi e^{\frac{\pi}{2}ai} \qquad \text{...(1)}$$

Now

$$\left|\int_{0}^{\pi} \frac{e^{a(R+iy)}}{\cos h(R+iy)}idy\right| \;<\; \int_{0}^{\pi} \frac{2e^{aR}dy}{\left|e^{(R+iy)} + e^{-(R+iy)}\right|}$$

$$<\; \int_{0}^{\pi} \frac{2e^{aR}dy}{\left|e^{R} - e^{-R}\right|}$$

$$=\; \frac{2\pi\, e^{aR}}{|\,e^{R} - e^{-R}\,|} \to 0 \text{ as } R \to \infty, \text{ since } a < 1$$

...(2)

Similarly

$$\left|\int_{\pi}^{0} \frac{e^{a(-R+iy)}}{\cos h(-R+iy)} dy\right| < \frac{2\pi\, e^{-aR}}{|e^{-R} - e^{R}|} \to 0 \text{ as } R \to \infty \ (a > -1) \quad ...(3)$$

Consider

$$\int_{-R}^{R} \frac{e^{ax}}{\cos h\, x} dx + \int_{R}^{-R} \frac{e^{a\pi i}\, e^{ax}}{-\cos h\, x} dx = \left(1 + e^{a\pi i}\right) \int_{-R}^{R} \frac{e^{ax} dx}{\cos h\, x} \quad ...(4)$$

From (1), (2), (3) and (4), we get

$$\left(1 + e^{a\pi i}\right) \int_{-R}^{R} \frac{e^{ax}}{\cos h\, x} dx = 2\pi e^{\pi/2\, ai}$$

Taking limit as $R \to \infty$

$$\int_{-\infty}^{\infty} \frac{e^{ax}}{\cos hx} dx = \frac{2\pi\, e^{\frac{\pi}{2} ai}}{1 + e^{a\pi i}}$$

$$= \frac{2\pi}{e^{\frac{-\pi}{2} ai} + e^{\frac{a\pi}{2} i}}$$

$$= \frac{\pi}{\cos\frac{\pi a}{2}} = \pi \sec\frac{\pi a}{2}.$$

EXERCISE

1. Evaluate the following integrals:

(*i*) $\displaystyle\int_0^{\infty} \frac{x^2\, dx}{x^4 + x^2 + 1}$ (*ii*) $\displaystyle\int_0^{\infty} \frac{dx}{\left(x^2 + a^2\right)\left(x^2 + b^2\right)}$

(*iii*) $\displaystyle\int_0^{2\pi} \frac{d\theta}{2 + \sin\theta}$ (*iv*) $\displaystyle\int_0^{\pi} \frac{d\theta}{(a + \cos\theta)^2}$, where $a > 1$

(v) $\int_0^\infty \frac{(\log x)^2}{1+x^2}dx$ (vi) $\int_{-\infty}^\infty \frac{e^{ax}}{1+e^x}dx$

(vii) $\int_0^\infty \frac{x\sin x\,dx}{\cos^4+4}$.

2. The integral $\int_{-\infty}^\infty e^{-x^2}\,dx = \sqrt{\pi}$ can be established using elementary calculus and polar coordinates. Use this result to show that

$$\int_0^\infty e^{-x^2}\cos\alpha\,x\,dx = \frac{\sqrt{\pi}}{2}e^{-\alpha^2/4}.$$

3. Show that $\int_{\Gamma_R} e^{iz^2}\,dz \to 0$ as $R\to\infty$ where Γ_R is the circular segment $z = Re^{i\theta}$, $0<\theta<\pi/4$.

4. Evaluate $\int_0^\infty \frac{\sin^2 x}{x^2}dx$.

ANSWERS

1. (i) $4\pi i$ (ii) $\frac{\pi}{2ab(a+b)}(a,\ b>0,\ a\neq b)$

(iii) $\frac{2\pi}{\sqrt{3}}$ (iv) $\frac{4\pi\left(a-\sqrt{a^2-1}\right)}{\sqrt{a^2-1}}$

(v) $\frac{\pi^3}{8}$ (vi) $\frac{\pi}{\sin\pi a}$

(vii) $\frac{\pi}{4e}\sin 1$.

4. $\frac{\pi}{2}$.

11.2. SUMMATION OF SERIES

This section is devoted to an application of residue in summation of series of the form

$$\sum_{n=1}^{\infty} \phi(n) \text{ and } \sum_{n=1}^{\infty} (-1)^n \phi(n)$$

where ϕ is suitable even function. In particular, we shall use Residue to sum the series $\sum_{n=1}^{\infty} \frac{1}{n^2}, \sum_{n=1}^{\infty} \frac{(-1)^n}{\alpha^2 - n^2}$ and $\sum_{n=1}^{\infty} \frac{1}{n^4}$ (and the corres-ponding function ϕ are $z \to \frac{1}{z^2}, z \to \frac{1}{\alpha^2 - z^2}, z \to \frac{1}{z^4}$). We shall sum these using one of the following.

***(i)* Using cot π *z*:** In some special cases, the residue at the simple poles of the trigonometric function cot π z are used to find the sum of an infinite series.

The zeros of sin z are real numbers $z = k\pi$, $k = 0, + 1, + 2, + 3, ...,$ therefore the function $\cot \pi z = \frac{\cos \pi z}{\sin \pi z}$ has simple poles at zeros of sin z, which are $\pi z = k\pi$ *i.e.*, $z = k$, $k = 0, + 1, + 2,......$ If a polynomial function $p(z)$ has (*i*) real coefficients (*ii*) degree $n > 2$ and (*iii*) no integer zeros, then the function

$$f(z) = \frac{\pi \cot \pi z}{p(z)}$$

has an infinite number of simple poles $z = 0, + 1, + 2,.......,$ from cot πz and a finite number of poles $z_{p_1}, z_{p_2},......., z_{p_r}$ from the zeroes of $p(z)$. Consider a rectangular contour γ with vertices $+(n + 1/2) + ni$ (Fig. 11.7). Where n is taken large enough so that γ enclosed the simple poles $z = 0, + 1, + 2, ..., + n$ and zeros of $p(z)$ $z_{p_1}, z_{p_2},......., z_{p_r}$. Applying Residue Theorem,

$$\int_{\gamma} \frac{\pi \cot \pi z}{p(z)} dz = 2\pi i \left\{ \sum_{k=n}^{n} Res\left(\frac{\pi \cot \pi z}{p(z)}, k \right) + \right. \qquad ...(1)$$

$$\left. \sum_{j=1}^{r} Res\left(\frac{\pi \cot \pi z}{p(z)}, z_{p_j} \right) \right\}$$

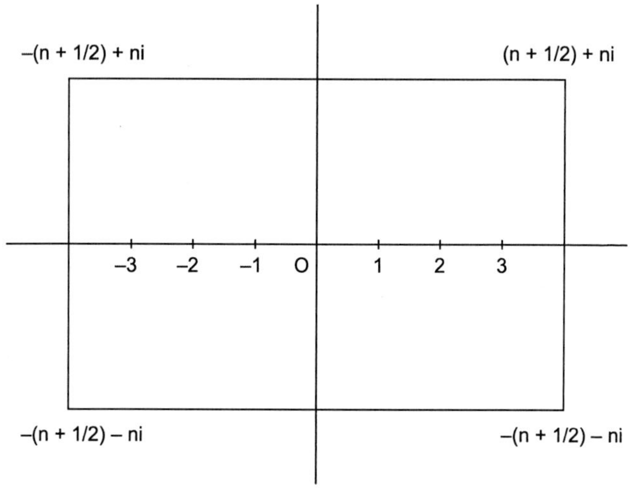

Fig. 11.7

We can also show $\int_{\gamma}^{0} \frac{\pi \cot \pi z}{p(z)} dz \to 0$ as $n \to \infty$, so from (1),

we get

$$\sum_{k=-n}^{n} Res\left(\frac{\pi \cot \pi z}{p(z)}, k \right) = -\sum_{j=1}^{r} Res\left(\frac{\pi \cot \pi z}{p(z)}, z_{p_j} \right) \qquad ...(2)$$

$$Res\left(\frac{\pi \cot \pi z}{p(z)}, k \right) = \lim_{z \to k} \frac{\pi \cos \pi \, z / p(z)}{(\sin \pi z)'}$$

$$= \frac{\pi \cos k\pi / p(k)}{\pi \cos k\pi}$$

$$= \frac{1}{p(k)}. \qquad ...(3)$$

From (2) and (3), we get

$$\sum_{k=-\infty}^{\infty} \frac{1}{p(k)} = -\sum_{j=1}^{r} Res\left(\frac{\pi \cot \pi z}{p(z)}, z_{p_j}\right).$$

Using cosec πz: cosec πz has poles at zeros of sin z *i.e.*, $\pi z = kz$ $k = 0, + 1, + 2, \ldots\ldots$ If $p(z)$ has finite number of zeros $z_{p_1}, z_{p_2}, \ldots\ldots, z_{p_r}$, where $p(z)$ is a polynomial of degree > 2 with real coefficient and having no integer zeros. Then, the function

$$f(z) = \frac{\pi \operatorname{cosec} \pi z}{p(z)}$$

has an infinite number of simple poles $z = 0, + 1, + 2, \ldots\ldots$ from cosec πz and finite number of poles $p_{z_1}, p_{z_2}, \ldots\ldots, p_{z_r}$. We can obtain similarly

$$\sum_{k=-\infty}^{\infty} \frac{(-1)^k}{p(k)} = -\sum_{j=1}^{r} Res\left(\frac{\pi \operatorname{cosec} \pi z}{p(z)}, z_{p_j}\right)$$

Example 11.7

Show that $\sum_{n=1}^{\infty} \frac{1}{n^2} = \frac{\pi^2}{6}$.

Solution

Let $p(z) = \frac{1}{z^2}$ and $f(z) = \frac{\pi \cot \pi z}{z^2}$. Then f has a simple pole at each integer n ($\neq 0$) and a pole of order three at 0.

$$Res(f(z);\, n) = \left[\frac{\pi \cos \pi z / z^2}{\pi \cos \pi z}\right]_{z=n} = \frac{1}{n^2}, n \in I, n \neq 0$$

We know $$\cot z = \frac{1}{z} - \frac{z}{3} + 0(z^3) \quad (0 < |z| < \pi)$$

Then $$\cot \pi z = \frac{1}{\pi z} - \frac{\pi z}{3} + 0(\pi z)^3$$

$$\Rightarrow \quad \frac{\pi}{z^2} \cot \pi z = \frac{1}{z^3} - \frac{\pi^2}{3z} + \ldots\ldots$$

Hence, $Res\left(\frac{\pi}{z^2}\cot\pi z\right) = \frac{-\pi^2}{3}$. There are no other poles. Consider a square contour γ with vertices $(+\,1+\mathrm{i})\left(n+\frac{1}{2}\right)(n \in I)$. By Cauchy's Residue Theorem,

$$\int_\gamma f(z)\,dz = 2\pi i\left(2\sum_{n=1}^{N}\frac{1}{n^2}-\frac{\pi^2}{3}\right) \qquad ...(1)$$

Now
$$\left|\int_\gamma f(z)\,dz\right| < \sup_{z\in\gamma}\left|\frac{\pi\cot\pi z}{z^2}\right| \times \text{length of the square}$$

$$< \sup_{z\in\gamma}|\cot\pi z|\frac{4(2n+1)\pi}{\left(n+\frac{1}{2}\right)^2} \to 0 \text{ as } n\to\infty$$

Thus from (1), we get

$$\sum_{n=1}^{\infty}\frac{1}{n^2} = \frac{\pi^2}{6}.$$

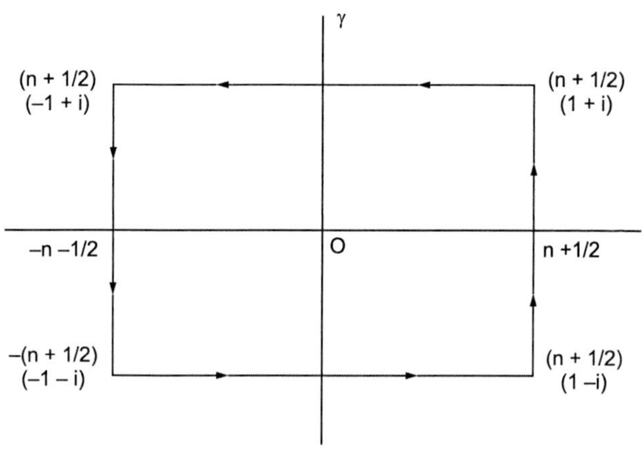

Fig. 11.8

Lemma 11.1

Let S_N be the square with vertices at $\left(n+\frac{1}{2}\right)(\pm 1 \pm i)$, ($n = 1, 2,.....$).

Then, there exists a constant C such that $|\cot \pi z| < C$ for all n and for all $z \in S_N$.

Proof

On the horizontal sides of the square $z = x + i\left(n+\frac{1}{2}\right)$

$$|\cot \pi z| = \left|\frac{e^{i\pi\left[x \pm i\left(n+\frac{1}{2}\right)\right]} + e^{i\pi\left[x \pm i\left(n+\frac{1}{2}\right)\right]}}{e^{i\pi\left[x \pm i\left(n+\frac{1}{2}\right)\right]} - e^{-i\pi\left[x \pm i\left(n+\frac{1}{2}\right)\right]}}\right|$$

$$< \left|\frac{e^{\pi\left(n+\frac{1}{2}\right)} + e^{-\pi\left(n+\frac{1}{2}\right)}}{e^{\pi\left(n+\frac{1}{2}\right)} - e^{-\pi\left(n+\frac{1}{2}\right)}}\right|$$

$$= \coth\left(n+\frac{1}{2}\right)$$

$$< \coth\frac{3\pi}{2} \quad \text{(because } \coth t \text{ is decreasing for } t > 0\text{)}$$

On the vertices sides $z = +\left(n+\frac{1}{2}\right) + iy$,

$$|\cot \pi z| = |\tan i\pi y| = |\tanh \pi y| < 1.$$

Example 11.8

Evaluate $\sum_{n=1}^{\infty} \frac{(-1)^n}{k^2 - n^2}$ where k is any complex number which is not an integer.

Solution

Let $p(z) = \dfrac{1}{k^2 - z^2}$ and $f(z) = \dfrac{\pi \operatorname{cosec} \pi z}{k^2 - z^2}$

f has simple pole at each integer n and simple poles at + k.

$$Res(f(z), n) = \lim_{z \to n} \frac{\pi / k^2 - z^2}{(\sin \pi z)'}$$

$$= \frac{\pi / k^2 - n^2}{(-1)^n} = \frac{(-1)^n \pi}{k^2 - n^2}$$

$$Res(f(z), k) = \lim_{z \to k} (z - k) f(z) = -\lim_{z \to k} \frac{\pi \operatorname{cosec} \pi z}{k + z}$$

$$= \frac{-\pi \operatorname{cosec} k\pi}{2k}$$

Similarly $Res\ (f(z), -k) = \dfrac{-\pi \operatorname{cosec} k\pi}{2k}$. There are no other poles.

Let $1/n$ be a square contour ($n > |k|$), $|z| > n + \dfrac{1}{2}$, so that for some constant C

$$\left| \frac{\pi \operatorname{cosec} \pi z}{k^2 - z^2} \right| < \frac{\pi c}{\left(n + \frac{1}{2}\right)^2 - |k|^2}, z \in \gamma_n$$

Thus, $\displaystyle\int_{\gamma_n} f(z) dz < \frac{\pi c}{(n + 1/2)^2 - |k|^2} . 4(2n + 1) \to 0$ as $n \to \infty$

By Residue Theorem

$$\int_{\gamma_n} f(z) dz = 2\pi i \left\{ \sum_{j=-n}^{n} Res\left(\frac{\pi \operatorname{cosec} \pi z}{k^2 - z^2}, j \right) + Res\left(\frac{\pi \operatorname{cosec} \pi z}{k^2 - z^2}, k \right) + \right.$$

$$\left. Res\left(\frac{\pi \operatorname{cosec} \pi z}{k^2 - z^2}, -k \right) \right\}$$

$$\Rightarrow \qquad 0 = 2\pi i\left\{\sum_{j=-n}^{n} \frac{(-1)^j}{k^2 - j^2} - \frac{\pi \operatorname{cosec} k\pi}{k}\right\}$$

Thus, $2\sum_{j=1}^{\infty} \frac{(-1)^j}{k^2 - j^2} + \frac{1}{k^2} = \frac{\pi \operatorname{cosec} k\pi}{k}$

$$\Rightarrow \qquad \sum_{j=1}^{\infty} \frac{(-1)^j}{k^2 - j^2} = \frac{1}{2k}\left\{\pi \operatorname{cosec} k\pi - \frac{1}{k}\right\}$$

$$= \frac{1}{2k^2}\{k\pi \operatorname{cosec} k\pi - 1\}.$$

Example 11.9

Find the sum of the series $\sum_{n=0}^{\infty} \frac{1}{n^2+1}$.

Solution

Let $p(z) = \frac{1}{z^2+1}$ and $f(z) = \frac{\pi \cot \pi z}{z^2+1}$.

$f(z)$ has simple poles at all integers n and also simple poles at + i.

$$Res(f;\ n) = \lim_{z \to n} \frac{\pi \cos \pi z / z^2+1}{\pi \cos \pi z} = \frac{1}{n^2+1};$$

$$Res(f;\ +i) = \lim_{z \to i} \frac{\pi \cot \pi z}{2z} = \frac{\pi \cot \pi i}{2i}$$

and $\quad Res(f;\ -i) = \lim_{z \to -i} \frac{\pi \cot \pi z}{2z} = \frac{\pi \cot \pi i}{2i}$

Now

$$\text{Res}(f;\ i) + \text{Res}\ (f;\ -i) = \frac{\pi \cot \pi i}{i}$$

$$= \frac{\pi}{i} \frac{\cos h(-\pi)}{(-i \sin h(-\pi))}$$

$$= \pi \coth\ (\pi)$$

Also $$\left|\int_{\gamma_n} f(z)\,dz\right| < \frac{c\pi}{\left(n+\frac{1}{2}\right)^2+1}\times 4(2n+1)\to 0 \text{ as } n\to\infty$$

where γ_n is a square contour $(n > 1)$, $|z| > n + \frac{1}{2}$. By Cauchy's Residue Theorem

$$2\sum_{n=1}^{\infty}\frac{1}{n^2+1}+1 = \pi\coth\pi$$

Thus, $$\sum_{n=1}^{\infty}\frac{1}{n^2+1} = \frac{1}{2}(\pi\coth\pi-1)$$

$$\Rightarrow \quad \sum_{n=0}^{\infty}\frac{1}{n^2+1}-1 = \frac{1}{2}(\pi\coth\pi-1).$$

EXERCISE

1. Find the sum of the series $\sum_{n=1}^{\infty}\frac{1}{n^4}$.

2. Evaluate the following sums:

(*i*) $\sum_{n=1}^{\infty}\frac{(-1)^n}{4n^2-1}$ (*ii*) $\sum_{n=1}^{\infty}\frac{(-1)^n}{n^2+1}$

3. Prove that

$$\sum_{k=0}^{\infty}\frac{1}{k^2+a^2} = \frac{1}{2a^2}+\frac{\pi}{2a}\coth a\pi.$$

Use this to evaluate the sum when $a = 2$.

4. **(*a*)** Obtain the general result

$$\sum_{k=-\infty}^{\infty}\frac{1}{(k-a)^2} = \frac{\pi^2}{\sin^2\pi a}$$

where $a \neq 0, +1, +2,$........

(b) Use part (*a*) to obtain $\sum_{k=1}^{\infty} \frac{1}{(2k-1)^2}$.

ANSWERS

1. $\frac{\pi^2}{6}$

2. (*i*) $\frac{-1}{4}(\pi - 2)$ (*ii*) $\frac{1}{2}\left(\frac{\pi}{\sinh \pi} - 1\right)$

❑❑❑

12

Conformal Mappings

The first part of the chapter concerns with an important and interesting geometric property of analytic function, known as angle-preserving property between regions in the complex plane. Such mappings are of intrinsic geometric interest and play an important role in solving the problems arising in fluid mechanics, electrostatics and many other physical situations which can be mathematically formulated in terms of Laplace's equation of the from

$$\frac{\partial^2 \phi}{\partial x^2} + \frac{\partial^2 \phi}{\partial y^2} = 0 \qquad ...(1)$$

in a certain region D of the z-plane. The function $\phi(x, y)$ in addition to satisfying equation (1) also satisfies certain boundary conditions on the boundary C of the region D. In such cases, it is necessary to find a conformal mapping that maps a disk into the half-plane $v \geq 0$. Such a mapping would have to map the circular boundary of the disc to the boundary line of the half-plane. A class of elementary conformal mappings that map circles to lines (and vice versa) are the linear fractional transformations called Möbius transformations, are defined and studied in the later part of the chapter.

12.1 CONFORMAL MAPPINGS

Suppose γ is a curve passing through the point a, which has a tangent at a. Apply a function f on γ which generates a new curve, denoted by $f(\gamma)$ (Fig. 12.1).

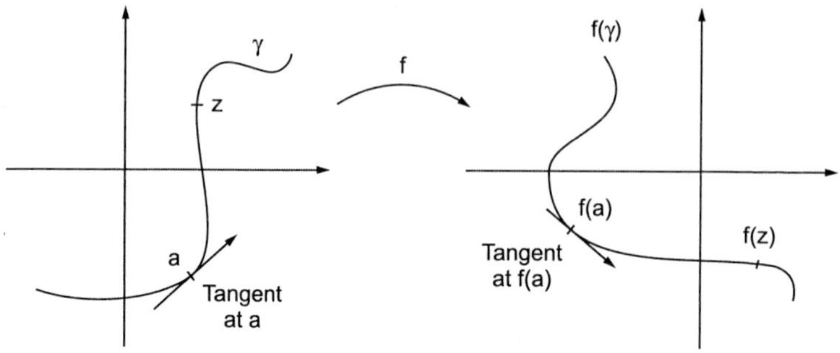

Fig. 12.1

The curve $f(\gamma)$ passes through $f(a)$; $f(\gamma) = \{f(z) : z \in \gamma\}$. Suppose γ has a tangent at a, then $f(\gamma)$ has tangent at $f(a)$, which may be thought of as the image of the tangent to γ at a. The tangent to $f(\gamma)$ at $f(a)$ is rotated, relative to the tangent to γ at a, through an angle Arg $f'(a)$.

A curve is visualised as a set of points in the plane, but also as the path traced out by a moving point. The tangent is then to be interpreted as the instantaneous velocity of the moving point. As the curve γ is traced out by one moving point, a corresponding moving point traces out the curve $f(\gamma)$. The number $|f'(a)|$ is the ratio of the instantaneous speed (or magnitude of instantaneous velocity) of the moving point on $f(\gamma)$ as it passes through $f(a)$ to the instantaneous speed of the moving point on γ as it passes through a.

So the function f has the effect of rotating and stretching tangents to curves or instantaneous velocity.

As a consequence of this result we have an important corollary: Suppose γ_1 and γ_2 are two smooth curves in a region D that intersect at a, the angle between their tangents at a serves as a measure of the angle at which the curves themselves intersect. Since $f(\gamma_1)$ and $f(\gamma_2)$ intersect at $f(a)$, and the two tangents are rotated by the same amount in going from a to $f(a)$, the angle between the image curves $f(\gamma_1)$ and $f(\gamma_2)$ at $f(a)$ is the same as the angle between the curves γ_1 and γ_2 at a. In this sense analytic functions preserve angles (at points where their derivatives are non-zero). The following example illustrates these concepts.

Example 12.1

Let $\gamma_1(t) = t + (2t - t^2)\, i$ and

$$\gamma_2(t) = t + \frac{1}{2}(t^2 + 1)\, i$$

be two curve from $[0, 2] \to \mathbf{C}$. Since $\gamma_1(1) = 1 + i = \gamma_2(1)$, therefore, the two curves intersect at $z = 1$. The tangent vectors at $z = 1$ are

$$\left[\gamma_1^1(t)\right]_{t=1} = [1 + (2 - 2t)i]_{t=1} = 1$$

and $\left[\gamma_2^1(t)\right]_{t=1} = 1 + i$, respectively. The angle between the two tangent is the angle between the two curves γ_1 and γ_2 *i.e.,* $\theta = \pi/4$.

Let $w = \bar{z}$ be a complex mapping. Then, the images of γ_1 and γ_2 under the map are

$$w_1(\text{t}) = t - (2t - t^2)i$$

and $$w_2(t) = t - \frac{1}{2}(t^2 + 1)i,$$

respectively. Also $w_1(1) = 1 - i = w_2(1)$. The two curves $w_1(t)$ and $w_2(t)$ intersect at $w_0 = 1 - i = f(z_0)$. The tangents at w_0.

$$w_1'(1) = [1 - (2 - 2t)i]_{t=1} = 1$$

$$w_2'(1) = [1 - ti]_{t=1} = 1 - i$$

to γ_1^1 and γ_2^1, respectively. The angle between γ_1' and γ_2' is also $\pi/4 = \phi$. Therefore, the angle θ and ϕ are equal in magnitude (Fig. 12.2).

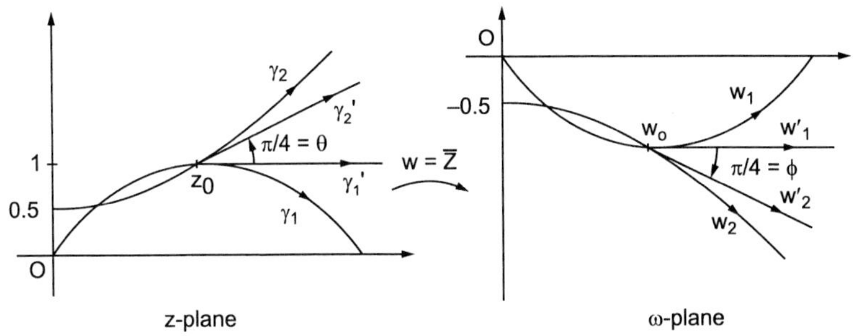

Fig. 12.2

The rotation of θ is in the counterclockwise direction whereas the rotation of ϕ is in the clockwise direction. Thus, ϕ and θ are equal in magnitude but not equal in direction. We are now in a position to define conformal mapping precisely in the following way:

Definition 12.1: Conformal Mapping

Let $w = f(z)$ be a complex mapping defined in a domain D and let z_0 be a point in D. Then f is said to be conformal at z_0 if for every pair of smooth oriented curves γ_1 and γ_2 in D intersecting at z_0 the angle between γ_1 and γ_2 at z_0 is equal to the angle between the image curves β_1 and β_2 at $f(z_0)$ in both magnitude and direction, we say f is conformal in D if f is conformal at all points $z \in D$.

Example 12.2

(*i*) The linear function $f(z) = az + b$, $a \neq 0$ is conformal at every point of the complex plane.

(*ii*) The map $f(z) = z^2$ is not conformal at $z = 0$ because the positive real axis and the positive imaginary axis are mapped onto the positive real axis and negative real axis, respectively.

(*iii*) The map $f(z) = \bar{z}$ is not conformal as shown in Example 12.1.

The Definition 12.1 is seldom used to prove that a complex mapping is conformal, rather we use the fact that an analytic function f is *a* conformal mapping at z whenever $f'(z) \neq 0$. But before proving this result we have the following definition.

Definition 12.2

(*i*) A function $w = f(z)$ is locally one-one at z_0 if for some $\delta > 0$ and for any two distinct complex number z_1 and z_2 in $D(z_0, \delta)$,

$$f(z_1) \neq f(z_2)$$

(*ii*) f is said to be locally one-one in the region D if f is locally one-one for all $z \in D$.

(*iii*) f is one-one function in D, if for every $z, z_2 \in D, f(z_1) \neq f(z_2)$.

Example 12.3

(*i*) The function $f(z) = z^2$ is not locally one-one at $z = 0$.

(*ii*) The function $f(z) = z$ is one-one in the complex plane **C**.

(*iii*) The map $f(z) = z^2$ is locally one-one at all points $0 \neq z \in \mathbf{C}$.

Theorem 12.1

Suppose f is analytic function in a domain D containing z_0 and if $f'(z_0) \neq 0$, then f is conformal mapping and locally one-one at z_0.

Proof

Suppose f is analytic in a domain D containing z_0 and $f'(z_0) \neq 0$. Let γ_1 and γ_2 be two smooth curves such that $\gamma_1(t_0) = \gamma_2(t_0) = z_0$. Assume that the map $w = f(z)$ maps γ_1 and γ_2 onto the curve $f(\gamma_1)$ and $f(\gamma_2)$.

To show: If θ is the angle between γ_1 and γ_2 at z_0 and ϕ is the angle between $f(\gamma_1)$ and $f(\gamma_2)$ at $f(z_0)$ then $\theta = \phi$ both in magnitude and direction. The angle θ is the unique value arg $(\gamma_1'(t)) - \arg(\gamma_2'(t))$ in the interval $[0, \pi]$.

Also $f(z_0) = f(\gamma_1(t_0)) - f(\gamma_2(t_0))$. The tangent vectors w_1' and w_2' are given by

$$w_1' = w_1'(t_0) = f'(\gamma_1(t_0))\,\gamma_1'(t_0) = f'(z_0)\,\gamma_1'(t_0)$$

$$w_2' = w_2'(t_0) = f'(\gamma_2(t_0))\,\gamma_2'(t_0) = f'(z_0)\,\gamma_2'(t_0)$$

Thus,

$$\begin{aligned}\arg w_2' - \arg w_2' &= \arg(f'(z_0)\,\gamma_1'(t_0)) - \arg(f'(z_0)\,\gamma_2'(t_0)) \\ &= \arg f'(z_0) + \arg \gamma_1'(t_0) - \arg f'(z_0) - \arg \gamma_2'(t_0) \\ &= \arg \gamma_1'(t_0) - \arg \gamma_2'(t_0).\end{aligned}$$

This expression has a unique value θ in $[0, \pi]$. Therefore, $\theta = \phi$ in both magnitude and direction. Consequently $w = f(z)$ is a conformal mapping at z_0.

To show: f is one-one in a neighbourhood of z_0.

Let $f(z_0) = a$ and choose $\delta' > 0$ sufficiently small so that $f(z) - a$ has no other zero in $D(z_0; \delta')$ (For if z_1 is the zero of $f(z) - \alpha$ in $D(z_0, \delta')$. Then $f(z_0) = f(z_1) = a$. Then f is constant in $D(z_0, \delta')$ and $f'(z_0) = 0$, a contradiction to the hypothesis). Let $\gamma = \gamma\,(z_0; \delta')$ and $\Gamma = f(\gamma)$.

By Argument Principle

$$1 = \frac{1}{2\pi i}\int_{\gamma} \frac{f'(z)}{f(z) - a}$$

$$= \frac{1}{2\pi i}\int_{\Gamma} \frac{dw}{w - a}$$

$$= \frac{1}{2\pi i}\int_{\Gamma}\frac{dw}{w-b}$$

(because the winding number is locally constant)

where b is in the disc $D(a; \in)$ for sufficiently small $\in > 0$.

Take $\delta \leq \delta'$ so that $D(z_0, \delta) \subseteq f^{-1}(D\ (a; \in))$. For any $z_1, z_2 \in D(z_0; \delta)$

$$1 = \frac{1}{2\pi i}\int_{\Gamma}\frac{dw}{w-f(z_1)} = \frac{1}{2\pi i}\int_{\Gamma}\frac{dw}{w-f(z_2)}$$

$$= \frac{1}{2\pi i}\int_{\gamma}\frac{f'(z)\,dz}{f(z)-f(z_1)} = \frac{1}{2\pi i}\int_{\gamma}\frac{f'(z)\,dz}{f(z)-f(z_2)}$$

i.e., $f(z_1)$ and $f(z_2)$ are inside C so that $f(z_1) \neq f(z_2)$ if $z_1 \neq z_2$.

Example 12.4

The function $f(z) = e^z$ has non-zero derivatives at all points of $\subset$. Thus, it is conformal and is locally one-one, but f is not globally one-one since $f(2 + 2\pi i) = f(z)$. We have shown in Chapter 4, that the net of horizontal and vertical lines are mapped to concentric circles under the map $f(z) = e^z$.

Example 12.5

Let $f(z) = z^2$. For $z \neq 0, f'(z) = 2z \neq 0$. Thus, f is conformal through $\mathbf{C} \sim \{0\}$. Set $f(z) = u(z) + iv(z)$.

If $z = x + iy$, then $u(z) = x^2 - y^2$, $v(z) = 2xy$.

If $Re\ z = \alpha\ (\alpha \neq 0)$, a line parallel to the imaginary axis, then the image of $Re\ z = \alpha$ under the map $f(z) = z^2$ is a parabola (in w-plane) $u = \alpha^2 - \dfrac{v^2}{4\alpha^2}$ (Fig. 12.3). The image of the imaginary axis is the non-positive real axis.

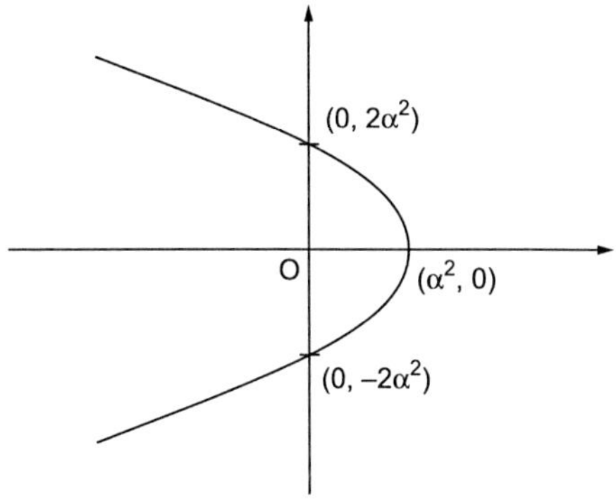

Fig. 12.3

Similarly, the image of the line $Im\ z = \beta(\beta \neq 0)$, parallel to the real axis, is the parabola (in the w-plane) $u = \dfrac{v^2}{4\beta^2} - \beta^2$ (Fig. 12.4). The image of the real axis itself is the non-negative real axis.

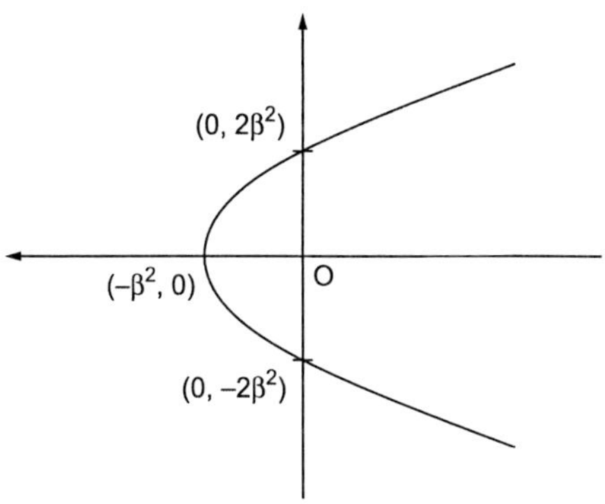

Fig. 12.4

The following diagram shows the images of several coordinate lines superimposed.

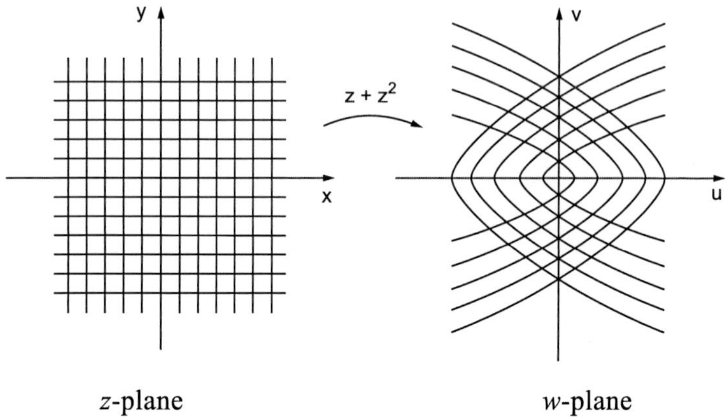

Fig. 12.5

Each parabola opens towards the right is the image of a line parallel to the real axis and so it intersects each parabola open to the left (which is the image of a line parallel to the imaginary axis) at right angles.

To study the mapping properties of functions at a point where its derivative vanishes, we define the following:

Definition 12.3

Let k be a positive integer. If f is a map from D_1 and D_2 such that for every $a \in D_2$, the equation $f(z) - a$ has k roots (counting multiplicity) in D_1 then f is said to be k– to – 1 mapping.

If $f'(z_0) = 0$, the analytic function f is not conformal at z_0, then the point z_0 is called critical point of f. The critical points are zeros of the analytic function f' therefore they are isolated. More specifically, we can show that the following magnification of angles occurs at critical points.

Theorem 12.2

Let f be analytic and non constant in a domain D of the complex plane. Suppose that $f'(z_0) = f''(z_0) = \ldots f^{(n-1)}(z_0) = 0, f^{(n)}(z_0) \neq 0, z_0 \in D$. Then, the mapping $z \to f(z)$ magnifies n times the angle between two intersecting differentiable arcs that meet at z_0.

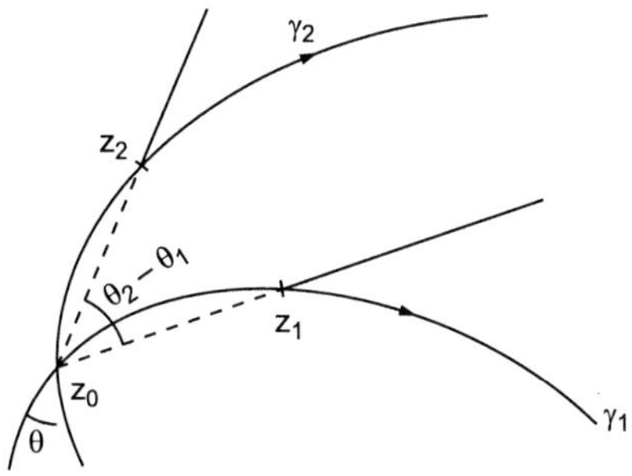

Fig. 12.6

Proof

Let $\gamma_1(t)$ and $\gamma_2(t)$ be the two curves intersecting at z_0. If z_1 and z_2 are points on these curves that have a distance r from z_0. Then,

$$z_1 - z_0 = re^{i\theta_1}, z_2 - z_0 = re^{i\theta_2}$$

Then, $$\frac{z_2 - z_0}{z_1 - z_0} = re^{i(\theta_2 - \theta_1)}$$

The angle $\theta_2 - \theta_1$ is the angle formed by the linear segments connecting the points $z_1 - z_0$ and $z_2 - z_0$. As $r \to 0$, this angle tends to the angle formed by the two intersecting arcs in the complex z-plane. If θ and ϕ denote the angles formed by the intersecting curves in the z-plane and w-plane, respectively.

Then,

$$\theta = \lim_{r \to 0} \arg\left(\frac{z_2 - z_0}{z_1 - z_0}\right),$$

$$\phi = \lim_{r \to 0} \arg\left(\frac{f(z_2) - f(z_0)}{f(z_1) - f(z_0)}\right) \qquad \text{...(1)}$$

Thus,

$$\phi = \lim_{r \to 0} \arg\left\{\left(\frac{\dfrac{f(z_2) - f(z_0)}{(z_2 - z_0)^n}}{\dfrac{f(z_1) - f(z_0)}{(z_1 - z_0)^n}}\right)\left(\frac{z_2 - z_0}{z_1 - z_0}\right)^n\right\} \qquad \text{...(2)}$$

Since f is analytic at z_0, therefore by Taylor's series

$$f(z) = f(z_0) + f'(z_0)(z - z_0) \;....\; + \frac{f^{n-1}(z_0)(z-z_0)^{n-1}}{(n-1)!} + \frac{f^{n}(z_0)(z-z_0)^{n}}{(n)!} + \frac{f^{n+1}(z_0)(z-z_0)^{n+1}}{(n+1)!} + ...$$

$$= f(z_0) + \frac{f^{n}(z_0)(z-z_0)^{n}}{n!} + ... \frac{f^{n+1}(z_0)(z-z_0)^{n+1}}{(n+1)!} + ...$$

So,

$$\frac{f(z_1)-f(z_0)}{(z_1-z_0)^n} = \frac{f^n(z_0)}{n!} + \frac{f^{n+1}(z_0)(z-z_0)}{(n+1)!} + ...$$

$$\Rightarrow \quad \lim_{r\to 0} \frac{f(z_1)-f(z_0)}{(z_1-z_0)^n} = \frac{f^n(z_0)}{n!}$$

Similarly $\lim_{r\to 0} \dfrac{f(z_2)-f(z_0)}{(z_2-z_0)^n} = \dfrac{f^n(z_0)}{n!}$

From (2), we get

$$\phi = \lim_{r\to 0} \arg\left(\frac{z_2-z_0}{z_1-z_0}\right)^n = n \lim_{r\to 0} \arg\left(\frac{z_2-z_0}{z_1-z_0}\right)$$

$$= n\theta.$$

Example 12.6

Consider a triangular region bounded by $x = 0$, $y = 0$ and $x + y = 1$. It's image under the transformation $w = z^2$ is given by the region shown in the Fig. 12.7.

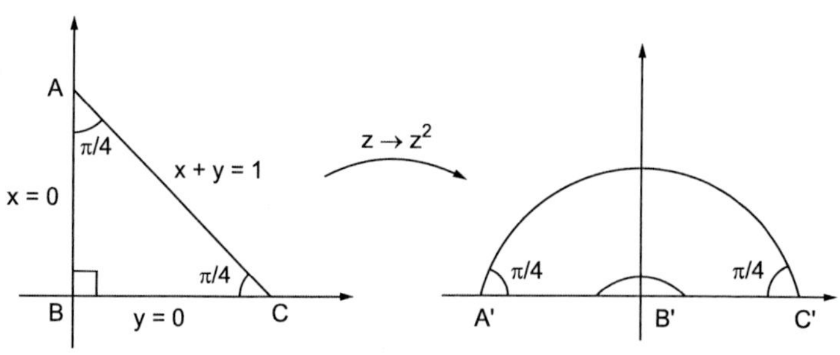

Fig. 12.7

Let $f(z) = u(z) + iv(z) = z^2$. If $z = x + iy$ then $u = x^2 - y^2$, $v = 2xy$. The line $x = 0$ is mapped to $v = 0$, $u \le 0$; the line $y = 0$ is mapped to $v = 0$, $u \ge 0$ and $x + y = 1$ is mapped to $v = \frac{1}{2}(1 - u^2)$. The function $f(z) = z^2$ is not conformal at $z = 0$. $f''(0) \ne 0$ and $f'(0) = f(0) = 0$. By using the Theorem 12.2, we conclude that the angle at B' is twice of the angle at B. (Note that $\angle B = \pi/2$ and $\angle B' = \pi$).

Critical points are also important in determining whether the function $f(z)$ has an inverse. Finding the inverse of $f(z)$ means solving the equation $w = f(z)$ for z in terms of w.

Theorem 12.3

Suppose f is a one-one analytic function in a region D. Then,

(*i*) f^{-1} exists and is analytic in $f(D)$.

(*ii*) f and f^{-1} are conformal in D and $f(D)$, respectively.

Proof

(*i*) Since f is $1 - 1$, therefore $f' \ne 0$ (otherwise if $f' = 0$, then f is constant and not $1 - 1$), Then by Theorem 3.4, f^{-1} is also analytic.

(*ii*) By Theorem 3.4,

$$(f^{-1})' = \frac{1}{f'}$$

So f^{-1} has a non-zero derivative. Thus f and f^{-1} are both conformal.

Using the above theorem, we define the following:

Definition 12.4

(*i*) A one-one analytic function is called conformal mapping.

(*ii*) Two regions D_1 and D_2 are said to be conformally equivalent if there exists a conformal mapping of D_1 onto D_2.

Remark

If f and g are two analytic function such that $R(f)$ C domain of g and if $f'(z_0) \ne 0$ for $z_0 \in$ domain of f and $g'(f(z_0)) \ne 0$ then $(gof)'(z_0) \ne 0$, using chain rule of derivatives. Thus, we conclude that the composition of two conformal maps is conformal.

Example 12.7

Verify that conformal equivalence satisfies the reflexive, symmetric and transitive properties of an equivalence relation.

Solution

Let D_1 and D_2 be two regions.

(*i*) **Reflexive:** Let $f: D_1 \to D_1$, then we can define $f(z) = z$ for all $z \in D_1$ such that $f'(z) = 1 \neq 0$.

(*ii*) **Symmetric:** Let D_1 be conformally equivalent to D_2. There exists $f: D_1 \to D_2$ such that f is $1-1, f'(z) \neq 0$ for all $z \in D_1$. By Theorem 12.3 f^{-1} exists and is analytic in $f(D_1)$. Thus, $f^{-1}: D_2 \to D_1$ is $1 - 1$ and is conformal. Hence, D_2 is uniformally equivalent to D_1.

(*iii*) If $f: D_1 \to D_2$ is a conformal map and $g: D_2 \to D_3$ is also conformal. Then, $gof: D_1 \to D_3$ is also conformal. Thus, D_1 is conformally equivalent to D_3.

Example 12.8

Find a conformal map from open upper half-plane $\pi := \{z : Im\, z > 0\}$ onto the open disc $D(0; 1)$.

Solution

By the definition $\pi := \{z : Imz > 0\}$

$$= \{z : |z - i| < |z + i|\}$$

Define $f(z) = \dfrac{z-i}{z+i}$. If $z \in \pi$ iff $|f(z)| < 1$ iff $f(z) \in D(0; 1)$.

Also $f'(z) = \dfrac{2i}{(z+i)^2} \neq 0$. Thus, f is conformal mapping.

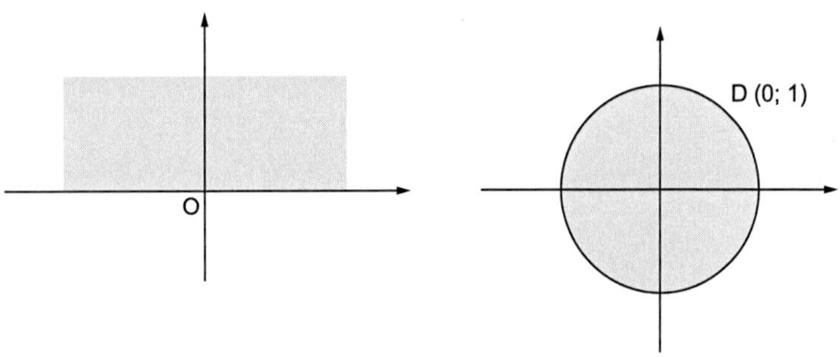

Fig. 12.8

EXERCISE

1. Determine where the complex mapping w = $f(z)$ is conformal

   (*i*) $f(z) = z^3 - 3z + 1$ (*ii*) $f(z) = 2z^2 + 3iz - 3$

   (*iii*) $f(z) = z - e^{-z} + 1 - i$ (*iv*) $f(z) = ze^{z^2-2}$.

2. Show that $f(z) = z^k$ is locally 1 – 1 for $z \neq 0$, k any non-zero integer.
3. Find the image under $w = e^z$ of the lines x = constant and y = constant.
4. Suppose $w = f(z)$ is a conformal mapping at every point in the complex plane. Where is the mapping $w = \overline{f(\bar{z})}$ conformal?
5. If $\omega = f(z)$ is a conformal mapping at every point in the complex plane. Where is the mapping $w = e^{f(z)}$ conformal?
6. Let D be the triangular region bounded by $x = 0$, $y = 0$ and $x + y = 1$. Find the image of D under the mapping $w = z^3$.

ANSWERS

1. (*i*) f is not comfomed at z = ± 1

   (*ii*) f is not conformed at $z = i$

   (*iii*) f is not conformed at z = (2n + 1) p i, n = 0, ± 1, ± 2, ...)

   (iv) f is not conformed at $z = \dfrac{\pm i}{\sqrt{2}}$.

2. Z^k is one-one in any of the form S = $\{z : a < \text{Arg } z < b;\ b - a < \dfrac{2\pi}{k}\}$.
3. $x = a$ is mapped into a circle centered at 0 and radius e^a. $x = b$ is mapped into the ray re^{ib}, $r > 0$.
4. $w = f(z^-)$ is conformal at every point of c.
5. $w = e^{f(z)}$ is conformal at every point in the complex plane.
6. $x = 0$ is mapped to $u = 0$, $v \leq 0$

   $y = 0$ is mapped to $u \geq 0$, $v = 0$.

   $x + y = 1$ is mapped to $v = u - 1$.

12.2 SPECIAL TRANSFORMATIONS

I. Elementary Transformations

(*i*) The linear map $w = f(z)$: $\mathbf{C} \to \mathbf{C}$ defined by $w = az + b$, is one-one analytic map.

(*ii*) **Magnification:** A map of the form $w = kz$, $k > 0$ is called a magnification. It sends each point onto another point along the same ray from the origin, multiplying its magnitude by a factor of k.

(*iii*) **Rotation:** The mapping $w = e^{i\theta} z$ is a counter clockwise rotation through an angle θ.

(*iv*) **Translation:** The map $w = z + b$ translates each point by the complex number b, therefore it is called translation.

(*v*) **Power:** The map $w = z^n$ $(n = 2, 3, ...)$ is conformal except at 0, where angles between paths are magnified by a factor of n. The function $w = z^n$ can be written as $z^n = e^{n \log z}$.

The point $z = re^{i\theta}$ is mapped onto $r^n e^{ni\theta}$ and hence $w = z^n$ maps the strip $S = \{z : \theta_1 < \text{Arg } z < \theta_2\}$ onto the strip $T = \{w : n\,\theta_1 < \text{Arg } w < n\theta_2\}$. If $n(\theta_2 - \theta_1) \le 2\pi$ *i.e.*, $\theta_2 - \theta_1 = \dfrac{2\pi}{n}$, the mapping is a conformal mapping S onto T.

(*vi*) **Exponential:** $w = e^z$. If $z = x + iy$. Then, $e^z = e^x e^{iy}$. This map is conformal in **C**. If $e^z = Re^{i\phi}$ where $R = e^z$ and $\phi = y$. Then, f maps a line $x = a$ to a circle $|w| = e^a$; a line $y = b$ to a half-line arg $w = c$.

f maps the vertical strip $\{z : a < Re\, z < b\}$ to the annulus $\{w : e^a < |w| < e^b\}$ (Fig. 12.9) and horizontal strip $\{z : c < Im\, z < d]$ to the sector $\{w : c < \arg z < d\}$ (Fig. 12.10). Moreover, if $b - a \le 2\pi$, the mapping is one-one. The strip $\{z : 0 < Im\, z < \pi\}$ is mapped conformally onto the upper half-plane (Fig. 12.11).

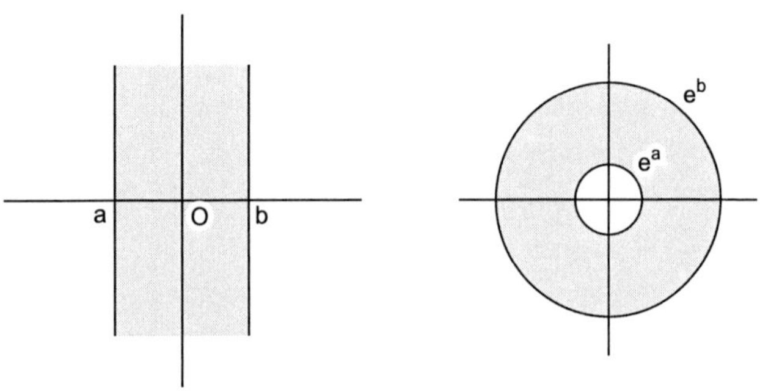

Fig. 12.9

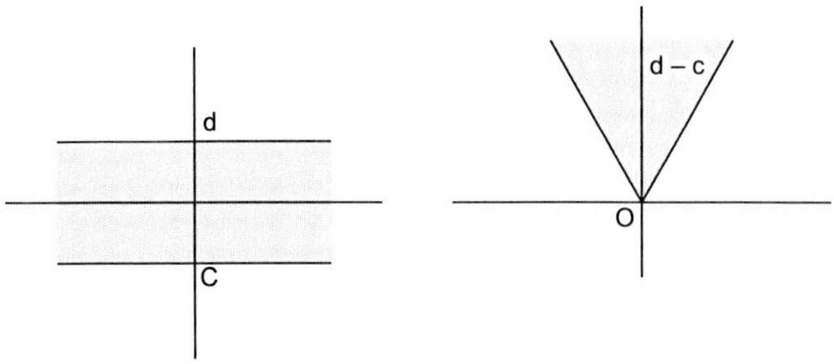

Fig. 12.10

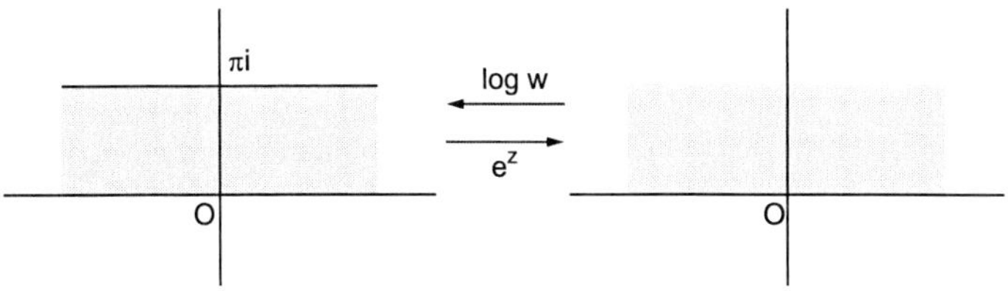

Fig. 12.11

Theorem 12.4

A linear transformation $w = az + b$ can be expressed as a composition of translation, rotation and magnification.

Proof

Let $w_1z = kz$, $k = |a|$, $w_2z = e^{i\theta}z$, $\theta = \arg a$, $w_3(z) = z + b$.

Consider
$$\begin{aligned} w_3 0 w_2 0 w_1(z) &= w_3 0 w_2(kz) \\ &= w_3(e^{i\theta}\, kz) \\ &= ke^{i\theta}z + b \\ &= az + b = w(z) \end{aligned}$$

where $a = ke^{i\theta} = |a|\, e^{i \arg a}$.

II. Möbius Transformation

A linear transformation $f: \mathbf{C} \to \mathbf{C}$ defined by

$$w = f(z) = \frac{az+b}{cz+d},\ ad - bc \neq 0 \qquad \ldots(1)$$

is a bilinear transformation. It is also called Möbius transformation. The condition $ad - bc \neq 0$ insures that f is neither identically constant nor meaningless.

Properties of Möbius Transformation

(i) f is locally $1-1$ and conformal.

For if $$f'(z) = \frac{ad-bc}{(cz+d)^2} \neq 0.$$

Thus, f is conformal on $\mathbf{C} \sim \left\{\frac{-d}{c}\right\}$.

(ii) f is globally $1-1$.

Let $$f(z_1) = f(z_2)$$

$$\Rightarrow \qquad \frac{az_1+b}{cz_1+d} = \frac{az_2+b}{cz_2+a}$$

$$\Rightarrow \qquad (ad-bc)(z_1-z_2) = 0$$

and hence, $z_1 = z_2$.

(iii) The Möbius Transformation can be viewed as a map from c_∞ to c_∞.

$$f\left(\frac{-d}{c}\right) = \infty \text{ and } f(\infty) = \frac{a}{c}.$$

Thus f is a $1-1$ mapping of Reimann sphere onto itself.

(iv) Inverse of bilinear transformation is also bilinear.

Since $$w = \frac{az+b}{cz+d}, \text{ then } z = \frac{dw-b}{-cw+a} \text{ and}$$

$$da-(-b)(-c) = da-bc = ad-bc \neq 0.$$

(v) The set of bilinear transformations forms a group under composition.

Let A denote the set of all bilinear transformations.

(a) **Closure property:** Let $f_1(z) = \dfrac{az+b}{cz+a}$, $ad-bc \neq 0$

and $$f_2(z) = \frac{Az+B}{Cz+D}, \ AD-BC \neq 0.$$

Then, $$(f_2 0 f_1)(z) = f_2\left(\frac{az+b}{cz+d}\right) = \frac{A\left(\frac{az+b}{cz+d}\right)+B}{C\left(\frac{az+b}{cz+d}\right)+D}.$$

$$= \frac{A(az+b)+B(cz+d)}{C(az+b)+D(cz+d)}$$

$$= \frac{(Aa+Bc)z+(Ab+Bd)}{(Ca+Dc)z+(Cb+Dd)}$$

Now $(Aa + Bc)(Cb + Dd) - (Ab + Bd)(Ca + Dc)$

$$= (AD - BC)(ad - bc) \neq 0$$

Thus, $f_2 \, 0 \, f_1$ is a bilinear transformation.

(*b*) **Associativity:** It can be easily shown that if $f_1, f_2, f_3 \in A$, then

$$f_3 \, 0 \, (f_2 \, 0 \, f_1) = (f_3 \, 0 \, f_2) \, 0 \, f_1.$$

(*c*) **Existence of identity:** If $f_1 \in A$ then there exists $I : \mathbf{C} \to \mathbf{C}$ such that

$$Iz = z = \frac{1.z+0}{0.z+1} \text{ then } I \in A \text{ and}$$

$$f_1 \, 0 \, I(z) = f_1(z) = I \, 0 \, f_1(z).$$

(*d*) **Existence of inverse:** Let $f_1 \in A$ such that $f_1(z) = \dfrac{az+b}{cz+d}$, $ad - bc \neq 0$. Define $sz = \dfrac{(-d)z+b}{cz+(-a)}$ such that $(-d)(-a) - bc = ad - bc \neq 0$

and $(s \, 0 \, f)(z) = s(f(z))$

$$= s\left(\frac{az+b}{cz+d}\right) = \frac{-d\left(\dfrac{az+b}{cz+d}\right)+b}{c\left(\dfrac{az+b}{cz+d}\right)-a}$$

$$= \frac{-adz - bd + bcz + bd}{caz + bc - acz - ad}$$

$$= \frac{(bc-ad)z}{bc-ad} = z = Iz \quad \forall \, z \in \mathbf{C}$$

Also $(f \, 0 \, s)(z) = Iz$.

(*vi*) If $c = 0$, then (1) can be written as $f(z) = \dfrac{az}{d} + \dfrac{b}{d}$ and this is a linear transformation, so a linear mapping is a special case of a bilinear transformation. If $c \neq 0$ then (1) can be written as

$$f(z) = \frac{az+b}{cz+d}$$

$$= \frac{bc-ad}{c} \cdot \frac{1}{cz+d} + \frac{a}{c}$$

Set
$$A = \frac{bc-ad}{c}$$

$$B = \frac{a}{c}$$

Then, $f(z) = f_1\ 0\ goh$ where $f_1(z) = Az + B$ and $h(z) = cz + d$ are linear transformation and $g(z) = \frac{1}{z}$ is the reciprocal function.

(*vii*) If $c \neq 0$, then

$$f(z) = \frac{az+b}{cz+d}$$

$$= \frac{\frac{az}{c} + b/c}{z + d/c}$$

$$= \frac{\phi(z)}{z + d/c}$$

where $\phi(z) = \frac{a}{c}z + \frac{b}{c}$. Since $ad - bc \neq 0$, therefore $\phi\left(\frac{-d}{c}\right) \neq 0$.

Thus, $z = \frac{-d}{c}$ is a simple pole of $f(z)$.

From Property (*iii*), we obtain that the definition of f can be extended to c_∞. In particular, if $c \neq 0$, then we regard T as a one-to-one mapping of the extended complex plane defined by

$$f(z) = \begin{cases} \dfrac{az+b}{cz+d}, & z \neq \dfrac{-d}{c},\ z \neq \infty \\ \infty, & z = \dfrac{-d}{c} \\ \dfrac{a}{c}, & z = \infty. \end{cases} \qquad \text{...(2)}$$

Remark

(*i*) We can define the bilinear transformation if $a = d = 0$, $b = c = 0$.

(*ii*) If $a = d = 0$, $b = c \neq 0$, then from (2) $f(z) = \frac{1}{z}$ is the reciprocal function.

Example 12.9

Find the images of the points 0, $1 + i$, i and ∞ under the linear fraction

$$f(z) = \frac{2z+1}{z-i}.$$

Solution

For $z = 0$

$$f(0) = \frac{-1}{i} = i;$$

$z = 1 + i$

$$f(1+i) = \frac{2(1+i)+1}{1+i-i} = 3+2i;$$

$z = i$

$$f(i) = \infty$$

$z = \infty$

$$\lim_{z\to\infty} f(z) = \lim_{z\to\infty} \frac{2+\frac{1}{z}}{1-\frac{i}{z}}$$

$$= 2.$$

Example 12.10

Find the bilinear transformation which send

(*a*) $1, i, -1$ onto $-1, i, 1$, respectively.

(*b*) $-i, 0, i$ onto $0, i, 2i$, respectively.

Solution

(*a*) Let $$f(z) = \frac{az+b}{cz+d}$$

Given: $f(1) = -1, f(i) = i, f(-1) = 1.$

Now $$f(1) = -1 \Rightarrow a + b = -c - d; \quad ...(1)$$

$$f(i) = i \Rightarrow ai + b = -c + di \quad ...(2)$$

$$f(-1) = 1 \Rightarrow -a + b = -c + d \quad ...(3)$$

(1) – (3) $\Rightarrow a = -d$. From (1) $b = -c$. From (2), we get

$$2di = b + c = 0 \Rightarrow d = 0$$

Thus, $a = d = 0$ and $b = -c$. Hence,

$$f(z) = \frac{-1}{z}.$$

(*b*) It is given that $f(-i) = 0, f(0) = i, f(i) = 2i.$

$$f(-1) = 0 \quad \Rightarrow \quad b = ai \quad ...(1)$$

$$f(0) = i \quad \Rightarrow \quad b = id \quad ...(2)$$

$$f(i) = 2i \quad \Rightarrow ai + b = -2c + 2id \quad ...(3)$$

From (1) and (2), we get $a = d$. From (3), we get $c = 0$. Thus,

$$f(z) = \frac{az+ai}{a} = z + i.$$

Circle Preserving Property

A very important and useful property of bilinear transformation is that they map circles and lines onto other circles and lines, we begin with the following:

Lemma 12.5

If S is a circle or line and $f(z) = \frac{1}{z}$, then $f(S)$ is also a circle or line.

Proof

Let S be a circle with centre a and radius r then the equation of S can be written as

$$|z - a| = r$$

$$\Rightarrow \quad |z - a|^2 = r^2$$

$$\Rightarrow \quad (z-a)\,(\bar{z}-\bar{a}) = r^2$$
$$\Rightarrow \quad z\bar{z} - z\bar{a} - a\bar{z} + a\bar{a} = r^2$$
$$\Rightarrow \quad z\bar{z} - z\bar{a} - a\bar{z} = r^2 - |a|^2 \qquad ...(1)$$

Let $f(S) = \left\{ w = \dfrac{1}{z} : z \in S \right\}$, then (1) becomes

$$\frac{1}{w\bar{w}} - \frac{\bar{a}}{w} - \frac{a}{\bar{w}} = r^2 - |a|^2 \qquad ...(2)$$

Case (*i*): If $r = |a|^2$ then the circle passes through the origin, (2) is equivalent to

$$1 - a\text{w} - \overline{aw} = 0$$
$$\Rightarrow \quad 2Re(aw) = 1$$
$$\Rightarrow \quad Re(aw) = \frac{1}{2}.$$

If $a = x_0 + iy_0$ and $w = u + iv$, then

$$ux_0 - vy_0 = \frac{1}{2};$$

it means $f(S)$ is a line in the w-plane.

Case (*ii*): If $r \neq |a|^2$, then (2) becomes

$$w\bar{w} - \left(\frac{\bar{a}}{|a|^2 - r^2}\right)\bar{w} - \left(\frac{a}{|a|^2 - r^2}\right)w = \frac{-1}{|a|^2 - r^2}.$$

Set $b = \dfrac{\bar{a}}{|a|^2 - r^2}$, then

$$w\bar{w} - b\bar{w} - \bar{b}w + |b|^2 = \frac{-1}{|a|^2 - r^2} + |b|^2$$
$$= \frac{-1}{|a|^2 - r^2} + \frac{a\bar{a}}{(|a|^2 - r^2)^2}$$

i.e., $$|w - b|^2 = \left(\frac{r}{|a|^2 - r^2}\right)^2$$

So that $f(S)$ is a circle with centre b and radius $\dfrac{r}{|a|^2 - r^2}$.

If S is a straight line, if $z = x + iy \in S$, then

$$ax + by = c \qquad ...(3)$$

where a, b and c are real-valued. Let $\alpha = a - ib$, then (3) becomes

$$\left(\frac{\alpha+\bar{\alpha}}{2}\right)x + \left(\frac{\alpha-\bar{\alpha}}{2i}\right)y = c$$

$$\Rightarrow \quad \frac{\alpha}{2}(x-iy) + \frac{\bar{\alpha}}{2}(x+iy) = c$$

$$\Rightarrow \quad \frac{\alpha\bar{z} + \bar{\alpha}z}{2} = c$$

$$\Rightarrow \quad \alpha\bar{z} + \bar{\alpha}z = 2c$$

Thus, $f(S)$ is either a circle or a line.

Lemma 12.6

The set of points satisfying the equation

$$|z - a| = \lambda\,|z - b|$$

represents a line if $\lambda = 1$ and is a circle if $\lambda > 0$ and $\lambda \neq 1$.

Proof

Consider $\quad |z - a|^2 = |z - b|^2$ if $\lambda = 1$, then

$$\bar{z}(\alpha - \beta) + z(\bar{\alpha} - \bar{\beta}) = |b|^2 - |a|^2 \qquad ...(1)$$

Let $c = \alpha - \beta$ and (1) becomes

$$c\bar{z} + \bar{c}z = |b|^2 - |a|^2;$$

it represents a line.

If $\lambda \neq 1$, then $|z - a|^2 = \lambda^2 |z - b|^2$.

$$i.e., \quad (z-a)(\bar{z}-\bar{a}) = \lambda^2(z-b)(\bar{z}-\bar{b})$$

$$\text{or} \quad z\bar{z} - \bar{a}z - a\bar{z} + a\bar{a} = \lambda^2[z\bar{z} - \bar{b}z - b\bar{z} + b^2]$$

$$|z|^2 - \frac{z\overline{(a-\lambda^2 b)}}{1-\lambda^2} - \frac{\bar{z}(a-\lambda^2 b)}{1-\lambda^2} + \frac{|a|^2 - \lambda^2|b|^2}{1-\lambda^2} = 0$$

$$\text{or} \quad |z|^2 - \frac{z\overline{(a-\lambda^2 b)}}{1-\lambda^2} - \frac{\bar{z}(a-\lambda^2 b)}{1-\lambda^2} + \frac{|a|^2 - \lambda^2|b|^2}{1-\lambda^2} + \left|\frac{a-\lambda^2 b}{1-\lambda^2}\right|^2$$

$$= -\left(\frac{|a|^2 - \lambda^2 |b|^2}{1-\lambda^2}\right) + \frac{(a-\lambda^2 b)(\overline{a} - \lambda^2 \overline{b})}{(1-\lambda^2)^2}$$

or $$\left|z - \left(\frac{\alpha - \lambda^2 b}{1-\lambda^2}\right)\right|^2 = \left(\frac{\lambda |a-b|}{(1-\lambda^2)}\right)^2$$

This represents a circle with centre $\left(\frac{a-\lambda^2 b}{1-\lambda^2}\right)$ and radius $\frac{\lambda|a-b|}{(1-\lambda^2)}$.

Theorem 12.7

If γ is a circle in z-plane and f is a bilinear transformation in the extended complex plane defined by

$$f(z) = \frac{az+b}{cz+d}, \; ad - bc \neq 0,$$

then, the image of γ under f is either a circle or a line in the extended w–plane. The image is a line if and only if $c \neq 0$ and the pole $z = \frac{-d}{c}$ is on the circle γ.

Proof

If $c = 0$, f is a linear map. We know that a linear function maps circle onto circle. If $c \neq 0$. Then,

$$\begin{aligned} f(z) &= \frac{az+b}{cz+d} \\ &= \frac{1}{c}\left[\frac{acz + ad - ad + bc}{cz+d}\right] \\ &= \frac{1}{c}\left[a - \left(\frac{ad-bc}{cz-d}\right)\right] \end{aligned}$$

Then, f is the composition of $f_1(z) = cz + d, f_2(z) = \frac{1}{z}$,

$$f_3(z) = \frac{a}{c} - \left(\frac{ad-bc}{c}\right)z \text{ such that } f = f_3 \, 0 \, f_2 \, 0 \, f_1.$$

f_1 and f_3 are linear. Hence, they map circles and lines onto circles and lines. By Lemma 12.5 f_2 maps circles to circles and lines to lines.

If pole $z = \frac{-d}{c}$ is on the circle γ then the origin $w = 0$ lies on the circle γ', the image of γ under f, then the image of γ' under $f_2(z) = \frac{1}{z}$ is either a horizontal or vertical line L and f_1 is a linear function, the image of the line L under f_1 is also a line. Thus, if the pole $z = \frac{-d}{c}$ lies on γ, then the image of γ under f is a line.

Conversely, assume that $z = \frac{-d}{c}$ is not on γ, then the origin $w = 0$ is not on γ'. Let γ' be the circle $| w - w_0 | = \rho$. Set $\xi = f(w) = \frac{1}{w}$, $\xi_0 = f(w_0) = \frac{1}{w_0}$, then for any point w on γ'.

$$| \xi - \xi_0 | = \left| \frac{1}{w} - \frac{1}{w_0} \right| = \frac{| w - w_0 |}{| w || w_0 |} = \rho | \xi_0 || \zeta | \qquad ...(1)$$

Since $w = 0$ is not on γ', therefore $| w_0 | \neq \rho$ or equivalently $\rho| \xi_0 | \neq 1$. Thus, by Lemma 12.6, (1) represents a circle. Since f_1 is linear, therefore image of a circle under f_1 is a circle. Thus, the image of γ under f is a circle.

Example 12.11

Find the image of the unit circle $| z | = 1$ under the bilinear transformation

$$f(z) = \frac{z+2}{z-1}.$$

What is the image of the interior ($| z | < 1$) of this circle?

Solution

$z = 1$ is a pole of $f(z)$ and it lines on the circle $\gamma = \{z : |z| = 1\}$. Thus, image of the unit circle is a line (using Theorem 12.7). Since $f(-1) = \frac{-1}{2}$ and $f(i) = \frac{-1}{2} - \frac{3}{2}i$. Thus image is the line $w = \frac{-1}{2}$. Interior of the circle $| z | < 1$ is either the left half-plane $u < \frac{-1}{2}$ or right half-plane $u > \frac{-1}{2}$.

But $f(0) = -2$ which lies in the left half-plane, so the image is the left half-plane $u < \frac{-1}{2}$.

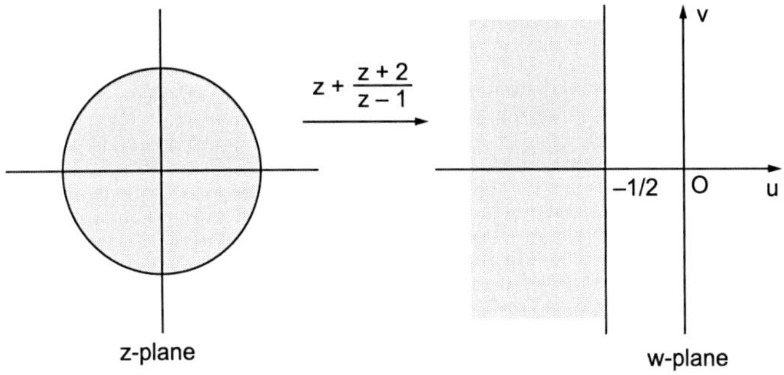

Fig. 12.12

Example 12.12

Find the image of the circle $|z| = 1$ under the mappings

(*i*) $w = \frac{1}{z}$ (*ii*) $w = \frac{1}{z-2}$.

Solution

(*i*) The unit circle $|z| = 1$ under the map $w = \frac{1}{z}$ is

$$z = \frac{1}{w}$$

$$1 = |z| = \frac{1}{|w|}$$

or $$|w| = 1$$

Thus, the image of $|z| = 1$ under $f(z) = \frac{1}{z}$ is a unit circle.

(*ii*) The map $w = \frac{1}{z-2}$ can be written as

$$z = \frac{1}{w} + 2$$

i.e., $$1 = |z| = \left|\frac{1}{w} + 2\right|$$

or $\qquad |2w+1| = |w|$. It represents a line $x = \dfrac{-1}{2}$

(by Lemma 12.6)

We give some examples in which we show how we can combine mappings from regions to disc or half-plane.

Example 12.12

Find a conformal mapping of the semi-circular region $G = \{z : Im\, z\,;\, |z| < 1\}$ onto $D(0\,;\,1)$

Solution

Step 1: We can express G as

$$\left\{z : \frac{\pi}{2} < \arg\left(\frac{z-1}{z+1}\right) < \pi\right\} \qquad \text{(See Chapter 1)}$$

Define $g(z) = \dfrac{z-1}{z+1} = \rho$ is mapped conformally to the Quadrant Q $= \left\{\rho : \dfrac{\pi}{2} < \arg \rho < \pi\right\}$.

Step 2: Let $\alpha = \rho^2$. Under the map $\rho \to \alpha$, Q is mapped to the open lower half-plane $\{\alpha : \pi < \arg \alpha < 2\pi)\}$

Step 3: The equation of the lower half-plane is $\{\alpha : |\alpha + i| < |\alpha - i|\}$ and so is mapped to $\{w : |w| < 1\}$ under $\alpha \to \dfrac{\alpha + i}{\alpha - i} = w$.

Thus, the map f is defined as

$$\begin{aligned} w = f(z) &= \frac{\alpha + i}{\alpha - i} \\ &= \frac{\rho^2 + i}{\rho^2 - i} \\ &= \frac{(z-1)^2 + i(z+1)^2}{(z-1)^2 - i(z+1)^2} \\ &= i\left(\frac{z^2 + 2iz + 1}{z^2 - 2iz + 1}\right) \end{aligned}$$

and f maps G onto $D(0;\,1)$ and is conformed.

Example 12.13

Find a conformal mapping between the regions $s = \{z = x + iy : -2 < x < 1\}$ and $T = D(0\ ;\ 1)$.

Solution

Step I: Define $f_1(z) = \frac{\pi}{3}(z+2)$, then $s_1 = \{z = x + iy : 0 < x < \pi\}$: Then, f_1 maps s to s_1.

Step II:

Define: $f_2(\zeta) = e^{i\zeta}$, then $|f_2| = e^{-Im\zeta}$ and $\arg f_2 = Re\zeta$.

Thus, f_2 is mapped by $z \to \zeta$ conformally onto

$$s_2 = \{\zeta : 0 < |\zeta| < \infty, 0 < \arg \zeta < \pi\}$$

Stage III: The upper half-plane is $\{\tau : |\tau - i| < |c + i|\}$ and so is mapped to $\{w : |w| < 1\}$ under the map

$$\tau \to \frac{\tau - i}{\tau + i} = w.$$

Thus, a suitable map f can be defined as

$$\begin{aligned} f(z) &= f_3\ 0\ f_2\ 0\ f_1(z) \\ &= f_3\ 0\ f_2\left(\frac{\pi}{3}(z+2)\right) \\ &= f_3\left(e^{i\frac{\pi}{3}(z+2)}\right) \\ &= \frac{e^{i\frac{\pi}{3}(z+2)} - i}{e^{i\frac{\pi}{3}(z+2)} + i}. \end{aligned}$$

Now we shall define a unique bilinear mapping sending three distinct point $z_1, z_2, z_3 \in c_\infty$ onto any three points $w_1, w_1, w_2 \in c_\infty$ respectively.

Definition: 12.5

A point $z = z_0$ is called fixed point of a function f if $f(z_0) = z_0$.

Example 12.14

Find the fixed points of the mapping

(*i*) $f(z) = \frac{z-1}{z+1}$ (*ii*) $f(z) = \frac{z}{z+1}$

Solution

If z_0 is a fixed point of f then

$$f(z_0) = z_0$$

$$\Rightarrow \quad \frac{z_0 - 1}{z_0 + 1} = z_0 \quad \Rightarrow z_0 - 1 = z_0^2 + z_0$$

$$\Rightarrow \quad z_0 = \pm\, i.$$

Thus, f has two fixed points i and $-i$.

(*ii*) $$f(z_0) = z_0 \Rightarrow \frac{z_0}{z_0 + 1} = z_0$$

$$\Rightarrow \quad z_0 = z_0^2 + z_0 \quad \Rightarrow z_0^2 = 0$$

Thus, 0 is the only fixed point of $f(z) = \dfrac{z}{z+1}$.

Theorem 12.8

A bilinear transformation

$$f(z) = \frac{az + b}{cz + d}, \; ad - bc \neq 0$$

has at most two fixed points.

Proof

If $c \neq 0$ then $f(z) = z$ gives $z^2 + (d - a)\, z + b = 0$.

Since *a* quadratic equation has two solution, thus f has at most two fixed points.

If $c = 0$, then $f(z) = \left(\dfrac{a}{d}\right)z + \dfrac{b}{d}$. If $\dfrac{b}{d} = 1$, then $f(z) = z$ has only one solution in the finite complex plane. Also $f(\infty) = \infty$, therefore f has two fixed points in the extended plane. But if $\dfrac{b}{d} \neq 1$ or in general $f(z) = z + \alpha$, then it has no fixed point.

Lemma 12.9

Let $(z_1, z_2, z_3) \in c_\infty$ be sets of distinct points then the unique mapping sending z_1, z_2, z_3 to ∞, 0, 1, respectively, is given by

$$Tz = \frac{(z - z_2)(z_3 - z_1)}{(z - z_1)(z_3 - z_2)}.$$

Proof

$$T(z_1) = \frac{(z_1 - z_2)(z_3 - z_1)}{(z_1 - z_1)(z_3 - z_2)} = \infty;$$

$$T(z_2) = \frac{(z_2 - z_2)(z_3 - z_1)}{(z_2 - z_1)(z_3 - z_2)} = 0;$$

$$z(z_3) = \frac{(z_3 - z_2)(z_3 - z_1)}{(z_3 - z_1)(z_3 - z_2)} = 1.$$

To Show: T is unique. Let S be any other bilinear transformation such that $Sz_1 = \infty$, $Sz_2 = 0$, $Sz_3 = 1$. Consider $T\,0\,S^{-1} = T_1$ is a bilinear transformation

$$T\,0\,S^{-1}(\infty) = T(z_1) = \infty$$
$$T\,0\,S^{-1}(0) = 0$$
$$T\,0\,S^{-1}(1) = 1$$

Thus, $T\,0\,S^{-1}$ has three fixed points. But a bilinear transformation can have at most two fixed points.

Thus, $T \equiv S$.

Remark

$$T(z) = \frac{z - z_2}{z_3 - z_2} \text{ if } z_1 = \infty$$

$$T(z) = \frac{z_3 - z_1}{z - z_1} \text{ if } z_2 = \infty$$

$$T(z) = \frac{z - z_2}{z - z_1} \text{ if } z_3 = \infty.$$

Thus, T can be defined uniquely in the extended complex plane.

Sometimes a conformal mapping is needed from a domain D that is bounded by circles onto another domain D' that is bounded by lines. For this we shall construct a bilinear transformation $w = Tz$, which map three distinct points (z_1, z_2, z_3) on the boundary of D to three distinct points (w_1, w_2, w_3) on the boundary of D'.

Definition 12.6

Cross Ratio

The cross ratio of the complex numbers z, z_1, z_2, and z_3 is the complex number

$$(z, z_1, z_2, z_3) = \frac{z - z_1}{z - z_3} \frac{z_2 - z_3}{z_2 - z_1}$$

This map sends $z_1, z_2, z_3 \to 0, 1, \infty$, respectively, (z, z_1, z_2, z_3) is the image of z under the bilinear transformation which maps z_1, z_2, z_3 to 0, 1, ∞, respectively.

Remark

(1) We must be careful about the order of the complex numbers while computing cross ratio. For example,

$$(0, 1, i, 2) = \frac{3}{4} + \frac{1}{4} i$$

$$(0, i, 1, 2) = \frac{1}{4} - \frac{1}{4} i.$$

(2) If

$$TZ = \frac{(z - z_1)(z_2 - z_3)}{(z - z_3)(z_2 - z_1)}$$

$$= \frac{z\left(\dfrac{z - z_1}{z_2 - z_1}\right) - z_1\left(\dfrac{z_2 - z_3}{z_2 - z_1}\right)}{z - z_3}$$

$$= \frac{Az + B}{Cz + D}$$

where

$$A = \left(\frac{z - z_1}{z_2 - z_1}\right), B = -z_1\left(\frac{z_2 - z_3}{z_2 - z_1}\right),$$

$$C = 1, D = 2,$$

$$AD - BC = \left(\frac{z - z_1}{z_2 - z_1}\right)^{z_3} + \left(\frac{z_2 - z_3}{z_2 - z_1}\right)^{z_1}$$

$$= \frac{-z_2 - z_3 + z_3^2 + z_2 z_1 - z_3 z_1}{(z_2 - z_1)}$$

$$= \frac{(z_2 - z_3)(z_1 - z_3)}{z_2 - z_1} \neq 0$$

because z_1, z_2, z_3 are distinet points. Thus TZ is bilinear transformation.

Proposition 12.10

The cross ratio is invariant under bilinear transformation *i.e.,* if S is a bilinear transformation, then

$$(Sz, Sz_1, Sz_2, Sz_3) = (z, z_1, z_2, z_3).$$

Proof

Let T be a bilinear transformation such that

$$T(z_1) = 0$$
$$T(z_2) = 1$$
$$T(z_3) = \infty.$$

Then, $T\,0\,s^{-1}$ maps Sz_1, Sz_2, Sz_3 to $0, 1, \infty$ respectively. Thus by the definition 12.6

$$(Sz_1, Sz_1, Sz_2, Sz_3) = Tz = (z, z_1, z_2, z_3).$$

Theorem 12.11

If $w = f(z)$ is a unique bilinear transformation that maps the distinct points z_1, z_2 and z_3 onto the three distinct points w_1, w_2, and w_3 respectively, then

$$\frac{z - z_1}{z - z_3}\,\frac{z_2 - z_3}{z_2 - z_1} = \frac{w - w_1}{w - w_3}\,\frac{w_2 - w_3}{w_2 - w_1}.$$

Proof

Let $w = f(z) = \dfrac{az + b}{cz + d}$ be the bilinear transformation such that

$$w_i = \frac{az_i + b}{cz_i + d}, \quad i = 1, 2, 3, 4.$$

Consider $$w - w_1 = \frac{az+b}{cz+d} - \frac{az_1+b}{cz_1+d}$$

$$= \frac{(ad-bc)(z-z_1)}{(cz+d)(z_1+d)}$$

Similarly $$w_2 - w_3 = \frac{az_2+b}{cz_2+d} - \frac{az_3+b}{cz_3+d} = \frac{(ad-bc)(z_2-z_3)}{(cz_2+d)(cz_3+d)}$$

Thus, $$(w-w_1)(w_2-w_3) = \frac{(ad-bc)^2(z-z_1)(z_2-z_3)}{(cz+d)(cz_1+d)(cz_2+d)(cz_3+d)}$$

Similarly $$(w-w_3)(w_2-w_1) = \frac{(ad-bc)^2(z-z_3)(z_2-z_1)}{(cz+d)(cz_1+d)(cz_2+d)(cz_3+d)}$$

Hence,

$$\frac{(w-w_1)(w_2-w_3)}{(w-w_3)(w_2-w_1)} = \frac{(z-z_1)(z_2-z_3)}{(z-z_3)(z_2-z_1)} \qquad ...(1)$$

Example 12.15

Construct a bilinear transformation that maps the point 1, i, –1 on the unit circle $|z| = 1$ onto the points –1, 0, 1 on the real axis. Determine the image of the interior of the unit circle under the transformation.

Solution

Put $z_1 = 1$, $z_2 = i$, $z_3 = -1$, $w_1 = -1$, $w_2 = 0$ and $w_3 = 1$ in (1)

$$\frac{(w+1)(0-1)}{(w-1)(0-(-1)} = \frac{(z-1)(i+1)}{(z+1)(i-1)}$$

$$\Rightarrow \quad \frac{-(w+1)}{w-1} = -i\left(\frac{z-1}{z+1}\right)$$

$$\Rightarrow \quad w = \frac{z-i}{iz-1} = Tz$$

Put $z = 0$, an interior point in $|z| < 1$, we get $T(0) = i$. Thus, the image of $|z| < 1$ is the upper half-plane $v > 0$.

Example 12.16

Prove that (z, z_1, z_2, z_3) is real-valued if and only if the four points (z, z_1, z_2, z_3) lie on a circle or a line.

Solution

Let $Tz = \dfrac{(z-z_1)(z_2-z_3)}{(z-z_3)(z_2-z_1)}$ maps z_1, z_2, z_3 to 0, 1, ∞, respectively and since it is bilinear, it maps the circle containing z_1, z_2, z_3 onto the real line. Thus, (z, z_1, z_2, z_3) is real-valued.

Conversely, if (z, z_1, z_2, z_3) is real-valued, then

$$sz = (z, z_1, z_2, z_3)$$

$$= \frac{Az+B}{Cz+D} = \text{Real.}$$

Thus, $$\frac{Az+B}{Cz+D} = \overline{\frac{Az+B}{Cz+D}}$$

$$\Rightarrow (Az+B)(\bar{C}\bar{z}+\bar{D}) = (\bar{A}\bar{z}+\bar{B})(Cz+D)$$

$$\Rightarrow (A\bar{C}-\bar{A}c)|z|^2 + (A\bar{D}-C\bar{B})z + (B\bar{C}-\bar{A}D)z + (B\bar{D}-\bar{B}D) = 0. \quad ...(1)$$

Case (i) If $A\bar{C}$ is real, then $A\bar{C}-\bar{A}C = 0$, then (1) represents a line

Case (ii) If $A\bar{C}$ is not real, then $A\bar{C} - A\bar{C} \neq 0$. From (1), we get

$$|z|^2 + \frac{A\bar{D}-C\bar{B}}{A\bar{C}-\bar{A}C}z + \frac{B\bar{C}-\bar{A}D}{A\bar{C}-\bar{A}C}\bar{z} + \frac{B\bar{D}-\bar{B}D}{A\bar{C}-\bar{A}C} = 0 \quad ...(1)$$

If $\bar{\gamma} = \dfrac{A\bar{D}-C\bar{B}}{A\bar{C}-\bar{A}C}$ and $\delta = -\left(\dfrac{B\bar{D}-\bar{B}D}{A\bar{C}-\bar{A}C}\right)$, then (2) can be written as

$$|z|^2 + \bar{\gamma}z + \gamma\bar{z} - \delta + |\gamma|^2 - |\gamma|^2 = 0$$

$$\Rightarrow |z+\gamma|^2 = \lambda \text{ where } \gamma = (|\gamma|^2+\delta)^{1/2} > 0 \quad ...(3)$$

Thus, (3) represents a circle with centre $-\gamma$ and radius λ.

EXERCISE

1. Find the image of

(i) $\{z : |z-1| > 1\}$ under $z \to \dfrac{z}{z-2}$,

(*ii*) $\{z : 0 < \arg z < \pi/4\}$ under $z \to \dfrac{z}{z-1}$,

(*iii*) $\{z : 0 < \arg z < \pi/6\}$ under $z \to (1 + i)\, z$

(*iv*) $\{z : 0 < \arg z < \pi/2\}$ under $z \to \dfrac{z-1}{z+1}$

(*v*) $\{z : |z - 1| > 1, |z + 1| > 1\}$ under $z \to \dfrac{i(z+2)}{z}$.

2. Find the Möbius transformation to map

(*i*) $-i, i, 2i$ onto $\infty, 0, \dfrac{1}{3}$, respectively,

(*ii*) $0, 1, \infty$ to $\infty, -1, 1$, respectively,

(*iii*) $-1, \infty, i$ to $0, \infty, 1$, respectively,

(*iv*) $1, i, 0$ to $1, i, -1$, respectively,

(*v*) $-1, 0, 1$ to $i, 0, \infty$, respectively,.

(*vi*) $-1, 0, 2$ to $0, 1, \infty$ respectively,

3. If $Tz = \dfrac{az+b}{cz+d}$, find necessary and sufficient conditions that $T(\Gamma) = \Gamma$ where Γ is the unit circle $\{z : |z| = 1\}$.

4. Let T be a bilinear transformation with two fixed points z_1 and z_2. If s is a also a bilinear transformation show that $s^{-1}z_1$ and $S^{-1}z_2$ are two fixed points of s^{-1} Ts.

5. Show that $Tz = \dfrac{az+b}{cz+d}$, $ad - bc \neq 0$ has 0 and ∞ as its only fixed points iff it is a dialation.

6. Show that a Mobius Transformation has ∞ as its only fixed point iff it is a translation.

7. Let T be a Möbius transformation $T \neq$ the identity. Show that a Mobius transformation S commutes with T if S and T have the same fixed points.

8. If T is a bilinear transformation and $T(0) = 0$, $T(1) = 1$, $T(\infty) = \infty$, then T must be the identity function *i.e.*, $T(z) = z$.

9. Let $Tz = \dfrac{az+b}{cz+d}$ is a bilinear transformation.

(*i*) If 0 is a fixed point of *T*, then what can be said about the coefficients *a*, *b*, *c* and *d*?

(*ii*) If 1 is a fixed point of *T*, then what can be said about the coefficients *a*, *b*, *c* and *d*?

(*iii*) If ∞ is a fixed point then what can be said about the coefficients *a*, *b*, *c* and *d*?

10. (*i*) Prove that linear formation maps polygons onto polygons.

(*ii*) Suppose *f* is analytic in **C** and, for some rectangle *R*, *f*(*R*) is a rectangle. Prove *f* is linear.

ANSWERS

1. (*i*) $Rez \leq 0$

(*ii*) Interior of the circle with center at $\left(\dfrac{1+i}{w}\right)$ and radius 1.

(*iii*) $\{w : (1+i)\, r < w < (w+i) r e^{i\pi/6}\}$

(*iv*) Circle with center *i* and radius $\sqrt{2}$.

(*v*) $\{w : |w+i| > |w-i|;\ |w-3i| > |w-i|\}$

2. (*i*) $TZ = 0$ (*ii*) $TZ = \dfrac{z-2}{z}$

(*iii*) $TZ = \dfrac{z}{2}(1-i)$

(*iv*) There is no such mobius transformation

(*v*) $TZ = \dfrac{2iz}{z-1}$ (*vi*) $TZ = \dfrac{2(z+1)}{2-z}$

4. $Tz_1 = z_1$; $Tz_2 = z_2$ $S^{-1}TS(S^{-1}z_1) = S^{-1}z_1$, $S^{-1}TS(S^{-1}z_2) = S^{-1}z_2$.

5. $T(0) = 0 \Rightarrow b = 0$, $T(\infty) = \infty \Rightarrow c = 0$. Then $TZ = \dfrac{az}{d}$ (drelation)

6. $T(\infty) = \infty \Rightarrow c = 0$, then $TZ = \dfrac{az}{d} + \dfrac{b}{d}$ (Tranolation)

7. If Z is find point of T and S, then Sz = Tz = z (TS) (z) = (ST)(z)

8. $T(0) = 0 \Rightarrow b = 0$, $T(\infty) = \infty \Rightarrow c = 0$, $T(1) = 1 \Rightarrow a = d$. Then, Tz = z

9. (*i*) $T(0) = 0 \Rightarrow b = 0$ and $ad \neq 0$

 (*ii*) $T(1) = 1 \Rightarrow a + b = c + d,\ b \neq d,\ c \neq a.$

 (*iii*) $T(\infty) = \infty \Rightarrow c = 0$ and $ad \neq 0$

❑❑❑

13

Schwarz's Lemma– An Automorphism of a Disc

In chapter 7, the Uniqueness Theorem tells us about the behaviour of a non-constant function in a region. It states that a non-constant analytic function in a region cannot be constant on any open set. Also, if f is non-constant in a region then $|f|$ is non-constant. Thus, a non-constant function in a region cannot map an open set into a point or a circular arc. In this chapter, we get stranger results with the help of Maximum-Modulus Theorem. In the later part of the chapter some applications of Schwarz-lemma are also given.

Theorem 13.1: Schwarz's Lemma

Let $D = \{z: |z| < 1\}$ and f be analytic on D with $|f(z)| < 1$ and $f(0) = 0$. Then, (*i*) $|f'(0)| \leq 1$ and $|f(z)| \leq |z|$ $\forall$ $z \in D$. Moreover, if $|f'(0)| = 1$ or if $|f(z)| = |z|$ for some $z \neq 0$, then there is a constant C, $|C| = 1$ such that $f(w) = Cw$ for all w in D.

Proof

Define $g : D \to \mathbf{C}$ by

$$g(z) = \begin{cases} \dfrac{f(z)}{z}, & z \neq 0 \\ f'(0), & z = 0 \end{cases}$$

We know g is analytic in D. Let $z \in D\,(0; 1)$ be fixed. Choose r such that $|z| < r < 1$,

$$|g(z)| < \max\{|g(z)| : z \in \gamma(0; r)\}$$

$$= \max\left\{\frac{|f(z)|}{|z|} : z \in \gamma\right\}$$

$$= \max\left\{\frac{|f(z)|}{r} : z \in \gamma\right\}$$

By Maximum-Modulus Principle

$$|g(z)| < \frac{1}{r} \text{ for } |z| \le r, 0 < r < 1$$

If $r \to 1$ then $|g(z)| < 1$ *i.e.,* $|f(z)| < |z|\ \forall\ z \in D$.

Also $|f'(0)| = |g(0)| < 1$

If $|f(z)| = |z|\ \forall\ z \in D, z \neq 0$ or $|f'(0)| = 1$, then g assumes its maximum value inside D. By Maximum-Modulus Theorem, $g(z) = C$ for some constant C with $|C| = 1$, then $f(z) = Cz$.

Proposition 13.2

If $|\alpha| < 1$ and $D = \{z : |z| < 1\}$ then $\phi: D \to D$ defined by

$$\phi_\alpha(z) = \frac{z - \alpha}{1 - \bar{\alpha} z}$$

is a $1 - 1$ map. Then inverse of ϕ_α is $\phi_{-\alpha}$. Furthermore, ϕ_α maps ∂D onto ∂D, $\phi_\alpha(\alpha) = 0$, $\phi_\alpha'(0) = 1 - |\alpha|^2$ and $\phi_\alpha'(\alpha) = \dfrac{1}{1 - |\alpha|^2}$.

Proof

If $|\alpha| < 1$ and $\phi : D \to D$ is defined by

$$\phi_\alpha(z) = \frac{z - \alpha}{1 - \bar{\alpha} z}$$

ϕ_α is a bilinear transformation. Also $\phi_\alpha(\alpha) = 0$, because $1 - \bar{\alpha}\ \alpha = 1 - |\alpha|^2 > 0$. Also,

$$\phi_{-\alpha}(\phi_\alpha(z)) = \phi_{-\alpha}\left(\frac{z - \alpha}{1 - \bar{\alpha} z}\right)$$

$$= \frac{\dfrac{z-\alpha}{1-\bar{\alpha}z}+\alpha}{1+\bar{\alpha}\left(\dfrac{z-\alpha}{1-\bar{\alpha}z}\right)}$$

$$= \frac{z-\alpha+\alpha-\alpha\bar{\alpha}z}{1-\bar{\alpha}z+\bar{\alpha}z-\alpha\bar{\alpha}}$$

$$= \frac{z\left(1-|\alpha|^2\right)}{1-|\alpha|^2} = z$$

Thus, $(\phi_\alpha)^{-1} = \phi_{-\alpha}$

Since $\partial D = \{z\,;|z|=1\} = \{e^{i\theta} : \theta \in [0, 2\pi]\}$. If $z \in \partial D$, then

$$\phi_\alpha(z) = \phi_\alpha(e^{i\theta}) = \left[\frac{e^{i\theta}-\alpha}{1-e^{i\theta}\,\bar{\alpha}}\right]$$

$$= \frac{1}{e^{i\theta}}\left(\frac{e^{i\theta}-\alpha}{e^{-i\theta}-\bar{\alpha}}\right)$$

$$\Rightarrow \qquad |\phi_\alpha(z)| = \left|\frac{e^{i\theta}-\alpha}{e^{-i\theta}-\bar{\alpha}}\right| = 1$$

Thus, ϕ_α maps ∂D onto ∂D.

Now $\qquad \phi_\alpha'(z) = \dfrac{1-\alpha\bar{\alpha}}{(1-\bar{\alpha}z)^2}$

$\Rightarrow \qquad \phi_\alpha'(0) = 1 - |\alpha|^2$

Also, $\qquad \phi_\alpha'(\alpha) = \dfrac{1-\alpha\bar{\alpha}}{(1-\bar{\alpha}\alpha)^2} = \dfrac{1}{1-|\alpha|^2}$.

The function ϕ_α can be used to solve various extermal problems for analytic functions.

Example 13.1

Suppose f is analytic in the unit disc such that $|f(z)| < 1 \ \forall\ z \in D$, $f\left(\dfrac{1}{2}\right) = 0$. Find an estimation for $\left|f\left(\dfrac{3}{4}\right)\right|$.

Solution

Since $f\left(\frac{1}{2}\right)=0$, define

$$g(z) = \begin{cases} f(z)\Big/\left(\dfrac{z-\frac{1}{2}}{1-\frac{1}{2}z}\right), & z \neq \dfrac{1}{2} \\ \dfrac{3}{4}f'\left(\dfrac{1}{2}\right), & z = \dfrac{1}{2} \end{cases}$$

is analytic in $|z| < 1$. Let $|z| \to 1$, by Maximum-Modulus Principle $|g(z)| < 1$.

i.e.,

$$|f(z)| < \left|\frac{z-\frac{1}{2}}{1-\frac{1}{2}z}\right| \quad \forall\, z \in D$$

Thus,

$$\left|f\left(\frac{3}{4}\right)\right| < \left|\frac{\frac{3}{4}-\frac{1}{2}}{1-\frac{1}{2}\times\frac{3}{4}}\right| = \frac{2}{5}.$$

Remark

$$\phi_{1/2}(z) = \frac{z-\frac{1}{2}}{1-\frac{1}{2}z}$$

and

$$\phi_{1/2}\left(\frac{3}{4}\right) = \frac{2}{5}.$$

Example 13.2

Show that if f is analytic and bounded by 1 in the unit disc, then $\max\left|f'\left(\frac{1}{3}\right)\right|$ is assumed when $f\left(\frac{1}{3}\right) = 0$.

Solution

Suppose $f\left(\frac{1}{3}\right) \neq 0$. Consider

$$g(z) = \frac{f(z) - f\left(\frac{1}{3}\right)}{1 - \overline{f\left(\frac{1}{3}\right)} f(z)}$$

If $w = f(z)$, then by Maximum-Modulus Principle

$$|g(z)| < 1 \text{ if } |w| = 1$$

Also $$g'(z) = \frac{f'(z)\left(1 - \left|f\left(\frac{1}{3}\right)\right|^2\right)}{\left(1 - \overline{f\left(\frac{1}{3}\right)} f(z)\right)^2}$$

and $$g'\left(\frac{1}{3}\right) = \frac{f'\left(\frac{1}{3}\right)}{1 - \left|f\left(\frac{1}{3}\right)\right|^2}$$

Thus, $$\left|g'\left(\frac{1}{3}\right)\right| > \left|f'\left(\frac{1}{3}\right)\right|$$

Now we prove a version of Liouville's Theorem using Maximum-Modulus Theorem.

Proposition 13.3

If f is an entire function satisfying

$$|f(z)| < \frac{1}{|Im\, z|} \; \forall \; z,$$

then $f \equiv 0$.

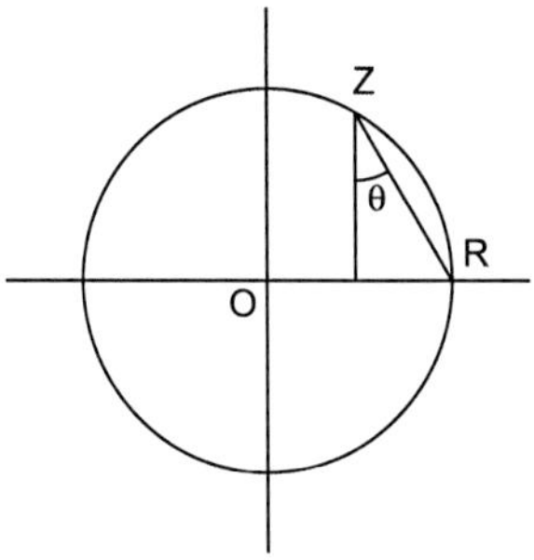

Fig. 13.1

Proof

If $|Im\, z| > 1$ then $|f(z)| < 1$. But if $|Im\, z| < 1$ then f could be unbounded. Let C be the circle $|z| = R$. Define a function $g(z)$ by

$$g(z) = (z^2 - R^2) f(z)$$

For any $z \in C$ and $Re\, z > 0$

$$|(z - R)f(z)| < \frac{|z - R|}{|Im\, z|} = \sec\theta \quad ...(1)$$

for some θ, $0 < \theta < \frac{\pi}{4}$. So from (1)

$$|(z - R) f(z)| < \sqrt{2} \quad \left(\because \sec \pi/4 = \sqrt{2}\right)$$

If $z \in \mathbf{C}$, $Re\, z < 0$, then

$$|(z + R) f(z)| > \sqrt{2}$$

Thus, $|g(z)| = |z + R|\, |z - R|\, |f(z)| < 3R$

for all $z \in \mathbf{C}$. But by Maximum-Modulus Theorem, the same upper bound holds for all z in $|z| < R$. Hence,

$$|g(z)| = |z^2 - R^2|\, |f(z)| < 3R$$

and $$|f(z)| < \frac{3R}{|z^2 - R^2|}$$

if $|z| < R$. If $R \to \infty$, $f(z) = 0$. Since this holds for all z. Thus, $f \equiv 0$.

Example 13.3

Suppose f is entire and $|f| = 1$ on the unit circle. Prove that $f(z) = Cz^n$.

Solution

Let $f(z)$ has zeros at $\alpha_1, \alpha_2, ..., \alpha_n$ inside the unit circle, therefore

$$f(z) = \left(\frac{z - \alpha_1}{1 - \overline{\alpha_1}\, z}\right)\left(\frac{z - \alpha_2}{1 - \overline{\alpha_2}\, z}\right) .... \left(\frac{z - \alpha_n}{1 - \overline{\alpha_n}\, z}\right) g(z)$$

where $g(\alpha_i) \neq 0$ and g is analytic, then

$$g(z) = \frac{f(z)}{\prod_{i=1}^{N} \left(\frac{z - \alpha_i}{1 - \overline{\alpha i}\, z}\right)} \quad ...(1)$$

Since $\left|\frac{z - \alpha_i}{1 - \overline{\alpha_i}\, z}\right| = 1$ (using Proposition 13.2) on $|z| = 1$, thus

$|g(z)| = 1$ on the unit circle

and by Maximum-Modulus Theorem, $|g(z)| = 1 \;\forall\; z \in D(0;\, 1)$ and hence, g is constant say C. Then, (1) implies

$$f(z) = C \prod_{i=1}^{N} \left(\frac{z - \alpha_i}{1 - \overline{\alpha_i}\, z} \right)$$

Since f is entire, therefore $\alpha_i = 0$. Then, $f(z) = Cz^n$.

Example 13.4

Suppose f is analytic in the annulus $1 < |z| < 2$, $|f| < 1$ on $|z| = 1$ and $|f| < 4$ on $|z| = 2$. Prove $|f(z)| < |z|^2$ throughout the annulus.

Solution

Let $g(z) = \dfrac{f(z)}{z^2}$, g is analytic in the annulus $1 < |z| < 2$. Also $|g(z)| < 1$ on $|z| = 1$ and on $|z| = 2$, $|g(z)| = \dfrac{|f(z)|}{4} < 1$. Thus, by Maximum-Modulus Theorem $|g(z)| = 1$ on the boundary of the annulus $1 < |z| < 2$ and hence on the annulus also. Thus,

$$|f(z)| = |z|^2 \quad \text{in} \quad 1 < |z| < 2.$$

Example 13.5

If f is analytic in the disc $|z| < 1$ and is boundary by 10 such that $f(1) = 0$. Find the best possible upper bound for $\left| f\left(\frac{1}{2}\right) \right|$.

Solution

Define $g(z) = \dfrac{1}{10} f(2z)$, then g is analytic and

$$|g(z)| = \frac{|f(2z)|}{10} < 1 \quad \text{on} \quad |z| < 1$$

Also $$g\left(\frac{1}{2}\right) = \frac{1}{10} f(1) = 0$$. By Proposition 13.2,

$$g(z) = \frac{z - \frac{1}{2}}{1 - \frac{1}{2} z}$$

and
$$|g(z)| < \left|\frac{z - \frac{1}{2}}{1 - \frac{1}{2}z}\right|$$

In particular $\left|g\left(\frac{1}{4}\right)\right| < \left|\frac{\frac{1}{4} - \frac{1}{2}}{1 - \frac{1}{8}}\right| = \frac{2}{7}$. Thus,

$$\left|f\left(\frac{1}{2}\right)\right| < \frac{20}{7}.$$

Example 13.6

Suppose f is entire and $|f(z)| < \dfrac{1}{|Re\, z|^2}$ for all z. Show that $f \equiv 0$.

Solution

If $|Re\, z| > 1$ then $|f(z)| < 1$. Let C be the circle $|z| = R$. Define

$$\begin{aligned} g(z) &= (z - iR)^2 (z + iR)^2 f(z) \\ &= (z^2 + R^2)^2 f(z) \end{aligned}$$

for any $z \in C$ and $Im\, z > 0$,

$$|(z - iR)^2 f(z)| < \left|\frac{z - iR}{Re\ z}\right|^2 = \text{cosec}^2\theta \qquad ...(1)$$

for some θ, $0 < \theta < \pi/4$, so

$$|(z - iR)f(z)| < 2$$

If $z \in \mathbf{C}$ and $Im\, z < 0$, then

$$|(z + iR)^2 f(z)| < 2 \text{ for all } z \in \mathbf{C}$$

By Maximum-Modulus Theorem, the same upper bound holds for $|z| < R$. Hence,

$$|g(z)| = |z + iR|^2\, |z - iR|^2\, |f(z)| < 8\, R$$

$$\Rightarrow \qquad |f(z)| < \frac{8R}{\left(z^2 + R^2\right)^2}$$

If $R \to \infty$,

$$f(z) = 0.$$ Since it holds for all z, thus, $f \equiv 0$.

13.1. AUTOMORPHISM OF THE DISC

Definition 13.1. Automorphism of a Region:

Let G be a region. A map f from G onto itself is called an automorphism of G. The set of all automorphism of G is denoted by Aut(G) and forms a group under composition of maps. The identity element is the map $z \to z$ and the inverses are the inverse functions. If $f, g \in$ Aut (G) then fog is also an automorphism and

$$(fog)^{-1} = g^{-1} \, 0 \, f^{-1}$$

We shall discuss an automorphism of the unit disc in the following Theorem.

Theorem 13.4

The only automorphism of the unit disc with $f(0) = 0$ are in the form $f(z) = e^{i\theta} z$.

Proof

Since f is automorphism, thus f maps the unit disc onto itself and $f(0) = 0$. By Schwarz's Lemma

$$|f(z)| < |z| \text{ for } |z| < 1 \qquad \ldots(1)$$

Since f^{-1} also maps disc onto itself and $f^{-1}(0) = 0$. By Schwarz Lemma again

$$|f^{-1}(z)| < |z| \text{ for } |z| < 1 \qquad \ldots(2)$$

(1) and (2) are valid only if $|f(z)| = |z|$. By Schwarz Lemma $f(z) = Cz$ where $|C| = 1$. Thus, $f(z) = e^{i\theta}z$.

If f is an automorphism of the unit disc with $f(\alpha) = 0$, for a fixed α, $0 < \alpha| < 1$. Assume f is bilinear transformation. Since f is globally $1 - 1$, therefore it maps unit circle onto itself. Hence, by Proposition 13.2, f must be of the form

$$f(z) = C\left(\frac{z - \alpha}{z - 1/\bar{\alpha}}\right)$$

where $|C| = 1$. Then $|f(1)| = |C| \left|\frac{1 - \alpha}{1 - \bar{\alpha}}\right| |\alpha| = 1$

We have $|C| = \dfrac{1}{|\alpha|}$. Thus f can be written as

$$f(z) = e^{i\theta}\left(\frac{z-\alpha}{1-\bar{\alpha}z}\right).$$

Theorem 13.5

The automorphism of the unit disc are of the form $g(z) = e^{i\theta}\left(\frac{z-\alpha}{1-\bar{\alpha}z}\right)$, $|\alpha| < 1$.

Proof

Let $g(z) = \dfrac{z-\alpha}{1-\bar{\alpha}\, z}$.

By Proposition 13.2, $|g(z)| = 1$ for $|z| = 1$, $g(\alpha) = 0$ and g is an automorphism from unit disc into itself. Let f be an automorphism of the unit disc with $f(\alpha) = 0$.

Set $h = fog^{-1}$ is also an automorphism with

$$h(0) = f(g^{-1}(0)) = f(\alpha) = 0$$

By Theorem 13.4, $h(z) = e^{i\theta}z$

or $$g(z) = e^{i\theta}\left(\frac{z-\alpha}{1-\bar{\alpha}\, z}\right)$$

Let $G = \{z: Im\, z > 0\}$ be the upper half-plane and $h: G \to D$ is an automorphism, then $h(z) = C\left(\frac{z-\alpha}{z-\bar{\alpha}}\right)$, $Im\, \alpha > 0$. This is proved in the following:

Theorem 13.6

The conformal mapping h of the upper half-plane onto the unit disc are of the form

$$h(z) = e^{i\theta}\left(\frac{z-\alpha}{z-\bar{\alpha}}\right), Im\, \alpha > 0 .$$

Proof

Let $f(z) = \dfrac{z-\alpha}{z-\bar{\alpha}}$. Since $|z-\alpha| = |z-\bar{\alpha}|$ for real z, thus f maps real axis onto unit circle. Also $f(\alpha) = 0$, $Im\, \alpha > 0$. Thus, f maps upper half-plane to the unit disc. Suppose g is an automorphism of the disc, therefore by Theorem 13.4, $g(z) = e^{i\theta}z$ for some real θ. Let $h = gof$, then h is an automorphism from upper half-plane to the disc. Also,

$$h(\alpha) = g(f(\alpha)) = g(0) = 0$$

and

$$h(z) = g(f(z)) = e^{i\theta}\left(\frac{z-\alpha}{z-\overline{\alpha}}\right).$$

A remarkable fact which is surprising is that the unbounded upper half-plane is conformally equivalent to the unit disc.

Theorem 13.7

The map F from upper half-plane, to the unit disc defined by

$$\mathrm{F(z)} = \frac{z-i}{z+i}$$

is conformed map with inverse G from unit disc to upper half plane, defined by

$$G(z) = i\left(\frac{1+z}{1-z}\right).$$

Proof

Both the functions $F(z)$ and $G(z)$ are analytic in their respective domains. The upper half-plane is $\{z : |z-i| < |z+i|\}$. Thus $|F(z)| < 1$ and F maps upper half-plane into the disc. Let $w = u + iv \in D$. Consider

$$Im\ (G(w)) = Re\left(\frac{1+u+iv}{1-u-iv}\right)$$

$$= Re\left(\frac{(1+u+iv)(1-u+iv)}{(1-u)^2+v^2}\right)$$

$$\frac{1-u^2-v^2}{(1-u)^2+v^2} > 0, \text{ since } |w| < 1.$$

Therefore G maps the unit disc to the upper half-plane

$$\text{Now} \qquad F(G(w)) = \frac{i\left(\dfrac{1+w}{1-w}\right)-i}{i\left(\dfrac{1+w}{1-w}\right)+i}$$

$$= \frac{1+w-1+w}{1+w+1-w} = w$$

Similarly $G(F(z)) = z$.

Theorem 13.8

The automorphism of the upper half-plane are of the form

$$f(z) = \frac{az+b}{cz+d}$$

where a, b, c, d are real and $ad - bc > 0$.

Proof

$$\text{Let} \qquad f(z) = \frac{az+b}{cz+d}$$

f maps real axis onto itself. Also,

$$Im\, f(i) = Im\left(\frac{ai+b}{ci+d} \times \frac{d-ci}{d-ci}\right)$$

$$= \frac{ad-bc}{c^2+d^2} > 0.$$

Hence f is an automorphism of upper half-plane. Define an automorphism of the form

$$h = f^{-1} 0\ gof$$

with $f(z) = \dfrac{z-i}{z+i}$ and $g(z) = e^{i\theta}\left(\dfrac{z-\alpha}{1-\bar{\alpha}\, z}\right), |\alpha| < 1.$

We want to show that $h(z) = \dfrac{az+b}{cz+d}$, $ad - bc > 0$.

Let $h = h_1\ 0\ h_2$ where

$$h_1(z) = \left(\frac{z-i}{z+i}\right)^{-1} 0\ e^{i\theta} z\ 0\left(\frac{z-i}{z+i}\right)$$

$$= i\left(\frac{1+z}{1-z}\right) 0\, e^{i\theta} z\, 0 \left(\frac{z-i}{z+i}\right)$$

$$= i\left(\frac{1+e^{i\theta}\left(\dfrac{z-i}{z+i}\right)}{1-e^{i\theta}\left(\dfrac{z-i}{z+i}\right)}\right)$$

$$= i\left(\frac{z\left(1+e^{i\theta}\right)+i\left(1-e^{i\theta}\right)}{z\left(1-e^{i\theta}\right)+i\left(1+e^{i\theta}\right)}\right)$$

$$= i\left(\frac{z\cos\theta/2\left(\cos\theta/2+i\sin\theta/2\right)+\sin\theta/2\left(\cos\theta/2+i\sin\theta/2\right)}{-iz\sin\theta/2\left(\cos\theta/2+i\sin\theta/2\right)+i\cos\theta/2\left(\cos\theta/2+i\sin\theta/2\right)}\right)$$

$$= \frac{z\cos\theta/2+\sin\theta/2}{-z\sin\theta/2+\cos\theta/2}$$

and
$$h_2(z) = \left(\frac{z-i}{z+i}\right)^{-1} 0\left(\frac{z-\alpha}{1-\bar{\alpha}\,z}\right) 0\left(\frac{z-i}{z+i}\right)$$

$$= i\left(\frac{1+z}{1-z}\right) 0\left(\frac{z-\alpha}{1-\bar{\alpha}\,z}\right)\left(\frac{z-i}{z+i}\right)$$

$$= i\left(\frac{1+z}{1-z}\right) 0\left(\frac{(z-i)-\alpha(z+i)}{(z+i)-\bar{\alpha}(z-i)}\right)$$

$$= i\left(\frac{1+\dfrac{(z-i)-\alpha(z+i)}{(z+i)-\bar{\alpha}(z-i)}}{1-\dfrac{(z-i)-\alpha(z+i)}{(z+i)-\bar{\alpha}(z-i)}}\right)$$

$$= i\left(\frac{z(1-\bar{\alpha}+1-\alpha)+i(1+\bar{\alpha}-1-\alpha)}{z(1-\bar{\alpha}-1+\alpha)+i(1+\bar{\alpha}+1+\alpha)}\right)$$

$$= i\left(\frac{z(2-2\,Re\,\alpha)-i(2i\,Im\,\alpha)}{z(2i\,Im\,\alpha)+i(2+2\,Re\,\alpha)}\right)$$

$$= \frac{z(1-Re\,\alpha)+Im\,\alpha}{z\,Im\,\alpha+(1+Re\,\alpha)}$$

Now
$$h = h_1 \, 0 \, h_2 = \frac{Az+B}{Cz+D}$$

where
$$A = (1 - Re\,\alpha)\cos \theta/2 + Im\,\alpha \sin \theta/2,$$
$$B = Im\,\alpha \cos \theta/2 + (1 + Re\,\alpha)\sin \theta/2,$$
$$C = (Re\,\alpha - 1)\sin \theta/2 + Im\,\alpha \cos \theta/2,$$
$$D = (1 + Re\,\alpha)\cos \theta/2 + Im\,\alpha \sin \theta/2$$

such that $AD - BC > 0$.

EXERCISE

1. Suppose that f is analytic and bounded by 1 in the unit disc with $f(\alpha) \neq 0$ for some $|\alpha| < 1$. Show that there exists a function g, analytic and bounded by 1 in the unit disc with $|g'(\alpha)| > |f'(\alpha)|$.
2. Find max $|f'(\alpha)|$ where f ranges over the class of analytic functions bounded by 1 in the unit disc, and α is a fixed point of $|z| < 1$. Show that
$$f'(\alpha) = \lim_{z \to \alpha} \left|\frac{f(z)}{z-\alpha}\right| < \lim_{z - \alpha} \left|\frac{\phi_\alpha(z)}{z-\alpha}\right| = \phi'_\alpha(\alpha).$$
3. Prove that
$$\frac{|f'(z)|}{1-|f(z)|^2} < \frac{1}{1-|z|^2} \quad \text{for all } z \in D$$
4. Let $f(z) = \dfrac{i-z}{i+z}$ and $f^{-1}(w) = i\left(\dfrac{1-w}{1+w}\right)$
   (*i*) Given $\theta \in R$, find real numbers a, b, c, d such that $ad - bc = 1$ and so that for any z in the upper half-plane
   $$\frac{az+b}{cz+d} = f^{-1}(e^{i\theta} f(z)).$$
   (*ii*) Let $\alpha \in D$, find real numbers a, b, c, d so that $ad - bc = 1$, so that for any z in the upper half-plane

$$\frac{az+b}{cz+d} = f^{-1}(\psi_\alpha\ (f(z))$$

where $$\psi_\alpha(z) = \frac{\alpha - z}{1-\bar{\alpha}\, z}, |\alpha| < 1.$$

5. What is the image of the upper half-plane under a mapping of the form

$$f(z) = \frac{az+b}{cz+d}, \ a, b, c, d \text{ real}; \ ad - bc < 0?$$

ANSWERS

1. Let $g(z) = \dfrac{f(z) - f(\alpha)}{1 - \overline{f(\alpha)}\, f(z)}$, then g is analytic & bounded by 1 in $D(0, 1)$ and $g'(\alpha) = \dfrac{f'(\alpha)}{1 - |f(\alpha)|^2}$. Then $|g'(\alpha) \geq |f'(\alpha)|$.

2. Since $|f(z)| \leq |f_\alpha(z)|$ for all $|z| \leq |$

Thus $$f'(\alpha) = \lim_{z\to\alpha}\left|\frac{f(z)}{z-\alpha}\right| \leq \lim_{z\to\alpha}\left|\frac{\phi_\alpha(z)}{z-\alpha}\right|$$

$$\Rightarrow \quad |f'(\alpha)| = |\phi_\alpha{}'(\alpha)| \qquad \left(\because \phi'_\alpha(a) = \frac{1}{1-|\alpha|^2}\right).$$

4. (*i*) $|f(z)| < 1$ & $|f^{-1}(w)| \leq 1$. $a = \cos\theta/2$, $b = \sin\theta/2$, $c = -\sin\theta/2$, $d = \cos\theta/2$

(*ii*) $a = 1 - Re\ \alpha$, $b = Im\ \alpha$, $c = Im\ \alpha$, $D = 1 + Re\ \alpha$

5. The lower half-plane

❑❑❑

Appendix–I
Mathematical–LAB WORK

'Mathematica' is a computational software program used in scientific, engineering and Mathematical fields and other area of technical computing. It was developed by Stephen Worlform in the year 1988 at Wolform Research of champaign, Illinois.

There are two parts of Mathematica system:

1. Mathematica Kernel: The part that actually perform computations.
2. Mathematica Front: The part that handels interactions with the user.

The most common type of front end for Mathematica is based on interactive documents known as "Notebook". A notebook is a collection of Mathematica statements, output and graphics.

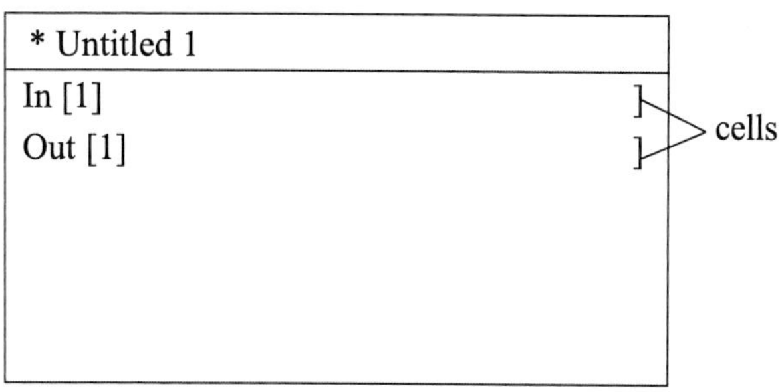

The Symbols] along the right side of the notebook is called a cell. The cell is the smallest unit of work in mathematica. A cell may contain input or output, math or comments, text or graphics.

Import: Shift + Enter to do a computation in Mathematica.

Opening of Mathematica

To open Mathematica, do the following:

Start → All Progress → Woldron Mathematica.

When we open Mathematica, an empty notebook appears on the screen of the computer. A cursor appears once we press a key.

Quitting Mathematica

To quit Mathematica, do the following:

- Quit Mathematica as other programs (by clicking on 'X')
- Or Write Quit
- File → Exit.

Important Conventions

- All built in Mathematica names start with a capital letter.
- Multiplication must be expressed by a space or an asterisk (*).
- All arguments are given in square brackets [ ].
- Parenthesis ( ) are used only for grouping terms.
- Curly braces { } are used for lists.
- Double brackets [[ ]] are used to extract elements from lists.

Various Symbols in Mathematica

Symbol	*Meaning in Mathematics*	*Meaning in Mathematica*
+	a + b	a + b
–	a – b	a – b
*	a × b	a * b, a b
/	a/b	a/b
^	a^b	a ^ b

Basic Constants

Symbol	*In Mathematica*	*How to type in Notebook*
π	Pi	ESC p ESC
e	E	ESC ee ESC
∞	Infinity	ESC inf ESC
i	I	ESC ii ESC

We calculate the decimal values of the above mentioned symbols in the following:

Pi // N — 3.14159

E // N — 2.71828

I ^ 2 — - 1

1/Infinity — 0

Referring to earlier results

% — Refers to the last result.

% % — Refers to the last to last result

% % ... % — Refers to the kth if there are k% marks.

Out [n] or %n — Refers to the result in the output line Out[n].

Basic Functions

Mathematical Meaning	*Mathematical symbol*	*Mathematica Expression*	*How to type in Mathematica*
Square rent	$\sqrt{x}$	Sqrt [x]	x ^ (1/2)
Exponential function	e^x	Exp [x]	e ^ x
Natural algorithm	$\log_{10}(x)$	Log [x]	Log [x]
Logarithmlog$_b$(x)	$\log_b^x$	Log [b, x]	Log[b, x]
Absolute value	$\|x\|$	Abs [x]	Abs [x]
Product of integer	$\underline{\lfloor n}$	Factorial	n!
Trigonometric function	Sin (x), cos (x),	Sine[x] Cosine [x]	Sin [x], Cos [x],
(With argument in radius)	tan (x)	Tangent [x]	Tan [x]
Inverse Trigonometric function	$\sin^{-1}$ x, $\cos^{-1}$ x, $\tan^{-1}$ x	Are Sin [x], ArcCos [x], Arc tan [x]	Arc Sin [x], Arc cos [x], Arc Tan [x]
Closest integer to	Round (x)	Round [x]	Round [x]
Modulus	n ≡ C(mod m)	modulus [n, m]	Mod [n, m]

Try the following:

In[1]:=25 + 56

Out[1]:= 80

In[2]:= 34 * 32

Out[3]:= 1088

In[3]:= 25 25

Out[3]:= 625

In[4]:= $\frac{4}{5}-\frac{2}{3}$

Out[4]:= $\frac{2}{15}$

In[5]:= I ^ 2

Out[5]:= – 1

In[6]:= Sqrt [125]

Out[6]:= $5\sqrt{5}$

In[7]:= Log [1234.5]

Out[7]:= 7.11842

In[8]:= $\frac{1}{\infty}$

Out[8]:= 0

In[9]: Abs [–23, 45]

Out[9]:= 23.45

In[10]:= Max [23, 67, 5, 46, 129, 390]

Out[10]:= 390

In[11]:= Min [90, 67, 45, 2, 0, 78]

Out[11]:= 0

In[12]:= Round [23.67]

Out[12]:= 24

In[13]:Sin [Pi/3]

Out[13]:= $\frac{\sqrt{3}}{2}$

Decimal Values

To calculate a decimal value for expression, we write **expr//n** or **N[expr]**

For example

In[14]:=625/466546;

Note that an expression ending with (;) does not give an output whereas it stores the expression.

In[15]:=% // N

Out[15]:= 0.0133959

In[16]:= E // N

Out[16]:= 2.71828

Defining Variables

While doing long calculations, it is convenient to given name to the intermediate results. We use the following:

x = Value – Assign Values for x

x – show the value of x

x = . or Clear [x] – clear the value of x

x = y = Value – Assign a value to both x and y.

For example

In[17]:= *x* = 16

Out[17]:= 16

In[18]:= 2x = 7

Out[18]:= 39

In[19]:= x =

Important: xy means x times y

xy without space is the variable with name xy.

5x means 5 times x

x^2y mean (x^2)y, not x^(2y).

Defining Functions

To define a function we type

In[20]:f[x–]: = x^2;

Where '–' refers to a blank.

In[21]:= % ^ 2

Out[21]:= x ^ 4

In[22]:= g[x_] = x ^ 3 + 4x – 5;

In[23]:= % % * %

Out[23]:= x ^ 4(x ^ 3 + 4x – 5)

Complex Numbers: The algebra on complex numbers is same as that of real numbers. For example.

In[24]:= 2 + 3I + 5 – I

Out[24]:= 7 + 2I

In[25]:= (1 – 2I) * (4 + 2I0

Out[25]:= 8 – 6I

In[26]:= (1 – I)/(3 + 2I)

Out[26]:= $\frac{1}{13} - \frac{5}{13}I$

In[27]:= Re[4 – 2I]

Out[27]:= 4

In[28]:= Im[3 + 6I]

Out[28]:=6

In[29]:= Arg [3 – 4I]

Out[29]:= $-\text{Arc tan}\left[\frac{4}{3}\right]$

In[30]:= Abs[2 – 3I]

Out[30]:= $\sqrt{13}$.

In[31]:= Complex Expand [(–1) ^ (1/3)]

Out[31]:= $\frac{1}{2} + \frac{I\sqrt{3}}{2}$

In[32]:= Conjugate [3 – 6I]

Out[32]:= 3 + 6I

Some Special Functions

Identity function we write

Identity function we write

Identity [x]

Inverse Function – Inverse Function [f][x]

For Example:

In[33]: Inverse Function [sin][x]

Out[33]:= Arc Sin[x]

Composite Function

Values of composite function can be calculated by writing f[g(x)] or composition [f, g][x]

In[34]:= f[x_]:= sin[x];

In[35]:= g[x_]:= x ^ 2;

In[36]:= f[g[a]]

Out[36]:= sin[a^2]

Trigonometric and Exponential Expressions

Trig To Exp [expr] – Write trigonometric function in terms of complex exponentials

Exp to Trig [expr] – Write complex exponentials in terms of trigonometric functions

In[37]: = Trig To Exp [cos [x]]

Out[37]: = $\frac{e^{-ix}}{2}+\frac{e^{ix}}{2}$

In[38]: = Exp To Trig [%]

Out[38]: = cos[x]

Differential and Integeral calculus

D[f, x] — Derivative of f with respect to x

D[f, x, x] — Second order derivative of f with respect to x

D[f, x, y] — Mixed Second-order-derivatives of f with respect to x and y

Series [f, {x, a, n}] –nth order Taylor series of f with respect to x at a

Limit [f, x → a] – Limit of f as x approaches a

In[39]:= D [x sin [y], x]
Out[39]:= sin [y]
In[40]:= D [x sin [y], y]
Out [40]:= x cos [y]

Integral Calculus

Integrate [f, x] – Indefinite integral of f with respect to x

Integrate [f, {x, a, b}] – Definite integral of f when x varies from a to b.

N Integrate [f, (x, a, b}] – Calculate the difinites integral by numerical methods

In[41]:= Integrate [sin [sin [x]], {x, 0, 1}]

Out[41]:= $\int_0^1 \sin[\sin[x]]dx$

In[42]:= N[%]
Out[42]:= 0.430606

Complex Integration

To integrate a complex-valued function along a curve we first use composition of functions and the integrate.

For example: Evaluate {Rez dz where $\gamma(t) = t + it^2$, $t \in [0, 1]$.

In[42]:= z = x + iy;
In[43]:= f[z–]:= ReZ;
In[44]:= g[z–]: = z + iz^2;
In[45]:= N Integrate [f(g[z]], {z, 0, 1}]
Out[45]:= 0.5 + .666i

Graphics

One of the important features of Mathematica is to graph the functions

Plotting one Curve

Plot[function, {Variable, min, max}]

In[46]:= Plot[sin[x], {x, –2Pi, 2Pi}]

Out[46]:=

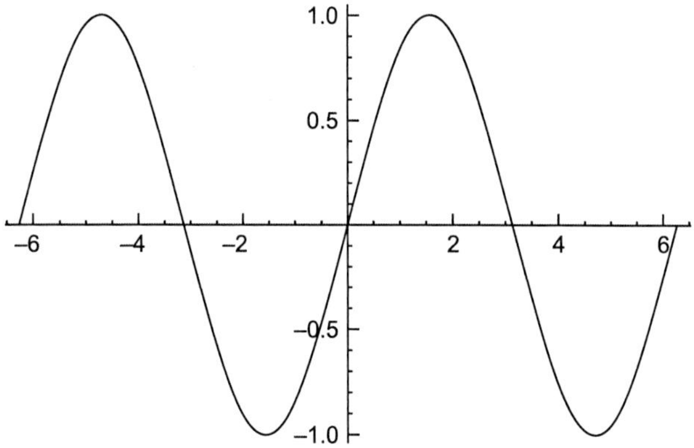

In[47]:= Plot[x ^ 2 – 2x – 3, {x, –5, 5}, Frame → True, Gridlines → Automatic]

Out[47]:=

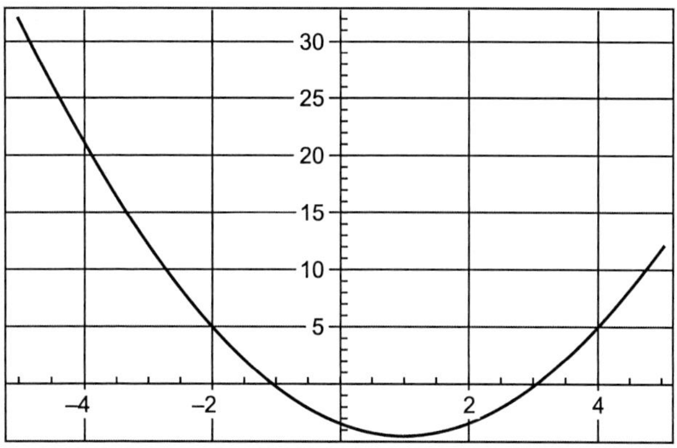

Options for Graphics

Axes → True: It shows x-axis and y-axes

Axes label → {"XTitle", "Y Title"} – To give titles to the axes

Axes Origin → {0, 0} – To give the coordinates of the origin

Axes Style → Arrowheads [{–0.5, 0.5}]

Axes Style → Directives [Red, Thick] – To have graph red in colour

Plot label → {"Plot Title"} – To give title to the graph

Plot Range → {{x axis range}, {y-axis range}}.

Plot Legend → {"graph 1", "graph 2", ...}.

Complex Function Graphs:

To plot an annulus $\{z : 1 < |z| < 2\}$ we write the following

In[42]: Parametric Plot [r cos [θ], r sin [θ]}, {r, 1, 2}, {θ, 0, 2, Pi}]
out [42]:=

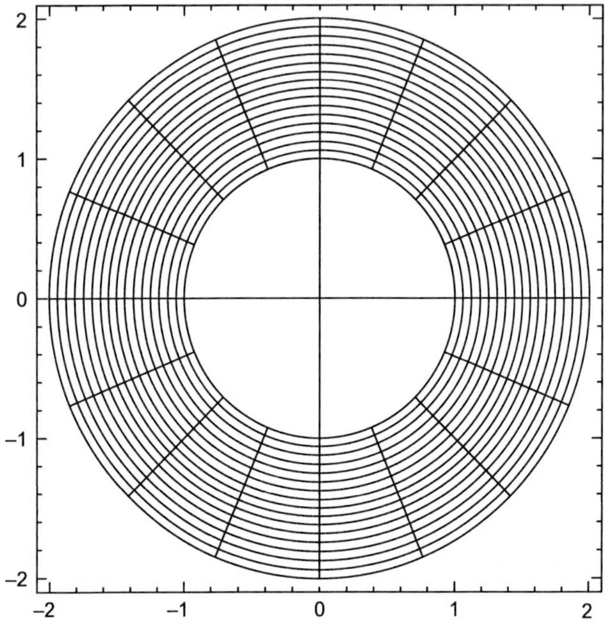

Graphs of Complex Functions:

If the function to be plotted has complex values of the argument, nothing is plotted for these values of argument. Thus, to plot complex values we use Re, Im or Abs to plot only the real or imaginary part or the absolute value.

Region Plot can be used for inequalities with complex variables.
For example

In[43]:= Set options [Region Plot, Frame → False, Axes → True};
P_1 = Region Plot [Abs [x + iy] ≤ 1, {x, –1, 1}, *y*, –1, 1}];
P_2 = Region Plot [Abs [1 – (x + Iy) ^ 3] ≤ 1, [x, –1, 1.3}, {y, –1.2, 1.2}];
Graphic Row [{p_1, p_2], Image Size → 420]

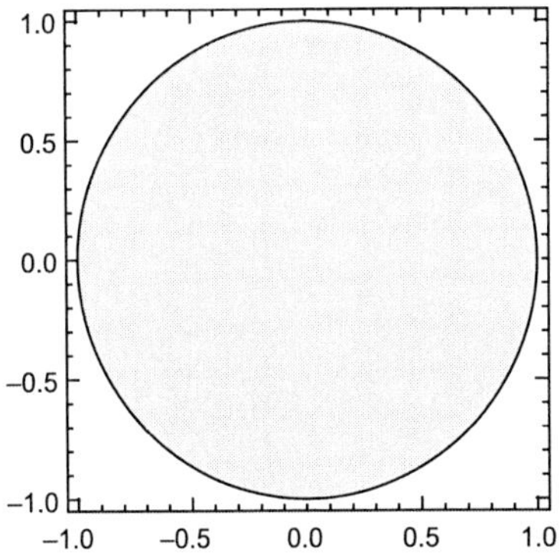

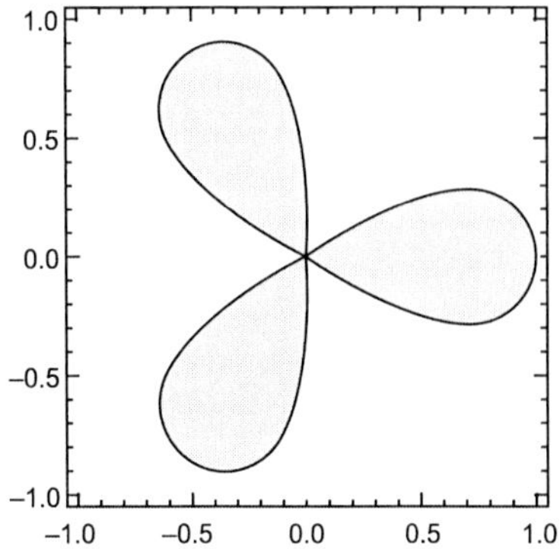

Contour Plot [Abs [f], {x, a, b], {y, c, d}]

Parametric Plot [Re[f], Im[f]}, {x, a, b} {y, c, d}].

For example

In[44]:= f = 1/x + Iy; {Contour Plot [Abs[f], {x, –1, 1}, {y, –1, 1},

Parametric Plot [{Re[f], Im[f]}, {x, –0.1, 0.1}, {y, –0.1, 0.1}]]

Out [44];=

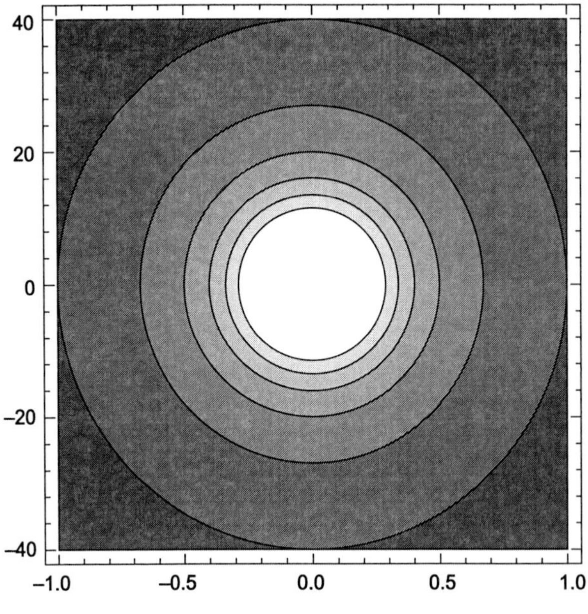

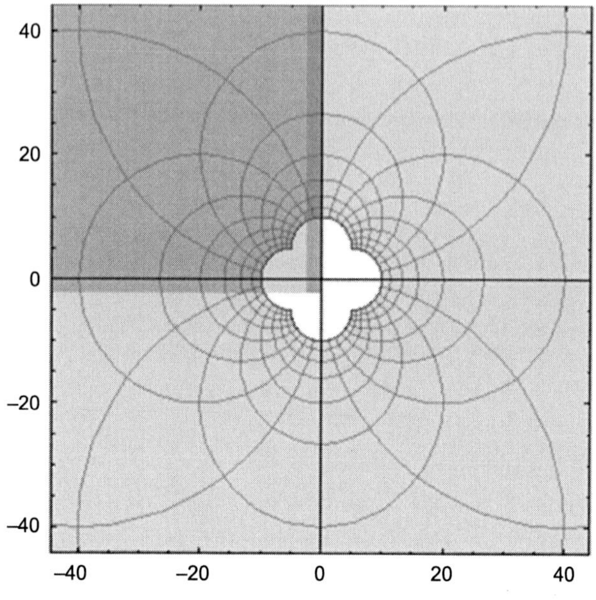
40
20
0
–20
–40
–40
–20
0
20
40

❑❑❑

Bibliography

1. L.V. Ahlfors, Complex Analysis, Mc Graw-Hill, New York, third Edition 1979.
2. J. Bak and D.J. Newman, Complex Analysis, Springer verlag, New York, Second Edition, 1997.
3. S.Lang, Complex Analysis, Springer-verlag, New York, Fourth Edition 1999.
4. H.A Priestley, Introduction to Complex Analysis, Clarendon Press, Oxford 1990.
5. E.M. Stein & Rami Shakarchi, Complex Analysis, Princeton Lectures in Analysis, Overseas press Pvt. Ltd.
6. D.G. Zill, P.D. Shanahan, A first course in Complex Analysis with Applications, 2nd Edition, Jones and Bartlett Publishers.

Index

A

B

C